More Auspicious Shores

More Auspicious Shores chronicles the migration of Afro-Barbadians to Liberia. In 1865, 346 Afro-Barbadians fled a failed post-emancipation Caribbean for the independent black republic of Liberia. They saw Liberia as a means of achieving their post-emancipation goals and promoting a pan-Africanist agenda while simultaneously fulfilling their "civilizing" and "Christianizing" duties. Through a close examination of the Afro-Barbadians, Caree A. Banton provides a transatlantic approach to understanding the political and sociocultural consequences of their migration and settlement in Africa. Banton reveals how, as former British subjects, Afro-Barbadians navigated an inherent tension between ideas of pan-Africanism and colonial superiority. Upon their arrival in Liberia, an English imperial identity distinguished the Barbadians from African Americans and secured them privileges in the republic's hierarchy above the other group of blacks. By fracturing assumptions of a homogeneous black identity, Banton ultimately demonstrates how Afro-Barbadian settlement in Liberia influenced ideas of blackness in the Atlantic World.

Caree A. Banton is Assistant Professor of Afro-Caribbean History at the University of Arkansas.

D1599117

More Auspicious Shores

Barbadian Migration to Liberia, Blackness, and the Making of an African Republic

CAREE A. BANTON

University of Arkansas

CAMBRIDGE
UNIVERSITY PRESS

CAMBRIDGE
UNIVERSITY PRESS

University Printing House, Cambridge CB2 8BS, United Kingdom

One Liberty Plaza, 20th Floor, New York, NY 10006, USA

477 Williamstown Road, Port Melbourne, VIC 3207, Australia

314-321, 3rd Floor, Plot 3, Splendor Forum, Jasola District Centre, New Delhi - 110025, India

79 Anson Road, #06-04/06, Singapore 079906

Cambridge University Press is part of the University of Cambridge.

It furthers the University's mission by disseminating knowledge in the pursuit of
education, learning and research at the highest international levels of excellence.

www.cambridge.org
Information on this title: www.cambridge.org/9781108453028
DOI: 10.1017/9781108556217

First published 2019
First paperback edition 2021

A catalogue record for this publication is available from the British Library

Library of Congress Cataloging in Publication data
NAMES: Banton, Caree A., 1982– author.
TITLE: More auspicious shores : Barbadian migration to Liberia, Blackness,
and the making of an African republic / Caree A. Banton.
DESCRIPTION: Cambridge, U.K. : Cambridge University Press, 2019. | Includes
bibliographical references and index.
IDENTIFIERS: LCCN 2018042765 | ISBN 9781108429634
SUBJECTS: LCSH: Barbadians – Liberia – History. | Liberia – History – 1847–1944. |
Liberia – Emigration and immigration – 19th century. | Barbados – Emigration
and immigration – 19th century.
CLASSIFICATION: LCC DT643 .B36 2019 | DDC 966.6200496072981–dc23
LC record available at https://lccn.loc.gov/2018042765

ISBN 978-1-108-42963-4 Hardback
ISBN 978-1-108-45302-8 Paperback

For Mama
Hilda Salmon and Isolyn Banton
For Papa
Joe Gayle and Claude Banton

"We are our grandmother's prayers.
We are our grandfather's dreamings."

"We Are," *Sacred Ground*, Sweet Honey in the Rock (1995)

Contents

List of Figures		*page* viii
Preface		ix
List of Abbreviations		xvii

Introduction: "Who Is This Man and from Whence Comes
He to Rule?"   1

PART I CARIBBEAN EMANCIPATION

1	Not Free Indeed	29
2	African Civilization and the West Indian Avant-Garde	74
3	The Liberian President Visits Barbados to Trade Visions of Freedom	102

PART II THE MIDDLE PASSAGE

| 4 | Middle Passage Baggage | 149 |

PART III AFRICAN LIBERATION

5	Barbadian Arrival and Social Integration in Liberia	185
6	Making Citizenship and Blackness in Liberia	233
7	A Changing of the Guards: Arthur Barclay and Barbadian Liberia Political Leadership	282
	Epilogue: British West Indians in Liberia from Edward Blyden to Marcus Garvey	326

| *Bibliography* | 333 |
| *Index* | 352 |

Figures

1.1 Anthony Barclay's Goods Sold in His Shop   *page* 36
1.2 Barclay Family Tree   41
2.1 Resolutions of the Barbados Colonization Society   95
3.1 N. M. Condy's Depiction of the Embarkation of the Liberian
     President J. J. Roberts from Plymouth on December 16, 1848   103
4.1 Ship Manifest List of Barbados Emigrants to Liberia   151
5.1 *The African Repository*'s Record of Migrant Ships to Liberia
     in 1865   186
5.2 Memorial of the Barbadians' Arrival   187
5.3 Sign Memorializing the Crozierville Settlement   202–03
5.4 Christ Church Episcopal, Named after the Parish of Christ
     Church in Barbados   222–23
6.1 Sarah Ann Bourne Barclay and Daughter, Laura Ann Barclay   271
6.2 Hon. S. E. F. Cadogan, Barbadian Attorney in Liberia   272
6.3 Map Showing African Polities and Migrant Settlements in
     Liberia   277
7.1 Liberian Territories Lost During the Scramble for Africa   291
7.2 Photograph of Arthur Barclay as Secretary of the Treasury   298
7.3 Arthur Barclay, Barbadian Migrant, 15th President of Liberia   305

Preface

This book began in a Latin American Studies Research course at Vanderbilt University. I had gone to Vanderbilt fully intending to write about the intersection of Jamaican music and politics. However, acting upon advice to change my research focus, I started to use the Latin American Studies course to explore an old interest in diplomatic history that had culminated in a curiosity about nineteenth-century Liberia. It was then that I discovered Gerard Ralston, a white Philadelphian colonizationist who served as Liberia's consul general in the mid-nineteenth century. I had started to write about Ralston and his efforts to negotiate trade and diplomacy on behalf of the imperiled black nation when I found a letter he wrote responding to a group of Barbadians who had expressed interest in emigrating to Liberia. Liberia's location just next door to Sierra Leone dramatized the Barbadians' odd interest. Overcome with curiosity, I found myself going down a rabbit hole: Why were British colonial Barbadians interested in migrating to Liberia? What made some emigrate to Liberia as others went elsewhere? What happened after they arrived?

An even more complex and fascinating story unfolded in my subsequent research. The story I uncovered brought together West Indians, African Americans, and Africans in ways that piqued my interest and encapsulated my passions. It struck me that while the Barbadians' story resembled that of other nineteenth-century migrants, theirs neither shared the common set of tropes nor the sense of narrative inevitability. My initial questions about Liberian diplomacy evolved to black colonization and emigration and were further complicated by the added layers of identity, which were also shaped by the ghosts of race and colonialism. Throughout the story, it became evident that as black migrants navigated the different structures in which they found themselves, they walked the tightrope that often revealed their conflicting human tendencies. Just as early African American black nationalists dreamt of creating an African utopia that often centered around American republican political ideals and Christianity, Afro-Barbadians were pan-Africanists whose ideas tended towards pro-royalist Anglophilia. These human contradictions became even clearer as black migrants increasingly slipped into more sanctimonious and oppressive positions as they took on the posture of white supremacy from which they sought to escape, and as the veneer of consanguinity and congeniality faded away.

One question loomed large throughout the research: why would previously oppressed blacks migrate to a new place to participate in acts that oppressed other blacks. I attempted to trace the path through which persons reeling from white supremacist abuse turned into its proponent and outline the ways in which blacks moved from the position of the dominated to the dominant. What became clear beyond the fact of white supremacy's global presence was also the seeming impossibility of escaping its ideals. As it permeated the social and discursive landscape, white supremacy shaped how black migrants thought about and approached certain issues. Consequently, its ideas would often be weaponized by blacks in their quest for racial uplift. As such, alongside the hopes of creating respectability for the black race, which was often at the heart of the migrants' redemption story arc, was also a desire to wield a kind of white power that had always felt physiologically distant.

In black colonizing and civilizing missions, indigenous Africans came to represent the depraved parts of what is perceived to be the "riven consciousness" of black people. They manifested the kinds of haunting abjection black migrants sought to redeem.[1] Diasporic migrants were thus willing to use them as collateral in the quest for black redemption. These initial research interests were further fueled by observations of a contemporary moment in which black migrants to the United States from the Caribbean, Africa, and Latin America have had to grapple with racism in the United States. They often find interesting ways to navigate the American racial landscape by pushing against and distancing themselves from historical constructs of blackness established relative to the native African Americans. Those who were not engaging in these kinds of gymnastics carefully sought other ways to overcorrect their behavior to offset the stereotypes associated with blackness. Naturally, as these

[1] Richard Wright, *Native Son* (New York: Harper Perennial Modern Classics, 1993), XXI.

various migrants wrestled with black history and identity, the past eerily continued to haunt the present.

Telling the story of Barbadian migration to Liberia required a wide array of documents. In Barbados, London, and Indiana, I discovered letters the Barbadians had written to Ralston, the American Colonization Society (ACS), and the Liberian government, as well as their numerous signed petitions to the British king. I also found the Barbadians' birth and church records, ship manifests, photographs, observations of colonizationists, missionary records, travel diaries, diplomatic records, African American news reports, Liberian presidential records, political and ethnographic databases, and maps at the various archives in Liberia, the University of Indiana, Bloomington, the Schomburg Center for Research in Black Culture, and the United States National Archives. When pieced together, these sources brought the story of the Barbadians into the larger discussion of nineteenth century black migration, thus enabling us to appreciate more deeply the contours of transatlantic black freedom movements, Liberian colonization, and ideas of blackness.

In archival documents, emigrants were often subsumed in numbers and represented as masses rather than as individuals and families with specific agendas. In recording the migrants in the ship's manifest, the ACS delineated the Barbadians by family unit, age, labor, and religion. Baptismal registers and ship manifests recorded the migrants' names, professions, and addresses in a way that catered to reconstructing the organizational structure of their households, family and kinship networks, work and religious affiliations, and community and class ties. What further gave the Barbadian emigrants significance were the meanings the ACS and the Liberian officials attached to these categories of classification. The Barbadian emigrants' locations within identifiable labor groups, communities, and institutions dictated their ambitions. Yet the 346 Barbadians who expressed interest in emigrating to Liberia were by no means homogeneous. They were a heterogeneous group whose identity as British subjects and Africans in the colonies were mediated by a myriad of differences surrounding gender, age, skill, education, religious affiliation, and social and political status.

Though the ACS had their own system of organizing the Barbadian migrants in its ship manifest (by name, age, occupation, and religious affiliation), it was necessary to be mindful of the silences. Demystifying the Barbadian emigrants and rendering them visible required disinterring their narrative from an archive as thorny as the racial and cultural mélange in which they found themselves. By listing the occupation of only the male passengers, the ACS ship's manifest rendered women's work invisible. Corroborating birth records, tax information, newspaper reports, and census data in Barbados often turned up differences. Religious ascriptions had to be considered within institutional, societal, religious, and cultural distinctions in which they were archived. For instance, the ACS designated the Barbadian emigrants as Episcopalian, which is the American term for their branch of Anglicans. Such designations and differentiations reflected the changing nature of cultural entanglements in which the migrants found themselves in their journey from British colonial Barbados to American colonial Liberia.

The archive, by unleashing a trail of designations and nomenclature in reference to the subjects of this study, shows the different ways in which black people were bound up in the records of the state. This fueled questions about how meanings changed not only in different archives but also across time and space. The absence of a racial category in the ship's manifest swept Afro-Barbadians up within the ACS's and African American ideas of blackness. This book, however, strives to give complexity to racial identity in numerous ways. I used letters, settlement patterns, architecture, labor, and nomenclature to tease out and trace transformations in the symbolic expressions of racial, cultural, and ethnic identity. In discussing the period before the end of slavery in 1834, I use terms such as enslaved Africans and free coloreds to denote Barbadians of both African and European ancestry who were free before the legal end of slavery and free blacks to denote Barbadians of African ancestry who were free during slavery. The members of the Barbados Company for Liberia (BCL) referred to themselves as "middle class," and so I refer to them accordingly. At times, I use Afro-Barbadians to specifically denote a link between African-ness and British-ness, both capturing complicated and challenged forms of identity, and social creations that have their own specific entangled lineages.[2] Such usage further served as a marker of difference to distinguish identity politics based on hegemonic views of race and nationality.

Nomenclature also reflected temporal and migratory changes. Identities did not always supersede prejudices. During slavery, some free Afro-Barbadians were referred to as "Congoes" as a means of denoting their darker color and proximity of African-ness. In Liberia, however, Afro-Barbadian colonial British identity became dominant. As a consequence,

---

[2] Agustin Lao, "Decolonial Moves: Trans-Locating African Diasporic Spaces," *Cultural Studies*, Vol. 21, Nos. 2–3 (2007), 320.

the Barbadians were often referred to as West Indians or Islanders. In the nineteenth century, African Americans were often politically referenced as "American Negroes," on one side of the Atlantic. Their designation as "Americo-Liberians" reflected the transatlantic shift in their citizenship status in Liberia and the ever-changing politics of nomenclature. In Liberia, African recaptives, also referred to as liberated Africans, received the designation "Congoes," which reflected not only their place of origin in Angola but also their rank in the Liberian caste. Native and indigenous ethnic Africans were sometimes identified by their distinct ethnic groups but were often simply referred to as "indigenes," and at other times "heathens." Other terms were used to represent different groups of blacks across class, ethnicity, and nationality.

Given the number of intersecting areas in the book, it took a long time, a lot of traveling, and assistance to come together. I am indebted to more people than there is space available for adequate acknowledgment. My husband, Roderick Stakley, who did extra chores and exercised the patience of Job throughout this process, is deserving of the heartiest gratitude. From time to time, he would enquire, how's the book coming along. The answers were already evident with the books, newspapers, and other documents that had begun to take over our house. Nonetheless, once he had seen my face, he would have had his answer. My parents, Prince Banton and Joan Gayle, family and friends, especially my cousins, have always been my source of determination and strength. My sincere appreciation also goes to my supervisor, Professor Richard Blackett, for the time he spent in directing, guiding, reading, editing my work, and answering my frantic panicked calls. At times, it tested his patience, sanity, and will to live. But he persevered. I thank him for his words of caution and advice and for being a role model through his research and scholarship. Occasionally, I would get emails from him, ranging from, "Look, I think this might be one of your Bajan people," to ribbings about the rivalry between Trinidad and Tobago and Jamaica to West Indies cricket and Premier League Football. Professor B paved the path before me, calling friends to host me on research trips at the University of Indiana and elsewhere. Mrs. Blackett, who always fed me and made sure my treat supply was never low, was like a surrogate mother during my time at Vanderbilt. The Blacketts' generosity and kind spirit have shaped not only my academic pursuits but also my life outside the walls of academy.

I would like to thank Vanderbilt University and the University of Arkansas for the generous support that helped to bring this project into being. The main libraries at both of these institutions played a significant role in the completion of the project. The Interlibrary Loan Department expedited requests for books and materials with lightning speed that enabled me to keep my momentum. At Vanderbilt University, Jane Landers, Moses Ochonu, and Jemima Pierre read early drafts of this book and provided thoughtful comments and feedback. I would also like to express my sincere thanks to Jim Gigantino, Michael Pierce, Trish Starks, and Randall Woods at the University of Arkansas who also read early drafts of this book.

Several fellowships helped to facilitate the creation of this book: The Albert Gordon Foundation and the Rotary International enabled the initial foreign research legs of this book in Liberia. The Herbert and Blanche Weaver Fellowship enabled research at the Historical Society of Pennsylvania and the Library Company of Philadelphia. The Andrew Mellon Foundation fellowship linked me with a group of scholars across a wide range of academic disciplines in the Sawyer Seminar—"The Age of Emancipation: Black Freedom in the Atlantic World" also served as a captive audience for early drafts of this book. During this year-long residency at the Robert Penn Warren Center where I drafted and workshopped early chapters, my fellow scholars—Richard Blackett, Teresa Goddu, Jane Landers, Catherine Molineux, Celso Castilho, Daniel Sharfstein, Herbert Marbury, Nihadf Farooq, and Emily August—offered valuable suggestions and critiques that moved the book beyond its initial narrow scope.

Through the Lapidus Center Fellowship, I was fortunate enough to spend time doing additional research and re-drafting this book at the Schomburg Center for the Study of Black Culture. Being in the center was inspiration enough but I also had the pleasure to meet and work with Sylvianne Diouf, who provided incredible advice and insight. My residency at the Schomburg was made all the more productive through regular seminar meetings facilitated by Farah Jasmine Griffin and the other residents, including Sonia Sanchez, Soyica Colbert, C. Riley Snorton, Tsisti Jaji, Kaiama Glover, Nicole Wright, Tanisha Ford, Sylvia Chan-Malik, Andrianna Campbell, and Jeff Diamant. They have provided advice and support above and beyond what was required of them. Aisha Al-Adawiya, Steven Fullwood, Mary Yearwood, Maira Liriano, and Cierra Bland also provided incredible assistance and support.

The generous support of Nancy Malkiel Weiss further facilitated the research and work that was necessary to complete this project. I would also like to thank the archivists at the Barbados National Archives, the University of the West Indies at Cave Hill, and the Barbados Library in Bridgetown. I am truly grateful not only for all their services rendered but also for the kind words and warm smiles with which they always greeted me. On the Barbados leg of my research journey, Professor Emeritus Sir Woodville Marshall provided a treasure trove of information that helped me to put together baptism records, residency, and place names of the migrants and often took me on little excursions for me to experience Barbados.

I am indebted to Verlon Stone at the Liberia Collection at the University of Indiana, Bloomington, who went above and beyond to digitize and share archival materials that were necessary for the start and completion of the manuscript. He was the one who pointed me in the direction of the Svend Holsoe Collection. I am deeply indebted to Holsoe, who over the course of his life worked in a variety of capacities in Liberia. He knew the book needed to be written and gathered many letters from the United States National Archives and gave copies to both the Liberia Collection at the University of Indiana and the Barbados Museum and Historical Society. Those documents helped me to forge the kinds of transatlantic connections in the story I had been trying to tell. Thanks to archivists and staff at the archives at the University of the West Indies at Cave Hill, the Barbados National Archives, the Barbados History and Museum Society, the Albert Porte Memorial Library in Liberia, the Historical Preservation Society of Liberia, and the University of Liberia. Kenneth Best at the *Liberia Observer* also directed me towards critical newspaper sources. I am grateful to Aren Ramirez, his grandmother Mai Barclay Roberts, and other family members of Barbadian migrants such as Tony Barclay Morgan, who gave their time and resources to this project.

It is a real honor that my manuscript found a home at Cambridge University Press. I would also like to thank Deborah Gershenowitz, Rachel Blaifeder and Ruth Boyes who guided me through the entire process. I would also like to thank the reviewers for their thorough review and thoughtful suggestions that were key for improving key theoretical aspects of the book even as they pushed me to keep the narrative centered on the Afro-Barbadians. My sincere thank you also goes to the administrative staff at Vanderbilt University and University of Arkansas: Heidi Welch, Brenda Hummell, Jane Anderson and Melinda Adams, Brenda Foster, and Jeanne Short. I am sincerely grateful for the support and advice from Scot Brown, Calvin White, Pearl Dowe, Linda Coon, Yvette Murphy-Erby, Valandra, and Kathy Sloan.

I also wish to big up Kadene Clarke-Gibbs, Camille Belgrave, and Desiree Ethridge, who not only provided love and support as friends and Hampton sisters, but also accommodation, hot meals, and shuttled me from one place to the next during my research in Barbados and New York. In Liberia, my fellow Yaadie, Denise Clarke, and her husband, Eden Charles Reeves provided accommodation and gave generously of their time and connections. In London, Dwayne Prince picked me up from the airport and showed me how to navigate the tube to get to and from the British Archives at the Kew. I am especially grateful that he created one of the highlights of my life by affording me the opportunity to witness Arsenal beat Chelsea in the FA Community Shield match. Professor Dennis Dickerson sent me connections with Liberia he discovered in his own research. Marie Ford, Jama Grove, and Imani Lewis transcribed many of the documents in this project. Sustained encouragement and moments of much needed laughter and joy came from my family, and an entertaining group of friends including, Amanda Johnson, Christina Dickerson-Cousins, Nicolette Kostiw, Angela Sutton, and Erica Rhodes Hayden. I thank them all for their moral support and for making this experience a very memorable one.

Abbreviations

AASS	American Antislavery Society
ACS	American Colonization Society
AME	African Methodist Episcopal Church
BCL	Barbados Company for Liberia
BCS	Barbados Colonization Society, also Barbados Colonization Society for Assisting in the Suppression of the Slave Trade and the Introduction of Christianity into Africa
BFASS	British and Foreign Antislavery Society
BMHS	Barbados Museum and Historical Society
CMS	Church Missionary Society
CO	Colonial Office
FUBES, also BES	Fatherland Union – Barbados Emigration Society
ICY	Institute for Colored Youth
PCS	Pennsylvania Colonization Society
TWP	True Whig Party

Introduction

"Who Is This Man and from Whence Comes He to Rule?"

Liberia was not prepared to accommodate the fullness of blackness. At its founding in the 1820s by the American Colonization Society (ACS), the colony only attended to one group of blacks – African Americans. However, with independence, internal pressures, and global developments, the nation progressively opened itself to others. The black nationalist Alexander Crummell then issued a call for all blacks in the diaspora to come to Liberia: "For myself I cordially invite Barbadians, Jamaicans, Sierra Leoneans as well as Americans to this common heritage of the Negro – as the Emigrant Commissioner of New York greet[s] the Germans, Italians, Swedes, English and Irish, who arrive at the port in the hundreds and thousands; and thus, every year swell the already vast population of the great Republic of America."[1] With such invitations framed in the language of black unity and equality, black migrants of different backgrounds and circumstances came to view migration to Liberia as an escape from white supremacist and colonial oppression, and made their way there expecting to be welcomed and embraced under a national canopy of blackness. The Liberian republic thus became a national receptacle for the deeply held aspirations of the African diaspora and a prescription for their historical traumas.

With the desires within and scrutiny from without, Liberia gradually came to be viewed as a state held together by blackness. But even with this racial guarantee, black nationalist migrants who had dreamt of escaping to a black Zion were haunted by the possibility of Liberia collapsing into

---

[1] Wilson Jeremiah Moses, ed. *Destiny and Race Selected Writings, 1840–1898* (Amherst: University of Massachusetts Press, 1992), 190.

a gaggle of fractious tribes. The piercing gaze of whites that had seemingly sealed Liberia's fate a priori made the anxieties all the worse. Given the elevated stakes, the republic could accept ordinary migrants. However, uneasy was the head who was chosen to wear the crown of the Negro Republic. Indeed, defining blackness at the level of the presidency required a level of exceptionality that unavoidably set in motion a revelatory process.

In an editorial published in the aftermath of the 1903 presidential election campaign, J. A. Tuning, a teacher in the Cape Palmas Methodist Episcopal Church common school, exposed the realities behind the feelings that had settled into the idea of Liberia: "The next important event that shall claim the undivided attention of the entire nation is the induction into the office of the newly elected president." But then Tuning inquired, "Who is this man and from whence comes he to rule?" It was his confident assessment that "this is the query going on in the circles, rounds, and claiming the attention of the most thoughtful Liberians whose interest in Liberia is most absorbing."[2] Such queries were to be expected as a part of the grandiosity of the occasion. But as Tuning gathered in the chatter about the president-elect, what many found newsworthy had little to do with either his past misdeeds or a previous appointment as the "head of the financial department." Instead, what was deemed odd was that the newly elected leader had "come *not* from the land of our forefather's nativity to fill that exalted post of the executive chair."[3] Through subjection to scrutiny in gossip and chatter, the primacy of the new president's heritage highlighted electoral expectations and indexed the terms of his othering.

Tuning was right. Up until the turn of the century, all of Liberia's leaders were of American heritage. White American colonizationists who created the colony governed until independence in 1847. Though all subsequent Liberian presidents had been African American migrants, the ACS maintained its hegemony in a nominally independent Liberia that co-opted rather than transformed the previous power dynamics. In the aftermath of the 1903 election campaign, Arthur Barclay, a migrant from the British Caribbean colony of Barbados, who emerged as the winner, became the first variance in Liberia's then fifty-year presidential history. Given the magnitude of changes wrought by the election, the inquiries of the pioneering Americo-Liberian community – and its gatekeepers like Tuning – might have been borne out of sheer curiosity. After all, Afro-

---

[2] *The Liberian Recorder*, December 1903. Liberia Collections, at Indiana University-Bloomington.
[3] Ibid.

Barbadians had arrived at the political negotiating table in Liberia with little more than the charm of being "Victorian Negroes." Yet, the inquiries also acted as a referendum that would unwittingly reveal emerging Liberian political ethics. Indeed, if Barclay, as a black migrant himself, was elected president of a country created for blacks, why was his impending presidency perceived as strange?

If Americo-Liberians were surprised and alarmed it was because Barclay's presidency announced not only a shift in the content of blackness in Liberia but also the ways in which it would be signified. Barclay's impending presidency signaled Liberia as no longer an African American fiefdom. Casting himself as a true patriot with a heritage supposedly traceable to the African American founding of Liberia with the arrival of the ship *Elizabeth* – the black *Mayflower* – Tuning positioned himself as a part of a group who could authorize what was good and respectable for the republic. By questioning Barclay's ascendance in the language of an inherited American colonial nationalism, it became clear that black ethnic divides had intervened to mark actions and attitudes as they heightened tensions that framed decisions. This revealed the Liberian pecking order and unwittingly laid bare the boundaries and hierarchies within blackness. Showing people like Barclay as foreign to the seat of the Liberian presidency was one thing. The implication of his foreignness to normative views of blackness in the idea of Liberian was quite another. By suggesting that Barclay lacked the requisite heritage and pedigree of past presidents, Tuning's fears about a non-American black leader revealed blackness in Liberia as hinging on the origin of certain blacks. Beyond its intended political formalities, Barclay's election and the hysteria it created served also to unsettle Liberia's dynamics as a black nationality by muddying the power relationships and processes that defined blackness. Thus, the suspicions and whispers about Barclay's impending presidency not only exposed the burden of intra-black power sharing but also how efforts to signify and represent the full spectrum of blackness became one of Liberia's biggest challenges.

Reflecting black migrant efforts to realize their dreams against clashing intra-racial and insider interests, the response to Barclay's election forces a reckoning with the kinds of provincialism that spurred ethnic biases within nineteenth century black spaces. What did it say about blackness and opportunity in Liberia when West Indian migrants like Barclay were viewed as strangers? White abolitionists and colonizationists as well as black nationalists and pan-Africanists had insisted that existence alongside whites was key to understanding the oppressive forces that created inequality for blacks. It was partly on account of this implicit concession that the black nationality of Liberia had been created. Revealing Liberia's vulnerabilities under a global gaze as the long arm of white supremacist and colonial forces were extended through blacks' internalization and embodiment of them, Barclay's rise to a position of power and visibility and his election controversy presents a counterpoint. Some black migrants had not rejected oppression but rather showed a predilection for the sort of black particularity and ethnocentrism imbued with the kinds of authoritarianism that benefited them. Indeed, if Liberia was supposed to represent a blow to racial oppression, it had instead become yet another site for it: its maintenance of previous power structures only benefited and valorized some groups of blacks, and forced others to assimilate or be excluded. As black migrants were pushed to discard some unsuitable parts of themselves, they probably pondered their reasons for going to Liberia in the first place. As some would discover, blackness was as much a color as it was an unsteady idea. And so was Liberia.

"A SPIRIT OF EMIGRATION TO LIBERIA"

Arthur Barclay's presidential controversy played out on the Liberian national stage, but it recalled decisions put in motion years before. They had not only altered the Barclay family path but provided the scaffolding for Arthur Barclay's rise to power in 1903. Only four years old in 1865 when his father, Anthony Barclay, made up his mind to leave Barbados with his family of thirteen and nearly 333 others, Arthur Barclay had yet to imagine a future as president of a nation. If anyone harbored those dreams, it was his father. Going against the public feelings of an era when black oppression seemed absolute and unchallengeable, the elder Barclay had imagined himself as a future ruler of a "Negro" nation. Given the nature of the circumstances under which he went to Liberia and the journey to get there, Barclay would without a doubt have been proud of his son's achievements. For Barbadian families who had journeyed to Liberia, the Barclays stood as the archetype of achievement and success. Yet, with the elder Barclay's own motives for leaving the Caribbean forming the beginning of his son's election dilemma, he would have also been shocked at the bitterness of the debate surrounding his election. Occurring nearly half a century later, Barclay's presidential election stood out of step with the underlying imperatives and circumstances that brought his family to Liberia.

In the 1840s, Anthony Barclay had suffered years of failure in advocating for post-slavery reforms in Barbados before he even considered leaving. He had hoped to convince the British monarchy that he and members of his class were loyal subjects who were fit for and deserving of their rights. In the midst of increasing white backlash against post-emancipation reforms, an anonymous writer, working under the pen name Africanus, wrote to the editor of *The Liberal*, a local newspaper, to suggest that Afro-Barbadians should broaden their horizons. The mysterious Africanus might have even outed himself as Barclay when he posed this question: "If political equality is denied to us in that land which gave us birth by those in whom rests the power to bestow it – how are we to obtain it?"[4] On one hand, Africanus suggested that Afro-Barbadians fight their way "as the braver spirits among us are doing – bringing all our moral energies to the good work." In another breath, however, he demanded that they seek it "on other and more auspicious shores, leaving behind the land of our birth – that land which is dear to our hearts, to be tilled by the tyrants who claim it as their own."[5] As Africanus's refrain of finding a "more auspicious shore" animated post-slavery life, it increasingly functioned to reset the limits placed on the desires and imaginative horizons of Barclay and other like-minded Barbadians.

Reacting to his discontent with a determination to fulfill his dreams, Barclay set his sights directly across the ocean to Liberia. Though on a distant shore, Liberia felt much closer to Barbadians. The Atlantic, the once shark-filled gulf that had swallowed up the bodies of chained Africans, did not appear so horrifying as to render chancing a crossing foolish. With the abolition of slavery and the emergence of Liberia as a possible alternative, the ocean appeared as a bridge drawn across two shorelines united by shared concerns about the future of blackness. Barclay's vision of life across the Atlantic was not as much about distance from Barbados as it was about envisioning his full and all-encompassing freedom. Staring across the vast ocean filled Barclay with the belief that he too could one day become governor of a Negro Republic. Having made up his mind to move there, Barclay and others began selling their cottages and giving up rented lands. But with no ships running between Barbados and Liberia and little or no financial resources, "sad disappointment" came over "the poor but well-meaning" group. The realization that their dreams of emigration could not "be achieved without foreign aid"

---

[4] *The Liberal*, February 17, 1841. Accessed at the Barbados National Archives, St. Michaels, Barbados.
[5] Ibid.

brought the Barbadians to the American Colonization Society (ACS), the very organization in the United States that had created the Liberia colony for blacks.[6]

Barbadians' longstanding interest in Africa proved valuable in approaching the ACS. Through institutions such as the Barbados Colonization Society for Assisting in the Suppression of the Slave Trade and the Introduction of Civilization into Africa, Barbadians had for a long time supported missionary ventures in hopes of serving as colonial agents of British abolitionism, civilizing, and imperial efforts. Due to their own experiences shaped from personal pathologies, British royalism appealed to many Afro-Barbadians after emancipation. Having enjoyed years of post-emancipation freedom, they were also most of all seduced by the possibilities of serving as representatives in the British imperial bureaucracy in Sierra Leone and other colonies in Africa. An awareness of imperial post-emancipation possibilities also mapped out "more auspicious shores," where Afro-Barbadians like Barclay could envision a future.

From Barbadians' early interests in Africa, two emigration movements had emerged. Anthony Barclay Jr. steered one group, serving as the chairman of the Fatherland Union – Barbados Emigration Society for Liberia (FUBES), while James T. Wiles served as secretary for the Barbados Company for Liberia (BCL). Unlike African Americans who had ready access to Liberia through the ACS, the Barbadians were forced to take a different route in order to make their emigration a reality. As Barbadians' interest in African emigration turned to an eagerness to flee the island in the 1860s, Wiles turned to Joseph Attwell, who he described as "not just a friend but a leading committee member and a fellow worker in a Scheme for officiating an Emigration to Liberia."[7] Attwell had left Barbados to study divinity at the Institute for Colored Youths (ICY) in Philadelphia, but due to the desperation of his friends, he quickly became their Liberia emigration agent.

Jolted into action in December 1864, Attwell, in a letter to the ACS, communicated the Barbadians' interests and concerns. "Invoking aid on behalf of the Company," he conveyed their "Urgent Appeal in Aid of Emigration ... from Barbados to Liberia."[8] He noted, "Were a free passage provided, several hundreds of worthy and industrious Barbadians

---

[6] *The African Repository*, Vol. 41 (1865): 19.
[7] James J. Wiles to George L. Armstrong Esquire, November 1, 1864. Svend Holsoe Collection, Indiana University, Bloomington.
[8] *The African Repository*, Vol. 41 (1865): 18.

would gladly and immediately seek the attractive shores of the African Republic."[9] As chairperson of the Fatherland Union, Barclay knew of over three hundred other Barbadians who were interested in emigrating to Liberia.[10] With concerns about respectability, he had largely chosen the potential migrants from artisans and professionals like himself who came from the political elite and socially mobile Afro-Barbadian middle class.[11] Single individuals formed the minority interest in a group of over fifty couples with large families. Though Barclay came from an older generation born during slavery, the majority members of his migrant group were young people and children born after slavery. Of the 346 total emigrants, 81 (23 percent) were between the ages of thirty and sixty-five, and 31 were born before slavery ended in 1834; 244 (70 percent) were born after slavery, and 24 (7 percent) were born during the period of apprenticeship (1834–1838). Despite divisions by age, the commonalities of class, religious affiliation, profession, and ambition forged in the crucible of their Caribbean post-emancipation experiences, formed a cohesive force that brought the group together as potential emigrants to Liberia.

For the ACS, a letter from the Barbadians was uncommon but not entirely surprising. Since launching in 1816, they had shuffled through piles of requests begging for some kind of assistance to emigrate to Liberia, but almost exclusively from African Americans. Hardly any letters were from black people outside of the United States, let alone from British colonial Barbadians, widely thought to be the most loyal of all West Indians. Having earned the reputation as the "gem of all the British Isles," travelers throughout the Atlantic world regularly mocked Barbados's loyalty by referring to the island as a "little London" and the provincial county of "*Bimshire*." Given this standing, the Barbadians' letter was truly an audacious move. Clearly, expectations of loyalty could not blunt the imagination of British subjects like Barclay when geographic pressure, familial aspirations, political goals, and racial consciousness helped him to conceptualize opportunities across multiple landscapes. Yet, surely, the ACS must have wondered: why were Barbadians who were treasured members of the British Empire interested

---

[9] Ibid. Also see reprint in the *Journal of the Barbados Historical and Museum Society* (Hereafter *BMHS*), Vol. 27 (1959): 76.

[10] "Emigration to Liberia," *The Times*, March 31, 1865; *BMHS*, Vol. 30 (1959): 199.

[11] See Jerome S. Handler, Frederick W. Lange, and Robert V. Riordan, *Plantation Slavery in Barbados: An Archaeological and Historical Investigation* (Cambridge, MA: Harvard University Press, 1978).

in migrating to Liberia (an American colony turned independent republic) instead of the British colony of Sierra Leone next door?

The Barbadians were new migrant terrain for the ACS. However, by the time their letter was received, it would become useful as propaganda to attract more blacks to Liberia. Printing the letter in bold headlines in *The African Repository,* the ACS boasted that "a spirit of emigration to Liberia is reportedly in existence in St. Kitts, Demerara, St. Thomas, and other islands of the West Indies."[12] Through their published letter, the Barbadians explained that they desired to emigrate to Liberia for two specific reasons: "One being the improvement of their condition by diligent labor, and two, the noble desire of assisting to elevate their fatherland, or building up a nationality, without which they consider their race can never attain their proper position in the family of nations."[13] With their letter, the Barbadians appeared to be both the typical and unusual prospective Liberian emigrants. Unlike many African Americans still enslaved in the United States, Barbadians who were already free were able to sketch out a future where they imagined using their labor to build a republic for the purpose of increasing black racial respectability. Drawing together the commonalities of a black racial identity that elevated the goals of the race, the Barbadians proposed a black freedom that included advancement for themselves, Liberia, and other blacks.

Though the Barbadians initially struggled in their quest to emigrate to Liberia, their interest boded well in the heady 1860s. The American Civil War had not only created a decline in financial support for the ACS but also caused waning African American interest in Liberian emigration. Yet, all the while concerns grew that "Liberia needs an intelligent and producing population."[14] Gripped with the fear of a possible failure of their colonization scheme, the ACS had begun to look for possible solutions when Edward Wilmot Blyden, a Liberian migrant from the British Virgin Islands, suggested that West Indians might fill the emigration void. In 1862, when Blyden returned to the Caribbean to circulate a pamphlet addressed to the "Descendants of Africa throughout the West Indian Islands," Liberian officials began to lure West Indians across the Atlantic, viewing their interest as mutually beneficial.[15] In a period in which a geographically fractured African diaspora began to see Liberia

---

[12] *The African Repository,* Vol. 41 (1865): 19.
[13] Ibid., 18.
[14] *The African Repository,* Vol. 51, July (1875): 65.
[15] Ibid.

with one vision, Blyden's black nationalist and pan-African motifs connected with the Barbadians' post-slavery frustrations and interest in efforts to civilize Africa. Barclay's subsequent appropriation of Liberian officials' rhetoric firmly planted Afro-Barbadians' desires in the very essence of colonizationists' goals. Thus, mutual pan-African desires to "build a nationality" brought together both parties into the cult of civilizing that had come to be regarded as central to the ACS's Liberia mission.[16]

Up to this point, all the stars were aligned to make Barbadians' emigration to Liberia a possibility. With the declining interest of African Americans and the Barbadians' growing interest, the ACS members were left with what appeared to be a simple decision. But they had yet another concern; the same one that Tuning would point out nearly forty years later during Arthur Barclay's presidential election. A clause in the ACS's 1816 constitution had outlined their objectives as an effort to "exclusively colonize ... the free people of color residing in our country [the United States]."[17] As West Indians, the Barbadians clearly fell outside the purview and aims of the ACS. But by 1863, as the Emancipation Proclamation began to foster feelings of hopefulness about life in the United States among African Americans who had shifted their focus away from Liberian emigration to a post-civil war future in the United States, the ACS ultimately revised the clause in their constitution to secure the Barbadians as potential migrants. Ultimately, this change brought together the Barbadians' interest in fleeing the Caribbean with the ACS's mission to increase Liberia's "civilized and productive" population.[18]

By the early months of 1865 when the ACS's migrant ship had still not shown up in Barbados, desperation began to set in. It was as if almost everything had given up on the Barbadians. A drought two years before that severely damaged crops had continued to cause "peculiar suffering and deprivation to all classes of the community." Newspaper editors across the island lamented the "unprecedented increase of the numbers of naked and starving poor in the island."[19] When it finally ended, James Walker – governor of Barbados and the Windward Islands – held

---

[16] Thomas C. Holt, *The Problem of Race in the Twenty-First Century* (Cambridge, MA: Harvard University Press, 2000), 176.

[17] See constitution of the ACS at "American Colonization Society with Abridged Proceedings of the Annual Meeting, and of the Board of Directors at Washington," January 18, 1842. Annual Report of the American Colonization Society: With Minutes. Vol. 25. 1842.

[18] *The African Repository*, Vol. 41 (1864): 150.

[19] BMHS, Vol. 30 (1959): 189; Extracts from *The Times*, Vol. XXX, 65.

a meeting "to consider the question of the distress" and aimed to "suggest, if possible, some practical measures of relief."[20] Walker's plans might have soothed some, but not Barclay and his group, who had already weighed life under the British Empire against other possibilities across the Atlantic. With dreams of freedom deferred in the Caribbean, Barclay and members of the FUBES and BCL shunned the paths taken by their nineteenth-century compatriots. They instead kept their sights on the "Negro Republic" of Liberia, viewing their migration there as the beginning of their full freedom.

FORGOTTEN STORIES OF LIBERIAN COLONIZATION

More Auspicious Shores takes the story of Liberian emigration – familiar to many in the United States and Liberia – and broadens our understanding of it by asking questions about the motivations and dreams of some of Liberia's migrants from a colonial Caribbean, post-emancipation, and African diaspora perspective. Barbadian migration to Liberia has been a lost but critical chapter of Liberian colonization, black freedom movements, and African diaspora history. Most studies on Liberian colonization and emigration have focused exclusively on the various facets of African American efforts. Claude Clegg's *The Price of Liberty: African Americans and the Making of Liberia* (2004)[21] and Kenneth C. Barnes's *Journey of Hope: The Back-to-Africa Movement in Arkansas in the Late 1800s* (2004)[22] represent two of the numerous works that explore the motivations of African American migrants to Liberia from different states in the USA. Eric Burin's *Slavery and the Peculiar Solution* (2005) explores the Liberian colonization project as an antislavery policy.[23] Marie Tyler-McGraw's *An African Republic: Black and White Virginians in the Making of Liberia* (2007) outlines the ways in which the politics of American Republicanism influenced Liberian nation building.

Even though these studies added much-needed nuance and richness to this complex subject, they altogether uniformly read Liberian emigration, colonization, and emergence as a black nationality strictly from an

---

[20] Ibid., 194. Extract from *The Times*, February 14, 1865.

[21] Claude Andrew Clegg, *The Price of Liberty: African Americans and the Making of Liberia* (Chapel Hill: University of North Carolina Press, 2004).

[22] Kenneth C. Barnes, *Journey of Hope: The Back-to-Africa Movement in Arkansas in the Late 1800s* (Chapel Hill: University of North Carolina Press, 2004).

[23] Eric Burin, *Slavery and the Peculiar Solution: A History of the American Colonization Society* (Gainesville: University Press of Florida, 2005).

African American cultural and political perspective. Tom Shick recognized the Barbadians as a migrant group as being separate from African Americans in *Behold the Promised Land: A History of Afro-American Settler Society in Nineteenth-Century Liberia* (1980)[24] but he relegated them to a footnote. Altogether, efforts to explore the black migrants in Liberia have failed to acknowledge West Indians as a community with its own identity, history, and relationship to race and blackness.

Today, the Barbadian migrants in Liberia remain largely forgotten. That only 346 Barbadians migrated in 1865, and only a few followed in subsequent years, possibly contributed to their consistent omission from and demotion in Liberian colonization narratives. Still, in spite of the small number, Barbadian migrants' presence shifted something in Liberia that has settled in its social and political landscape, memory, and other facets of national life. The way in which all-encompassing labels such as "America-Liberian" operate suggests a second and more probable explanation for the Barbadians' invisibility. Used to describe the customary African American migrant in Liberia, the designation of America-Liberian flattened and simplified the content of Liberian emigration in its attribution of black migrants' identity and place of origin to the United States. It thus privileged the interest, experiences, and positions of African Americans in Liberia. For scholars thinking about nineteenth-century migrants to Liberia, it became more apt to envision African American migrants while safely associating West Indians with the neighboring colony of Sierra Leone. As a consequence, historians have not really had the opportunity to fully acknowledge the diversity of Liberia's migrants, let alone process and integrate them into frameworks, theories, and analysis around migration, race, diaspora, or blackness.

Additionally, parallel analyses of the Barbadian emigrants in the Caribbean and in Africa have operated in isolation to one another. Consequently, the Barbadian transatlantic experience has been subject to a fragmented discussion in both Caribbean post-emancipation and Liberian colonization narratives that is routinely dismissed as insignificant. Because scholars rarely looked at the interconnected nature of the lives of Liberia's Afro-Barbadian migrants, we also know relatively little about the transatlantic dimensions of Caribbean post-emancipation. This has served to diminish and disregard the impact of their migration. For Barbadians, emancipation was not a singular moment in which all was resolved and fulfilled in the ways

---

[24] Tom W. Shick, *Behold the Promised Land: A History of Afro-American Settler Society in Nineteenth-Century Liberia* (Baltimore: Johns Hopkins University Press, 1980).

that they imagined. After the legal end of slavery, the quest for liberty among blacks in the Caribbean remained an active endeavor that persisted across space and time. Afro-Barbadians aspired to leave the Caribbean for what they assumed would be greener pastures in Liberia. Wishing for a future unburdened by the past, they discovered the impossibility of separating the two. When looked at from the vantage point of the Caribbean or Liberia, the story of Barbadian migration appears to be an insignificant, micro-historical event. However, when traced across the Atlantic their movement reveals dynamics not usually visible within national or regional frames of study. A transatlantic analysis illustrates that the Barbadian transition from a Caribbean post-emancipation society to life in the West African Republic of Liberia cultivated a development that extended far beyond what one might have expected from a group of 346 migrants. As a social, economic, and political movement that embodied the temporal and spatial breadth of the British post-emancipation project, Barbadian migration to Liberia produced a watershed moment in the black Atlantic world.

One epistemological problem that has contributed to the uneasy placement of Barbadians in Liberian colonization history has much to do with the view of Caribbean emancipation as a temporally specific and spatially constrained phenomenon. Phillip Curtin, in his work *Two Jamaicas* (1955), argued that following the Morant Bay Rebellion in 1865, "the defeat admitted by the assembly which saw the introduction of Crown Colony government was a mark that signaled the end of the post-emancipation epoch."[25] Scholars within this field have done critical work in redefining the struggles of the post-slavery period and have offered various frameworks for understanding Afro-Caribbean peoples' fight against oppression that pushed against the boundaries of freedom. For instance, Melanie Newton's *The Children of Africa in the Colonies* (2008) has established a foundational reframing of Afro- Barbados post-emancipation experiences. Meanwhile, Nemata Blyden's *West Indians in West Africa, 1808–1880: The African Diaspora in Reverse* (2000) has shown the outcome of West Indians' migration to Sierra Leone and other West African colonies.

Still, regional and national historical frameworks continue to create analyses of the Caribbean with a kind of parochialism that treats the experiences of emancipation as spatially bounded. Such geographical strictures that foster narrow regional and national frameworks have continued

---

[25] Phillip Curtin, *Two Jamaicas: The Role of Ideas in a Tropical Colony* (Westport, CT: Praeger,1968), 101.

to misconstrue the study of post-emancipation by concealing more than they reveal. Cutting off the transatlantic dimensions necessarily obscures the scope of Afro-West Indian post-emancipation demands and the array of desires they centered in their struggle to find freedom, citizenship, and nationhood. A reduced geography and chronology thus unwittingly purports emancipation to be a narrow, singular moment of resolution and fulfillment for West Indians. Afro-Barbadians, however, by considering their relations to blacks in other transnational spaces and the larger structural problems of freedom that collectively afflicted them had developed a diasporic imagination through which they considered remaking their lives and affecting larger social and political transformations.[26] The ways in which the Barbadians imagined and remade themselves in relation to other blacks buttressed a significant part of the politics of Caribbean emancipation. It animated the very nature of how they conceived of the nature of their own subjectivity – themselves as political agents, the nature of their agency, and how they thought it should be used. The transatlantic migration of some of Newton's documented "children of Africa in the colonies" attests to the expansive transatlantic resistance carried out by black people to achieve a more meaningful freedom during the post-emancipation period. By reorienting how we think about Caribbean post-emancipation, African colonization, and Liberia as a black nation, this narrative of Barbadian migration illuminates these previously unexamined challenges. As such, it illustrates the African diaspora's ever shifting and differential experiences of freedom, citizenship, nation building, and blackness across the Atlantic world.

HISTORIOGRAPHICAL INTERSECTIONS IN LIBERIA

Historiographical intersections make it possible to recover the historical connections, continuities, discontinuities, and mutabilities in the movement of the Barbadians and their ideas from one side of the Atlantic to the other. Furthermore, the Barbadians constituted but one fragment of the African diaspora who ended up in Liberia. Upon arrival, in addition to the African Americans who were either forcefully colonized or had emigrated voluntarily, they also encountered various ethnicities of Liberian indigenes as well as displaced African recaptives liberated

---

[26] Henrietta Moore, *Still Life: Hopes, Desires, and Satisfaction* (Cambridge, UK: Polity Publishers, 2011), 2.

from slave ships. Thus, in addition to a transatlantic dimension, the Barbadian migration yokes together several other historiographies.

Firstly, the Barbadians' migratory move was less a radical creation of something new than a recovery of timeless African diasporic efforts towards resistance. Mobility had always been a means of insurgency for enslaved and free Africans throughout the diaspora. Maroons (escaped slaves) in Jamaica, Cuba, Brazil, and Suriname fled slavery in search of new spaces of freedom in mountains, swamps, and even urban areas. African Americans escaped slavery to create new societies in Nova Scotia, Haiti, and Sierra Leone and fled unfair contractual arrangements in the South for better wages after the Civil War.[27] Similar factors also drove migratory workers from the British West Indies to the Spanish Caribbean. From Jamaican peasants escaping to the foothills of the Blue Mountains to the Exodusters of the United States, the logic of movement was inexorable. Movement was a metaphor for freedom and Africans in the diaspora radically claimed the right to move about freely for themselves in slavery and freedom. Mirroring these hemispheric movements, Barbadian emigration represents freed people's continued subversion of systems of oppression in "freedom."[28] The Barbadian migrants' story builds on histories of African diasporic freedom movements. It joins many other narratives in the field of African Diaspora Studies, where scholars have increasingly sought to explore the diverging nature of black freedom strategies to address more broadly black movements to resist domination, inequality, and injustice.

The integration of Barbadians and the post-emancipation context out of which they emigrated shows the Liberian post-independence period as one negotiated by a wide cross-section of blacks with different experiences and aspirations. Re-telling the story of American colonization of Liberia from a Caribbean post-emancipation perspective highlights the different

---

[27] The works of Stephen Hahn, Thomas Holt, Rebecca Scott, Lee Bettis, and Patricia Fumerton have together further shown that such movements of laborers in the nineteenth century point to broad similarities throughout the Atlantic.

[28] See Nell Irvin Painter, *Exodusters: Black Migration to Kansas after Reconstruction* (New York: Knopf, 1977); David L. Golbert and Jerome Handler, "Barbados in the Post-Apprenticeship Period: The Observations of a French Naval Officer," *Journal of the BMHS*, Vol. 35, No. 4 (1978): 243–266 and Vol. 36, No. 1 (1979): 4–15; James Haskins, *The Geography of Hope: Black Exodus from the South After Reconstruction* (Brookfield, CT: Twenty-First Century Books, 1999); Ira Berlin, *The Making of African America: The Four Migrations* (New York: Viking Press, 2010); Lara Putnam, *Radical Moves: Caribbean Migrants and the Politics of Race in the Jazz Age* (Chapel Hill: University of North Carolina Press, 2013).

sets of motives and calculations within which different members of the African diaspora viewed migration to a black republic. While different segments of the African diaspora emigrated to Liberia, their motivations were not all the same. Flattening black migrants to Liberia and their motivations into a single anachronistic rationale alienates them from the historical restrictions, cultural bases, and material realities of their own motivations and desires. The particular nature of the constellation of subjective forces around them, including material conditions, played a clear role in why different groups within the African diaspora pursued African emigration. It shaped the worlds they drew from and carried with them. African Americans who migrated to Liberia before the Emancipation Proclamation of 1863 sought to escape the travails of an American slave society. Barbadians who pursued a more expansive form of freedom, citizenship, and belonging through Liberian migration in 1865, only did so after experiencing over thirty years of a Caribbean post-slavery period and failed attempts to negotiate their status and rights under the auspices of the British Empire through royalist appeals. A microhistory of the African diaspora in Liberia thus serves to delineate the differences in the subjectivities, imaginaries, and contexts from which the migrants imagined their migration.

Ultimately, Liberian colonization brought historically and culturally specific forms of black subjectivity side-by-side in one of the most critically scrutinized political settings of the African diaspora in the nineteenth century. This opens up new spaces of inquiry to understand the genealogies of power and political economy that accompanied different streams of black migrants. The wide-ranging means by which the different groups of blacks arrived in Liberia – enabled by different types of cultural, social, economic, and political technologies – attest to the scope of African diasporic struggles for freedom, citizenship, and nationhood. The interconnected conversations and historiographies in the African diaspora and transatlantic and black Atlantic history that come together in Liberia recover the links between African American and Caribbean freedom movements. Piecing them together also recasts new conceptual and theoretical boundaries that further our understanding of Liberia's complex history. Being a migratory destination for the African diaspora meant that Liberia also became the resting place for not only the crises of freedom, labor, and race but also racial and ideological sensibilities whose expansive nature are not readily perceptible through national narratives. As a layered story of Caribbean emancipation, migration, and African liberation, Barbadian emigration revives some elements of the debates in African diaspora history by forging new connections and paths between ideas about freedom, citizenship, and nationhood, black nationalism and pan-Africanism, and meanings of blackness.

Barbadian emigration to Liberia, told within the story of Liberian colonization, highlights other compelling aspects of an African diaspora framework. Liberia stood at the center of an intersection between the diaspora and Africa. In this new commingling of diaspora where overlapping layers of experiences laced various histories together, the different historical and intellectual genealogies of interest in Liberia were shaped by and, in turn, also shaped the evolution of the black nationalist and pan-African discourse through which black people exchanged ideas. Different African diasporic groups came to ideologies of pan-Africanism and black nationalism in different ways. Each version was largely dependent on how the different localities within the diaspora constructed meaning through the dynamics of their sociopolitical maps. The Barbadians emigrated with local forms of racism that served as the antecedent to their ideology that also propped up monarchism, colonialism, and capitalism, thus making visible the constitutive role of their British colonial experience.

To the extent that the Barbadians' story became an indispensable component of the Liberian nation-building process, their historiographical exclusion negates the various ways in which ideals of British colonialism affected the Republic and shaped its ideologies. Whereas African Americans expressed themselves from an American Republican position, Afro-Barbadians tended to articulate race consciousness and ideas about Africa from a British royalist and imperial perspective. Unlike African Americans who were black nationalists, Afro-Barbadian emigrants were instead pan-Africanists who did not necessarily believe in the necessity of a nation state, and as a consequence, buried British royalism and colonialism within their ideologies of liberation. The complex nature of the challenges that defined the Liberian experiment over time, differentially positioning the migrants within black nationalist and pan-African ideologies, was also bound to affect relationship formation and coexistence upon arrival in Africa. The juxtaposition of the migrants' dissimilar impulses reveals the ways in which their seemingly cohesive visions had begun to fracture even before they had even arrived in Liberia.

FROM DOMINATED TO DOMINANT/ OF VICTIMS TURNED VICTIMIZERS

The story of Afro-Barbadian migration to Liberia shows the continuities from slavery to freedom that moved across space from the Caribbean to

Africa and worked in ways that complicated aspirations. Having been faced with the oppressive forces of colonialism and white supremacy, black migrants were seduced by the thought of removing themselves from whites to create a black-only nation. An ethnically black nationality, it was believed, would create a sociopolitical contract that would ensure the equal experiences of freedom, citizenship, and nationhood for blacks. In these ideas that promoted blacks' removal from white spaces, anti-black racism appeared as a passive rather than an active system, a vestigial impulse that would inevitably fade with distance. The hope that a racially homogenous future would result in a paradise where white racism miraculously declined was misleading at best. At worst, thoughts of Liberia as a uniform mass of blacks reinforced the "racist witchcraft"[29] that had created ideas about "blackness" in particular and race in general. The triumphant lore of escaping white supremacy and overcoming racism went to the core of a mistaken perception and ignored a durable feature of these oppressive forces. People who were once the objects of imperial and white supremacist oppression often became accomplices in their own victimization and enablers of a system they had once sought to resist.

When black migrants believed they had gotten away from the dread and terror of white supremacy and colonialism, different aspects of the ideologies traveled to Liberia through black migrants' own internalization of them. White supremacist and colonial discourse and other efforts to discipline blackness moved from the colonies across the Atlantic through black migrant thoughts and actions. Despite British half-hearted reforms and various revolutions that gripped the Caribbean, migrants often primarily understood freedom through the models and choices that capitalism offered. Thus, aspects of white racism and imperialism were integrated in their quest for black redemptive efforts to colonize and civilize Africa. As pioneers, some African American migrants served as the ambassadors of white supremacy, colonialism, and imperialism. The social, cultural, and political complexity and tensions produced by the Barbadians' arrival in Liberia marked the ways in which British colonialism presented itself in new spaces. Though Africa featured prominently in pan-African motifs, it did not animate the central political mission in Liberia. Altogether, the migrants' civilizing plan rested on the view that certain color, culture, and labor practices were markers of inferiority. In a republic designed to foster black empowerment, the only

[29] See Karen E. Fields and Barbara Jeanne Fields, *Racecraft: The Soul of Inequality in American Life* (London: Verso, 2012).

redeemed blacks were diasporic migrants whose aim was to defend blackness against the threats of barbarity and savagery. Recaptive Africans and
indigenes, who were viewed as culturally backward and uncivilized,
would have to prove themselves to the civilizing troop of diasporic
migrants who had come to remediate black pathology.

As diasporic migrants journeyed into "uncivilized Africa," they entered
an African world to which they presumed affiliation but from a superior
position. In a peculiar sense, the diasporic migrants were cultural strangers. For this reason, their civilizing efforts struggled to sway African
indigenes and recaptives who did not perceive the migrants as being
a part of them, and instead viewed them as an alien force. Having been
previously marginalized, the migrants did with freedom what had been
done to them. Sanitized of their enslavement, the diaspora's turn to
African civilization was conditioned by their desire to exercise a power
begotten by their proximity to whiteness. Adopting white supremacist and
colonial hegemonic traditions became a way of untangling themselves
from its power so as to become individuals and not the collective "others"
that the discourse had categorized them as. In the process, the pernicious
ideologies adopted a spectral presence almost as if their hold and persistence were inevitable.[30]

Positioned at the nexus of an interwoven narrative that reveals the
transatlantic boundaries of freedom, Liberia also simulated the diverging
and contrasting experiences of black oppression and empowerment. In the
blurred lines of oppressed and oppressor, diasporic migrants were both
victims and fiends. As ideas of black liberation gave way to oppression, the
circumstance rather than the race of the victimizer proved to be the most
revealing. Out of all the wounds of Liberia colonization, black oppression
of other blacks pierced the deepest. In the flattening of race, black colonizationists discarded a more complex truth, which offers a loose guide into
understanding the inevitable results of Liberia's later conflicts. Power is
not static, and like most social relationships, hierarchies determined by
race also embodied the practices carried out within them.[31] As race was
transmogrified into class, blacks who had migrated on account of racial
bonds could resent others and covet their political and economic progress.

---

[30] See Jean Paul Sartre, "A Theatre of Situations." *Vol IX: Melanges* (Paris: Gallimard Press,
1972), 101.
[31] Gayatri Chakravorty Spivak, "Can the Subaltern Speak?," in *Marxism and the
Interpretation of Culture*, eds. Cary Nelson and Lawrence Grossberg (Urbana: University
of Illinois Press, 1988), 271–313.

"Not all black subjects liked to hear all subalterns speak." Differences in experiences of subjectivity – "power differentials compounded further by subjective levels of vulnerability" – shaped even relationships within groups.[32] The experience of oppression either made migrants sympathetic to other oppressed groups or made them "the worst of all tyrants."[33] As Ayi Kwei Armah declared in *The Beautyful Ones Are Not Yet Born*, those who once struggled to destroy the masks that hid the truth often became the same ones who, once they tasted power, found those veils useful. In the same way, blacks who had resisted white supremacy, once they were in charge, found that their actual desire all along was to be like them and "live above all the blackness in the big old slave castle."[34] Yet, with the negation of Liberia's diversity in the flattened fiction of nation building, the black migrants who took up these positions rarely understood themselves as engaging in a power struggle. For them, the end goal of racial respectability justified the colonization, civilization, and imperialism means. As this permeated Liberia's political codes, it unraveled black nationalist ideas of racial purity as a panacea against black oppression.

The oppression at the base of the black identity has its roots in slavery and colonialism where migrants witnessed and endured oppression that cemented their blackness. The ontology of Liberia does not account for the violence that is foundational to the formation of blackness as well as the creation of the republic. Since the diasporic black being does not exist without violence, the creation of Liberia produced through migration must take into account these forces that shape it. The reworking of this political ontology to account for the foundational violence in the formation of blackness is necessary to understanding Liberia. Additionally, the possibility of a holistic universal category of human freedom, citizenship, and nationhood never existed in diaspora. These were only possible at a racially tribal level. As a consequence, this created an understanding of these categories as depending upon hierarchies. Thus, even when migration shifted the racial balance of power under their feet, it mapped new

---

[32] Agustin Lao, "Decolonial Moves: Trans-Locating African Diasporic Spaces," *Cultural Studies*, Vol. 21, Nos. 2–3 (2007): 315.

[33] Frances Anne Kemble, *Journal of a Residence on a Georgian Plantation, 1838–1839*. Ryan Memorial Library of the St. Charles Borromeo Seminary (May 24, 2004 [EBook #12422]).

[34] Ayi Kwei Armah, *The Beautyful Ones Are Not Yet Born* (Boston, MA, Houghton Mifflin, 1968).

and even-deeper tribalism, thus fostering new struggles. Freedom within the context of the tribe necessarily created other tribes to oppose.

WHO DEFINES BLACKNESS?

It might appear counterintuitive to explore blackness and race in a black African republic. Working from a post-colonial African perspective, Jemima Pierre's *The Predicament of Blackness: Post-Colonial Ghana and the Politics of Race* (2013) has shown how global white supremacy informed the ongoing construction of racial identity in Ghana. In the same way, an African diasporic reading of Liberia enables a radically different interrogation of the relations of power inscribed in historically variable forms of black subjectivity and the ways in which they came together in Liberia. This enables us to "develop frameworks to understand the articulations of power and culture embedded in different definitions of blackness and distinct forms of black politics."[35] The outcome of these entanglements, as West Indians triangulated their British, Caribbean, and African identities and joined the social, economic, and political struggle for resources and rank with African Americans who negotiated their American and African identities and liberated Africans and indigenes who identified with different ethnic and kingdom affiliations, are indeed valuable. Putting these various identities in service of policies towards Africa's civilization and modernity transformed experiences of freedom, citizenship, and nationhood, as well as the meanings of blackness. Thus, Barbadian emigration and efforts to define their place in Liberia offer complex and valuable ways of understanding and disturbing theoretical configurations around black ethnic and racial formations.

Uniting the neglected and unconnected dimension of Caribbean postemancipation shows the ways in which nineteenth-century Liberia became new grounds out of which different ways of knowing blackness emerged. The crises of post-emancipation that brought together differently emancipated black subjects in Liberia and created a new kind of fraught sociopolitical diasporic space also highlighted the shifting nature of black identities across space and time. As colonizationist and panAfrican rhetoric and efforts defined and solidified the nation's borders, ethnicity and race became wrapped up in the Liberian nationality and the nation-state began to play a significant role in the generation of racial knowledge. Racial politics in Liberia were especially complicated because

[35] Lao, "Decolonial Moves," 325.

of the ways in which desires for shared solidarity and understandings of racial experiences were driven apart by different histories of identity that rendered some migrant groups unrecognizable. Consequently, when the post-independence government sought to foster the idea of Liberia as the black man's republic, it also became a project to craft a unified national racial identity.

Liberia became the stage for the kind of diverse blackness that assumed the absence of dissimilar identities. In ideology, if not always in politics, the black republic sought to cast a liberating image that aimed to invert racial and colonial hierarchies as it countered oppressive whiteness. Overlooking migrants' discrete political prerogatives, the Liberian state produced a false logic of homogeneity and an artificial view of its diverse black community. Instead of acknowledging the different subjective cultures, all the different groups of black migrants, for better or for worse, were lumped together in Liberia, irrespective of their experiences. Liberia sought to replicate the fictive boundaries of race, class, and gender. In doing so, it thereby obscured the interconnected nature of these categories and reinforced their differences by encouraging the uncritical acceptance of the essentialization of race not only as normative and fixed but as expressions of power that were nonetheless intimately intertwined. Migrants thus contended with a Liberian nationality created to reflect the shared cultural codes of blackness through the essentialism and universalized versions proffered by pan-Africanism and black nationalism.[36] With ideas about black racial homogeneity, the Barbadians, like other non-American blacks, were incorporated into the Liberian nation-building project without much thought of the social, cultural, and political ramifications. Those on the outside looking through the flattened lens of blackness came to see Liberia as a stable entity without parts that bumped up against one another. The presumption of an undifferentiated "blackness" functioned to cover up the diversity of black migrants and the variety of ideas that circulated within the Liberian nation-building project, thus underscoring a significant problem in how we understand Liberian colonization, black nationalism, and pan-Africanism.

Much of the ideas and representations of black homogeneity in Liberia came to rely upon an essentialized idea of blackness read through African Americans. Elevated into leadership in Liberia, African Americans

---

[36] Jason McGraw, *The Work of Recognition: Caribbean Colombia and the Postemancipation Struggle for Citizenship* (Chapel Hill: University of North Carolina Press, 2014), 2.

enmeshed the republic with their meanings.[37] The experiences of other groups came to be regarded as peripheral. Under the white gaze, ideas about blackness in Liberia were organized around the positive affirmations of African Americans against African indigenes. Reading blackness through a mobilized African American identity reduced its rich meanings. However, by further bifurcating it into the categories of black and "politically black," it further determined accommodation in the republic. As blackness defined through African Americans shaped the legal construction of citizenship in Liberia, it produced the ideological and racial terrain that other migrants entered in Liberia and the basis by which they would be included or excluded. How then would other members of the African diaspora construe their identity as black people if African Americans had already posted the markers and symbols? As blackness fused with Liberian-ness, non-American migrants took on a derivative black identity. In reinventing themselves from place to place, they privileged or eschewed certain elements of blackness to fulfill Liberia's new expectations of civilization and modernity. The silence of ACS officials, Liberian statesmen, and cultural arbiters – the very people who decided policies around accommodation and citizenship – intervened in the theoretical debate about blackness and its representation on the national landscape. Thus, reframing Liberian colonization from the perspective of Barbadian emigration offers new opportunities to theorize citizenship across different spatial and temporal landscapes as well as understanding its particularities in a black republic.

The struggles of the different groups to articulate and maintain their distinctions rendered the nationalist project of Liberia incomplete. Created on the presumption of blackness as the great and necessary homogenizing force, differences among blacks became apparent when efforts to integrate the various migrant groups into the nation produced uneven results. Liberia revealed the tensions between the ubiquity of black racial codes and inclinations to over-determine racial identity. Though we can discern through the intersections afforded by overlapping experiences the subjugation produced by racist discourses and practices, their particularities were evident. Points of similarities and important distinctions of self-identification, culture, and subject-hood became readily discernible as each wave of culturally different black migrant shifted the bounds of racial determinism and innovated Liberia's racial and ethnic imagination. Thus, rather than racial

---

[37] See Carlos Nelson Coutinho, *Gramsci's Political Thought* (Leiden: Brill, 2012).

coherence, migration to Liberia recreated processes that strengthened separate ethnic formations among diasporic blacks. The political and sociocultural outcomes of uniting "negroes" in the Caribbean, the United States, and Africa in Liberia exerted pressure on ideas of blackness in the Atlantic world and produced new meanings to what it meant to be black. Unveiling Liberia as an Afropolity with multiple groups of black people cordoned off into new ethnic locales inverts conventional thinking about black identity that usually centers African American and white colonizationist views. When our attention is geared toward the qualitatively different experiences of Liberia's various black migrants, the prevailing wisdom about blackness and race loses its luster.

The tendency to view Liberia as a "black" nation despite its various cultural divisions exposes blind spots within understandings of race and ethnicity. Homogenization of emigrants to Liberia undermines the theoretical implications of differential black subjectivities in shaping the Liberian nationality. The resulting relationship between race, ethnicity, and nationality that emerged from the making of Liberia's cosmopolitan black community usurped the categories and concepts on which racial identity prided itself. As it cultivated ethnic formations along sociocultural and political lines, migrant encounters also unlocked new explanations for differences within the African diaspora. The presence of these multiple groups of blacks in Liberia fostered a complex discussion of blackness that sometimes pushed popular opinions in the Atlantic world toward narrower conceptions of race and kinship. Unlike the West where the one-drop rule and the association of culture with biology made blackness capacious in efforts to restrict access to whiteness, blackness in Liberia became a narrow racial category that had to be earned. The sociopolitical and cultural implications of black migration and settlement in Liberia dispelled the biologically deterministic arguments about race that had dominated the thinking of white racists, abolitionists, and colonizationists who created Liberia. Liberia's black migrants discovered that the larger strictures of race "inhere[d] neither in biology nor culture." They realized instead that it must be called to mind by "their encounters in social space and historical time."[38]

As assumptions of black homogeneity fractured, rendering a more complex picture of the black identity visible, the chimerical nature of a single, unified black identity revealed itself. Evelyn Brooks Higginbotham has

---

[38] Thomas Holt, "Marking: Race, Race-making, and the Writing of History," *American Historical Review*, Vol. 100, No. 1 (1995): 1.

suggested that "we should challenge the overdeterminancy of race vis-à-vis social relations among blacks themselves and conceptions of the black community as harmonious and monolithic."[39] The distinctions produced through the intertwining and contestations of migrants' experience call into question the conceptual applicability of Black Atlantic and diaspora theories in Liberia. Diaspora in essence has come to represent a historical logic without the means of showing the struggles within different cultural transformations. Including in diaspora similar occurrences that differ from its core meaning has threatened the idea of it as a framework of understanding. Without engagement with the politics of its different cultural parts, diaspora history becomes an evenly evolving process without spheres of conflict. In recent times, the term Afropolitanism has also emerged to fill some of the gaps in diaspora theory. Afropolitan has come to mean an African way of being amenable to difference in ways that rise above race. It at once replaces the voices of a broader cross-section of Africans with that of a few black elites driven by Western interests which center whiteness and Western colonial ideas in an effort to remake Africa in that image. Afropolitanism has thus proven incapable of taking on that kind of conceptual duty. Without a focus on shared culture rather than racial classification, it prohibits analysis of the various black freedom movements that converged in Liberia and the definitions of black identities structured by multiple and varying connections and the difficulties of diasporic affiliation and pan-African politics.

The migration of the various groups of blacks, each with different points of entry into and out of the Atlantic, signals the limits of frameworks often used to describe places like Liberia. A broader view of Liberian colonization reveals a layered, nuanced field of black experiences that provides us with a variety of theoretical points of view. Black Atlantic and Afropolitan theories fail to provide the kinds of full theoretical accounting for Barbadians' experiences that would explain the kinds of fragmentation and responsibilities of their identity calling for a "triple consciousness" that was necessary for them to assimilate into Liberia.[40] The Caribbean as a point of departure for Liberian migrants produced situational issues that produced consequential action and particular

---

[39] Evelyn Brooks Higginbotham, "African-American Women's History and the Metalanguage of Race," *Signs*, Vol. 17, No. 2 (1992): 255.

[40] Fanon alludes to this idea: "Thus assaulted from all sides, he was made not a double but "a triple person." Frantz Fanon, *Peau noire, mosques blancs* (Paris, 1952), 89–90. Quoted in Thomas Holt, "Marking: Race, Race-making, and the Writing of History," *American Historical Review*, Vol. 100, No. 1 (1995): 1.

meanings, which when enacted and shared in the social and political spheres of the Liberian republic produced epistemic breaks and dissimilar visions of blackness. By acting out their different framing of blackness upon arrival, Liberian migrants animated the shifting divisions within the African diaspora that lingered beneath its veneer of shared codes of black racial references. Liberia ultimately became a black migrant borderland project with each migrant group holding on to its own customs and peculiarities in their settlements. To the extent that we can see the "various black communities living and working in a world of overlapping diasporas," the notions of black homogeneity and undifferentiated blackness unravel.[41]

****

The chapters that follow trace the interlaced chain of events that shaped the Barbadians' journey. Part I (chapters 1–3) outlines one Atlantic dimension of the migrants' lives by examining Caribbean post-emancipation experiences and Barbadians' imaginations of possibilities elsewhere. Understanding Barbadian migration to Liberia means exploring why they desired to leave in the first place, how they were finally able to leave, and what they took with them. Chapter 1 shows the particularities of Afro-Barbadians' post-emancipation subjugation in the Caribbean and their unsuccessful efforts to find solutions within the scope of the monarchal system, which partially cultivated their interest in Liberian emigration. Chapter 2 shows the ways in which colonial subjectivity shaped Barbadians' thoughts on British efforts to civilize Africa and dictated how they navigated their identities as British West Indian subjects and the "children of Africa." Civilizing Africa also played a role in Barbadians' attempts to reclaim the prestige they lost after the end of slavery. By using colonial subjecthood to leverage their importance to the African civilization project, Barbadians positioned themselves at the nexus of the African-European relationship and mapped a new vision of pan-Africanism onto Liberia. Chapter 3 outlines the ways in which communication with African Americans furthered Barbadians' interest in Liberia over other emigration destinations. In mutually imagining a community, these communications forged West Indian and African American ideas about duty to race, thus highlighting the different genealogy of interests in Liberia that shaped strains of black nationalist and pan-

---

[41] Earl Lewis, "'To Turn as on a Pivot': Writing African Americans into a History of Overlapping Diasporas." *American Historical Review*, Vol. 100, No. 3 (1995): 767.

African discourse. Part II (Chapter 4) uses the "middle passage" as a metaphoric space to show the kinds of social, cultural, and political baggage that Barbadian Anglophiles carried to Liberia as they embraced black nationalist ideas for African redemption.

Part III (Chapters 5–7) explores the point where imagined possibilities met realities and illustrates the changing transatlantic ideas and experiences of freedom. Chapter 5 describes Barbadians' settlement and the ways in which they sought to fulfill their dreams of emancipation as they fashioned themselves as Liberians. Chapter 6 highlights the challenges for citizenship in Liberia as Barbadians who helped in the creation of the True Whig Party protested against African American republicanism. Land acquisition and settlement patterns that displaced indigenes physically marked new meanings of blackness onto the landscape and architecture in ways that transformed Liberia's ethnocultural identity. As Liberia struggled to project a civilized black identity, Barbadians' labor served as a new way to claim citizenship. Chapter 7 bookends Barbadians' transatlantic experiences with Arthur Barclay's rise to the presidency, representing the triumph of Barbadian political ideals in Liberia. As West Indian colonial culture worked its way into Liberian culture, law, and nation-building policies, their "English" heritage challenged the legitimacy of their leadership and attracted suspicion as the British encroached on Liberian territory during the scramble for Africa that saw European nations divide the continent among themselves for the purpose of expanding empire and exploiting natural resources.

The experiences of the Afro-Barbadian migrants to Liberia remain formative to understandings of blackness and twentieth-century black freedom movements. Liberia, too, in its development, remained central to black liberation. In the early twentieth century when the Jamaican leader, Marcus Garvey, created the Universal Negro Improvement Association (UNIA) and renewed the call for a back-to-Africa movement, the 1865 group of West Indian migrants in Liberia would serve as a source of connection for Garvey's pan-Africanist vision. Much time had separated early nineteenth-century pan-Africanists from their twentieth-century counterparts. But while the circumstances had changed, the underlying experiences had in many ways remained the same. Liberia, from Blyden to the group of Barbadians and to Garvey, reflects the ongoing linkages and challenges of global African freedom movements.

PART I

CARIBBEAN EMANCIPATION

I

Not Free Indeed

When Anthony Barclay first thought about leaving Barbados, he changed his mind. He briefly entertained the idea of going to Haiti a few years after the end of slavery. But swayed by the new air of optimism among his peers, he stayed in Barbados to see what was in store. On August 2, 1838, when his acquaintance, Thomas Harris Jr., called for them to meet to celebrate the official arrival of full freedom, a large number of free colored men anxiously congregated at the Barbados Bible Society in Bridgetown. Harris' invited guests included other respectable men in the emerging Afro-Barbadian middle class, such as Samuel Prescod, a human-rights rabble-rouser, editor, and co-owner of *The Liberal* newspaper with Harris. While Prescod chaired the meeting, Harris gave the keynote address, one shaped by his expectations of the post-emancipation period.

Brimming with optimism, Harris marked the purpose of the meeting for the group of largely "former free people." As a class, they expected the first of August to be a day that would bring them as well as their previously enslaved brethren the full breadth of freedom. Harris was grateful he had lived to see the day where he could "celebrate our Emancipation." He clarified: "I say *our* emancipation, gentlemen, because I do assert, and that too, without fear of contradiction, that this day in which [...] the legislature of this island has granted freedom of the slave – also made us free indeed."[1] Harris's deliberate use of the word "our" highlighted non-slave blacks views on class, race, and emancipation.

---

[1] *The Liberal*, August 4, 1838. Quoted in Melanie Newton, *The Children of Africa in the Colonies: Free People of Color in Barbados in the Age of Emancipation* (Baton Rouge: Louisiana State University Press, 2008), 2.

For the class of blacks who had been formerly free before legal emancipation, the abolition of slavery was a sign of better things to come. Harris felt quite sure that those who had gathered would agree with his view that their freedom up to that point had only been provisional and all along they were only "nominally free." Harris also pointed out "That [the newly emancipated class] are our brethren by the lieu [*sic*] of consanguinity, of suffering, and of wrong." Despite defining his class apart from other blacks, Harris viewed their kinship through common ancestral descent and experiences of grief, misery, and suffering. But the Queen had now removed "that disgraceful stain of slavery and its horrors." Harris was optimistic that emancipation would mean the improvement of "the colored body," and that "the other class" of whites would change the island's laws to grant colored people equal privileges, rights, and their proper respect. "Long may she reign to witness the good effects of the blessings she has conferred upon a grateful though calumniated people," Harris told the gathering. Harris hinted to an awareness of similar class dynamics in the United States when he admitted that he employed the "use of the language embodied in an admirable resolution to the colored people of America."[2] He harbored the hope that changes for all of them would be enacted through legal changes and new economic opportunities.

Nearly thirty years later, Harris's sense of hopefulness about postemancipation turned into despair. Barclay too, upon realizing that his dreams of freedom would not be fulfilled in the Caribbean, considered leaving again. Pushed to breaking point, Barclay, on December 14, 1864, sent a long list of grievances to Governor James Walker. As the representative of "a body of respectable, intelligent, and industrious persons," Barclay explained their "present position in this Island as a suffering people from the want of employment by which means alone they have to expect their daily bread." He pointed out that their deep interest in migration was due to "pinching want and adversity which cannot be well seen, but is severely felt amongst the middle classes who now exist without hope for the present or future generations, occasioned by the want of good, suitable, constant and remunerative employment." Barclay deduced that overpopulation in Barbados would "eventually lead to [a] rise in crime or some awful crisis." He thus concluded that if means were not speedily "devised for effecting some desirable change," they would be

---

[2] Ibid.

therefore compelled "if possible to remove so as to improve their condition with emigration."[3]

Barclay laid out the factors that drove many to consider emigration. But he also invoked emigration because it was so frequently cited in the era that it had become synonymous with freedom. Barbadians took advantage of the new post-emancipation culture and helped to shape it. Statistics capturing the emigration of the formerly enslaved from Barbados, revealing their strong reactions to abolition, support historians' contention that movement psychologically became synonymous with freedom.[4] Between 1834 and 1864, newly freed Afro-Barbadians thought through their frustrations at the inadequacies of post-emancipation and took up the cause of defining freedom for themselves by turning to migration. As a consequence, in the period following slavery, Barbadians formed the largest migratory group in the Caribbean. While the 1851 Barbados census recorded a population of 160,000, nearly 10 percent migrated in the post-slavery years: 9,814 Barbadians went to British Guiana; 1,495 to Demerara; 3,500 to St. Croix; and 999 to Antigua. Some went to other places unlike Barbados in size and over-population that were new frontiers of development in the British Empire.[5] By 1871, more than 13.4 percent of the Barbadian population lived in other places.[6] Indeed, one writer in a letter to the editor of *The Times* declared that "Barbados is the Ireland of the West Indies, its population poor and prolific descending forth a constant stream to other places, and yet increasing numbers in poverty."[7] Through migratory efforts aimed at resolving post-emancipation contradictions, Afro-Barbadians conjured up what the colonial bureaucracy failed to do. This quest for their vision of freedom reoriented the ability to define freedom away from white British abolitionists and articulated a view that centers an Afro-Caribbean perspective.

Interest in Liberian migration – which was unlike the migrations of the newly freed – emerged out of a social class whose stories are often

---

[3] Anthony Barclay to his Excellency Governor James Walker Esq. C.B. December 14, 1864. Svend Holsoe Collection, Indiana University, Bloomington.

[4] Steven Hahn, *A Nation Under Our Feet: Black Political Struggles in the Rural South, from Slavery to the Great Migration* (Cambridge, MA: Belknap Press of Harvard University Press, 2003); Patricia Fumerton, *Unsettled: The Culture of Mobility and the Working Poor in Early Modern England* (Chicago: University of Chicago Press, 2006).

[5] *Census Report of the Population of Barbados 1851–71* (Barbados: Barbados National Archives, 1872), 1.

[6] Ibid.

[7] *The Times*, October 10, 1865.

excluded from post-emancipation narratives. This is largely because the experiences of the post-slavery period tend to be viewed through race rather than class. Different classes of Afro-Barbadians responded to the failures of the post-slavery period in starkly dissimilar manners. Barclay, Harris, and their class did not share the same sets of post-emancipation circumstances that led to their interest in Liberia. Differing experiences of post-emancipation across social groups in Barbados underlay the dissimilar reasons they were motivated to leave. Thus, to consider the interests of the 346 emigrants to Liberia merely as part of a general euphoria that drove the appeal of emigration across Barbados would falsely suggest racial uniformity in Afro-Barbadian post-slavery expectations.[8]

The ways in which the expressed priorities, decision making, and reasoning of Barclay and Harris – the self-identified formerly free, emergent members of the middle class – differed from those of their newly freed counterparts suggest that migratory catalysts were not the same for all groups. New freedmen's understanding of free labor carried them on migration paths in the circum-Caribbean region in search of higher wages and a better living. For the most part, Afro-Barbadians who were newly freed from the legal and physical constraints of slavery had been denied mobility and wages in their previous existence as slaves. As a consequence, they embraced a "negative freedom" because this aspect of freedom occupied a higher priority in their lives. Conversely, for the Afro-Barbadian middle-class, who were free before the legal end of slavery and exercised mobility among a series of other privileges, freedom defined as a release from another's control was obviously important but was simply taken for granted. With the creation of class consciousness during slavery and its mediating role in the black community, their expectations for post-slavery were much higher. Anticipating an even broader spectrum of rights than black laborers, they centered access to civil and political rights, respectability, social mobility, citizenship, and nationhood as fundamental to the meaning of freedom.

Since they experienced post-slavery for over thirty years, migration that attracted land acquisition and political agency would mean not only

---

[8] Walter Rodney and Woodville Marshall have used the appeal of emigration to show how laborers envisaged the experiences of freedom. See Woodville Marshall, "We be Wise to Many More Things: Blacks Hopes and Expectations of Emancipation"; Rebecca Scott, "Former Slaves: Responses to Emancipation in Cuba"; Sidney Mintz, "The Origins of the Reconstituted Peasantries," all in Hilary Beckles and Verene Shepherd, eds., *Caribbean Freedom: Economy and Society from Emancipation to the Present a Student Reader* (Princeton, NJ: Wiener, 1996).

gaining rights but also regaining their status lost by a flattened hierarchy that lumped the formerly distinct free colored class into the crude post-emancipation racial designations of black and white. In the nearly thirty years since slavery had ended, the Afro-Barbadian middle class had been engrossed in one post-slavery disappointment after the other. The economic and political advancement they understood to be part of abolition slavery never came. The political and institutional processes that reshaped Barbados society post-emancipation created restrictions and barriers to freedom that members of the Barbadian emigration societies sought to escape. Ideological motivations, added to frustrations with post-emancipation, shaped an identity through which they envisioned the benefits and trade-offs of undertaking such a long journey. Men like Barclay and Wiles, ultimately gaining little with emancipation, imagined Liberia from these imperial, sociocultural, racial, religious, and class contexts in which they were bound. Their willingness to take on the risk inherent in Liberian emigration outlines the extent of their dissatisfaction and disappointment with the Caribbean post-emancipation era.

MAKING THE AFRO-BARBADIAN MIDDLE CLASS

Approximately eighty of Barclay's emigrant cohort who declared an interest in Liberia were born before the legal end of slavery. Holborn Jessamy, born in 1800, Catharine McClean and James Gittens, five years later, and John T. Worrell, in 1806, represented some of the oldest among the group who were born during slavery and came of age in a slave society. In 1810, at the height of slavery, a freedman named Anthony Barclay Sr. had a son and namesake, Anthony Barclay Jr. The institution of slavery cast its long shadows over the potential emigrants to Liberia and served as a fundamental element in shaping their worldviews.[9] The nature of their lives before slavery ended greatly shaped expectations of emancipation and interest in emigration. Though much is unknown about many of the other migrants, evidence suggests that like Barclay, Harris, and Wiles, they were also members of the black middle class.

The Afro-Barbadian middle class sprang from free coloreds and free blacks. In Barbados, "free coloreds" was used to designate the mixed-race status of individuals like James J. Wiles. Wiles highlighted his mixed-race heritage when he described himself, in a letter to ACS member George

---

[9] See Elsa V. Goveia, *Slave Society in the British Leeward Islands at the End of the Eighteenth Century* (New Haven, CT: Yale University Press, 1965).

Armstrong, as "the Reputed colored son of your old and esteemed friend R.J. Wiles, Esquire."[10] Wiles's keenness to identify himself as mixed-race, thereby positioning himself alongside whiteness, betrays the consciousness, anxieties, and constraints of his class. Because they were not slaves, free coloreds, in theory, were British subjects who could claim the rights held by whites. Though not equal to their white counterparts, free coloreds' position above slaves and free blacks afforded a series of privileges that fueled their sense of superiority. But even so, the efforts of whites geared towards social and racial control, fixed their status and shaped their lives.[11] In slavery, these kinds of peculiarities conferred upon them an inbetween and undesignated status that rendered them an "unappropriated class."[12]

Barclay's cohort were aware of their position in an unappropriated intermediary class, a position determined by skin color as much as income or profession. Their geographical location in Bridgetown between poor blacks and whites reinforced their sense of being stretched between two worlds. Because free coloreds and free blacks, for the most part, were city dwellers in the Barbadian capital, at least half of the migrant families interested in Liberia hailed from areas around Bridgetown and the largely urban parish of St. Michael.[13] In Bridgetown, free coloreds and blacks often came in contact with a diversity of sojourners in the British Atlantic world, including black

---

[10] James J. Wiles to George L. Armstrong Esquire, November 1, 1864 in Svend Holsoe Collection, Bloomington, Indiana University.

[11] Edward L. Cox, *Free Coloreds in the Slave Societies of St. Kitts and Grenada, 1763–1833* (Knoxville: University of Tennessee Press, 1984).

[12] See Jerome Handler, *The Un-Appropriated People: Freedmen in the Slave Society of Barbados* (Baltimore: John's Hopkins University Press, 1974).

[13] Established by English settlers in 1628 as a launching point for the expansion of the British Empire, Bridgetown became the economic and political center not only of Barbados but of the British Atlantic world. Given its strategic geographical location and commanding favorable trade winds, Bridgetown serviced the early slave trading economy of North America and other Caribbean islands. The city's lively maritime culture, trade, and a centrality to colonial governance reinforced its vital connection to the Metropole and wider Atlantic networks. To understand Cis-Atlantic communities in the British Atlantic World, see David Armitage and Michael J. Braddick, eds., *The British Atlantic World, 1500–1800* (Basingstoke: Palgrave Macmillan, 2002); Elizabeth Mancke and Carole Shammas, *The Creation of the British Atlantic World* (Baltimore: Johns Hopkins University Press, 2005); Karl Watson, *The Civilised Island, Barbados: A Social History, 1750–1816* (Ellerton, Barbados: Caribbean Graphic Production, 1979); Stephen Hornsby, *British Atlantic, American Frontier: Spaces of Power in Early Modern British America* (Lebanon, NH: University Press of New England, 2005); Patricia Stafford, "The Growth of the Black and Brown Middle Class, 1838–1988, and its Role in the Shaping of Modern Barbados." PhD thesis (Cave Hill: University of the West Indies, 2005).

seamen and mariners who worked on the wharves in the city. Families like the Barclays lived on the famous Roebuck Street in Bridgetown that boasted some of the better housing available in the urban area, suitable to the respectable tastes of people of their ilk.[14] Roebuck Street also achieved fame for its small huckster shops. Samuel Skeete, one of the prospective Liberian emigrants, had started out on the same street peddling goods, ranging from furniture to trinkets and wares, and parlayed those efforts into ownership of small shops, (See Figure 1.1).[15] An American prisoner of war detained at Barbados during the war of 1812 observed these kinds of urban activities among the "large number of free Negroes residing in Bridgetown, most of them in comfortable circumstances." He noticed the popular vocations of the growing class, pointing out that "these free Negroes carried on all the mechanical trades, such as tailors, shoemakers, jewelers, and were expert workmen. Many of them were shopkeepers. Indeed, I should think that the largest numbers of shops were kept by them."[16]

Other visitors also noted that a large proportion, if not a majority, of Bridgetown merchants were colored. Many mechanics in the city were enterprising colored or black men. All skills needed by the plantations, including blacksmithing and coopering, were performed by black men. The taxes levied by the parishioners through the St. Michael Parish Vestry ran especially high, which meant that black professionals who lived there could afford the high rates. Indeed, black merchants and shopkeepers of Bridgetown paid about one-third of the entire taxes, while the white proprietors and planters paid the other two-thirds. Given that the majority of the emigrants were from this area, we can assume that they were taxpayers in one way or another. Being corralled into the economies of the state in this way unwittingly offered some sense of participation in citizenship. By contrast, other migrant families from the up and coming parish of Christ Church that bordered the Barbadian capital to the south, as well as the rural areas like St. Thomas, St. Phillip, and St. Joseph, would not have had the same kind of experiences as urbanites like Skeete and Barclay.

---

[14] *The Times*, September 19, 1865.
[15] See "The City of Bridgetown," *The Sunday Advocate*, June 30, 1996.
[16] Warren Alleyne, "Old Bridgetown's Black Businessmen in it so Happened, *Barbados Advocate*," quoted in Cecilia Karch Brathwaite, "London Bourne of Barbados (1793–1869)," *Slavery and Abolition*, Vol. 28 (2007): 30.

Anthony Barclay

Has, in addition to former supplies received per

Don Juan

THE FOLLOWING ASSORTMENT OF GOODS

GENUINE GOODS

Which he offers for sale on terms the most reasonable and

moderate, viz;

West of England BROAD CLOTH in black, blue, green, Roman Purple and violet

Wooled CASSIMERES, in fancy plaids and lavenders, and Slate
Black and fancy Cable Cord BUCKSKINS
Black CRAPP and Clerical LASTINGS
GAMBRETTS in various colours
Superior White MOLESKIN
White fancy-ribbed STRIPES
Coloured MOLESKINS, and printed Diagonal
      DRILLS
Black Silk SERGE
Coloured Silesian LININGS
Raven Sewing SILK in Blue, white and assorted
      Light dyes
Best Black MOHAIR
Black, White, Brown and all colour THREADS
Fancy Textile BUTTONS, and Tailors incl
Measures
A Few dozen superior plain satin STOCKS, mirth
And a neat and substantial assort
Ment of Gentlemen's black, coloured, kidd
And other GLOVES, warranted Real Hitichins
Make

No. 12 High Street, Oct 25, 2n

FIGURE 1.1: Anthony Barclay's Goods Sold in His Shop
Source: Barbados National Archives, Black Rock, St James, Barbados

The identity and sense of self of free coloreds and blacks was tied directly to their inbetween status in a clearly defined race and class hierarchy in Barbados. They derived their power not from race or wealth but from a hierarchically sanctioned dominance in the public sphere and the virtue of having dependents under them. In their position over enslaved Africans, they gained a sense of paternalism. They made a living exploiting this middling position. Free coloreds grew to become as class conscious as the plantocracy from whom they had received their freedom. This traces a pattern of behavior that was common among the gentry in Europe, where, as soon as they acquired freedom from the bondage of the lords, they sought to exercise their positive freedom by dominating and exploiting the very slaves and lower classes from which they had come. Free coloreds exhibited a similar behavior in their thinking towards Africans. Having escaped oppression, they quickly became oppressors themselves.[17]

Yet, slavery created numerous problems for them socially and politically. Discriminatory laws barred them from legally testifying in civil proceedings involving whites, though whites could testify against them. Other pieces of legislation prohibited them from voting, holding elective office, or serving on juries. Worse yet, they were excluded from political and religious leadership positions, could not take communion at the same time as whites, and were forced to sit in segregated seats in church. Though excluded from these social, civil, and political privileges of citizenship, they were forced to pay taxes for schools that excluded them, serve in the militia, and to contribute to other general societal upkeep. The Barbadian governor once railed, in 1802, that "for though not the property of other individuals, they [free coloreds] do not enjoy the shadow of any civil right."[18] To add insult to injury, the white planter fathers of free coloreds often did not acknowledge them. Though these issues may have caused free coloreds to despise whites, they were also grounds on which they coveted white social status and power. As skilled and taxpaying families with "proximate whiteness," their exclusion from its privileges only magnified their grief.

Free coloreds' unclear status carried a certain ideological indefinability and political suspiciousness that compromised their desires for more inclusion into the privileges of whiteness. As a safeguard between themselves and the mass of darker enslaved Africans, whites used free coloreds as a buffering zone to keep the enslaved population in check. To further secure their place in the hierarchy, free coloreds clarified their position by going back and forth between siding with enslaved Africans and disparaging them. The distinctions between free colored men like Harris, Barclay, and

[17] Orlando Patterson, "The Ancient and Medieval Origins of Modern Freedom," in Steven Mintz and John Stauffer, eds., *The Problem of Evil: Slavery, Freedom, and the Ambiguities of American Reform* (Amherst: University of Massachusetts Press, 2007), 40–41.
[18] Ibid.

other blacks were most visible during the era of slaves' rebellious struggle for freedom. Like their counterparts in colonial Haiti, some free coloreds in Barbados also owned slaves. Though he was born a slave, Thomas Harris, who led the post-slavery free colored dinner gathering, became a slave owner before later campaigning for the rights of free coloreds.[19] In 1816, with the memory of the Haitian Revolution still hanging over the Caribbean, General Bussa drew Barbados into the popular uprising mood by inciting the "Bussa Rebellion," one of the three big rebellions that brought an end to slavery in the British world. In this instance, black social distinctions seemed more visible than ever as free colored elites sought to distance themselves even further from slaves. Men like Harris revealed the ways in which colonial royalism was strengthened by the support of former slaves who had once been subjected to imperial oppression.[20] Ex-slaves like Harris ultimately prevented their own slaves from participating in rebellions not only to distinguish themselves from enslaved Africans but also to prove the kinds of loyalty to the interests of the crown deserving of citizenship.[21] Rather than discrimination based on race, their expressed support of slavery rendered them visible as deserving subjects of the Empire.

In 1819, economically prosperous free colored men like Harris seemed to be separated from the black underclass by an un-crossable chasm. In what became known as the Belgreave Address, free coloreds again revealed their royalist positions by showing their disdain for enslaved Africans. Headed by Jacob Belgreave, the group of free coloreds sent a letter denouncing slave uprisings throughout the Caribbean and actively undermined the voices of black rebels and the work of British abolitionists.[22] Free coloreds used the address to demonstrate their acceptance of the British colonial order, declaring their "loyalty to the land of our nativity and to the institutions and forms of government under which hitherto had the happiest of lives." They declared their opposition to "insurrectionists and other radicals" and vowed to "assist with all their power in the maintenance and subordination of good order."[23] During

---

[19] Newton, *The Children of Africa in the Colonies*, 2.

[20] Marcela Echeverri, *Indian and Slave Royalists in the Age of Revolution: Reform, Revolution, and Royalism in the Northern Andes, 1780–1825* (New York: Cambridge University Press, 2016), 2.

[21] C. L. R. James, *The Black Jacobins; Toussaint L'Ouverture and the San Domingo Revolution* (New York: Vintage Books, 1963); Laurent Dubois, *Avengers of the New World: The Story of the Haitian Revolution* (Cambridge, MA: Belknap Press of Harvard University Press, 2004).

[22] Newton, *The Children of Africa in the Colonies*, 80.

[23] *The Barbadian*, February 25, 1824.

the same time, Anthony Barclay Sr. and 172 other freemen signed "a petition requesting the privilege of testifying, and supported the Belgreave Address."[24] As a payoff for helping to crush the rebellion, free coloreds briefly won the right to testify while the voices of other blacks were kept marginalized. In 1831, the Barbadian legislature further responded to Afro-Barbadian middle-class petitions by passing what became known as the "Brown Privilege Bill." The bill repealed "all acts or such parts of acts that impose any restraints or disabilities whatsoever on his majesty's free colored and free black subjects ... to which his majesty's white subjects ... are not liable."[25] Thus, during slavery in Barbados, free coloreds improved their status by rejecting the type of blackness they would later invoke to justify migration to Liberia.

By May 6, 1833, the shifts created by a burgeoning emancipation reversed the political stance of the free colored community from disavowal to an embrace of the enslaved as their "brethren." It was within the crucible of heightened abolitionist activities that Anthony Barclay Jr. emerged as a political leader. At a protest of the Belgreave Address, Barclay Jr. supported "strong resolutions at a public meeting of freedmen" and was granted the opportunity as one of the few selected to present a statement to the governor of Barbados.[26] The tone of the address was such that the Barbadian governor branded Barclay and his cohort of agitators as "dangerous men who desired to throw the colony into anarchy and confusion."[27] Perhaps Barclay Jr. supported the new resolution out of a realization that if slavery persisted not only would he not truly be free but he would also be expected to maintain "a respectful deference to whites [as an] indispensable duty and stay in the position accorded to them by whites."[28] As long as slavery continued, he would not be entitled to all the rights and privileges of citizenship, and his legal position would remain in a peculiar place. This hostile background against which the Afro-Barbadian middle class emerged during slavery set up their expectations for the post-emancipation period in which they were forced to act.

---

[24] Jerome Handler, Ronnie Hughes, and Ernest M. Wiltshire, *Freedmen of Barbados: Names and Notes for Genealogical and Family History Research* (Charlottesville, VA: Virginia Foundation for the Humanities and Public Policy, 1999), 67–68.

[25] See the resolutions of the Barbados House of Assembly, February 18, 1824, printed in *The Barbadian*, 25 February 1824. Quoted in Karch Braithwaite, "London Bourne," 31.

[26] Handler et al., *Freedmen of Barbados*, 8.

[27] Karch Braithwaite, "London Bourne," 31.

[28] Handler, *Un-Appropriated People*, 197.

EMANCIPATION'S DISCONTENT

Afro-Barbadians' interests in Liberian emigration were also largely influenced by the distorted efforts to enact emancipation. In determining the terms of Caribbean freedom, neither the Queen nor Liberal Whig politicians had consulted the self-important free coloreds.[29] Instead, far removed from day-to-day life in the Caribbean, Whig liberals in the British parliament sourly debated the provisions of the Emancipation Act.[30] Whiggish views on abolition had proven less significant to emancipation than the everyday rebellions of enslaved Africans like Bussa, whose uprisings against the prevailing force of slavery had roused the concerns of colonial administrators.[31] Even so, the stronghold of the Barbadian white planter elite ensured the Barbadian legislature's reluctance to introduce emancipation. While colonies like Jamaica quickly moved to enact the legislation to abolish slavery, "changes had to be virtually imposed from the outside on a dissenting Barbadian judiciary."[32] On August 1, 1834, within this gloomy climate of dissension and reluctance, slavery finally came to a "legal" end in Barbados and across the British Empire.

On September 6, 1835, a year after abolition, Barclay, then superintendent of St. Mary's Asylum and a "penman," professionally skilled in handwriting, married Bourne's daughter Sarah, a confectioner.[33] They grew to be a family of thirteen, including eight daughters and five sons, one of whom, Samuel Gerald, died in Bridgetown on June 17, 1854, at age five, before the family could depart for Liberia.[34] Barclay Jr. ranked among the educated, having descended from a line of educated freed blacks, (see Figure 1.2 Barclay Family Tree). Barclay family members' levels of education and training secured social and political affluence, an important metric for how the Barclays would fare in Liberia. Mary shared her mother's profession as a confectioner; Antoinette became a school mistress; Elizabeth, a teacher; Melvina was a fancy worker who helped in the making of exquisite material goods; and Sarah was a music teacher. The other daughters, Laura, Florence, and Ellen, were twelve, ten,

---

[29] Anthony Phillips, "The Parliament of Barbados, 1639–1989," *Journal of the Barbados Museum and Historical Society (BMHS)*, Vol. 38, No. 4 (1990): 422.

[30] Lisa Lowe, *The Intimacies of Four Continents* (Durham, NC: Duke University Press, 2015), 13.

[31] Ibid.

[32] Phillips, "The Parliament of Barbados," 422.

[33] Gerald K. Barclay, "Brief Life Sketch of the Late Malvina Barclay", August 10, 1973, in the original papers of L.A. Grimes, Accessed at the University of Liberia Library, Monrovia, Liberia.

[34] Ibid.

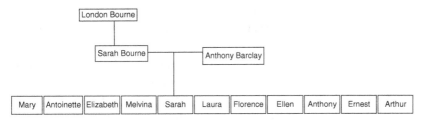

FIGURE 1.2: Barclay Family Tree

and eight years old, respectively. Of the three surviving sons, Anthony was a merchant clerk, Ernest was a coppersmith, and Arthur Barclay was still a child. That both males and females in the Barclay family were educated and trained meant that their family was adaptable to new circumstances and dynamics.

Members of the free colored class like Barclay looked on as white planter interests pervaded abolitionist efforts and undermined the radical agenda necessary for full freedom. British discussions of individual rights had neither considered the societal obstacles nor the materials necessary for the realization of those rights. British officials decided that the parts of the freedmen's lives necessary to support a capitalist system were to be encouraged.[35] Planters aimed to socialize former slaves to become wage laborers, reasoning that because they had not yet become rational actors they should be kept out of political and private economic spheres. Viewing post-emancipation through a racial lens, colonial administrators turned their attention away from securing the rights of the newly freed and towards ensuring their powerlessness. Without political and economic rights, the freedom offered through abolition essentially lacked any modicum of independence and power.

In 1837, James Thome and Thomas Kimball, two American abolitionists, went on a six-month tour of Antigua, Barbados, and Jamaica to assess the workings of "the great experiment of freedom."[36] Kimball and Thome met with some members of the black middle class, who enjoyed a great degree of social and economic success and had essentially established themselves as a petit bourgeois group. They dined with London Bourne and his family. London Bourne, the son of William Bourne, was a slave who later became a wealthy cooper. The younger Bourne was also born a slave

[35] Ibid.
[36] James A. Thome and Joseph Kimball, *Emancipation in the West Indies: A six months' tour in Antigua, Barbadoes, and Jamaica in the year 1837*, New York, Published by the American Anti-Slavery Society, 1838 (New York: Cambridge University Press, 2010), iii.

but, like his father, found success as a merchant in Bridgetown. Kimball and Thome noted that "he owns three stores in Bridgetown, and lives in very genteel style in his own house and is worth from twenty to thirty thousand dollars."[37] The abolitionists described the Bournes as "genuine and unadulterated Negroes," whose eleven-year-old son was about to set out to Edinburgh in Scotland to study at the university. Bourne had become a part of the middle class in typical fashion, exhibiting the kinds of education and literacy often noted in the Afro-Barbadian middle class.

Barclay and Harris worried about the social and political ramifications of having experienced no radical altering of their status. Samuel Prescod, their friend, trusted ally, and leader in Afro-Barbadian circles, tracked the struggle to define the nature of freedom in post-emancipation. In the early 1840s, at one public meeting where Barclay was present, Prescod "rose to propose a toast and sentiment" that was cordially responded to by those in attendance. He declared that he "needed not remind them of the indissoluble ties between them and the lately emancipated classes. These were the stock from which they as branches had sprung, and in the degradation of that stock they had necessarily been degraded." Hailed with cheers, he declared, "Their own freedom had only been nominal – and it had produced, and could produce, none of the political advantages of freedom, so long as their brethren remained in slavery (applause). They were now both free and on to moral and social improvement."[38] Prescod's confirmation of post-emancipation's minor rewards only compounded Afro-Barbadians' anxieties. His reference to the "indissoluble ties" with the newly freed illuminated the collapse of the class hierarchy that meant the loss of the social advantages of the free colored's mediating role. Emancipation did much to erase the lines of social demarcation by eliminating the distinctions that existed during slavery between free blacks, coloreds, and slaves. The refocusing of imperial citizenship away from class to race further threatened to plunge middle-class Afro-Barbadians downward in status, toward the treatment those below them experienced. With the social distinction achieved from direct economic coercion erased in the absence of slavery, bourgeois mediating roles lost their function.

Not only were the needs of Afro-Barbadians not codified into law, but more than on any other island, the continued presence of whites in Barbados, who aimed to sustain the material vestiges of the plantation

---

[37] Ibid., 307. See also Caree A. Banton, "1865 and the Incomplete Caribbean Emancipation Project: Class Migration from Barbados in the Long Nineteenth century," *Cultural Dynamics*, 2019. SAGE Publications.

[38] *The Liberal*, August 3, 1839.

complex, foiled the Afro-Barbadian middle class's post-emancipation desires. There was no encouragement of new kinds of political power or land and property ownership. The white planter class's majority ownership of the land and wealth gravely constrained the kinds of land redistribution that middle-class Afro-Barbadians desired. Such control of land barred freedmen from bargaining on equal terms as economically independent, self-sufficient citizens. The endurance of the plantation economy further secured a minimal post-emancipation freedom through retrograde ideas about free labor, land tenure, social status, and political rights. The landlessness of Afro-Barbadians provided the means by which white elites in the colonial establishment indoctrinated social, civil, and labor habits while keeping the lower classes in their proper social place.[39] Because landless freedom in Barbados ensured continued rule of planters, abolition had merely raised the Afro-Barbadians to the status of landless wage earners.[40] As Prescod prophesied, the future of the newly freed would be low wages and mandatory labor enabled through vagrancy and other forms of legal enactments, "the maximum being fixed by the very party interested in keeping down wages to the lowest point."[41]

Another blow to Afro-Barbadian post-emancipation dreams came through the enactment of a period of apprenticeship. Ostensibly geared towards facilitating a smooth transition out of slavery, it created an environment in which Barbadians would be properly conditioned into being wage laborers. Apprenticeship not only stifled the emergence of an unrestrained free labor, but also sanctioned the kinds of coercion that secured unfree labor. Ultimately, it represented capitalism's efforts to police its way out of abolition with the result being the giving over of labor to its service. The change in designation from slaves to apprentices released the formerly enslaved into a post-emancipation imagined as a new kind of slavery that maintained the dynamics of its power by changing the rules and rhetoric. Abolitionists' promise of freedom, whose general terms sounded beguiling, turned out to mean "freedom for the pike, not for the minnows."[42] One writer noted that apprenticeship was meant to "tame the man and preserve the slave" and was "a

---

[39] Hilary Beckles, *Great House Rules: Landless Emancipation and Workers' Protest in Barbados, 1838–1938* (Kingston, Jamaica: Ian Randle, 2004).
[40] Eric Williams, *Capitalism and Slavery* (Worcester: Andre Deutsch Limited, 1964), 191.
[41] *The Liberal*, February 24, 1838.
[42] George Monbiot, ""Neoliberalism – the ideology at the root of all our problems." *The Guardian*, April 15, 2016. https://www.theguardian.com/books/2016/apr/15/neoliberalism-ideology-problem-george-monbiot.

deliberate action to ensure that the plantation owners were provided with free labor even after slavery was abolished."[43] Its very manifestation reflected fears that ex-slaves would flee to areas beyond the control and supervision of the plantation.

As the economic and social mechanisms sought to maintain the political status quo, the Afro-Barbadian middle class gained little during apprenticeship. While the peasantry slipped into a reality of wage labor, the Afro-Barbadian middle class found themselves with a limited range of options for advancement.[44] Given that they were already free, the slow implementation of changes after slavery was even more frustrating for them. Middle-class families looked on in horror at the future of their children as some slipped out of what had been a clearly defined status in slavery into social and financial ruin. Emancipation had done much to erase the lines of social demarcation by eliminating the distinctions that existed during slavery between free blacks, coloreds, and slaves. The refocusing of imperial citizenship away from class to race further threatened to plunge middle-class Afro-Barbadians downward in status, toward the treatment those below them experienced.

Post-emancipation threatened to send the middle class to work on the plantations. That a "colored" man captained the schooner that brought Sturge and Harvey to Barbados convinced them that the middle-class people had already commandeered these kinds of occupations.[45] The British observers noted: "The competition of the colored people has driven [poor whites] out of almost every field where free laborers were wont to exercise their skills and industry."[46] The archdeacon of St. Michael's Cathedral corroborated the "they are taking our jobs" familiar refrain in a sermon delivered in 1833. He noted that the "free blacks have, by their superior industry, driven down the lower order of whites from almost every trade requiring skill and continued exertion. I believe that not one in twenty of the working shoemakers is a white man. The working carpenters, masons, tailors, smiths *et cetera,* are for the most part men of colour."[47] With emancipation realignment of racial

---

[43] Anne-Marie Sharman, 1993 ed., *Anti-Slavery Reporter* (13) No. 8, P.35. London: Anti-Slavery International. See also Capt. Richard H. Pratt's "Kill the Indian, and Save the Man." A Speech delivered in 1892.

[44] See Diane Barnes, *Artisan Workers in the Upper South: Petersburg, Virginia, 1820–1865* (Baton Rouge: Louisiana State University Press, 2008), 2.

[45] Joseph Sturge and Thomas Harvey, *The West Indies in 1837* (London: Hamilton Adams, 1838).

[46] Sturge and Harvey, *The West Indies in 1837*, Appendix E, Section 1.

[47] Jill Sheppard, *The Redlegs of Barbados* (New York: KTO. Press, 1977), 46.

hierarchies, the competition between the artisanal middle class and poor whites seemed to now favor the latter, threatening to push the former into positions previously below their station.

For politically affluent and educated middle-class families in this position, emigration promised more than upward mobility; it preserved dignity. Middle-class families were bound to react, given their reliance on the patriarch. With businesses that were usually controlled by the father, whose power bonded the family together, diminishing opportunities for the head of household put the family in a dangerous economic position. As free-labor habits became an important predictor of black racial ability during the apprenticeship period, it also intensified Afro-Barbadians' familial concerns for their children's future. With land unavailable and other avenues of advancement unopened, many Afro-Barbadian middle-class families were forced to a decision between making their children apprentices or facing violence. Children were especially affected by the new laws enacted to control families after emancipation, laws that allocated food and housing on the basis of the number of family members apprenticed. Of the 346 total Afro-Barbadian emigrants, 244 (70 percent) were born after the end of slavery and 24 were born during the period of apprenticeship. The pressing question of legacy became a new kind of moral compass that shaped their desires to leave Barbados.

Samuel Prescod published widely on the effects of apprenticeship on families. In a column in *The Liberal* titled "The Blessings of the Apprenticeship System," Prescod criticized a "Mr. Tinling, Special Justice of District G" who had "sentenced four women with young children to give three Saturdays' labor each to the estate for having been a little late to the field."[48] Their punishment was "deemed a very mild punishment, a tender mercy sort of an affair; and they were threatened to be more severely dealt with should they similarly offend again." Prescod concluded with a jab: "We should like to know the decrease in the infant population since the commencement of apprenticeship. Of course, it is to be entirely attributed to the careless inattention of the parents."[49] These harsh conditions geared towards securing a labor supply throughout the colonies rendered the post-slavery household a significant decision-making unit. Given the vulnerability of children during apprenticeship, the loss of a child in efforts to find a better life on a migration journey was easier to face than the loss of a child because

---

[48] *The Liberal*, March 21, 1838.
[49] Ibid.

of the hardships of emancipation. For Afro-Barbadian families, migration became a way of negotiating a post-slavery labor market that seemed determined to keep them in peonage. The post-slavery decline of the family thus played an important role in Afro-Barbadians' conception of Liberian migration.

As Afro-Barbadians grimaced at their declining household capabilities, Liberia's pull assuaged their anxieties. Because mortality often exceeded natural population increase, the migration of families was central to Liberia development. Indeed, whole families were encouraged to emigrate as a means of addressing population challenges. Families were not only a pivotal concern in decisions to emigrate, but they also figured significantly in the establishment of support networks at the destination. The extent to which migration could provide the means for success largely depended on the capacity of migrants and their households to mobilize support through their established kinship networks. The ACS encouraged whole families to emigrate to create stability, but they also did not want to be associated with breaking up families as was the case with American slavery. Families such as the Barclays, who started to have children during slavery, were able to keep their families together thirty years after the institution ended.[50] These domestic arrangements for Barbadian families highlight an important difference from African American migrants who, in many cases, were forced to emigrate, sometimes leaving family members behind.[51] These variances underscore the multiple social forces that would shape Liberia's power dynamics as constituted through the various ruling families who dominated economic and political life in the republic.

Post-emancipation, punctuated as it was by the shortcomings of abolition, the legalization of racial inequality, and the realignment of labor and capital, demonstrated a clear lack of commitment to black material well-being. With its own inherent flaws and with pressure from the newly freed class, the apprenticeship system came to a premature end in 1838 only to

[50] Laurence Brown and Tara Inniss, "The Slave Family in the Transition to Freedom: Barbados, 1834–1841," *Slavery and Abolition*, Vol 26 (2005): 257–269. Also see Elizabeth Ann Regosin, *Freedom's Promise: Ex-Slave Families and Citizenship in the Age of Emancipation* (Charlottesville: University Press of Virginia, 2002).

[51] See Tom W. Shick, Roll of the Emigrants to the Colony of Liberia Sent by the American Colonization Society from 1820–1843 [computer file]. Madison, WI: Tom W. Shick [producer], 1973. Madison, WI: Data and Program Library Service [distributor], 1973 and 1996; Peter J. Murdza, *Immigrants to Liberia, 1865* Emigrants Database, Virginia Emigrants to Liberia. Liberian Studies Research Working Paper. No 4. Virginia Center for Digital History, University of Virginia.

be replaced by a system of tenancy.[52] As a brutal scheme of labor management, representing a balance between a desire for black self-sufficiency and the planter's demand for a productive labor force, tenancy curbed competition and hindered free labor through the use of terror and other extralegal force against workers.[53] Contractual arrangements for subsistence and housing that meant the ever-present possibility of removal from plantation property formed a dynamic that ensured that freedmen continued dependence for survival. This system of paternalistic dependency – the refusal to sell freedmen land – thwarted the industry and secured the cheapness of labor in Barbados. The system had achieved success by absorbing the new generation of children as laborers. At the end of 1839, Joseph Evelyn, the police magistrate for Christ Church, reported: "I am happy to say that the labourers are beginning to feel the necessity of rearing up their children in habits of industry."[54]

In 1840, members of the British and Foreign Antislavery Society (BFASS) held a convention at Exeter Hall, London.[55] The convention was organized by the British abolitionists Joseph Sturge and Thomas Harvey, who had visited Barbados in 1837 and ultimately came to view the post-emancipation period with much deserved suspicion. Sturge and Harvey, in their observations of Barbados, were intrigued by parents' encouragement of their free children to pursue the trades over agriculture. They reckoned: "The boon of freedom granted, as if in mockery to their helpless infants has proved a source of misery and bitter persecution to the Negro mothers."[56] The two London abolitionists also drew heavily from Prescod, whom they likely met during their trip to Barbados. Prescod told them about laborers' gravitation toward independence by pointing to the differences in their productivity when they were required to work on the plantations without wages and when they worked for themselves. When land was available for peasant agriculture or other enterprises, apprentices interpreted free labor as

---

[52] In 1837, the publicizing of James Williams' experiences as an apprenticed laborer in Jamaica, in a short pamphlet, *A Narrative of Events since the First of August, 1834* helped to bring apprenticeship to a premature end in 1838. See Diana Paton, *A Narrative of Events Since the First of August, 1834* (Durham, NC: Duke University Press, 2001).

[53] See Jonathan M. Wiener, *Social Origins of the New South: Alabama, 1860–1885* (Baton Rouge: Louisiana State University Press, 1978), 16.

[54] CO 28/140, 17 June 1841, Brathwaite to Russell, attached Police Magistrates Reports, 1 October–31 December 1839. Quoted in Laurence Brown, and Tara Inniss, "The Slave Family in the Transition to Freedom: Barbados, 1834–1841," *Slavery and Abolition*, Vol. 26 (2005): 5.

[55] *The Colored American*, January 23, 1841.

[56] Sturge and Harvey, *The West Indies in 1837*, 8.

reaping the fruits of their labor. Contrary to the view that freedmen were lazy, Prescod argued that they did, in fact, enjoy work; they merely desired "a fair standard that could guide" them.[57]

Unavailability of land had long plagued blacks in Barbados. Barbadians were wont to face greater post-emancipation frustrations because the majority of issues revolved around the politics of land. In Prescod's observations, landlessness especially compounded the problems of post-emancipation for Barbadians. Peasant farming, which had created an alternative economy on larger islands such as Jamaica, might have worked if land was available for such ventures in Barbados. In 1841, a St. Michael magistrate testified in parliament that "little progress has been made by the laborers in establishing themselves as freeholders, not from any disinclination on their part to become so, but circumstanced as our island is, there is little probability of any great number being able to obtain freeholds."[58] According to the magistrate, "the reason is obvious; there is not in the whole island a spot of wasteland fit for cultivation, and as the land is principally divided into plantations, the proprietors are not likely to sell off small plots for that purpose; and there being no public lands available, it is plain that freeholders to any extent cannot be established in this country."[59] The inability to access land on which to establish their communities and families opened laborers' eyes to possibilities elsewhere.[60]

MIDDLE-CLASS POST-EMANCIPATION DECLINE

On December 26, 1840, Prescod and twenty-three Afro-Barbadians sent a dispatch via governor John McGregor to Queen Victoria congratulating her on her marriage to Prince Albert. They also used their congratulatory offerings to the royals to also seek an extension of the elective franchise.[61] However, as the Afro-Barbadian middle class sought to make post-emancipation laws less restrictive and more accessible to their goals,

[57] *The National Era*, September 16, 1858.
[58] Parliamentary Papers, 1842 (479). XIII. Appendix VI. Report of Police Magistrates of St. Michael's Parish, June – December, 1841 (Grey to Stanley, 18 April, 1842. No. 12, Enc.No.1.) in Select Committee on West India Colonies, 1842.
[59] See Janet Momsen, "Rural Post-Emancipation Rural Settlement in Barbados." (Thesis. Department of Geography, Newcastle: Newcastle University, 1988.)
[60] Ibid.
[61] CO 28/135/50, Despatches from Evan Murray John McGregor, Governor of Barbados. Accessed at the British National Archives. Kew Gardens. UK.

white elites in the Barbadian Assembly had used racial, ideological, economic, and imperialistic rationales to exclude them from the body politic. The real and deep political nature of property and land holding manifested when white elites made political rights commensurate with owning them. In large contrast to Afro-Barbadians' desire for political rights, the Assembly of landed white aristocrats enacted stricter voting laws. The 1842 "Franchise Act" moved to set new qualifications for representation and voting. According to the act, "a member of the House of Assembly had to possess at least thirty acres of land with a house worth at least 500 pounds or control property with an annual value of 200 pounds." They could also possess "annual income of no less than 300 pounds." On the other hand, "freehold property worth twenty pounds, leasehold property with a rental value of 100 pounds, an annual income of twenty pounds, or occupancy of urban house or business place with a rental value of fifty pounds, or payment of parochial rates of five pounds" formed the minimum qualifications for the vote.[62] Because they did not own sufficient property and land, these provisions in effect disqualified them from citizenship, political power, and social mobility, which they could not acquire if they remained in Barbados.

The would-be Barbadian emigrants to Liberia complained bitterly about these post-emancipation issues to their American patrons. A signed letter to the ACS by John T. Worrell, J. T. Wiles, C. Aug Lawrence, A. Barker, and W. W. Burnett – chairman, secretary, vice chairman, and treasurer, member of the committee respectively, of the BCL – noted that Governor James Walker had referenced their interest in migration from Barbados as the "use of persons actuated by very different views than those of labor." The letter's authors also noted that when the BCL solicited his assistance to emigrate, Governor Walker had "offered us every inducement to remain or to direct our energies to any of the British Colonies. But we refused to avail ourselves of his offers. Our object being to go to no other place than the land of our forefathers." One of their primary reasons for wanting to emigrate was this: "We are all renters of small spots of land which we cultivate ourselves." They noted that Barbados was quite limited in this regard as "a country of twenty-one miles long by fourteen wide and a population of 153,000 inhabitants."[63]

[62] Woodville Marshall, "List of Voters for Barbados 1873: A Comment," *BMHS*, Vol. 51 (2005): 187.

[63] ACS, Reel 96. National Archives. Available in the Svend Holsoe Collection. Indiana University-Bloomington.

When Joseph Attwell wrote to the ACS, he pointed to the size of Barbados in explaining why members of the BCL were interested in Liberia. "The Island of Barbados, West Indies, with an area of 166 square miles, has a population of nearly 160,000 persons, of whom one hundred and thirty-six thousand are colored. It will readily be perceived, therefore, that this class of its population is excessive, and the natural consequence of which is emigration!" Indeed, Attwell pointed out in his letter that "several thousands have already gone to neighboring colonies."[64]

With the island's population density at 966 per square mile, Barbadian wages were among the lowest in the Caribbean. The island's small land mass and overpopulation were such that Barbados was one of the only islands to refuse recaptured Africans and Asian indentured laborers after slavery.[65] In an island that had limited land, lack of access meant either low-wage work on the plantations or emigration. These unfavorable circumstances in Barbados pushed many migrants to neighboring islands in search of higher wages, land, political rights, better living conditions, and other post-emancipation opportunities. The unavailability of land ensured that they could only understand free labor in its alienated, waged sense. By reeling in the boundaries of freedom sought by freedmen, emigration laws not only preserved the continued rule of the plantocracy, but also blocked mobility, the literal and metaphorical condition on which blacks anchored their new freedom. Writing their way out of a Barbadian society thirty years into emancipation, these Barbadians were no longer content to be just free laborers. Through their emigration, they hoped to construct a free society and become a free people.[66]

The possibilities of acquiring land made emigration to Liberia especially attractive to farmers. The many "planters"[67] listed among the Barbadians interested in Liberia underscored the centrality of land as an impetus for emigration. Sixteen emigrants were planters or small farmers. They included thirty-five-year-old John Nurse, James Briggs, thirty-three, and John Braithwaite Weeks, forty. William Edward Tull, a forty-four-year-old married to Sarah Ann Tull, aged forty, was also

---

[64] *The African Repository*, Vol. 41, December 8 (1864): 19.

[65] See Roseanne Marion Adderley, *"New Negroes from Africa": Slave Trade Abolition and Free African Settlement in the Nineteenth-Century Caribbean* (Bloomington: Indiana University Press, 2006); Lisa Yun, *The Coolie Speaks: Chinese Indentured Laborers and African Slaves in Cuba* (Philadelphia: Temple University Press, 2008).

[66] Holt, *The Problem of Freedom*, 170.

[67] Planters connoted large scale farm holdings. This was designation of the Barbadian farmers by the ACS.

among them. Together they had five children: Joshua, Esther, Catherine, Henry, and Vashti. The family resided in Tull's Land in St. Thomas. Guy Brown, a forty-year-old married to Delia Brown, thirty-eight, lived in Rawlins Land with their four boys: Albert, Nathaniel, Ernest, and Frederick. Planters such as Isaac William Denny, twenty-nine, John Brathwaite, twenty, and John Adamson, twenty-two, represented the average age of single Barbadians who were interested in Liberian emigration.

The value of these farmers was wrapped up in Barbados historic centrality of Barbados to the British Empire. Americans in the ACS marveled that the island had "the most industrious population under the sun, [and] there is not an uncultivated acre of land in the island ... every part not devoted to these products is cultivated with vegetables, fruit, cattle, and poultry." This kind of productivity no doubt raised the cost of living as "land near Bridgetown rents for twenty-four dollars per acre."[68] A statement meant to highlight Barbadian industry instead thrust the issue of land scarcity to the forefront:

The secret of this astonishing prosperity is that there are no Crown lands[,] vacant fields and districts belonging to the Government on which idle people squat, and with the aid of the gun and the fishing rod or line, together with a shabby cultivation of a little ground for gardens, earn a precarious and uncertain living, as is customary in Tobago, Antigua, St. Kitts, Dominica, Trinidad, and other islands where Crown lands abound.[69]

Barbadians who looked to migration sought to escape the political and economic constraints in an island as small as Barbados that blocked access to land and forced many into low-wage plantation labor. A smaller land mass complemented by the demographic pressures of overpopulation exacerbated Afro-Barbadian efforts to take hold of already vague promises of emancipation.[70] The post-slavery period trained freedmen for social, economic, and political positions at the bottom of the class system and conditioned them for lives with few second chances, little support, limited opportunity, and subordination and control. Viewing the Barbadians' efforts to migrate as a move to right the disappointments of emancipation – even at a time when British planters were calling for

---

[68] *The African Repository*, Vol. 40 (1864): 367.
[69] Ibid.
[70] Governor C.B. Rowson, "Census Report of the Population of Barbados 1851–71." (Bridgetown, Barbados: Barbados, Barclay and Fraser Printers, 1872), 1. Accessed at the Barbados National Archives.

increases in Asian indentured laborers to offset labor shortages – paints a broader picture of freedmen's efforts to shape the conditions and meanings of freedom in the post-slavery era.

By the mid-nineteenth century, post-emancipation fostered a sense of stagnation, societal disassociation, and a gloomy view of a Caribbean future for black families. The Abolition Act of 1833 proved to be an empty gesture for the black middle class. As they were largely not slaves, they had little to gain from legislation decided and passed in the British Parliament largely without their input. Furthermore, there were few if any changes in an increasingly restrictive political atmosphere. At the very least, enslaved Africans had received tangible gains. While abolitionists had hinged freedom on the economic potential of free labor, judicial enactments unleashed newer forces of coercion. With this, the middle class was forced to determine the risks of achieving freedom elsewhere. With increasing interest in Africa, London Bourne, Anthony Barclay Jr.'s father-in-law, founded the Fatherland Union–BES, setting a precedent that his son-in-law would later revive.

The confines of the island's rigid economic, social, and political structure made emigration especially appealing to households like the Barclays. The ideas shaping their expectations of a future home were about more than finding a new society. The list of the skills and trades underscored their perceptions of the utility of their labor, ethic of independence, and a dedication to work as dogged as the Protestant work ethic. Although some Afro-Barbadian middle class had economic success, members of the black middle class were ever mindful of the racial hierarchy in Barbadian society that confined them to an uncomfortable place. For example, although London Bourne was commercially successful, racism initially denied him membership in Commercial Hall, an early forerunner to the Chamber of Commerce in Barbados.[71] Despite the success of nonwhite merchants, the governor refused to endorse the passage of an "act for constituting a Corporation for the better ordering and managing of the Barbados Chamber of Commerce," reasoning that "no mercantile gentlemen of the coloured body were to be members of that institution."[72] Kimball and Thome noted these kinds of prejudices in their observations, writing that "the prejudice against color is stronger in Barbados than in any other colony, although the colored class of its population is

---

[71] Karch Braithwaite, "London Bourne," 26.
[72] Ibid.

numerous, wealthy, and respectable, and comprises some of the first merchants of the island."[73]

Kimball and Thome also met with Prescod, whom they described as "chiefly devoted to the interests of the colored community." As the son of a wealthy planter and lawyer and of a slave woman, Mary Smith, Prescod had come to the middle class in a typical fashion, but his upbringing did not mirror that of the majority of Bridgetown's darker inhabitants. He was initially apprenticed to a joiner in Barbados but later went to study at the Inns of Court in England.[74] The abolitionists highlighted that both Mr. and Mrs. Prescod had English education but complained of being excluded from white society.[75] Before 1843, when he became the first Afro-representative in the House of Assembly, Prescod had been ejected from the gallery of the House of Assembly while observing a legislative session. During a discussion of the Franchise Bill in 1829, the precocious twenty-two-year-old Prescod was promptly struck by a fellow attendee with an umbrella for having yelled out an appeal for Afro-Barbadian civil liberties.[76] An English visitor to Barbados who witnessed Prescod's ridicule commented that if Prescod lived in England he would be "esteemed as a gentleman, whilst in Barbados he is to some degree a despised colored man."[77]

The abolitionists left Barbados believing that the "star of hope" was rising in the black and brown community.[78] Yet this was not altogether true for the middle class. The institutional shifts and social processes necessary to bring about such outcomes in post-emancipation never came. Despite their persistent petitioning for post-slavery reforms and efforts toward inclusion in the body politic, they were rejected by the ruling white oligarchy. Race routinely blocked and denied Afro-Barbadian middle-class access to political power, citizenship, and their meaning of freedom; that they could never achieve it made it all the more valuable. The gap between their ambitions and the kind of freedom that emerged during post-emancipation created a sense of societal disassociation that made life in Barbados unbearable.

---

[73] Sturge and Harvey, *The West Indies in 1837*, 154.

[74] Samuel Prescod's course was unfortunately interrupted by his ill health.

[75] F. A. Hoyos, *Builders of Barbados* (Basingstoke: MacMillan Education, 1972) 46.

[76] Glenn O Phillips, "The Beginnings of Samuel J. Prescod, 1806–1843: Afro-Barbadian Civil Rights Crusader and Activist," *The Americas*, Vol. XXXVIII, No. 3 (1982): 366.

[77] William Lloyd, *Letters from the West Indies* (London: Darton and Harvey, 1838), 17. See Glenn O. Phillips, "The Beginnings of Samuel J. Prescod," 364.

[78] Stafford, "The Growth and Development of the Black Middle Class," 4.

BARBADOS POST-EMANCIPATION LABOR EMIGRATION

If emancipation meant status anxiety for the Afro-Barbadian middle class, emigration became the salve. The failure of British emancipation to sanction full freedom, and the resulting unavailability of land and political frustrations, created a rapid rise in emigration. Migration became the single most important feature of freedom making. Caribbean migration patterns caught the attention of Thome and Kimball.[79] They noted that freedmen "may leave the island if they choose and seek their fortunes in other parts of the world." Barbadians had been exploiting their post-slavery privileges through migration to the colony of Demerara.[80] Increasingly, however, migration became a nuisance to Barbadian colonial authorities who had grown increasingly anxious about losing "many of the laboring population." In the midst of their travels, the abolitionists noted that "the question was under discussion . . . whether it should not be unlawful to prohibit emigration."[81]

For the different classes of Barbadians, interest in migration became a form of post-emancipation progressive rationality that carried a different set of calculations, risks, and rewards. With a significant portion of the labor force freed, abolition had effectively caused a labor shortage in many islands. This opening of the labor market generated labor competition among the islands and created a confidence in freedmen's labor at odds with the colonial administration. Low wages in Barbados, compounded by issues of high population density and unavailability of land, pushed Barbadian freedmen to seek opportunities in other islands where labor was in short supply, higher wages were offered, and land was available. Leery of working agreements in Barbados and having experienced no radical transition from slavery, freedmen sought to take their freedom into their hands.

Large numbers of black laborers departed Barbados, but unlike the middle class who were interested in Liberia, they migrated to other parts of the Caribbean, a world within their reach. Other islands cunningly used emigration agents and newspaper advertisements to lure Barbadian laborers to their shores. One such agent, J. H. Shannon, frequently ran emigration advertisements in *The Times*: "Notices to laborers out of employment wishing to go to St. Croix in search of work; offered free

---

[79] Thome and Kimball, *Emancipation in the West Indies*, 133.

[80] Ibid., 186. Demerara became a county of British Guiana in 1838 but continued to be treated as a separate colony by the Barbados census.

[81] Ibid., 133.

passages to [said] island where they can make their own terms." Laborers would be "accompanied by Mr. Shannon or his agent to protect their interests," and "if terms offered are not satisfactory they will be brought back to Barbados at a moderate charge." He stipulated that "only those in earnest for work need apply ... able-bodied men with families are preferred" and that "a limited number to be taken on the first voyage all of whom must be vaccinated."[82] Shannon followed with many other advertisements offering work in Antigua and other islands.

Laborers formed the majority of emigrants from Barbados, but sought-after artisans also tried the Caribbean waters before signing up to go to Liberia.[83] Shannon switched the target of his emigration advertisements, promising to send artisanal middle-class men to places like Jamaica.[84] Samuel Inniss sought to "quit the island" through these schemes before his interest in Liberia. Inability to access land threatened to plunge artisans like Inniss into the soul-destroying work that would ruin their valued sense of independence. In British Guiana, artisans such as boat builders, smiths, joiners, house carpenters, and masons could earn $1.50 per day. The fee for shoemakers, bakers, and tailors was between 80 cents and $1.00 per day.[85] About a hundred young men left under this scheme in 1839, and a further 2,000 had left by 1841. It was only after conditions in British Guiana became less attractive, later in 1841, that the outflow lessened and artisans began to consider other possibilities.

Other emigration agents would be put off by the Barbados government. On October 30, 1863, the Government of British Guiana appointed Edward Walcott as an agent to make arrangements with those desirous of obtaining employment in that colony. Walcott joined the group of emigration agents advertising for laborers. He offered "a bounty of fifteen dollars and a free passage to themselves and families to those disposed to comply with the terms of the contract, which will be fully explained to every intending emigrant by one of H[is] M[ajesty's] justices of the Peace before signing the agreement."[86] Objections from the Barbadian government forced Walcott to withdraw the bounty. As a notice reprinted in *The Times* on November 6, 1863, highlighted, "A letter from the colonial

[82] Extracts from the *Times*, Friday July 17, 1863 in *BMHS*, Vol. 30 (1959): 156.
[83] Ibid., 159.
[84] Ibid.
[85] Extracts from *The Times*, Friday Nov. 6, 1863 in *BMHS*, Vol. 30 (1959): 161.
[86] Ibid., 160.

secretary under the direction of the governor to Mr. J. H., Shannon objected to the offering of a bounty as an improper inducement for leaving the island."[87]

In the subsequent issue of *The Times,* Walcott withdrew his fifteen dollars proposal to emigrants to British Guiana but maintained that "the offer remains of a free passage, certain employment on arrival, comfortable houses, and hospital care in case of sickness."[88] The following December, Shannon resumed advertisements of "free passages for laborers to Surinam and Nickerie," offering wages of forty cents per day and "the usual advantages of housing. Free passages back if employment is unfavorable."[89] The *Mirror,* the St. Vincent newspaper, reported on the government interest in Barbadian laborers. Similar largely empty promises were also made to migrant laborers to Central America. Migrants arrived already in debt to the company for their passage and became essentially indentured labor trapped in a new place.

Yet, the appeal of emigration for Barbadians was not solely geared towards securing economic benefits from better wages and land. The political capital derived from the ability to control and claim the fruits of one's labor and to make claims on larger society were also critical. Not only were landless Afro-Barbadians at the mercy of the planter elite who were their former enslavers, they were legally tied to the reconstituted plantation.[90] The promises of higher wages, accommodation, land, and other enticements to which Barbadians were unaccustomed proved effective in defining the ways in which the free labor market would now operate. They had been forced into a strictly alienated, wage-based interpretation of free labor, and, as the census report highlighted, "pestilence or emigration is apparently the alternative as an escape from starvation."[91]

Barbadians in these other countries sometimes found the freedom they sought. Others who did not returned home. Charles Henry Strutt, a stipendiary magistrate on a tour of British Guiana commissioned by

[87] Ibid.

[88] Ibid., 161.

[89] Ibid., 163.

[90] Paper given by Pedro Welch at the 41st Annual Conference of the Association of Caribbean Historians (ACH) at the University of the West Indies at Cave Hill, "The Forgotten Dimension: Barbadian Emigration to Suriname in the Nineteenth Century." Also see Frank Harcourt, "Early Post-Emancipation Migration from the Caribbean with Particular Reference to Official Attitudes to Emigrant Agents, 1838 -1842." Master's thesis Kingston, Jamaica: University of the West Indies at Mona, 1998.

[91] Governor C.B. Rowson, "Census Report of the Population of Barbados 1851–71." (Bridgetown, Barbados: Barbados, Barclay and Fraser Printers, 1872), 4. Accessed at the Barbados National Archives.

Governor Henry Light, found thirty Barbadians at the Woodley Park Plantation in Berbice to be "sulky and out of humour ... a few of them appear[ing] to be slightly suffering from fever." On inspecting the Barbadians on the Blairmont Plantation in British Guiana, he "found thirty-five of these people located here in very comfortable well-built detached cottages raised upon brick pillars, floored and shingled; found some of them sickly and complaining of the climate; two or three appeared very cheerful and contented." He noted that "none had any complaints to make against their manager."[92] News about these bare-minimum migratory achievements within the circum-Caribbean must have pushed the Afro-Barbadian middle class to look elsewhere for better conditions. As concerns for material and political advancement made middle-class blacks receptive to taking greater risks, it drew Liberia into the migratory marketplace of possible destinations.

Artisans were a self-reliant and independent group, and the economic exigencies of post-emancipation society in Barbados compromised social relations by eroding artisans' sense of self-sufficiency, threatening to remake them into workers dependent on wages.[93] Artisans' sense of the value of their labor had as much to do with social dynamics as it did with politics. Enlightenment ideas of personal property and of the self inspired how they perceived individual freedom. T. H. Marshall has argued that "heavy and excessive labor" characterized the working classes, while skilled artisans' labor was not "deadening and soul-destroying." This distinction rather than a simple wage increase decided whether or not artisans could move into a "civilized status." In developing a self-sufficiency and a sense of self-respect that they extended to others, artisans came to an understanding that they were men and "not producing machines,"[94] and thus they increasingly accepted the "private and public duties of citizens."[95] This made artisans, as a group of workers, central to their communities. By organizing themselves into guilds and societies, they commanded further societal respect.[96]

---

[92] House of Commons Papers, Vol. 16, 234–236. Accessed at the British National Archives. Kew Gardens.

[93] Bruce Laurie and Eric Foner, *Artisans into Workers: Labor in Nineteenth-Century America* (New York: Hill and Wang, 1989), 15.

[94] T. H. Marshall, *Citizenship and Social Class and Other Essays* (Cambridge: Cambridge University Press, 1950), 150.

[95] Ibid., 7.

[96] For instance, when His Royal Highness, Prince Alfred, second son of Queen Victoria, and the first member of the Royal family visited Barbados between February 21 and March 1, 1861, his procession included groups such as the Shipwrights Provident Union, and bricklayers.

As organizers of brotherhoods, guilds, and labor unions, artisans were
a politicized group in Barbados. The importance and prestige associated
with artisanal organizations such as the Shipwrights and Bricklayers
Union were recognized when the group marched in a procession when
Prince Alfred, the second son of Queen Victoria, visited Barbados in
1861.[97] Barbadians and blacks on all sides of the Atlantic joined these
organizations to forge connections that would enhance their status.[98]
These fraternal organizations and the kinds of fictive kinships forged
within them factored greatly in political organizing.[99] Their value as
migrants in terms of their skills and community went beyond what their
meager numbers suggest, stretching from the family unit and rippling
outward to broader communities and the nation.

William Inniss, Edward Blackett, and Samuel Holder, who joined
Barclay's emigration movement, were among the Barbadian artisans
interested in Liberia. They lined up next to carpenters, shoemakers, wheel-
wrights, printers, teachers, and several who understood the cultivation of
cane and the processing of sugar.[100] The possibilities they saw in the
promises of land acquisition in Liberia reflected their Western understanding of holding property and the ways in which it would attract the
kinds of freedom, citizenship, and respectability they hoped for as individuals and families. Members of the large body of the artisanal social class
had specific post-emancipation aspirations for citizenship. Together with
their ambitions to improve themselves by diligent labor, Barbadians projected a high degree of industry and civilization.

The Barbadians appealed to the ACS via the constructive image they
portrayed through the wide array of the listed artisanal skills and professions, and, in turn, the ACS considered Barbadians beneficial to the
growth of Liberia. In addition to being highlighted on the ship manifest,
nearly all other communication between the Barbadians and the ACS

---

[97] "The Visit of HRH, Prince Alfred to Barbados, February 21–March 1, 1861," *BMHS*,
Vol. XXVIII (1959), 56.
[98] See Philip A. Howard, *Changing History: Afro-Cuban Cabildos and Societies of Color in
the Nineteenth Century* (Baton Rouge: Louisiana State University Press, 1998);
Ivor Miller, *Voice of the Leopard: African Secret Societies and Cuba* (Jackson:
University Press of Mississippi, 2009).
[99] See James Robert Spurgeon, *The Lost Word; or, The Search for Truth; Oration
Delivered Before the Grand Lodge of the Most Ancient and Honorable Fraternity of
Free Masons in the Republic of Liberia*, Dec. 27, 1899, Monrovia (Monrovia, Liberia:
Press of the College of West Africa, 1900).
[100] Ibid. Emigrant List Reference of Brig Cora: Vessel #141, *The African Repository*,
Vol. 41 (1865): 236–242.

emphasized that the interested emigrants were artisans.[101] The Barbados Company collected the names of "mechanics, sugar traders, distillers of spirits and useful agents in raising and manufacturing the products of the tropical countries." Of the 346 emigrants, 115 were males who possessed skills necessary for Liberia's development. The ACS rejoiced that among the interested families that all the head of households had some kind of skill related to agriculture. As such, they were always keen to list the male head of household first on the ship manifest. This was the model exhibited on the ship manifest for almost all of the Barbadian emigrant families. How the ACS allocated the Barbadians' labor revealed attitudes about gender roles and the sexual divisions of labor and how this would affect Liberia's civilization and their integration into the larger economy.

Though family acted as the fundamental organizing principle within the ship manifest, the emphasis on the importance of male labor encoded the nature of patriarchy in Liberian nation building. In the Blackett family, the ACS listed the father, Edward Blackett, as a blacksmith and listed no profession for his wife, Mary Elizabeth Blackett. As was customary in the nineteenth century, the wife's role was to care for the four young children: Catharine Jackman Blackett, six years; Alonzo Horatio F. H. Blackett, five years; Alfred Eleazer F. G. Blackett, three years; and Alberta Lavinia Blackett, one year. This was the same for the Padmore family. While the father, Jacob Padmore, was listed as a carpenter on the birth record of his daughter Ruth Padmore and as a farmer on the ship manifest, no occupation was listed for the mother, Lucretia Padmore, on either the baptism record or the ship manifest. Of the eleven Padmore children, one of the sons, Jacob Padmore, was listed as a mason. This highlighted the male role as the economic core of the family. Positioning males as heads of household inversely highlighted the females' domesticity. The primacy accorded to males and their labor highlights the kinds of patriarchy that would underpin the makings of the Liberian nation. In keeping with the Atlantic age of emancipation, white elites in the ACS envisioned freedom as male subjects becoming wage laborers, then heads of households, and eventually political subjects. Masculine labor was a tool for economic and political development in Liberia.[102] Women, on

---

[101] See Letter from Jas. Walker to William Coppinger, ACS Reel 96, domestic Letters, Letter no. 67. Folder 63417. Svend Holsoe Collection. Accessed at Indiana University-Bloomington.

[102] Herbert Gutman, *Work, Culture, and Society in Industrializing America: Essays in American Working-Class and Social History* (New York: Knopf, 1976); Rowland Berthoff, *British Immigrants in Industrial America, 1790–1950* (Cambridge:

the other hand, would serve in social roles in the households as domesticated dependents.

CRIMINALIZING MIGRATION

In the midst of increasing migration, the colonial government began instituting new aggressive preventative measures. On February 4, 1841, amid the circulation of reports from other islands and increasing emigration statistics, the Barbadian governor, Evan John Murray MacGregor, who had been observing the effects of emigration, moved to regulate the meaning of free labor. In addressing a legislative session, MacGregor referred to the departure of 2,157 laborers to other islands as "deceitful allurements practiced on the inexperience and credulity" of laborers.[103] He pleaded with the Barbadian Assembly, "for the sake of humanity," not to impede the Barbadian free labor experiment. He suggested that they curb further the colonial contest emerging through labor migration "by steadily persevering in the gradual amelioration of interior relations and peaceful pursuits of agriculture and commerce, that the credible station may be ever prosperously maintained through the favor of providence."[104] As a further caution, MacGregor pointed to the census guide to curbing emigration: "A well regulated emigration system, which shall provide for the admixture of a fair proportion of females and of old and young of both sexes in the ebbing flood, appears to be the only safe course by which the escape from the evils which [might come from] either an unhealthy emigration, such as has been in progress during the last ten years."[105]

In the aftermath of these recommendations, Barbadian legislature, in a bid to keep its low-paid labor force, increasingly contested emigration. In the subsequent period, "slavery was transformed rather than annulled."[106] New legislations ensured the continuation of slavery in freedom. Though emancipation promised mobility, the right to move about became a legally constituted process. Barbadian anxiety about

---

Harvard University Press, 1953); Alan Dawley, *Class and Community: The Industrial Revolution in Lynn* (Cambridge, MA: Harvard University Press, 1976).

[103] *The Colonial Magazine and Commercial-maritime Journal*, Vol. 4 (1841): 510. Also see Pedro L.V. Welsh, 2009. "An Overlooked Dimension: The Emigration of Barbadian Labourers to Suriname in the Nineteenth Century," *The Journal of Caribbean History*, Vol. 43, No. 2: 246–264.

[104] *The Colonial Magazine and Commercial-maritime Journal*, Vol. 4 (1841): 510.

[105] Ibid.

[106] Saidiya V. Hartman, *Scenes of Subjection: Terror, Slavery, and Self-Making in Nineteenth-Century America* (New York: Oxford University Press, 1997), 10.

labor movement resulted in several pieces of legislation. On April 26, 1839, the legislature passed "an Act to prevent the clandestine deportation of young persons from this island."[107] On February 24, 1840, in order "to regulate the hiring of servants and to provide for the recovery and security of their wages," colonial officials passed the Master and Servant Act, a piece of post-emancipation legislation that sought to control the hiring of labor.[108] Through these legal instruments, the meaning of emancipation was further removed from the desires of those who were meant to experience it. As the right of free persons to move became a legal matter, post-emancipation became an atmosphere of restrictions masquerading as freedom.

For much of the post-emancipation period, the tension between freedom and labor played out in emigration laws. More gruesome labor laws, meant to discipline the labor force, followed policies against emigration. Laws exercised power directly over the person of the colonist rather than property. In attempts to contractually tie freedmen to plantations, colonial officials created contractual agreements between laborers and planters that eschewed the necessity of a written contract.[109] They sanctioned that "any such contract shall be entered into for one month, and at the expiration thereof, any such servant . . . shall with the consent of his or her employers, either expressed or implied, continue in such service either after the first month or after any subsequent month, every such continuance shall be deemed and taken in every such case to be a renewal of the contract of the service."[110] One month later, the legislature further amended "the Act to prevent the clandestine deportation of young persons," so as "to regulate the Emigration of Labourers from this Island and to protect the Labourers in this Island from impositions practiced on them by Emigration Agents."[111] In undermining freedmen's ability to sell their labor, these legislations further designated laborers as wards of the state. The periodic re-issuing of new emigration laws in Barbados during post-emancipation reflected their relative ineffectiveness.

---

[107] Government House, *Laws of Barbados: Laws Statutes and Compilations* (London: William Clowes and Sons, 1875).

[108] Ibid., 191.

[109] B. Hawes, *West India Colonies: Copies of the Laws, Ordinances and Rules Not Hitherto Printed, Now in Force in Each of the West India Colonies, for the Regulation of Labour between Masters and Labourer, and Stating the Dates of Their Being Put in Force* (London: Colonial Office, 1848).

[110] Public Acts in Force, 1837–1841, 175–188. Accessed at the Barbados Department of Archives, St. Michael. Barbados.

[111] Ibid.

Naturally, Barbadian colonial officials started to reign in those they believed to be emigration agent provocateurs. Efforts to prosecute persons believed to be promoting emigration from Barbados exposed how ordinary Barbadians had come to think about migration and labor after slavery. Shortly after the passage of the act, while "passing in the street," the Bridgetown police magistrate overheard Jane Dayrell, "a poor Bridgetown widow," haggling with a laborer who was attempting to charge her "an exorbitant price for a bundle of fuel." Dayrell supposedly jokingly told the laborer that he should "go to Demerara where he would make a better living."[112] Though the proposition was purportedly innocent, the observing magistrate insisted that the widow had breached the newly decreed Emigration Act and summoned her to the courthouse to stand trial on April 2, 1840.[113] Operating under the guise of protecting Afro-Barbadians from the machinations of speculators and emigration agents, colonial officials acted as if they were looking out for the best interest of the laboring class as they tried to solve the emigration problem.

The passing of the Emigration Act signaled new imperial tactics in an arena of shifting social change where individuals who supported emigration incurred the wrath of the colony's elite. On May 10, a month after Dayrell's trial, police magistrate Applewhaite from St. Phillip's Parish charged and convicted Thomas Day, an emigration agent from British Guiana, £50 or three months in jail for acting as such an agent. That same day, "John Thomas Brown, a shopkeeper in the parish examined as a witness in Day's case was convicted by the same magistrate for aiding and abetting Mr. Day in his agency." While giving testimony, the shopkeeper incriminated himself when he disclosed that "he had served laborers in the parish about to migrate with provisions from his shop by order of Mr. Day."[114] The court convicted Brown on the additional charge of his "hiring out his cart to Mr. Day to take the baggage of emigrants to town from whence they embarked for British Guiana."[115] The shopkeeper appealed his verdict, which the court subsequently reversed, but the emigration agent

---

[112] Colonial Office Records (CO) 28/137, "Letter of Prescod to Right Honourable Lord John Russell, Her Majesty's Principal Secretary of State," November 26, 1840, in University of the West Indies at Cave Hill, Barbados Archives.

[113] C. V. H. Archer and Wilfred K. Fergusson, *Laws of Barbados* (Barbados: Advocate Co, 1944).

[114] *The British and Foreign Anti-Slavery Reporter*, Vols. 1–3 (1841) (London: Kraus Reprint, 1969), 23.

[115] Colonial Office Records (CO) 28/137, "Letter of Prescod to Right Honourable Lord John Russell, Her Majesty's Principal Secretary of State," November 26, 1840, in University of the West Indies at Cave Hill, Barbados Archives.

experienced no such fortune. The Assistant Court of Appeal reduced Day's fine to £25, but the Court of Error sentenced him, citing the "clandestine" and "fraudulent" operations.[116] Day recognized that the freedom dreamed up in the Abolition Act had been won in name only because the restriction of movement was meant to restrict labor. He thus argued that the legality of his actions as an emigration agent rested on a natural assumption of emancipation: "The right of the free laborer to seek employment wherever he can obtain the best return for his labor."[117] With the ideas of old plantocracy still holding sway, Day's words rang hollow.

Deliberations over emigration outlined the varying understandings of post-emancipation. During his trial, Day used what he viewed as Barbadian laborers' enthusiastic desire to sell their labor to the highest bidder to challenge allegations that he had "fraudulently" or "clandestinely" motivated laborers to emigrate. He cited instances where prospective emigrants had "walked upwards of 800 miles in the course of their repeated applications before they eventually succeeded."[118] It was planters' interests, reinforced by a "system of terrorism," rather than the need to "protect" laborers, that Day saw as the real obstacle to applicants' desires for emigration. Day viewed his actions as simply facilitating the "opening [of] the labor market of the West Indies to general competition." This, he felt, would ensure "the emancipated classes the full and entire benefit of the act for the abolition of slavery."[119] But by viewing the efforts of neighboring colonies to attract their laborers as "an unnatural inter-colonial contest," this "opening up of the labor market to general competition" was exactly what Barbadian planters feared.[120] Instead of fears of the mistreatment of laborers by emigration agents, as the wording of the laws suggested, laborers' empowerment alongside competition with other islands underlined planters' and colonial government officials' view of Day's business deals. As an instrument of control, emigration legislation thus served larger Atlantic economic and political ends.[121]

---

[116] The Court of Error was comprised of the Barbadian Governor and council. See CO 28/139 Memorial of Thomas Day to the Right Honourable Lord John Russell, in University of the West Indies. Cave Hill, Barbados Archives.

[117] CO 28/139 Memorial of Thomas Day to the Right Honourable Lord John Russell, in University of the West Indies at Cave Hill, Barbados Archives.

[118] Ibid.

[119] Ibid.

[120] Minutes of Assembly from meeting of February 4, 1841, quoted in Frank Marshall's "Early Post-Emancipation Emigration with particular reference to Official Attitudes." Master's Thesis. UWI-Cave Hill, Barbados, 1998, 61.

[121] The *Census Report of the Population of Barbados 1851–71* lists these groups as a representation of the varying "complexion" of the population.

Barbadian planters had other reasons to fear the opening of the labor market. Movement from Barbados had much to do with the internal dynamics of different islands and played an important part in augmenting geopolitical shifts during post-emancipation.[122] The pervasiveness of legal cases like Day's demonstrated that the opening of the labor market had shifted the arena of the colonial contest in the post-emancipation era. In this new period, the social, political, and economic conditions of different islands influenced freedmen's emigration tendencies. Whereas the predominant issue in slavery had been competition over sugar production, labor became the central rivalry among West Indian territories in the post-emancipation period. From the governor's viewpoint, Barbados's density of population was a non-issue.[123] Barbadian colonial officials were also concerned, as the census highlighted, that "the withdrawal of one class of the population, of a large excess of that class, of the sex and age most valuable to the community and the consequent increase of the non-productive and infirm proportion of the population is a matter of grave consideration."[124] Facts from the 1851 census countered this view, showing that "Barbados could well spare this number, and still a greater number, without injury to the agricultural, or any other interest."[125] This more than anything else confirmed speculations that the planter class's desire to maintain low labor costs drove emigration legislation.

AFRO-BARBADIAN POST-EMANCIPATION POLITICAL AGENDA

While legal statutes like the Emigration Act were directed at the black laboring class, it was the Afro-Barbadian middle class who mobilized to rail against it. Legal contestations in the post-slavery period had moved to a judicial and political realm in which the impoverished and illiterate laboring counterparts could neither make claims nor seek redress. However, more resources and education, the middle class was not going to take what they perceived to be an attack lying down. Throughout the period, the Afro-Barbadian middle class largely channeled their anger towards the law. Yet, this was not so much about enabling the poor

---

[122] Karen S. Dhanda, "Labor and Place in Barbados, Trinidad and Jamaica: A Search for a Comparative Unified Field Theory Revisited," *New West Indian Guide*, Vol. 75, No. 3–4 (2001): 229–256.

[123] Census Report, 1851–1871. Accessed at the Barbados National Archive.

[124] Ibid.

[125] Ibid.

masses to have a political voice. In many ways, the voices of the middle classes continued to be privileged, and their political authority persisted as a kind of vestige of the slavery era. As a group that had been free for longer, they had developed an awareness of rights and a mastery of the legal system that facilitated their ability to initiate legal action. Taking action was also a way to continue the kind of paternalistic patron-client relationship between the Afro-Barbadian middle class and the lower classes that kept the latter voice marginalized and allowed the former to dictate the agenda.

Samuel Prescod sought to "fully avail himself of this constitutional means" to make the king "acquainted with the following facts illustrative of the spirit in which the said [Emigration] Act has been and is yet being carried into effect by the magistrates and others in authority." With their positions at the margins of society, the black middle class came to the realization that "access to justice was an attribute of citizenship ... and that the law was the foundation of a free society."[126] Serving as mediators between the colonial administrators and freedmen and speaking for others below them also represented efforts to clearly define and empower their class. The shrinking ambit of middle-class power ensured their reliance on these kinds of political tactics.

Prescod used numerous cases to outline the legally restrictive and oppressive nature of Barbadian post-emancipation. In November 1849, when John Candler, a representative of the BFASS, visited the West Indies, Prescod explained that "laborers are not suffering from the operation of laws against them, but from the absence of laws to protect them."[127] He showed that though they "hire houses, and land for provision grounds," they still "have no security of tenure for either," as they "can be ejected at a day's notice."[128] The charges levied in Day's emigration case also became an example. Prescod noted that "it was not stated in the charge, nor shown in evidence that any particular person or persons had been contracted with, enticed, or persuaded by the defendant to leave the island, but simply that he acted as such an agent." He further noted that "neither before the magistrates in the first instance nor in either of the subsequent appeals was it shown that he had promoted his object by falsehood or fraud."

---

[126] *The British and Foreign Anti-Slavery Reporter*, Vol. 1–3, 1841, (London: Kraus Reprint, 1969), 23.

[127] Joseph Borome, ed., "John Candler's Visit to Barbados, 1849," *BMHS*, Vol. 50 (1960): 128.

[128] Ibid.

Indeed, in almost all of the cases, "the law was invariably imposed by the convicting magistrates; in none of them did it appear in evidence that the party had promoted his object by falsehood or fraud."[129]

Prescod's expression of concerns about the welfare of the Barbadian underclass, the quality of their freedom, and interpretations of free labor attracted efforts to silence him. In 1840, Magistrate Frederick Watts filed a libel suit against Prescod, who had come to be seen as "the most clamorous adviser of the peasantry." The suit stemmed from an incident on July 8, 1839, when Prescod in a letter to the *British Emancipator* spoke to laborers on a plantation in St. George Parish. He reported that the laboring classes were suffering from oppression and fraud and that, in a new post-slavery society, not only were laborers now less free than any other class, they were also further driven to desperation.[130] Prescod's story reached Governor MacGregor, who then hired Magistrate Watts to examine the allegations. Like with the Belgreave counter-address, Anthony Barclay was appointed as chairperson of a committee of inquiry into the statements of the St. George delegation of laborers and was asked to present a report to the governor.

After conducting his interviews, Watts, in reporting to the governor, brought a deputation of laborers to bear out that they were reasonably well treated, contrary to Prescod's claims. The document read to the governor in the presence of the laborers, supposedly with their acknowledgment and consent, stated that "far from being improperly interfered with, as free we have every advantage that any class of subjects possesses, the same laws that govern us, the same magistrates to guide us, and in fact every privilege enjoyed by every other citizen of the state."[131] From the perspectives of the newspaper editors, the laborers' acknowledgment clearly refuted Prescod's slanderous comments and intentions to "blacken the characters of the White inhabitants from the Governor down to the lowest grade of the official authorities and especially the planters of the island."[132] The white elites punctuated their dissatisfaction with Prescod by labeling him an unpatriotic and disloyal mischief-maker whose letter had only sought to disrupt the "mutual good feeling" that existed between the planters and the laborers.

---

[129] CO 28/139, Memorial of Thomas Day to the Right Honourable Lord John Russell, in University of the West Indies at Cave Hill, Barbados Archives.
[130] *The Liberal*, February 10, 1838.
[131] *The Liberal*, November 27, 1839.
[132] Ibid.

For his part, Prescod's criticism of Watts's deceit highlighted the larger social implications of the grave power imbalance that defined efforts legally to create a post-emancipation society. Watts had been selective in the plantations he visited, which meant that he deliberately ignored the views of over 90,000 laborers in Barbados. During his trial, Prescod sought to transcend the simple charge of having printed false information. He explained that in writing the letter, he had merely sought "redress for the laboring class by supplying his friends in England at the Anti-Slavery Society with the necessary information regarding the state of the colony and the conditions of the people so that the society could use its influence to exert pressure on behalf of these members of his country."[133] He pointed out that the case had an impact not only on his own rights but also on those "of every man of every class in the community who knew himself a free man and desired to maintain his freedom."[134]

Issues of race linked the fates of laborers and the middle class in the post-slavery period. The middle class felt that, although the plantocracy directed the legislation toward the peasantry, it also compromised their own sense of political security. Laborers recognized the significance of their racial connection to middle-class men like Prescod. Writing to *The Liberal* under the pseudonym Defensor, one supporter of Prescod noted that although the laborers had been questioned, they had not known that their answers were geared toward vilifying Prescod, making him out to be an enemy to their cause. In fact, according to the writer, the laborers became aware of the true intent of the address only when it was read in their presence to the governor. As far as the daily gossip within the laboring community went, headmen had only shown up to tell them that it was necessary that they sign the address so as to cultivate good relations between themselves and their employers.[135] Some laborers subsequently sought to make it publicly known that they had not signed any address against Prescod.

Members of the middle class also called several public meetings in Bridgetown in the months following Dayrell's case. Prescod chaired the meetings and helped to focus the various post-emancipation discontents of the black community into cogent political action. At the meeting, Jane Dayrell informed Prescod that, "in a letter which was published at the time, one of the magistrates held out a threat to her that they would bear the charge in mind if she ever appeared before them again for the

---

[133] Thome and Kimball, *Emancipation in the West Indies*, 9.
[134] Marshall, "Early Post-Emancipation Emigration from the Caribbean," 51.
[135] Ibid.

slightest offence."[136] Prescod and others held several other public meetings. Post-emancipation meetings in which the Afro-Barbadian middle class represented the interest of the larger laboring population did much to create a sense of cross-class unity. In one of the subsequent emigration petitions to Lord John Russell, secretary of state for the colonies, Prescod highlighted not only Dayrell's case but others he deemed illustrative of the legally restrictive and politically exclusive post-emancipation atmosphere in Barbados. In a later complaint to the British king, Prescod along with several of the prospective Liberian migrants – William F. Thomas, Joseph Kennedy, Thomas J. Cummins, Thomas Harris, and Anthony Barclay Jr. – signed the petition on behalf of the free colored and free black populations.

Snubbing the middle class's efforts to legally insert themselves into the power structure of post-emancipation society affected their class psyche. Other petitions challenging the constitutionality of post-slavery denial of rights illustrate middle-class efforts to create a space for dialogue over their own issues and interest in achieving respectability. In a letter to Colonial Secretary Lord Russell, the group complained about the "certain disabilities they suffer." They stated that members of the House of Assembly were not pleased with their suggestion that "free coloured and free Black Companies of Militia should be commanded by Officers of their own caste."[137] At another meeting, Prescod appealed "the present very restricted and partial enjoyment of the elective franchise." One of the prospective Liberian migrants, Henry Dayrell, "addressed the company on the advantages which emancipation had conferred on them; and after a few observations on the state of the Elective Franchise, and the necessity of unceasing exertions for the extension of the suffrage, conclud[ed] with expressing a hope that every succeeding of that day would be celebrated as a sacred day of liberty."[138]

The Barbadians' criticism of post-emancipation colonial life and loyalty to the British king constituted a particular kind of "royal justice."[139] Efforts to make claims on citizenship by extending their orbit of power through the appropriate legal and political channels established the

---

[136] Ibid.
[137] CO 28/111, Sir Lionel Smith to the House of Assembly, May 2, 1833. Accessed the British National Archives, Kew Gardens, UK.
[138] *The Liberal*, August 3, 1839.
[139] Also see Marcela Echeverri, *Indian and Slave Royalists in the Age of Revolution: Reform, Revolution, and Royalism in the Northern Andes, 1780–1825* (New York: Cambridge University Press, 2016).

middle class as respectable people entitled to rights. Though excluded from the franchise, by appealing to the British king, the middle-class blacks were in a small way already imagining themselves as imperial citizens. But Dayrell was unsatisfied with symbolic acts of freedom and longed for more concrete gains. In another of their petitions, the middle class complained about "the partial and unequal constitution of the government" and "the many serious abuses and evils resulting therefrom."[140] They wrote that the abolition of slavery had "effected no alteration in the state of things, as the franchise had continued to be limited to 1,200 out of 130,000 persons."[141] Furthermore, the limited number of those who could vote included absentee white planters who did not reside in Barbados.[142] With this in mind they complained that "there are certain parts of our colonial code which except us from participating with our white brethren in certain privileges, and to which, as British subjects we humbly conceive we have a claim; and that it is our intention, in a less agitated state of the colony, to pray for a removal of such parts which by the several enactments of the legislature materially affect us."[143] Inspired by Victorian behaviors deserving of citizenship, middle-class petitioners often described themselves as exercising proper social and religious conduct. As they noted in one plea, "Your petitioners ... have all been baptized and brought up in the religion of the established church of England and their general conduct has been met with universal approbation and upon no occasion whatever have they shewn an unwillingness to comply with the rules and restrictions that the legislature have thought proper to lay upon them."[144] Even as middle class Afro-Barbadians protested their post-slavery status of freedom, they were actively distinguishing themselves as a certain type of colonial subject. Even as they sought to improve their lives and expose the injustices of post-emancipation, their protest was not altogether anticolonial.

[140] Minutes of Assembly, Meeting of July 14, 1840, accessed at the Barbados Archives, St. Michael Barbados.
[141] Ibid.
[142] CO 28/230/24. Colonial Office and predecessors: Barbados, Original Correspondence. Accessed at the British National Archives, Kew Gardens, UK.
[143] Resolutions of the Barbados House of Assembly, February 18, 1824, printed in *The Barbadian*, 25 February 1824, quoted in Karch Brathwaite, "London Bourne," 30.
[144] CO/32, Government Gazettes from the Colonies. The British National Archives, Kew Gardens, UK.

In their appeal to England for a reprieve, middle-class blacks took their cues from news of gains in other islands.[145] A Caribbean-wide consciousness surrounding the struggles of contemporaries in other colonies informed the Afro-Barbadian middle class about the possibilities for freedom. The Afro-Jamaican middle class had fared better than Barbadians in acquiring liberties and moving into positions of social, economic, and political power. By the early 1800s, Jamaica's free coloreds were active participants in the island's economic life. A few had even inherited plantations from their fathers. Others who were educated at universities in Britain achieved some measure of upward mobility and social acceptance. In Kingston, the children of free coloreds outnumbered whites in schools. Of the 500 students at the Wolmers Free School in 1837, 430 were children of free coloreds.[146] By contrast, according to Kimball and Thome, in Barbados "no colored student has yet been admitted within the walls of Codrington College."[147] The abolitionists nonetheless found a class of free colored, small independent freeholders and some brown and black schoolteachers in Barbados. Land mass shaped the critical differences in the experience of freedom on the two islands. Freedmen in Jamaica who acquired land through Baptist missionaries or squatting were able to build numerous free villages and community institutions.[148]

Using their keen awareness of the diverging political geography across the Caribbean, the Afro-Barbadian petitioners outlined the unique traumas of their post-emancipation experiences. "Your petitioners with due pleasure beg leave to observe to your honorable and worshipful house that there are some laws and restrictions laid upon them that the legislature of the sister colonies have found necessary to adopt for the government of the

---

[145] See Julius Scott, *A Common Wind: Currents of Afro-American Communication in the Era of the Haitian Revolution* (New York: Verso Books, 2018); Phillip Troutman, "Grapevine in the Slave Market: African American Political Literacy and the 1841 Creole Revolt" in *The Chattel Principle: Domestic Slave Trades in the Americas*, ed. Walter Johnson (New Haven, CT: Yale University Press, 2004), 203–233.

[146] See Gad J Heuman, *Between Black and White: Race, Politics, and the Free Coloreds in Jamaica, 1792–1865* (Westport, CT: Greenwood Press, 1981).

[147] Sturge and Harvey, 154. Codrington College was set up under the will of a wealthy West Indian planter, Christopher Codrington who left his plantations in Barbados to the Society for the Propagation of the Gospel. In 1829–1830, under the leadership of Bishop Coleridge, it became a predominantly theological college which was affiliated to the University of Durham in 1875. Sean Carrington, Henry Fraser, John Gilmore, and Addington Forde. *A-Z of Barbadian Heritage* ([1990] Oxford: MacMillan Caribbean, 2003), 47.

[148] See Gad Heuman, "Slavery and Emancipation in the British Caribbean," *The Journal of Imperial and Commonwealth History*," Vol. 6, No. 2 (1978): 166–171.

same class of persons." They pointed to the fact that "respectable and influential merchants, storekeepers, and freeholders" were denied rights enjoyed by their counterparts.[149] In keeping with middle class expectations of changes they expected to follow abolition, they noted, while "those restrictions may have been necessary a century and a half ago, they trust that [you] will see the utility of adopting laws more suitable to the improvement of the present age ... putting us on the like footing of people of color in Jamaica, and the other sister colonies of their royal master and king."[150] These observations of developments in Jamaica became the crowning step in the middle-class disillusionment with freedom in Barbados. Given the sense of deprivation they felt when they compared their position to counterparts in other islands, it is of little wonder that some members of the BCL who had intended to go to Liberia ended up in Jamaica.[151]

The white oligarchy consistently unleashed a range of economic forces that excluded the black middle class from the body politic and inhibited their socially mobility. Indeed, they found that no matter how powerful or vociferous they were, they could always be put in their place by the small white oligarchy. With no kind of leverage, they feared sliding down into the peasant class. Afro-Barbadians' frustrations with the futility of their efforts to enact franchise and other reform efforts increasingly moved toward a noticeable boiling point. Countless members of the middle class, including many who had expressed interest in Liberian emigration, were displeased with franchise reforms. Samuel Prescod, as much as he had been doing since the end of slavery, decried the lack of traction on proposed reforms. One columnist, in a letter to the editor "invite[d] the calm and serious attention of his readers to a speech reprinted by special request delivered at a public meeting held in May, 1849, by the most talented and energetic member of the colored class, Samuel J. Prescod from whose arguments moderate and prudent reformers may gather valuable hints for pressing on our legislation an extension of the franchise, a lowering of the qualifications."[152]

As members of the same social class, Prescod often entertained Anthony Barclay Jr., who "considered it an honour to be personally

---

[149] Quoted in Howe and Marshall, eds, *The Empowering Impulse*, 46.
[150] Ibid.
[151] ACS, Reel 96, Domestic Letters, Letter no. 50, folder 63389. National Archives. United States.
[152] *The Liberal*, Friday, Oct. 13, 1865 reprinted in the *BMHS*, Vol. 31 (1964): 156.

acquainted with" him. In a report of one of their meetings, "Mr. Anthony Barclay felt great pleasure in proposing [a toast to] the health of Mr. Samuel Prescod." Barclay announced that he "had become acquainted with his liberal principles and seen his zealous endeavours to promote the advancement of his brethrens." Barclay outlined that "to the present moment he had all along found him through good report and through evil report, opposed and culminated the same unflinching uncompromised consistent advocate of their rights and protector of their liberties." Indeed, Barclay felt certain that Prescod would always "merit the grateful respect, the confidence, and the support of the respectable coloured community, in addition to the well-earned love of his emancipated brethrens."[153]

GIVING UP ON BARBADOS

Throughout the post-emancipation era, the façade of a secure Afro-Barbadian middle-class existence deteriorated into an uncertain reality that many did not know they could continue to face. The Afro-Barbadian middle class felt they had been barred from the formal corridors of power and had grown impatient with the colonial establishment. Despite their frequent "petitions to the two houses of parliament," their prayers "for a reasonable and just reform" had not been answered.[154] Many of them thus came to the belief that racism under Empire was the reason for their continued subordination and second-class status in Barbados, but a status they could leverage to achieve their dreams elsewhere. That the monarch in his response to the Barbadian governor observed that "their tone was impatient" highlights the degree to which they had grown exasperated with the British colonial establishment.[155]

In the end, the desires among those who were delighted with the prospects of "building up a nationality of the descendants of Africa" were enough to overrule other objections.[156] The idea that freedom could only be attained where they could enjoy private ownership of land, property, and material aspects of freedom had gained sway. They came to believe that self-ownership was not simply a release from chains

---

[153] CO 28/111/42. Printed copy of an address from the free coloured and free Black Population. Accessed at the British National Archives, 2015.
[154] Ibid.
[155] Ibid.
[156] ACS Reel 96, domestic letters letter. No 51. Folder 63391. National Archives. United States. Svend Holsoe Collection. Accessed at Indiana University-Bloomington.

and could only be made possible if truly enabled by legal policy. For Afro-Barbadians inspired by ideas of the self and personal property, freedom was the ability to participate actively in the political system that shaped their world. They, like others in the Caribbean, "insisted that political and economic freedom did not function in separate domains. To neglect one was to damn the other."[157] It was not just the emphasis on labor that foreclosed freedom; the imposition of policies entailed a powerful political authority that controlled their labor while excluding them from political participation. To inhabit life wholly on the same terms as white men, they could not remain in the Caribbean.

As post-emancipation anxieties reached a tipping point, this changed the landscape of options for the middle class. As Prescod continued to carry on the fight for civil and political rights, others like Barclay instead looked abroad for a better life. For men like Barclay who were deeply concerned about self-determination, the conciliatory, planter-friendly terms of Caribbean post-emancipation had lost their sway. Barclay reflected an imagination about emancipation that would continue to harden through possibilities denied in the Caribbean. After a petition to the Barbadian legislature that received no response, they called a public meeting in Bridgetown and started an emigration subscription list. Many attended the meeting, including James Barclay, who spoke against plans to leave.[158] Shannon, who had been involved in recruiting emigrants to go to Demerara and other Caribbean territories, mentioned that many at the meeting expressed concerns about migrating to a "foreign flag," to which they would have to take the oath of allegiance. Four interested emigrants asked the Barbadian government for assistance to go to Liberia but were informed that the governor could not help to build up a foreign government.

[157] Holt, *The Problem of Freedom*, 397.
[158] Ibid.

2

African Civilization and the West Indian Avant-Garde

If post-emancipation crises pushed the Barbadians out of their Caribbean homeland, the desire to spread Christianity, civilization, and modernity also pulled them towards Africa. In an 1864 letter, Anthony Barclay outlined as much to Governor James Walker:

I beg to inform Your Excellency that our desire to emigrate to Africa and assist in the glorious work of regenerating and civilizing our Fatherland is not of recent date. It has been manifested on several occasions by those of the children who have never ceased to believe it a sacred duty devolved on them, and the time appears now to have fully arrived after years of great hardship, toilsome study and strict enquiry that a movement should be made in that direction.[1]

Barclay pointed out that he had finally come to believe that "the fact that our presence and our aid is much required there, and will be of advantage to all the parties concerned – these, therefore, encourage us onwards." Still, in addition to their obligations to Africa, Barclay also acknowledged their responsibilities to the British Empire. Soliciting the governor's assistance, Barclay noted that the emigrants, "knowing their duty to our Sovereign and the veneration and respect due to her representative, have in this instance with as much propriety solicited your Excellency's patronage."[2]

Casting the emigration of the 346 Barbadians within the context of attempts to civilize Africa highlights how West Indians negotiated different post-emancipation forces in their efforts to find a freedom that was of their making and to their liking. Increasing post-emancipation dilemmas might

---

[1] Anthony Barclay to His Excellency James Walker Esq. C.B 14th of December 1864, in Svend Holsoe Collection. Accessed at the University of Indiana at Bloomington.
[2] Ibid.

have pushed the Barbadians to a realization about the mutual benefit of their support and presence in Africa. However, such insights emerged from their longstanding curiosity about African emigration, as well as an interest in being involved in the British imperial initiatives in colonies such as Sierra Leone. Liberia's location just next door to Sierra Leone dramatizes the ideological evolution of the group. As Barbadians thought about the new era of emancipation under the duress of stagnation and oppression, they reframed their conceptions of freedom from petitioning the British monarchy for special status as colonial subjects to pronouncements about the importance of their involvement in African civilization through emigration initiatives. Emanating from the emigrants' own religious and ideological beliefs, these views, which became additional persuading factors for the emigrants, developed both inside and outside the context of the economic and political pressures of post-emancipation Barbados. Among the host of factors that influenced them, their interest in civilizing Africa proved especially critical. Providing a more personal reflection of who the emigrants were, it unveils how they conceived of themselves and what image they had crafted and projected onto Africa as they imagined creating a Christian Negro republic. Furthermore, for an interest that started in Sierra Leone and other places, the turn of the migrants' attention to Liberia is particularly instructive.

THE WEST INDIES AND SIERRA LEONE

In the late eighteenth century, Barbadians first organized efforts to civilize Africa through Sierra Leone. Working through the Society for Effecting the Abolition of the Slave Trade, British abolitionists, including Thomas Clarkson, Granville Sharpe, and William Wilberforce, had waged a vigorous campaign to abolish slavery. They soon had other concerns, most notably black loyalists who had fought for the British during the American Revolutionary War who had turned into the black poor in England and Nova Scotia. In 1787, through efforts designed to ameliorate their condition while also aiming to abolish slavery, British abolitionists established the colony of Sierra Leone. Having institutionalized the idea of African colonization, the British began to use Sierra Leone as a solution for the problems of blackness in Britain as well as for other problems connected to the empire.[3] As a result, West Indians became some of the

---

[3] See David Lambert, "Sierra Leone and Other Sites in the War of Representation over Slavery," *History Workshop Journal*, Vol. 64, No. 1 (2007): 103–132; See Zoe Laidlaw, "Heathens, Slaves and Aborigines: Thomas Hodgkins's Critique of Missions and

earliest emigrants to Sierra Leone. In 1796, Jamaican maroons who had been deported to Nova Scotia and exiled to Sierra Leone went on to play a military role in the development of the colony. Unruly enslaved Africans, particularly those who had participated in the 1816 Bussa Rebellion, the largest slave revolt in Barbadian history, were also exiled to Sierra Leone. Several Barbadian members of the West India Regiment also petitioned the British seeking to take up different administrative positions after their retirement in the Sierra Leone colony.

When British abolitionists created Sierra Leone, they intended for it to become a "province of freedom" for poor blacks.[4] Sierra Leone, however, came to represent one of the contradictory spaces within British abolitionist designs. The advent of the Sierra Leone colony as a symbol of freedom not only stood in stark contrast to an African coast overrun by slave trafficking but also contradicted the kinds of racial bondage maintained by the British in the Caribbean.[5] By exposing the glaring loopholes in the abolitionist campaign, these inconsistencies exposed British hypocrisy. As the lieutenant governor of Gambia warned, barring a more harmonious course of action, "the blacks in the West Indies will . . . receive his emancipation at the expense of his brethren in Africa."[6] The governor's words served as a kind of foreshadowing when the British abolished slavery in 1834. By the time West Indians began to carve out their lives as freedmen after emancipation, the slave trade had revitalized with force on the West African coast, sending many more Africans into slavery in Cuba and Brazil, contrary to the Abolition Act.[7]

While British West Indies territories struggled with labor problems and political protest after slavery, British West African territories such as

Antislavery," *History Workshop Journal*, Vol. 64, No. 1 (2007): 133–161; Simon Schama, *Rough Crossings: Britain, the Slaves, and the American Revolution* (New York: Ecco, 2006); James T. Campbell, *Middle Passages: African American Journeys to Africa, 1787–2005* (New York: Penguin, 2006).

[4] Lambert, "Sierra Leone and Other Sites," 105.
[5] Laidlaw, "Heathens, Slaves and Aborigines," 154.
[6] Quoted in J. Gallagher, "Fowell Buxton and the New African Policy, 1838–1842," *Cambridge Historical Journal*, Vol. 10, No. 1 (1950): 36.
[7] For more on the "second slavery" and the campaign to abolish the Atlantic slave trade, see: Dale Tomich and Michael Zueske, eds., The Second Slavery: *Mass Slavery, World-Economy, and Comparative Microhistories*, Special Issue, Review: A Journal of the Fernand Braudel Center, Vol. 31, No. 3 (2008), 297–343; Karen Racine and Beatriz G. Mamigonian, *The Human Tradition in the Atlantic World, 1500–1850* (Lanham, MD: Rowman & Littlefield, 2010); Rebecca J. Scott, *Degrees of Freedom: Louisiana and Cuba After Slavery* (Cambridge, MA: Belknap Press of Harvard University Press, 2005).

Sierra Leone grappled with the issues of slave trading and self-government. The British Empire combined these two problems by hiring West Indians to fill governmental positions in Sierra Leone.[8] Even as the British brazenly hindered freedom efforts in the Caribbean, they used West Indians as middlemen to maintain their colonial endeavors in Sierra Leone. For instance, in 1818, the Afro-Barbadian Thomas Carew acted as an agent of the British colonial project when he became the mayor of Freetown, Sierra Leone. Alexander Fitzjames, who had trained as a lawyer in Trinidad, also emigrated to Sierra Leone. In the 1830s, before migrating to Sierra Leone, he had brought attention to the ills of the British colonial system in Trinidad and planters' inability to transition from their roles as slaveholders. He believed this affected freedmen's effort to experience full freedom.[9] In the absence of the white British governor, Stephen Hill, Fitzjames often assumed the middle-man position of acting governor in Sierra Leone.

The crucible of transatlantic exchanges in Sierra Leone animated the consolidation of British views on race. Adopting an imperial policy on labor and race, the British established a link between their territories in the West Indies and West Africa by 1834. While freedmen came to occupy positions of prominence in Sierra Leone that were closed to them in the West Indies, they soon realized that the British colonial office often viewed them in ways similar to Africans. The British excluded both West Indians and Africans from some of the highest political offices in the Caribbean and Sierra Leone; these were reserved for the British colonial officials. West Indians who agitated and fermented discontent were rebuffed and dismissed.[10] The colonial establishment in Sierra Leone labeled William Drape, a West Indian emigrant in Sierra Leone and the first editor of the newspaper *The New Era,* as an agitator. His dismissal as "an adventurer from the West Indies" highlighted a status outside of the satisfactory norms of British transatlantic behavior.[11] Increasingly, Fitzjames, too, came to be regarded as too excitable, over-zealous, and unsuitable for leadership. Fitzjames's dismissal from his position as Queen's advocate in Sierra Leone signified the strident forms of racism that bolstered the new British imperial colonial order in Africa.[12] In an increasingly tense racial

---

[8] Nemata Amelia Blyden, *West Indians in West Africa, 1808–1880: The African Diaspora in Reverse* (Rochester, NY: University of Rochester Press, 2000), 43.

[9] Ibid.

[10] Ibid.

[11] Ibid.

[12] Ibid.

climate, such accusations undermined the position of West Indians in authority who came to be viewed as threats to the colonial establishment. As a result, Britain slowly changed its attitude towards West Indian emigration to its West African colonies.

Before going to Liberia, several members of the Barbadian cohort had petitioned for similar positions of prominence. On January 4, 1848, Charles Phipps sent a petition to Earl Grey, the British Secretary of State for the Colonies who was in charge of emigration schemes to Sierra Leone, Australia, and elsewhere.[13] Through approximately six petitions sent to the governor and the colonial office, Phipps had requested imperial appointments as either a magistrate or provost marshal in another Caribbean island or Sierra Leone. In response to his request, Earl Grey sent a note to the secretary of state highlighting that Phipps' "station in society, though quite respectable, does not adapt him to be added to the existing body of magistrates in this Island, and despite his qualifications, it would be difficult to find a 'suitable' appointment for him in Barbados." Grey along with other British officials concluded that a position that entailed regulating the immigration of recaptives and other laborers from Africa on the West African coast, or on another island would best suit him. Whether or not he had sufficient funds Phipps was sufficiently wealthy to occupy the post he had requested. Furthermore, he was led to believe that if he were white he would have received a more favorable response from the colonial office.[14]

THE BARBADIAN RELIGIOUS IMAGINARY

Despite the early exile and migration of West Indians in Sierra Leone, the connections shaped by churches and other institutions created more direct and long-lasting links between the West Indians and British colonies in Africa. Given the dominance of established churches, religion came to serve as one of the most powerful factors that shaped the Afro-Barbadian emigrants and their ideas of civilizing Africa. Religious identity was especially cherished by members of the Barbados Company. In his letters to the ACS describing the potential migrants to what many called "the Christian Negro Republic," Joseph Attwell wrote, "A large proportion was the professed followers of Christ, prompted by the love of souls, as

[13] CO 28/81/23 and CO28/169, Misc. Folio no. 399, "Response of Earl Grey to Charles Phipps." British National Archives. Kew Gardens. UK.
[14] Newton, *The Children of Africa*, 202.

well as the desire to improve their temporal condition, many Christian people of the Episcopalian, Wesleyan, and Moravian Churches, are desirous of emigrating to Liberia."[15] Even as they were attempting to emigrate to Africa, the Barbadians highlighted their affiliation to established European denominational churches.

Churches, then, staged the tensions between Christian religious beliefs and African spiritual traditions. The establishment of churches throughout the Caribbean formed a countervailing influence against the development of African religious practices in the Caribbean. Central to life in the colonies, churches served as ideological institutions that inculcated ideas of virtue, hard work, morality, abolitionism, and missionary duty and labor. Churches and missionary endeavors also provided the context in which Barbadians perceived Africa, and African religious practices, as backward and in need of civilizing from a superior doctrine. The Barbadians had their own personal conversion experiences as examples to inform further their views of native Africans.

Unsurprisingly, the majority of the interested Barbadian emigrants were Anglicans. When the first batch of English settlers arrived in Barbados, they established the Church of England as one of the earliest English institutions. As the oldest established church, the Anglican Church had more prestige than any other religious institutions on the island.[16] Many of the Barbadian emigrants went to the same parish churches, and the same ministers baptized their children. The growing presence of blacks in Christian churches highlighted the Afro-Barbadian duality as Africans and imperial subjects. In turn, affiliation with churches provided a way for Barbadians to acquire a higher social status. The respectability politics inherent to different religious orientations, particularly Anglicanism, created obstacles that became a part of the Barbadian baggage that would hinder relationships with other blacks. Religious and social connections created ties among the emigrants that reinforced and unified their sense of vision for Africa. Given that many of the emigrants were from St. Michael's parish, their children were baptized at St. Mary's or St. Paul's Chapel, the only two Anglican churches in the parish.

While the early doctrine preached in many Christian churches served to strengthen the institution of slavery, several of them later played a role in

---

[15] "The Barbados Expedition," *Annual Report of the American Colonization Society*, Vol. 46 (1863): 10

[16] Gordon K. Lewis, *The Growth of the Modern West Indies* (New York: Monthly Review Press, 1968).

its abolition. However, ideas of abolitionism varied from church to church. The Anglicans tended to differ from the Methodists, who followed the teachings of John Wesley.[17] Moravian and Methodist churches had become increasingly known as the "dissenting churches," opposing the more mainstream Anglicans doctrinally and in worship practices.[18] In the early nineteenth century, Methodist missionaries traveled to Barbados to proselytize and set up churches. A prominent missionary, Reverend William Shrewsbury, was thought by Barbadian planters to be an agent of "the villainous African Society" and someone who frequently communicated with the abolitionist Thomas Buxton. Assumed to have had a role in the 1816 Bussa Rebellion, Shrewsbury and his wife were almost killed by white planters after the uprising and were later expelled from Barbados. Buxton, who defended him after the rebellion, also lauded him with praises for his abolitionist work.

Notwithstanding the early troubles, Methodism established traction in Afro-Barbadian religious traditions in a manner similar to how it gained its foothold in African American communities. In a movement they defined as "Emancipation in Action," Methodism began as a radically equalitarian institution catering to Christian conversion and the education of Afro-Barbadians. The church held regular services that featured various speakers. For instance, on December 30, 1861, *The Barbadian* reported that "the new Wesleyan Chapel called Belmont on My Lord's Hill will be opened for divine service on Wednesday morning at eleven am, 1st January 1862, in the presence of H[is] E[xcellency] the Governor," who laid the cornerstone of the chapel on October 14, 1861.[19] Reverend Henry Bleby, who played a prominent role in the social and spiritual lives of Barbadian Wesleyans and had preached in various parts of the Atlantic world, led the opening sermon.[20] Ideas about African indigenes and their need to be civilized would also be filtered and widely distributed to diasporic audiences through iterant ministers such as Bleby. It was in these kinds of settings that the trope of native heathenism and savagery would be taken up by Barbadians.

---

[17] See Kenneth Cracknell and Susan J. White, *An Introduction to World Methodism* (Cambridge: Cambridge University Press, 2005); Frederick A. Dreyer, *The Genesis of Methodism* (Bethlehem, PA: Lehigh University Press, 1999).

[18] Alvin Thompson, *Emancipation I: A Series of Lectures to Commemorate the 150th Anniversary of Emancipation* (Barbados: University of the West Indies, 1984), 91.

[19] *The Barbadian*, December 30, 1861.

[20] Ibid.

In Bridgetown, the capital of Barbados, Wesleyan ministers used the popular gathering place, Marshall Hall as a site for their many lectures in religion and world affairs. On one occasion, "the talented and popular lecturer, Reverend Bleby, describing the rise and progress of Assyrian Archeology gave a lecture on Nineveh: Its Ruined Palaces and Sculptures" to a large audience.[21] Again on Friday, November 13, 1863, *The Times* noted the occurrence of an "interesting lecture on The Wonders of the Deep" given at Marshall Hall by Reverend Bleby.[22] British missionaries also pushed their West Indian parishioners to embrace Britishness through instructions on moral values surrounding marriage, sobriety, labor, and loyalty to the British monarchy. Some Afro-Barbadians followed these values, especially members of the middle class who either sought to use Britishness and British values more strategically or rejected them outright.[23] Isaac Graves, a sugar boiler from Lower Collymore Rock in St. Michaels, along with his wife, Rebecca Graves, a seamstress, and their seven children were a part of this tradition as members of the Wesleyan church in Barbados. So too was the twenty-nine-year-old Samuel Inniss, a boot-maker, and his brother, Charles Inniss, a twenty-three-year-old cabinet maker. They all likely heard such sermons from Bleby and others before emigrating.

Though the ACS ship manifest's records omitted baptism, it nonetheless formed an important part of the religious dynamic of the emigrating Christian Afro-Barbadian families. Parents engaged in these kinds of religious rituals as a sign of devotion and also to enmesh themselves in kinship networks that would help them gain respectability. Samuel Skeete's baptism in St. Michael's Cathedral, recorded on July 19, 1856, was perhaps done for these kinds of religious and social purposes.[24] He was the son of Samuel and Sarah Jane Skeete, who lived on Baxter's Road in Bridgetown, not too far away from the cathedral. The names of the father and mother, the profession of the father, and the abode were always registered in the baptismal records of the children. In this way, the records of these Barbadian emigrants challenge one of the classic stereotypes of black families, in that none of these women bore children to unnamed fathers. The only exception was Sarah Jane Graves, twelve years old, born

---

[21] *The Times*, November 13, 1863.
[22] Ibid.
[23] Christienna Fryar, Nicole Jackson, and Kennetta Hammond Perry, "Windrush and Britain's Long History of Racialized Belonging," *Black Perspectives*, July 31, 2018, www.aaihs.org/windrush-and-britains-long-history-of-racialized-belonging/.
[24] Record of Baptisms. Accessed at the Barbados National Archives, St. Michaels, Barbados.

in 1853, whose baptism the officiating minister, H. R. Redwar, solemnized in the district of St. Paul's in the parish of St. Michael on June 15, 1854.[25] Sarah was her mother's namesake, and on this occasion it seemed as if only her mother, who lived in Lower Collymore Rock and worked as a domestic, was present.

The evolution of St. Mary's Church is particularly important in understanding the efforts of the church to accommodate the social demands of people of color in Barbados. Located in Lake Folly, the St. Mary's Anglican Church was built to accommodate the growing population of the city, particularly its colored constituents. The expansion of services to blacks occurred against the backdrop of a coming emancipation. In 1816, the Bussa Rebellion led to "a proclamation by the Prince Regent denying that emancipation had been ordered, but recommending to the local authorities in the respective colonies to ... promote the moral and religious improvement, as well as the comfort and happiness of the Negroes."[26] William Harte, who became a part of the clergy at St. Mary's, had been known to emphasize the doctrine of equality between the races. One of his sermons led parishioners to accuse him of "trying to alleviate the slaves of their duty by including doctrines of equality inconsistent with their obedience to their masters and the policy of the island."[27] As a consequence of the doctrinal conflicts, the parish later separated into two ecclesiastical districts.

St. Mary's Chapel also became a cornerstone in Barbadian religious life. The children of Anthony and Sarah Barclay, including the young Arthur Barclay with his twin sister, Florence, were baptized on November 29, 1854, by F. B. Grant in St. Mary's Chapel.[28] On February 14, 1865, just a few months before they emigrated, Minister Grant also baptized another pair of twins – Helen Beatrice and Ella Alberta Wiles – the daughters of James Thomas and Mary Elizabeth Wiles.[29] The Wiles, having moved from Chapman's village, lived in Lake Folly, where their father worked as a blacksmith. With this move, St. Mary's Chapel became an important part of their family life. On August 9, 1854, F. B. Grant also baptized their other daughter, Laura Editha Wiles, who was born in 1853 and was twelve

[25] Ibid.
[26] Arthur Charles Dayfoot, *The Shaping of the West Indian Church 1492–1962* (Gainesville: University Press of Florida, 1999), 152.
[27] See Sehon Goodridge, *Facing the Challenge of Emancipation: A Study of the Ministry of William Hart Coleridge First Bishop of Barbados, 1824–1842* (Bridgetown, Barbados: Cedar Press, 1981), 8.
[28] Baptism record. Accessed at the Barbados National Archives, St. Michaels, Barbados.
[29] Ibid.

years old at the time of her emigration. Two years later, on February 10, 1856, Florence Irene, another daughter of the Wiles, was also baptized at the same church.[30]

Several other children and families were from St. Thomas in Central Barbados. The Holy Innocents Church became significant for many parishioners, especially the many emigrant children from this parish who would be baptized in this church. This was where William Edward, a carpenter, and his wife, Sarah Ann, from Tull's Land, baptized their son Henry Herdle Tull, who was born on December 16, 1858.[31] Born on April 27, 1856, and baptized just a few months later on June 12 by the officiating minister, H. N. B. Blankett, Ruth Padmore was nine years old at the time of her emigration.[32] Her parents, Jacob and Lucretia Padmore, lived near Kew, where her father worked as a carpenter. Adriana Alberta Louisa Thorpe, born in 1853 and baptized September 13, 1853 by H. H. B. Bovell at the Chapel of the Holy Innocents, was twelve years old at the time of her emigration.[33] She was the daughter of John Isaac and Elizabeth Maria Thorpe, who lived in Billain, where her father worked as a mason. Nine years old in 1865, Frances Eliza Bourne, the daughter of Francis and Susan Bourne from Codrington Hill, was born on July 11, 1856 and was baptized by M. C. Chrinkett. Like John Thorpe, Francis Bourne was also a mason. Seven-year-old Amelia Moore was born on June 14, 1858, and baptized by H. H. B. Bovell the same year on September 9 in St. Thomas parish. Amelia and her parents, Edward and Maud Moore, lived on the plantation at Clefts Handle Mill, where the father worked as a freight carrier.[34]

In the parish of St. Phillip, on July 7, 1863, Samuel Brown, a laborer, and his wife, Catherine Brown, from Rawlin's Land, went to H. M. Collymore at the Chapel of St. Martin to baptize their son, Frederick Augustus Brown. Similarly, in St. Joseph, Thomas Henry Eastman, a laborer, and his wife, Rebecca Ann, from Joe's River, called upon Minister John Bradshaw from the St. Joseph parish church to baptize their daughter Laura Matilda Eastman, who was born on April 4, 1861. Three years later in the same community of Joe's River in St. Joseph, the plumber, John Abraham Cox, and his wife, Molly Ann, also had minister Bradshaw baptize their son

[30] Ibid.
[31] Ibid.
[32] Ibid.
[33] Ibid.
[34] Ibid.

Josiah Cox, who was born on December 15, 1864. On that same day, Reverend Bradshaw also baptized two other children from Joe's River, a watchman's daughter christened as Helena Jane Clarke and a blacksmith's son named Josiah.[35] These factors not only enhanced the stature of the 346 Barbadians as emigrants, they also laid the groundwork for future tensions. Such class status, skills, and education cultivated a sense of religious self-righteousness that created an unequal relationship between the Barbadians and Africans.

AFRO-BARBADIANS AND MISSIONARY WORK

The Barbadian religious imaginary was defined through the ways in which Barbadians' religious beliefs reproduced pre-existing discourses of dominance. In the mid-eighteenth century, the series of evangelical revivals that swept across the British colonies during the First Great Awakening had done much to convert enslaved Africans and had served to connect multiple black communities, especially those in Barbados who continued to live and work on plantations after slavery. The Second Great Awakening that followed nearly half a century later stressed the importance of human agency and reform, introduced perfectionism, through ideas of creating a perfect world that would usher in the return of Christ. Through Reverend Rawle, the principal of Codrington College in Barbados, West Indians harnessed and refined the religious ideas of the time. In 1703, Christopher Codrington, a West Indian sugar planter, had made a will leaving three plantations and over three hundred slaves to the Society for the Propagation of the Gospel in Foreign Parts. The college had long been known for its philanthropy via the Anglican Church on Barbadian plantations.[36] William Colebrook, who was appointed as a governor of the island in 1848 and was impelled by the missionary impulse, also participated in similar philanthropic endeavors. White planters believed it was the primary duty of the church to spread the gospel, and they felt even more secure in their view that the West Indies owed a special debt to Africa because of the slave trade. The Barbadian planters had not only provided an idea of a "dark Africa" in need of civilization but

---

[35] Ibid.
[36] Frank Joseph Klingberg, *Codrington Chronicle; An Experiment in Anglican Altruism on a Barbados Plantation, 1710–1834* (Berkeley: University of California Press, 1949); Angela Cole, *God Have Mercy: The Codrington Trust* (Barbados: s.n., 2003); Nina Langley, *Christopher Codrington and His College* (London: SPCK, 1964).

further facilitated their self-serving mission by providing the resources for Afro-Barbadians' missionary training. These ideas would be deployed as West Indian missionaries established themselves as some of the early proselytizers in African communities in areas around the Rio Pongo in Sierra Leone.[37]

White Barbadians increasingly supported the works of various missionary societies in Africa. They eventually forged a more concrete religious relationship with the continent through the Church Missionary Society.[38] William Knibb, the British abolitionist missionary in Jamaica, connected West Indian missionary impulses to the efforts of the Basel Mission in Akrapong near the Guinea Coast.[39] Afro-Barbadians did seek to carve out spaces of independence within the British religious imperial terrain. As the "children of Africa in the colonies," Creole Barbadians broke through the dichotomy of European and African to fashion their own movement.[40] In 1851, Afro-Barbadians formed their own missionary societies through their Anglican church memberships. They eventually established a cross-Caribbean mission to West Africa. Founded in 1855, the West Indian Church for the Furtherance of the Gospel in Western Africa would be incorporated by 1857, after which it came to be commonly referred to as the Pongas Mission.[41]

When blacks started to promote their own movements to return to Africa, it gave white missionary societies the perfect vessels through which to make their doctrine look familiar and attractive to Africans. British missionary society soon began to deploy blacks, whom they viewed as racially amenable to the African environment, as the new missionary

---

[37] See Kristin Mann and Edna G. Bay, eds., *Rethinking the African Diaspora: The Making of a Black Atlantic World in the Bight of Benin and Brazil* (London: F. Cass, 2001); Ana Lucia Araujo, Mariana P. Candido, and Paul E. Lovejoy, eds., *Crossing Memories: Slavery and African Diaspora* (Trenton, NJ: Africa World Press, 2011); José C. Curto and Paul E. Lovejoy, eds., *Enslaving Connections: Changing Cultures of Africa and Brazil During the Era of Slavery* (Amherst, NY: Humanity Books, 2004).

[38] For African missions see Waibinte E. Wariboko, *Ruined by "Race": Afro-Caribbean Missionaries and the Evangelization of Southern Nigeria, 1895–1925* (Trenton, NJ: Africa World Press, 2007); J. F. Ade Ajayi, *Christian Missions in Nigeria, 1841–1891: The Making of a New Élite* (Evanston, IL: Northwestern University Press, 1965); P. R. McKenzie, *Inter-Religious Encounters in West Africa: Samuel Ajayi Crowther's Attitude to African Traditional Religion and Islam* (Leicester: University of Leicester, 1976).

[39] Dayfoot, *The Shaping of the West Indian Church*.

[40] Newton, *The Children of Africa in the Colonies*, 2.

[41] James Ebenezer Reece and Charles Guilding Clark-Hunt, *Barbados Diocesan History* (London: West India Committee, 1928).

agents of European abolitionism and colonizationism. They decided that "a mission to West Africa would be a work peculiarly suitable to the church in the West Indies, where the population consists so largely of persons deriving their origin from that country."[42] While Reverend J. Bradshaw became the society's secretary, Reverend Rawle became its vice president, and S. J. Hill, the governor of Sierra Leone, a vice-patron. Rawle provided accommodation at Codrington College for the training of the mission students. Shortly after the first group of missionaries were deployed, *The Barbadian* published a gloomy report: "Mr. Phillips, a young, simple-hearted, well-educated, and brave son of Barbados and Codrington College, who went out to Africa between one and two years ago to join the Pongas Mission ... was soon obliged to retreat from the field of operations in consequence of a severe attack of illness."[43] While the broadly held assumptions among whites about blacks' ease of adjustment to African environments and disease had not worked, Reverend H. J. Leacock followed suit, arriving in Sierra Leone shortly afterwards. On November 15, 1857, it was reported that the first church of the Pongas mission at Fallangia was "solemnly opened for divine service."[44]

Barbadians of all economic classes supported the Pongas missionary works. One of its more prominent founders and subscribers was Anthony Barclay's own father-in-law, the wealthy Afro-Barbadian merchant London Bourne, who contributed an annual subscription of ten pounds.[45] But less well-off Afro-Barbadians also supported the Pongas as well as other missions. One administrator of the missionary society in Barbados noted that "those from the Egertons' Estate deserve particular notice, as the laborers there again manifested their interest in the evangelization of their fatherland by contributions."[46] So extensive was the support of efforts that the planters were forced to remark on even the support of the young children. As they observed, "There is something

[42] J. J. Halcombe, *Mission Life*, Vol. IV. Part II (London: W. Wells Gardner, 1873), 561.

[43] "Mr. Phillips and the Pongas Mission," *The Barbadian*, December 9, 1857, reprinted in the *BMHS*, Vol. 29 (1963): 28; Pongas Mission Reports and Papers, 1857–1874. Accessed at the Barbados Archives, St. Michaels, Barbados. See also Alfred Henry Barrow, *Fifty Years in Western Africa: Being a Record of the Work of the West Indian Church on the Banks of the Rio Pongo* (London: Society for Promoting Christian Knowledge, 1900), 79.

[44] Pongas Mission Reports and Papers, 1857–1874. Accessed at the Barbados Archives, St. Michaels, Barbados.

[45] Karch, "A Man for all Seasons: London Bourne," *BMHS*, Vol. XLV (1999): 1.

[46] Pongas Mission Reports and Papers, 1857–1874. Accessed at the Barbados Archives, St. Michaels, Barbados.

peculiarly interesting in such liberality as has been exhibited by these laborers, or by the children of the St. Thomas's Sunday School, already to their beneficence." The mission administrators compared the poor Afro Barbadians to "the Macedonian Christians" mentioned in St. Paul's letter to the Corinthians, who, they said, were "shining forth from amidst their poverty, as fine gold in a rugged rock."[47] Moved by children's actions, the administrator commented that "such facts are not simply interesting. They are highly encouraging and instructive, as showing how ready the great bulk of the people and even their children are to interest themselves and to help in works of piety and charity, if the appeal be only made to them judiciously and kindly."[48] The missions held a parochial association at Holy Innocents Church, where several of the prospective Liberian migrants were members.

Barbadian missionaries were not only keen on spreading the gospel; they were also preparing themselves for improving the social and material needs of the African societies they would encounter. Many considered skilled blacks of exemplary character to be especially suitable as missionaries, and this highlights the reasons why the Fatherland Union and Barbadian Company for Liberia were so well-regarded. Missionary work united religion, labor, and virtue to inculcate the "Protestant work ethic" in Africans. One missionary society remarked that, "having pointed out the necessity of having some help to the mission such as artisans and agriculturists, steps have been taken for sending out a Christian family of exemplary character and industrious habits, the head of which is a carpenter of repute in his trade, while his wife and children are helpful in various ways, he and they knowing something of agriculture and other pursuits, and being willing to make themselves generally useful."[49]

Missionary experiences in Africa were often met with misfortune for a variety of reasons. As was the case with some of the early Pongas missionaries, blacks neither showed more tolerance for the African environment nor experienced the success initially anticipated. Indeed, it was highly likely that like the Jamaican missionaries to Southern Nigeria in the early twentieth century, the Afro-Barbadians who were interested in Liberia would also fail. The Jamaican men and their wives who went to Africa under the aegis of the Church Missionary Society (CMS) had a mission of "improving the spiritual and moral conditions of Africans"

[47] Ibid.
[48] Ibid.
[49] *The Barbadian*, November 7, 1863.

but were also motivated by economic and social interests.[50] Assumptions about Africans as well as diverging views on racial identity eventually ruined the mission. Joseph Harris has argued that "the idea of return is one of the key features of the African diaspora," as it formed the "completion of the circular process that is inherent to the diaspora."[51] That African liberation did not feature highly among the Jamaican missionaries, who felt no close affinity to the Africans they sought to spiritually uplift, departs from Harris's argument about diasporic return. In this case of West Indian emigration, views of Africa structured by British imperialism interrupted the closing of the diasporic circle.

Because Barbadian migration to Sierra Leone prefigured and informed the migrants' choices, it is likely that the prospective Liberian migrants knew that Barbadian missionaries struggled to find common ground with native Africans. The *Barbadian* newspaper reported news of "the burning down of the W[est] I[ndian] African Mission buildings in the Pongas country, and the destruction of all or nearly all, the personal property of the missionaries." While they noted that "the calamity was a purely accidental one," they also saw it as "a calamity which every Christian believer in this land will most deeply deplore."[52] On May 8, 1863, *The Times* reported in its ecclesiastical news on the arrival of the Reverends Phillips and Duporte from the Pongas Country in West Africa on the troopship *Adventure*. The missionaries were on six months' leave of absence as they had "been unremittingly devoted to missionary labor in the Pongas Country for the last seven years."[53] On their return, the missionaries met with other Barbadians who were eager to hear about their experience. A report of a meeting held at Marshall Hall noted that Barbadians filled it to its maximum capacity. As various newspapers reported, "The Reverends Duporte and Phillips, the missionaries recently arrived from West Africa, spoke on all their experiences, telling of the benefits brought to the people of the region and the necessity for continued support for the mission."[54] The missionaries paid tribute to the late Reverend Leacock, who many described as the martyr of the Pongas. Newspapers frequently reported on the favorable impression made by the missionaries at the various meetings held during their visit. Notices printed in the *Times* about mission sermons show that the proselytizers certainly

---

[50] Wariboko, *Ruined by "Race,"* XIII.
[51] Joseph E. Harris, *Global Dimensions of the African Diaspora* (Washington, DC: Howard University Press, 1982), 3.
[52] *The Barbadian Newspaper*, December 9, 1843.
[53] Extracts from *The Times*, May 8, 1863, reprinted in *BMHS*, Vol. 30 (1962): 155.
[54] Ibid.

sought to spread the word about civilizing Africa throughout Barbados. For instance, the Reverend J. N. Durant preached two sermons at the St. Leonard's Chapel during the season of Advent on the subject of missions. In a number of Sunday services, the missionaries noted that "the offertory collection will be made in aid of the Pongas Mission."[55]

WHITE DEATH AND BLACK SAVIORS

The early period of transatlantic relations between British Colonial Sierra Leone and the West Indies laid a direct foundation for renewed Afro-Barbadian interests in emigration. Through Sierra Leone, middle-class Barbadians like Anthony Barclay, James Wiles, and other middle-class Afro-Barbadians started to formulate ideas about how life in the British Empire had endowed them with the kind of "civilization" and a certain Afro-European "double-consciousness" that would easily lend itself to efforts in Africa. But it was the post-slavery abolitionists' climate and initiatives that created the tipping point. By adopting British abolitionism and civilizationist sentiments, Barclay and his Barbadian emigrant cohort, who had been keenly following British imperial efforts in Africa, progressively broadened their migratory horizons.[56]

By the 1840s, Thomas Buxton had succeeded William Wilberforce as the new leader of British abolitionist efforts in parliament.[57] In his publication *The African Slave Trade and Its Remedy* (1840), Buxton sought to "ascertain why it is that our gigantic efforts and costly sacrifices for the suppression of the slave trade had proved unavailing."[58] Many problems beleaguered abolitionists' efforts.[59] However, Buxton's focus

---

[55] *The Times*, November 19, 1870.

[56] See Alexander Byrd, *Captives and Voyagers: Black Migrants across the Eighteenth-Century British Atlantic World* (Baton Rouge: Louisiana State University Press, 2008).

[57] William Hague, *William Wilberforce: The Life of the Great Anti-Slave Trade Campaigner* (Orlando: Harcourt, 2007); Eric Metaxas, *Amazing Grace: William Wilberforce and the Heroic Campaign to End Slavery* (New York: Harper San Francisco, 2007); Stephen Tomkins, *William Wilberforce: A Biography* (Grand Rapids, MI: Eerdmans, 2007).

[58] Private Letter on the Slave Trade to the Lord Viscount Melbourne and the Other Members of Her Majesty's Cabinet by Thomas Fowell Buxton (London: John Parker and West Strand XXXVIII, 1838), VII. Also see Thomas Fowell Buxton, *The African Slave Trade and Its Remedy* (London: Dawsons, 1840).

[59] See Eric Williams, *Capitalism and Slavery* (New York: Capricorn Books, 1966); Christopher Brown, *Moral Capital: Foundations of British Abolitionism* (Chapel Hill: University of North Carolina Press, 2006); Seymour Drescher, *Econocide: British Slavery in the Era of Abolition* (Pittsburgh, PA: University of Pittsburgh Press, 1977).

on Africa as the lone site from which to implement abolition policies yet again highlighted the kinds of one-dimensional and short-sighted thinking that seemingly handicapped the British abolitionist movement.[60] Buxton formulated a new approach to British abolition, alongside the Church Missionary Society (CMS) and the Society for the Extinction of the Slave Trade, that West Indians like Barclay would later replicate in the Caribbean. In 1841, Buxton planned to eradicate the slave trade once and for all through an organized expedition up the Niger River. He put together a trip with agriculturalists, scientists, and missionaries, with liberated Africans as interpreters, in hopes of spreading the three C's – civilization, Christianity, and commerce – that would promote free-produce cultivation as "legitimate commerce" and an alternative to slave-trade-derived capital among Africans living along the Niger. After a few days on the Niger River, however, the chief medical officer of the expedition logged that "fever of a most malignant character" had broken out and "paralyzed the whole expedition."[61] At this moment, the expedition encountered the realities behind the belief popular in missionary circles that Africa was indeed the "white man's grave."

If not Europeans, who then could draw Africa into a modern, civilized future? As white mortality rates halted the Niger trip, organizers increasingly embraced a belief that linked race with civilizationism in Africa. White missionaries on the Niger came to believe that blackness would have inoculated them against African diseases. British abolitionists responded to the failure of the Niger Expedition with new standards for choosing missionaries for fieldwork.[62] Their new ideas partly came from blacks themselves, especially Afro-Barbadian missionaries and those in the United States who had petitioned to go back to Africa after the American Revolution for the purpose of working to abolish the slave trade. Likewise, British abolitionists came to a conclusion that civilized blacks with Christian experience and other facets of European enlightenment would be especially beneficial given their ability to identify with their "African brethren." Their race would further enable them to weather

[60] Howard Temperley, *White Dreams, Black Africa: The Antislavery Expedition to the River Niger 1841–1842* (New Haven, CT: Yale University Press, 1991).

[61] See William Simpson, *A Private Journal Kept During the Niger Expedition from May, 1841, Until June, 1842* (London, 1843), 56.

[62] Mark Harrison, "The Tender Frame of Man: Disease, Climate, and Racial Difference in India and the West Indies, 1760–1860." *Bulletin of the History of Medicine*, Vol. 70, No. 1 (Spring 1996): 68–93.

the dangers of the African environment.[63] Following the failure of the Niger Expedition in 1841, abolitionists turned to Africans liberated from slave ships on the Atlantic to become the new forces of missionary work geared towards African civilization. Shortly after the Niger failure, Samuel Crowther, who became one of the first recaptive missionaries, started to proselytize to native Africans as the new purveyor of civilization, Christianity, and commerce in Africa.[64]

Thomas Buxton's idea of taking the gospel to Africans stirred missionary and emigrationist sentiments in the Caribbean. In the same letter to the editor of *The Liberal* in which Africanus advised Barbadians to seek more auspicious shores, he also directed their attention to "a rumor afloat of a scheme of the British people for the civilization of Africa." Pointing to the civilizing spirit of the mid-nineteenth century, Africanus surmised that "the energies of the British people, pent up for years, now seek an outlet in philanthropic acts."[65] Reflecting on these efforts filled Africanus with feelings of indebtedness to the British: "How exalted ought to be the emotions of gratitude, in the breast of every descendant of Africa to the British nation that so disinterestedly, so humanely, extends the hands of succor to the sons of that despised land, with a view of raising them to a station among the civilized nations of the earth!" When Africanus discovered that British abolitionists had plans underway to instruct Africans rescued from slave ships to work as civilizing missionaries among natives engaged in the slave trade, he countered by outlining the critical necessity of West Indian participation. Indeed, Africanus insisted, "It is necessary for the practical success of the scheme that the children of Africa in the colonies should lend their zealous cooperation in this gigantic undertaking." As Africanus encouraged Barbadians to find "more auspicious shores," he rallied them to emigrate for the cause of African civilization by invoking a globalized black racial identity that transcended the local. "We are not borne down by the paltry considerations of locality. No! Wherever our species is found, there we instinctively feel to be our

[63] See John Turner, "A Black-White Missionary on the Imperial Stage: William H. Sheppard and Middle-Class Black Manhood," *Journal of Southern Religion*, Vol. 9 (2006), https://jsr.fsu.edu/Volume9/Turner.htm.

[64] See James Schön and Samuel Crowther, *Journals of the Rev. James Frederick Schön and Mr. Samuel Crowther: Who, with the Sanction of Her Majesty's Government, Accompanied the Expedition Up the Niger in 1841 on Behalf of the Church Missionary Society* (London: Cass, 1970); Duke Akamisoko, *Samuel Ajayi Crowther: His Missionary Work in the Lokoja Area* (Ibadan, Nigeria: Sefer, 2002).

[65] *The Liberal*, February 17, 1841.

home because with them we are identified. When we raise our voices in that cause, they awaken a responsive chord in the breast of the Negro in every part of the world."[66]

Africanus's suggestion that the diaspora should be thankful for British imperial efforts in civilizing Africa reflected the ways in which Barbadians' colonial identity sometimes drafted them into imperial projects. Africanus's designation of West Indians as "the children of Africa in the colonies" represented a broad umbrella that permitted Afro-Barbadians to enable or disable parts of their multiple identities as they desired.[67] Yet the title of "children of Africa in the colonies" also animated the ways in which a colonial identity complicated the relationship to Africa for some members of the African diaspora.[68] Afro-Barbadians' interest in the British civilizing project exposed how colonialism politically and culturally divided West Indian identity.

Barclay, in particular, had long openly embraced the growing pan-Africanist and black nationalist sentiments of the mid-nineteenth century through the consciousness of British colonialism. In 1839, "in an eloquent speech" at a public meeting, Barclay "reviewed the greatness of ancient Africa, the cradle of Arts and Sciences, whose visible remains were even now the admiration of the world." Out of his frustrations with post-emancipation, Barclay embraced a nostalgia for an African golden age within his emigration desires. "The revolutions of time had dimmed her glory, and she was degenerate," Barclay explained, "but her sons having obtained a footing in the new world, and been brought within the influence of modern civilization, would be actuated by the noble ambition of recovering for themselves a part of that ancient glory."[69] The solutions furnished by Barclay's juxtaposition of past and present showed an Africa ruptured by the process of diaspora but producing its saviors in the process. Barclay and the others ascribed their importance to the civilizing project to their historical connection to both Africa and Europe and the space they occupied between them.[70] Afro-Barbadians were infantilized but also ennobled by their colonial association to Britain. As British subjects, the Barbadians

---

[66] Ibid.
[67] See Judith Butler, The *Psychic Life of Power: Theories in Subjection* (Stanford, CA: Stanford University Press, 1997).
[68] Deborah Kimmy quoted in Jennifer Lynn Gilchrist, "Houses on Fire: Late Modernist Subjectivity and Historical Crisis." Thesis. (New York; Fordham University, 2008), http://fordham.bepress.com/dissertations/AAI3314561.
[69] *The Liberal*, February 17, 1841.
[70] Newton, *The Children of Africa in the Colonies*, 8.

shared status with other members of the Empire who vowed fealty to the crown and were subject to the authority of the monarchy but who were also othered and excluded on the basis of race.[71] As children of Africa in the colonies, they could use the British Crown's imperial influence and moral superiority to alleviate the problems that plagued Africa and the diaspora.

Barbadians' creative capacity to produce colonial fantasies of Africa further shaped the beliefs and realities of their African emigration interests. Indeed, convinced that West Indian involvement would draw Africa closer to its destiny, Africanus used Afro-Barbadians' colonial subjectivity to leverage their importance to the African civilization project. Afro-Barbadians entrusted themselves with the task of recovering Africa's past and unlocking its great destiny. As Africanus declared: "There is nothing in the least unreasonable in the idea that in the far regions of the continent another China may be concealed from the vision of the great European nations who, at present, consider themselves the monopolizers of learning and science."[72] Subscribing to the assumption of Africa's separation from the West and its place outside of the purview of civilization and modernity, the Barbadians' idealistic depictions failed to contest white supremacy.[73] Barbadians believed that their location in what many referred to as Little London placed them in a position of power to influence the global and transnational spheres of black culture that would define the course of African civilization and black racial modernity. Their particular embodiment of African blood civilized through racial slavery and proximity to whiteness made them valuable in the efforts towards African progress and to the quest to recover Africa's past and unlock its civilized destiny. Caught between the burdens of colonialism and the duties of diaspora, the Barbadians froze Africa in time, rendering it static to receive the blessings of their modernity. In this way, changing the complexion of the missionaries did not somehow change the underlying dynamic of African civilization. For Afro-Barbadians, participation in British imperial efforts became a way for them to switch their identity, overcome racial discrimination, and achieve their desired respectability.

---

[71] Ibid., 13.
[72] *The Liberal*, February 17, 1841.
[73] Yogita Goyal, "Africa and the Black Atlantic," *Research in African Literatures*, Vol. 45, No. 3 (2014): v–xxv.

First. *Resolved,* That this meeting has for some years past, watched with deep anxiety the efforts of Her Majesty's Government to suppress the slave trade, put down slavery, and civilize the untutored inhabitants of the continent of Africa.

Second. That although these efforts have not altogether been crowned with success, owing in some measure, to the generally received opinion, that the climate of that portion of the continent, to which Great Britain has directed her attention, is pernicious to the constitution of the inhabitants of Europe, yet there is room for the hope, that Her Majesty's government have not abandoned their original designs, but will continue to employ those means, which occasionally present themselves, of attaining their object, and which are now abundantly offered by the capacity and disposition of the descendants of Africa, inhabitants of the British West India colonies.

Third. That the philanthropic objects which Her Majesty's Government have in view, and the measures which they have adopted for the carrying out of the same, have, for some time, engaged the attention of a considerable portion of Her Majesty's loyal subjects in the Island of Barbados, and awakened in them, not only a deep feeling of gratitude for the great measure of emancipation, whereby their brethren in bondage were generally raised from a state of abject slavery to the proud position of British freemen, but also a disinclination to remain passive spectators of the great work of moral regeneration already commenced for the benefit of their brethren on the continent of Africa, to whom they are closely bound by the ties of consanguinity, affection and sympathy.

Fourth. That whilst this meeting deeply deplore the wrongs that are continually inflicted on the helpless inhabitants of Africa, the atrocities which are daily perpetrated on them by the continuance of the slave trade as well as the dark clouds of ignorance and superstition which overspread the land, they cannot but conceive it a duty which they owe to God, the British Government and themselves to make a voluntary offer of their personal efforts, to advance as far as in their power lies, the grand work of the moral regeneration and civilization of Africa, by proceeding with the assistance of the Government to the scene of action, by planting a colony, or settling a district in the Colony of Fernando Po, or on any other or more suitable spot which the Government might select, by introducing amongst the inhabitants our manners and customs, by studying the language of the surrounding nations, by making known to them the folly and wickedness of continuing the slave trade, by establishing schools of general instruction, by instilling into their minds the knowledge of the benefits to be derived from the cultivation of their lands, by introducing systematic culture, by endeavoring to establish the most friendly relations with the native tribes, by opening a mart for British commerce, and by our examples, moral, religious, and social, to form a nucleus from which instruction may be radiated around, and the well-disposed be induced to amalgamate with us.

Fifth. That under the protection, and with the assistance of the British Government and people, we are of opinion that success will attend our efforts, because we are certain that if liberal grants of land be made, proper encouragement given to industry, and a regular communication be opened between the western coast of Africa and the British West India colonies; but more especially with the Island of Barbados, a stream of emigration will commence to flow hence to Africa of numberless persons who are already civilized, and who will carry with them their various trades and professions, and their capabilities of every degree of instruction necessary for the formation of a newly settled colony.

Sixth. That emigration from this Island cannot at all interfere with the measures of Government now in progress for facilitating emigration from Africa to the colonies in the West Indies, inasmuch as the want of labor is not known here, this country being over stocked with inhabitants, who are increasing in such a degree, that it will be morally impossible, in a short time, for them to find adequate employment; in fact, in the present depressed state of the Island, there are hundreds who are in this predicament, and who could well be spared; and, therefore, in the event of our meeting with attention in the proper quarter, through which alone, under God, success can attend our efforts, the said emigrants must ultimately benefit themselves as well as others, as the means will thus be afforded of effecting a mutual interchange of the already civilized to a place where civilization and industry are required, and of the uncivilized to already civilized countries.

Seventh. That for all the foregoing important considerations, we forthwith form ourselves into a committee for the purpose of addressing a memorial to Her Majesty's Secretary of State for the colonies, through the medium of His Excellency Governor Reid, therein stating our wants, wishes, and suggestions, and earnestly and sincerely offering ourselves a devoted band (considering no sacrifice too great) to proceed to the continent of Africa, for the accomplishment of the object of our wishes, the British Government assisting us, and Providence being our guide. On behalf of the Committee.

FIGURE 2.1: Resolutions of the Barbados Colonization Society
Source: *The African Repository*, April (1865): 242

AFRO-BARBADIAN IDEAS OF AFRICAN CIVILIZATION

In the aftermath of the failed Niger Expedition, desires to abolish the slave trade and to civilize Africa mobilized Afro-Barbadians to join emigration societies and organizations geared toward missionary efforts on the continent. Barclay and other middle-class Afro-Barbadians began to form their emigration societies. Barclay's father-in-law, London Bourne, who had been actively involved in the Church Missionary Society as well as West Indian Church missionary activities in Africa, began to lay the foundation for the Fatherland Union Barbados Emigration Society (FUBES). Though the emigration society failed to galvanize enough financial and political support, upon his death, Bourne left a sum of money in his will for five pounds to be paid to support the efforts of the British and Foreign Antislavery Society (BFASS) and the Rio Pongas Mission.[74] While James Wiles and others created the Barbados Company for Liberia (BCL), Barclay later also followed up on the aims of his abolition and civilization society by reviving the Fatherland Union, the emigration society started by his father-in-law, London Bourne, in prior years.

Barclay and his peers formally began to express and reproduce their own civilizing projects for Africa through institutions in Barbados. Ideas about Africa and understandings of their duties as members of the diaspora shaped the Barbadian imaginary but often entered it through the

[74] Karch, "A Man for All Seasons," 19.

context of British colonial subjectivity. Civilizing Africa became the crucible through which the diaspora could mask their colonizing and imperializing sentiments within pan-Africanism. The same Christianity that grounded the mission and served as a moral scaffolding also created the patriarchal hierarchy that would enable the Barbadians to establish their dominance. The beliefs in Christianity around gender manifested not only in the Barbadians' ideas of Africa but also in their institutions designed to bring civilization to the continent. Within their institutions, Afro-Barbadians anchored a masculinist African diasporic politics of British imperialism within their mission to emigrate for the cause of African colonization. In the overwrought male narrative in which blacks in diaspora viewed the quest for autonomy and respectability as a confrontation between men of the African diaspora and the West, women were only accorded sentimental roles. In other ways, Barbadians who tended to view Africa as their "fatherland" were at odds with other black nationalist projects that tended to feminize Africa as a motherland to be protected and rescued.

Barclay and his committee's ideas about African civilization revealed the very making of the Caribbean imperial subject who was shaped by the politics of not only claiming rights but also carrying out the responsibilities of imperial subjecthood.[75] Bound by colonialism, their relationship to other Africans became one of simultaneous distance and embrace. Barbadians interested in African emigration negotiated a double movement between acknowledging and denying the effects of Empire and strategically highlighting, rejecting, or spinning the relevance of issues and events that indexed African culture. In their efforts to triangulate their identity and ideological positions around British subjectivity, West Indian-ness, and an African-ness, Barbadians navigated an inherited hostility to Africa. Barbadians, by virtue of colonial education and training, absorbed an Africa invented by the British and used this invention in their desires of creating a republic that would earn respectability for the race.

In an effort to fulfill the positions previously occupied by white Britons that were now left wide open, Afro-Barbadians made another pitch for a role in the British imperial service. During this period, like the societies created by Buxton and others in England, the ambitious Barclay, Thomas Cummins, and Charles Phipps who had petitioned for an imperial position, alongside a number of prominent white, wealthy Barbadians, created

---

[75] Janis Ho, *Nationhood and Citizenship in the Twentieth-Century British Novel* (New York: Cambridge University Press, 2015), 5.

the Barbados Colonization Society for Assisting in the Suppression of the Slave Trade and the Introduction of Civilization into Africa that was also locally known as the Barbados Auxiliary Antislavery Society, similar to societies created by Buxton and others in England. The British imperial imaginary and the assumptions and objectives of its colonial project were reflected in the Barbadian consciousness in multiple ways. The social imaginary of the Barbadian colonial project for Liberia was defined through the ways in which their ideas reproduced and appropriated already existing intellectual and political dialogues and their meanings and assumptions of dominance. This eliminated any chances that Afro-Barbadians would break the mold with British imperialism by creating something altogether new. West Indians shared British imperial ideas of abolitionism and African civilization and used their subjectivity to create gaps in the African civilizing campaign in which they would be regarded as important stakeholders.

The Afro-Barbadians placed the weight of their colonial ethos into a series of ideas about civilizing Africa. Assimilating their colonial views on race, religion, civilization, nature, and culture, the Afro-Barbadian middle class developed a series of seven resolutions to civilize Africa, (See Figure 2.1). In developing their civilizationist ideas within their emigration efforts, the Barbados emigrants captured their ideology and goals in their resolutions. As a vision for Africa that sprang from colonized minds, the series of resolutions passed by the Barbados Colonization Society for Assisting in the Suppression of the Slave Trade and the Introduction of Civilization into Africa reflected the particularity of Afro-Barbadians' brand of civilizing. Like Africanus, Anthony Barclay, the chairman, along with committee members Charles Phipps and Edward Archer, praised the efforts of "Her Majesty's Government to suppress the slave trade, put down slavery, and civilize the untutored inhabitants of the continent of Africa." To prove their worth to African civilization, Barbadians adorned themselves in valuable accoutrements of British cultural capital. In the language, aspirations, and self-image, a superior sense of "Englishness" pervaded every aspect of the Barbadians' goals as they presented an image of religiosity, family values, and skillfulness.

In the first of the resolutions passed by the committee of the Barbados Emigration Society (BES), they expressed that "the philanthropic objects which Her Majesty's Government have in view and the measures which they have adopted for the carrying out of the same have for some time engaged the attention of a considerable portion of Her Majesty's loyal

Subjects in the Island of Barbados."[76] West Indians, by inserting themselves into this transatlantic dialogue, claimed and rearticulated their subjecthood, a move that served as the platform for the active citizenship they demanded during post-emancipation. Members of the Barbadian company were deeply concerned about the development of the race. The granting of emancipation prompted Afro-Barbadians' perceptions of diasporic duty that were further exacerbated by anxieties about African civilization. In another resolution, the Barbadians claimed that British philanthropic efforts had "awakened in them ... a deep feeling of gratitude for the great measure of emancipation, whereby their brethren in bondage were generally raised from a state of abject slavery to the proud position of British freemen." This not only disclosed the free status of members of the FUBES and BCL, it further showed their embrace of British identity. As they noted, freedom fueled their disinclination to "remain passive spectators of the great work of moral regeneration already commenced for the benefit of their brethren on the continent of Africa, to whom they are closely bound by the ties of consanguinity, affection, and sympathy."[77] In addition to claiming an identity as "British freemen," the Barbadians also claimed a blood kinship to Africans.

Citing the ruinous effects of climate on British efforts in Africa, the Barbadians noted that the diaspora had produced a remedy. There was "hope now abundantly offered by the capacity and disposition of the descendants of Africa, inhabitants of the British West India colonies." They acknowledged the impact of the continuation of the slave trade in Africa, but also highlighted that equally responsibility for the continent's underdevelopment was placed on the "dark clouds of ignorance and superstition." The resolutions also illustrated the ways in which Barbadians navigated their various identities. Not only did they owe it "to God and the British government, but also to themselves to offer their personal services in the efforts to regenerate Africa by planting a colony in Fernando Po or elsewhere."[78] Fernando Po, strategically located off the coast of West Africa, was used by the Royal Navy as the base for their anti-slave-trading campaign. The British had abolished the slave trade in 1807 and slavery throughout the Empire in 1834. The Royal Navy squadrons

---

[76] "Resolutions Unanimously Passed by the Committee of the Barbados Colonization Society," reprinted in *The African Repository and Colonial Journal*, Vol. 24 (1848): 241.
[77] Ibid.
[78] Ibid., 242.

worked in overseeing these legislations on the West African coast, and Fernando Po was often the first port of call for slaves confiscated from illegal slavers. When many more slaves were being shipped to Cuba and Brazil during the "Second Slavery" and the numerous river deltas and coves gave cover to slave traders, Fernando Po became a perfect base from which the Royal Navy patrols could intercept and interdict slave traders. Because of the ravishes of disease, the base was never a popular destination for British sailors. However, the numbers of freed slaves substantially increased the population of the island.

In the post-emancipation era, instead of assimilating into the existing norms of Empire or being passively tolerant, as previous generations born into slavery had done, Afro-Barbadians envisaged an active double citizenship as both British subjects and members of the African diaspora.[79] They saw themselves as bringing important religious and social values to the continent. They hoped to introduce the natives to "our manners and customs, making known to them the follies of continuing the slave trade, building schools to introduce 'systematic culture,' to teach land cultivation and introduce commerce." They expected that "by our examples, moral, religious, and social, to form a nucleus from which instruction may be radiated around, and the well-disposed be induced to amalgamate with us."[80] The aphorism of leading by example in Africa disguised the denial of African ways of being and structured a hierarchy that valorized the diaspora as civilized and modern people from whom Africans should learn. In this way, African emigration under the banner of civilization appeared to be a thinly veiled cover for black imperialism in Africa. The resolution with its well-intentioned language perhaps inspired hope in the face of an incredible sense of great expectations. It can also be read as the statements of subjects who had lost control in post-emancipation using another theater to assert power through the mechanism of Empire.

By offering themselves up to the British efforts in Africa, Barbadians hoped to fill the gap between the abolition of the slave trade in Africa and the persistence of slavery in the Caribbean and the abolition in the Caribbean while the slave trade persisted in Africa. As members of the BCL reasoned, were they given land, their industry would encourage a relationship between the African coast and British West Indian colonies like Barbados that would cause a flow of emigration to Africa of

---

[79] Janis Ho, *Nation and Citizenship*, 24.
[80] "Resolutions Unanimously Passed by the Committee of the Barbados Colonization Society," 242.

"numberless persons who are already civilized, and who will carry with them their various trades and profession and their capabilities of every degree of instruction necessary for the formation of a newly settled colony."[81] Praising the Barbadians' skill and industry contrasted with the demonization of African indigenes. Through this formulation, characteristics were attached to different black ethnicities. In the adoption of this framework, these groups became the prisoners of an identity constructed on biological essentialism. At the same time, in this lopsided construction, the Barbadians converted the horrors of slavery into tools of civilization and modernity. In this formulation, slavery and colonialism became crucibles within which West Indians acquired enlightenment, industry, and moral elevation. They noted that their actions would not interfere with the labor program for recaptured Africans in Barbados. They would only be affecting "a mutual interchange of the already civilized to a place where civilization and industry are required, and of the uncivilized to already civilized countries."[82] The Barbadians' emigration project, shaped as it was by notions of British superiority, outlined how they viewed their relationship with Africa and Africans and foreshadowed future problems. While the Barbadians' approach to civilizing Africa positioned itself as being joined by the ties of kinship, it ironically perceived Africans as too backward to know what was good for them. It differed from white civilizing only in relying upon a different set of "elite" black saviors to come to their rescue.

Barbadians' efforts to civilize Africa placed the locus of control in their hands. Offering solutions and directing choices in the efforts to civilize Africa placed them in a position of power that they did not have ready access to in the diaspora. But the resolutions for civilizing Africa invoked some crucial questions not only about pragmatism but also about the functionality of the Afro-Barbadian brand of pan-Africanism. While the emigrants saw their individual economic and social successes as important to the development of Liberia, this success would not come if they lived on equal terms with native Africans. Diasporic visions for African development operated on the assumption of native Africans' weaknesses and cultureless heathenism. Africa's place as the birth of blackness as abject, degraded, and uncivilized could be shifted with colonialism.[83] Thus, while Africa and African development were the focus in the Barbadians' brand

---

[81] Ibid.
[82] Ibid.
[83] See Richard Wright, *Native Son* (New York: Harper Perennial Modern Classics, 1993).

of pan-Africanism, its doctrines rendered Africans as subjects, not actors, in the process of Liberian nation-building. The perceived superiority of British imperialism in Barbadians' conception of pan-Africanism, when juxtaposed to African Americans' Republicanism, created other ruptures in the ideological terrain. Here, pedigree and class distinctions emerged, and the question became about "who" rather than "what" would lead African development.[84] The implication, when brought to Liberia, fueled tensions on the ground.

[84] E. Franklin Frazier, *Black Bourgeoisie, The Book That Brought the Shock of Self-Revelation to Middle-Class Blacks in America* (New York: The Free Press, 1997).

3

The Liberian President Visits Barbados to Trade Visions of Freedom

In 1848, in the midst of their post-emancipation frustrations, Afro-Barbadians interested in emigration to Liberia received a visitor who brightened their prospects. Declaring independence from the ACS a year earlier, Liberia's first president, Joseph Jenkins Roberts, a mixed-race migrant from Virginia, United States, embarked on a mission to recruit and gather support for his young nation (See Figure 3.1). In London, Roberts met with Gerard Ralston, a white Pennsylvanian colonizationist serving as Liberia's consul general, negotiating diplomatic treaties and trade agreements as well as recruiting new migrants.[1] On his way to the United States, Roberts stopped over in Barbados. Given the nature of Atlantic currents, his layover was as fortuitous as it was unavoidable. But after ten years of post-emancipation without much traction in their agitation for full freedom, the dissatisfied Afro-Barbadians saw Roberts's visit as a balm. It served to affix their gaze on the newly independent nation.

If Afro-Barbadians, fueled by their interests in African civilization, were pushed out of the Caribbean by post-emancipation frustrations, African Americans in Liberia also persuaded them to African shores. Roberts's timely visit extended beyond his nation-building priorities to bring a level of clarity to the geographical possibilities of post-emancipation freedom for the Barbadians. The experiences of African American migrants like Roberts, who had risen to the highest positions in Liberia, not only counteracted missionary stories of Africa but cemented Barbadians' hope that one day they, too, could push past the barriers of oppression to achieve their dreams. More than anything else, Roberts's

[1] *The African Repository and Colonial Journal*, Vol. 24 (1848): 240.

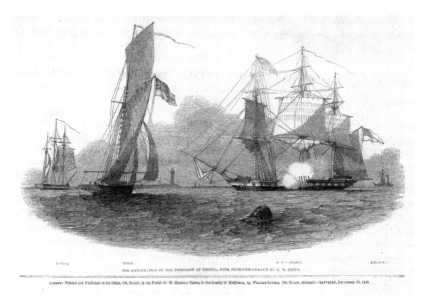

FIGURE 3.1: N. M. Condy's Depiction of the Embarkation of the Liberian
President J. J. Roberts from Plymouth on December 16, 1848
Source: Plymouth Museums Galleries Archives, Plymouth City Council, United
Kingdom

visit convinced Barclay that he, too, could become a ruler. At a time when
there were increasing post-emancipation failures and the creation of
a more rigid post-slavery hierarchy, Afro-Barbadians capitalized on
Roberts's visit to re-imagine their freedom.

As chairman of FUBES, Barclay met with Roberts and used the opportunity to raise Afro-Barbadians' concerns to him. Barclay, in a lengthy
address on behalf of his association, expressed his joy at the president's
safe arrival in Barbados at a time "when a large portion of our brethren . . .
have formed themselves into a society for the purpose of emigrating to the
Western Coast of Africa with the intention of forming a settlement in the
land of our forefathers."[2] In his address, Barclay used British imperial
efforts on the continent as a point of self-recommendation. He pointed to
the group's "intention of forming a settlement in the land of our forefathers, and for assisting, as far as in our power lies, the great work of the
moral regeneration of Africa; already commenced by the British
Government, under which we have the happiness to live, by the friends

---

[2] Ibid.

of the African race in England, and by a colony such as yours, from which under God we expect the happiest results."[3] Barclay does not place Afro-Barbadians outside of British imperialism. Rather, by seizing upon and appropriating the vocabulary of what Barclay perceived as British altruism and philanthropy, he cleared space for Barbadians in Africa by way of their colonial subjecthood. By suggesting that West Indians by virtue of their British colonial status had gained sensibilities that enabled them to participate in civilizing Africa, Barclay portrayed British imperialism as a part of Afro-Barbadian heritage.[4]

Barclay's address to Roberts reflected African diasporic counter discourses of subjectivity.[5] Barclay's references to the British civilizing project as well as popular black millenarianism exemplified the particularities of Barbadians' complex identity, and relationship with other members of the diaspora and Africa. His invocation of British imperial efforts in Africa instantiated a moment of contrast: that Barbadians and Roberts were not exactly alike in their experiences and interests in Liberia. Barclay, however, skillfully bridged this divide with pan-Africanism, using facets of its ideological rhetoric to point out the commonalities and interests shared between Barbadians and Roberts. "Trusting that we exchange reciprocal feelings when we state that [we are] bound to each other by the ties of our common origin and feeling the same deep interest in the enlightenment and civilization of our fatherland," Barclay requested that Roberts provide "information and advice from the results of your experience as may assist us in our labor of love." Barclay's turn to pan-Africanism was telling in the ways he recognized his shared heritage with Roberts, albeit one of a different sort. In closing, Barclay presented Roberts with a copy of the resolutions unanimously passed the year before by him and the other committee members of the Barbados Colonization Society for assisting in the suppression of the slave trade and the introduction of Christianity into Africa. He concluded by beseeching Roberts to "occasion us to hail with joy! the day when Ethiopia may emphatically be said to stretch forth her hands to God," while also sending the "best wishes for your Excellency's future success and the health and happiness of your Excellency and family, we have the honor to remain, Your Excellency's very humble servants."[6]

---

[3] Ibid.

[4] *The African Repository and Colonial Journal*, Vol. 24 (1848): 236.

[5] See Michelle Wright, *Becoming Black: Creating Identity in the African Diaspora* (Durham, NC: Duke University Press, 2004); James C. Scott, *Weapons of the Weak: Everyday Forms of Peasant Resistance* (New Haven, CT: Yale University Press, 1985).

[6] *The African Repository and Colonial Journal*, Vol. 24 (1848), 240.

As Barbadians considered the elevated stakes of remaining in Barbados and what it would take to find a more expansive freedom, Roberts's stay in Barbados served as a determining factor in their decision making. Announcing Liberia's recent independence in unambiguous terms to Barclay's crew of interested emigrants, Roberts's visit eliminated the more culturally and politically familiar British Crown colony of Sierra Leone as a migratory option as it encouraged Barbadians towards Liberia. By seeing Roberts in the flesh, Barbadians more than ever became confirmed in their beliefs that the issues faced by Africa could be solved. Liberia's independence signaled new promises of freedom for the young nation, and enticed blacks on the other side of the Atlantic interested in emigrating to a self-governing African republic. As Barclay told Roberts: "We request your Excellency to accept our assurance that we have received the intelligence of the formation of your settlement, the progress you have made under many difficulties, and the establishment of your independence with inexpressible joy as another demonstration to the world, that the descendants of Africa, when placed in a fair position, are not inferior in civilization, religion, and morality, to those nations, amongst whom it was their lot to be cast for a given time."[7]

In the wake of Roberts's departure, as Barclay sought more information about Liberia, exchanges between Barbadians and African American emigrants cemented their bond. Newspapers, letters, gossip, propaganda, and other forms of communication created a discursive space through which African American experiences of emigration and colonization in Liberia crossed national boundaries and penetrated the wider public conversation in Barbados. Through these mediums, West Indians and African Americans envisioned themselves as similar even before they ended up in Liberia. African Americans' experiences of colonization and emigration served to shape Afro-Barbadians' migratory visions and sense of diasporic duty. The flow, exchange, and cross-pollination of ideas between the United States, the Caribbean, and Africa informed the "practice of diaspora" by helping to establish and maintain consciousness about how choices of migratory destinations aligned with diasporic duty to Africa.[8] Dialogue in which African Americans deliberated over Liberia not only shaped Afro-Barbadians' imagination of the possibilities there but further passed on an additional collection of insights that broadened

---

[7] Ibid.

[8] See Brent Hayes Edwards, *The Practice of Diaspora: Literature, Translation, and the Rise of Black Internationalism* (Boston, MA: Harvard University Press, 2003).

their understanding of freedom. As rising uncertainty in the Caribbean synergized with the American Civil War and the incentives offered in Liberia, possibilities the Barbadians had only dreamed of began to materialize, facilitated by increased communication with African Americans and the ACS. As they carved out circuits of communication through black nationalism and pan-Africanism, Barbadians and African Americans shaped ideas of black identity and race.

BARBADIANS' MIGRATORY CHOICES

Barbadians' particular interest in Liberia emerged in an era of bristling migratory movements filled with large numbers of black migrants driven by pan-African and black nationalist philosophies. Finding camaraderie in the revolutionary nineteenth century, Barclay and his cohort navigated a wide array of ideologies and migratory destinations in their decision making. The institutional intent and transnational masculine imaginary of the BCL and FUBES matched those of other black emigrationist ventures to Haiti, Nova Scotia, and Central America, as well as those of the later colonizationist movement in Liberia. Barclay and other Afro-Barbadians interested in Liberia were aware of the prerogatives of the numerous emigration movements and what each of them could offer.[9] At the same meeting that Barclay glowingly spoke about Africa, he also toasted the "infant Haiti"; both were reportedly met with "hear, hear, and great applause." Barclay used the republic's successes as an example of black people's capacity to overcome struggles. Barclay declared: "The Republic of Haiti with her yet virgin resources had the means especially in her power and would employ them to expose the modern fallacy which would make moral and intellectual greatness to depend upon complexion." After much more cheering, Barclay concluded: "She had established her rights in defiance of the two most powerful nations of modern times – she had produced a Toussaint, (applause) and he trusted that her poets, her philosophers, and her artists were not far behind." Barbadians at the meeting may have imagined themselves as being in some ways similar to the Haitian revolutionary leader, given that Barclay's "toast was drunk with three hearty cheers."[10] In spite of his glowing views, Barclay and his cohort in the BCL discounted Haiti, even though it was a closer migratory

---

[9] Ibid. Also see "Colonization in Canada and Hayti, Compared to Colonization in Liberia." *The African Repository and Colonial Journal*, Vol. 8 (1832): 225–229.
[10] *The Liberal*, August 3, 1839.

destination. Rather, they looked to Liberia and were willing to take the risk of an Atlantic crossing in their quest.

The original mission through which Liberia emerged as a possible destination came out of the emigration impulses of black freedom movements in the late eighteenth century. In the 1780s, Paul Cuffe, an American sailor of Indian, black, and Quaker heritage, became one of the earliest advocates of British imperial efforts to subcontract African colonies to deal with issues of race and citizenship through the colonization of black loyalists in Sierra Leone.[11] By 1811, Cuffe visited Sierra Leone in search of information on how the United States could develop a similar arrangement for its own black population. In experiences and ideology, Cuffe was not unlike Barclay, whose original intent was to create a colony like Sierra Leone in the Fernando Po area. Cuffe eventually transported thirty-eight former slaves in his boat the *Traveller* to Sierra Leone, and planned a return trip in which he proposed to carry free blacks desirous of going back to Africa, but he died before his plans could materialize.[12] As black emigration evolved as a radical, grass-roots movement, plans similar to Cuffe's were developed to varying degrees of success in the early nineteenth century.

By 1816, white interest in the black emigration efforts resulted in an intrusion that would wrestle leadership of the movement away from blacks.[13] In a larger reform era, Liberia came to be seen through a colonizationist lens as a place that could deal with problems of free blacks' presence in an American slave society. Proponents of Liberian colonization ranged from US presidents James Monroe and Andrew Jackson to Bushrod Washington, the nephew of George Washington; Francis Scott Key, who authored "The Star-Spangled Banner"; and to other luminaries such as Henry Clay, Daniel Webster, and John Randolph. Following the creation of the ACS in 1816, the following year, the ACS sent two white members, Samuel Mills and Ebenezer Burgess, to the African coast to choose a location to set up a Liberia colony.[14] Finding an initial settlement near Sierra Leone, the

---

[11] See Floyd Miller, *The Search for a Black Nationality: Black Emigration and Colonization, 1787–1863* (Urbana: University of Illinois Press, 1975).

[12] Paul Cuffe and Rosalind Cobb Wiggins, *Captain Paul Cuffe's Logs and Letters, 1808–1817: A Black Quaker's "Voice from within the Veil"* (Washington, DC: Howard University Press, 1996).

[13] See "Congressional Debate Regarding Paul Cuffe's Petition," *Niles Weekly Register*, April 2, 1814.

[14] "Sketch of the History of Liberia," *The African Repository*, Vol. 28, No. 5 (1852): 129.

organization began to relocate African Americans to a colony they called Liberia, naming the capital Monrovia after then president James Monroe.

The aims of the ACS varied, vacillating between the different motivations and visions of the colonizationists. In arguments over whether philanthropy, religion, political pragmatism, or racism drove the interest of its members, some historians attribute the organization's beginning to members of the clergy like Robert Finley and Philadelphia philanthropist, Robert Ralston. Eric Burin has credited the founding of the ACS to American politicians who were southern conservative slaveholders, such as Charles Mercer, Clay, and Webster, arguing that their interest grew out of an alarm at the surging free black populations in several states.[15] Slaveholding members believed that freed blacks posed a problem to the institution of slavery and hoped to maintain the institution through the expulsion of free black Americans to Liberia. As slaveholders sought to colonize African Americans to Liberia against their will, Liberia became a space of exile for racially disruptive African Americans in the same way Sierra Leone had been for Jamaican maroons and rebellious slaves of the Bussa Rebellion.

On the other hand, some colonizationists believed that the creation of a nation would not only help blacks to develop but also eliminate slavery. Abolitionists believed that were blacks given a chance and a suitable environment, they could prove their humanity and thereby furnish the circumstances that would end slavery. Some viewed colonization as a way to reverse the violence and inhumanity wrought by the slave trade. As one of the first colonizationists, Reverend Finley advocated for the movement with the idea that "our forefathers brought the Negroes to American soil, and we are bound if possible to repair the injuries inflicted on Africa."[16] He surmised that "Africa was a grieving mother who would forget her sorrows and bless the hands of her benefactors for returning her kidnapped children. Americans owed a moral debt which they could pay by transporting thousands of African progeny."[17] Attorney James S. Green (son of Ashbel Green, president of Princeton University from 1812 to 1822) explained colonization in more reparative terms, suggesting that "slavery was a moral debt and colonization was the sinking fund, by the gradual operation of which, this debt will be ultimately charged."[18] In this

[15] See Douglas R. Egerton, "'Its Origins Is Not a Little Curious': A New Look at the American Colonization Society," *Journal of the Early Republic*, Vol. 5 (1985): 463–480.
[16] Quoted in P. J. Staudenraus, *The African Colonization Movement, 1816–1865* (New York: Columbia University Press, 1961), 17.
[17] Ibid., 20.
[18] Ibid., 85.

way, Liberian colonization also became a project of white guilt. In reality, the combined interests and investments of both slaveholders and abolitionists manifested the reality of Liberia as a colony.

During the first third of the nineteenth century, African Americans restored their search for a black nationality as Cuffe had done in the early years. African American emigration to Liberia continued, though it was not exclusive. African Americans forged leadership through emigration projects to find opportunities that would free them from white paternalism. These became a viable alternative for blacks who wanted to be a part of a movement that was free from the economic control of whites. African Americans primarily responded to repression in the United States through two leaders who differed in their solutions. At the center of this discourse was a larger debate about black advancement. Frederick Douglass came to represent assimilationist ideals in his belief that blacks should remain in the United States and destroy slavery from within the belly of the beast. For Douglass, leaving the country was tantamount to abandoning those blacks who were still in chains.[19] On the other side, Martin Delany argued that "only through wielding the national helm could Africans in the Americas achieve their quest for representation and preserve their distinctiveness."[20] For black leaders like Delany, African emigration should be aimed towards finding economic opportunities and political development outside the sphere of white control. Douglass's and Delany's differences over emigration not only put them at odds but also fractured the pan-Africanist and black nationalist visions of nation building in the nineteenth century.[21]

CHOOSING LIBERIA OVER SIERRA LEONE

Those efforts that directed diasporic flows to Africa in the early nineteenth century likely also informed the Barbadians' emigration choices. Despite their desires to escape the travails of Caribbean emancipation, West

---

[19] Howard Bell, "Negro Nationalism: A Factor in Emigration Projects, 1858–1861." *Journal of Negro History*, Vol. 47 (1962) 42–53.

[20] Herman L. Bennett, "The Subject in the Plot: National Boundaries and the History of the Black Atlantic." *African Studies Review*, Vol. 43, No. 1 (2000): 105.

[21] Kwando Kinshasa, *Emigration Versus Assimilation: The Debate in the African American Press, 1827 – 1861* (London: McFarland, 1988); Martin Delany and Robert Campbell, *Search for a Place; Black Separatism and Africa, 1860* (Ann Arbor: University of Michigan Press, 1969); Martin Robison Delany, *The Condition, Elevation, Emigration, and Destiny of the Colored People of the United States; And, Official Report of the Niger Valley Exploring Party* (New York, Arno Press, 1968).

Indians were not actively trying to subvert the will of the British Empire. In writing to the colonization society, Joseph Tracy, a director of the ACS, noted "some of the West India blacks are determined to colonize in Africa. Their plan is to do it under British protection, but they are resolved to do it whether they have that or not."[22] Desiring to remain under British protection, the Barbadians' pan-African ideology and subsequent interest in Liberia grew, in part, out of their earlier misadventures in Sierra Leone. British attitudes towards West Indian migrants in Sierra Leone and Roberts's visit to Barbados opened up a space for a counter imaginary to arise. Still, the fact remained that British imperial and racial subjectivities limited transatlantic experiences of freedom. While Barbadians saw themselves as imperialistically connected to Sierra Leone, the ethos of independence drew them closer to Liberia. Certainly, diplomatic changes in Sierra Leone made Liberia an alternative destination attractive to Barbadians. However, the fact that Liberia was an independent black republic, while neighboring Sierra Leone operated as a British crown colony, reveals one of the reasons Barbadians viewed it as "more auspicious."

Barbadians would have heard the changing rhetoric of travelers to the West African coast who touted Liberia's rising status as a republic. Such news about Liberia also helped to steer the Barbadians away from Sierra Leone. Indeed, as the ACS turned the *African Repository* into a Liberian propaganda machine, they published letters from visitors who praised Liberia for surpassing "her larger and older neighbor, Sierra Leone in learning the arts of civilized life."[23] F. Harrison Rankin, an English visitor to Liberia, praised the Republic for exceeding Sierra Leone as a colony.[24] On January 8, 1858, *The Liberal* reprinted an article from an American paper on the slave trade, "in which Mr. Rainey, the commissioner who went to Africa with the returned Negroes spoke highly of the fine appearance of the country, of the industry, intelligence and refinement of the people of Liberia."[25] Accounts of Liberia's economic status might have also further influenced the Barbadians' interests. In a lecture to New York City colonizationists, Reverend Thomas Gallaudet hailed "Liberia's commercial growth as astonishing," further insisting that "even the British

---

[22] Letter 270. ACS Domestic Letters reel 55, folio 31060. Svend Holsoe Collection. Accessed at the Barbados Museum and Historical Society, 2014.
[23] Staudenraus, *The African Colonization Movement*, 167.
[24] Ibid., 167.
[25] Karch, "London Bourne of Barbados (1793–1869)," 87.

conceded that Liberia was better poised than Sierra Leone to garner the unfathomed interior trade."[26] With these kinds of images of Liberia emerging in response to various other emigration and separatist black nationalist movements, Barbadians' turn away from Sierra Leone underscored the importance of black nationhood to them.[27]

Following independence in 1847, Liberia gained traction among would-be diasporic migrants to Africa. The appeal was visible to those already enthralled with the existence of a black nationality at all. Prominent pan-Africanists and black nationalists harnessed black anxiety over Liberia's success. They held up the republic as the national manifestation of blacks' identity and potential as a race.[28] In a speech titled "The Significance of Liberia," Edward Blyden highlighted the meaning of Liberia and the duty of diasporic blacks to the nationality. He outlined: "I am free to say that as Africans in the land of our fathers, hence our own land, with the advantages gained in slavery, we have special duties and glorious privileges. It is not our part to be looking backward across the ocean, but forward into the great continent, our ancestral home." Blyden associated Liberian migration with blacks' self-affirmation, arguing: "Our brethren in foreign lands are striving by all possible unnatural means to become white, while we are looking eastward and are determined to remain natural."[29] For Blyden, Liberia was the national embodiment of black liberty to which all blacks should aspire. Such ideas articulated by black nationalists helped to further convince Barbadians interested in Liberia.

To be sure, Liberia appealed to the Barbadians because it was also a relatable colonization project. In the already established colonial project of Liberia, Barbadian middle-class migrants could control the indigenous masses through the guise of civilization. The conditions propelling the Barbadians' flight, which also made it possible to establish Liberia as a viable colonial project founded upon "systems of knowledge, values,

---

[26] Ibid., 158.

[27] Bell, "Negro Nationalism."

[28] For explorations of emigration and colonization movements see Graham Russell Hodges, *The Black Loyalist Directory: African Americans in Exile After the American Revolution* (New York: Garland Publishers, 1996); Leon D. Pamphile, *Haitians and African Americans: A Heritage of Tragedy and Hope* (Gainesville: University Press of Florida, 2001); Cassandra Pybus, *Epic Journeys of Freedom: Runaway Slaves of the American Revolution and their Global Quest for Liberty* (Boston, MA: Beacon Press, 2006).

[29] Edward W. Blyden, *The Significance of Liberia, an Address Delivered in the Senate Chamber, Monrovia, Liberia, 20th May 1906* (Liverpool, John Richardson and Sons: 1906).

beliefs, and ideologies of power," called upon a Barbadian imaginary shaped by British imperialism.[30] Furthermore, not only did Barbadians recognize that their dreams could be realized outside of the Caribbean, they also saw a way to regain the mediating role they had lost after slavery in their journey as emigrant civilizers in Africa. In their new positions, the civilized worked to uplift the uncivilized. African American migrants to Liberia and members of the ACS appealed to prospective Barbadian emigrants using a familiar language of civilizing and Christianizing long established in old colonization and imperialist motifs. Within blacks' own initiatives and pan-African aspirations were also desires of rescuing the native Africans from their backwardness in the same way that the English had sought to rescue Indians in the Americas. As prospective black migrants worried about the fate of the nation they were going to build, the United States stood as a reminder and model for their ideals.

Barbadians were also enticed by African Americans in Liberia who circulated calls for others to join their colonial project. In this way, the Barbadians envisioned themselves as being a part of an Empire run by fit blacks. "Come Over and Help Us, we have a gem of an empire," read an editorial that was reprinted in the *African Repository* from *Africa's Luminary*.[31] The editorial further highlighted:

The Macedonian cry, "Come over and help us," is continually ringing and echoing in our ears from the natives of the adjacent country. Almost every breeze brings upon its wings the same sound; we hear it alike in the still small voice and in the strong roar of hundreds of the heathens around us; and we may not refuse to prolong the joyful news, lest possibly, we prove ourselves to be dumb and unworthy watchmen.

Viewed through these lenses, the rhetoric co-opted by the African diaspora as emancipatory and the driving force for African civilization was not new. The Puritans' use of similar rhetoric, for example, was enshrined on the seal of the company that had established Massachusetts Colony. It depicted a dejected Indian with his arrows turned down, entreating whites to "come over and help us." The long history of colonizationist impulses had grown out of interpretations of Acts, chapter 16, verse 9, where Christians were told: "And a vision appeared to Paul in the night; There stood a man of Macedonia, and prayed him, saying, Come over into

---

[30] Keith Sandiford, *Theorizing a Colonial Caribbean-Atlantic Imaginary: Sugar and Obeah* (New York: Routledge, 2011), 54.
[31] "Help Needed," *The African Repository and Colonial Journal*, Vol. 17 (September 15, 1841): 280.

Macedonia and help us." As the African American pioneers pointed out, "Africa, Western Africa stands forth in an imploring attitude, and begs and entreats that her voice may be heard, that her petition may be granted; which is that the Gospel be preached unto her."[32]

Race and the moral necessity of abolition complicated the black imperialist pull of emigrants to the African coast. Civilization through the prism of black nationalism endeavored to portray indigenes as docile beings waiting to be reinvigorated with the religion and culture of the returning migrants: "She only asks to be taught the way of salvation. Her condition is pitiable, indeed, is miserable in the extreme – dark, gloomy, and peculiar. Much has been done by different denominations of Christians, and yet comparatively speaking, nothing has been accomplished. Millions are yet without having so much as heard of the 'new and living way.'" Along with the idea that this was their duty as the diaspora, prospective migrants believed they were needed and that the indigenes would welcome them. Religion and black millenarian ideology were further infused with these ideas of civilization to achieve this end. The popular millenarianism that ultimately became the hallmark of pan-Africanism would be wielded towards this end: "Ethiopia is stretching forth her hands unto God, and hundreds of her sons and daughters, are imploring the Christian Church to send life and salvation to them." African Americans pointed out what they were witnessing on the ground: "We see and know that the harvest is already ripe and that the laborers are few. We pray the Lord of the vineyard and his co-workers to send forth more laborers."[33] The civilization of Liberia would be the lighthouse that would show the way for the regeneration of the whole continent. Pamphlets, newspaper, and other publications invited blacks to migrate to Liberia with the clarion call: "We desire to blow the trumpet, if happily the sounding thereof may reach unto those who are ready, and willing to send and come to the relief of perishing thousands." Even in the face of untold dangers, advocates hoped for this: "Notwithstanding God in his providence and wisdom sees proper to remove by death, one and another of the laborers sent here by the different Mission Boards[,] their ranks will still be filled ... [and] though a thousand die, Africa will not be given up."[34]

Forged through the efforts of other blacks, Liberia had gained independence in 1847 while neighboring British-run Sierra Leone languished

[32] Ibid., 280.
[33] Ibid.
[34] Ibid.

as a colony. This alone rendered the black nationality as a credible position from which to deploy the British colonial project and affect African civilization. The Barbadians' interest endorsed the persistent associational tendencies of the British colonial project and its tropes of "civilization." With their migration constructed as a sacred two-way obligation that melded the duty of the diaspora into the burden of imperial subjectivity, Afro-Barbadians came to see their migration to a black republic as one filled with great purpose. Afro-Barbadians saw themselves as bearers of the kind of civilization central to Africa's ability to reach its great destiny. As Liberia became intricately intertwined with blacks' identity and sense of progress, the Barbadians surmised that their migration would position the republic as a modern political symbol reminiscent of Africa's glorious past and future.

Such views were welcomed by American colonizationists like John Latrobe, who had begun attempts to make Liberia into an Americo-African country and a black Christian Republic. Latrobe, who had imperial designs, specifically desired that the United States, in time, would supplant all its great European rivals in Africa. Liberia's president also provided the Barbadians with reasons for why Liberia was the best choice for them. Liberian officials pointed to the acknowledgment of the republic's sovereignty by leading nations. For Barbadians seeking to throw off some of the yoke of empire but also use it in service of their savior complex, Liberian officials provided a familiar draw. They highlighted that the republic was "the most suitable starting point from which the returning exiles may begin to take possession of and civilize this long-neglected land, and thus aid in restoring this ancient cradle of civilization to her pristine glory."[35] The Liberian republic rather than the Crown colony of Sierra Leone offered a superior theater of freedom. As a migratory destination, Liberia provided the possibilities for British West Indians to escape the socio-economic and political encumbrances of imperial and racial subjectivity even as they leveraged its value for their benefit. By taking part in African civilization and the black nation-building project, they would also make their freedom more meaningful. Liberia fulfilled Afro-Barbadians' migratory vision of helping to build up a black republic that would gain respectability for the race.

---

[35] Ibid.

GERARD RALSTON AND THE BARBADIANS

In 1864, several committee members of the BCL – John Worrell, Charles Lawrence, and Samuel Griffiths – wrote to Gerard Ralston, the Liberian consul in London.[36] In his reply to the "Gentlemen," after reading their "interesting letter," perhaps to help them decide between the various available migration ventures and to clarify information on Liberia's specific offerings, Ralston enthusiastically promoted Liberia as the up-and-coming Negro nation. He "rejoiced that as many respectable inhabitants of Barbados are willing to emigrate to Liberia to strengthen the Negro nationality on the West Coast of Africa in conjunction with their African brethren of the United States of America, who have preceded them in establishing a highly vigorous representative Republican Government."[37] Ralston assumed that the Barbadians might be interested in forms of citizenship they had been denied in the British Empire and would be enticed by Liberia's republican form of government. Nonetheless, like they had with Roberts, the Barbadians added him to the broad network of people that could help them achieve their dreams.

Ralston attempted to paint a picture of life among whites as opposed to blacks by convincing the Barbadians that the advancement of a black nationality could only occur on the African coast. He believed no such nation could exist in the "United States, neither in Jamaica, nor Trinidad, nor Demerara, nor Hayti, nor Cuba, nor Central America, nor in short in any other country but Liberia." He further cautioned: "Whatever country the white man inhabits the black man ought to avoid."[38] Afro-Barbadians could relate to the follies of white supremacy, but Ralston moved to provide concrete eye-witness accounts of the failures and setbacks of black emigration schemes that had emerged to counter the work of the ACS in Liberia.[39] In the 1850s, after explicitly condemning Liberia colonization, Martin Delany and Robert Campbell developed efforts to plant a colony in Abokeuta, near today's Nigeria. African American emigrationists formed their own brand of colonization and manifest destiny by taking into account commerce, Christianity, and civilization in their black

---

[36] Gerard Ralston's father was a founding member of the Pennsylvania Colonization Society (PCS).

[37] *The African Repository*, Vol. 40 (1864): 368.

[38] Ibid., 369.

[39] *Niles Weekly Register*, July 3, 1824 as quoted in Miller, *The Search for a Black Nationality*, 8. Emigration projects developed rapidly as African Americans sought to escape the onslaught of the Fugitive Slave Act (1850), the Kansas-Nebraska Act (1854), and the Dred Scott Decision (1857).

nationalist pursuits.[40] In 1855, James Holly, an emigrationist, missionary, and bishop, negotiated with Faustin Soulouque, the self-proclaimed Emperor of Haiti, to promote African American emigration to the first black Republic.[41] Many African Americans who shunned Liberia advocated Canada, Central America, and Haiti as alternative sites of emigration.

In his response to the interested Afro-Barbadians, Ralston had probably helped to convince them. As he told the Barbadians, their migration to Liberia would "assist in putting a stop to the slave trade, establish a nationality, and labor for the civilization and Christianization of Africa."[42] For the cause of abolition alone, Ralston advised them not to choose Haiti, further highlighting that Liberia "had as fine, or better, climate, as regards atmosphere than the West Indies."[43] Ralston assured the Barbadians, "I write this in the interest of a Negro nationality which is the cherished wish of my heart to succor." Like many colonizationists, his reason rested on the improbability of forming a successful interracial democracy in the West. "The experience of 245 years proves that whites and blacks cannot live comfortably together. The whites dominate the blacks, and it is important they should live separately if both [are] to prosper."[44] Ralston had come to the conclusion that in no other country but Liberia can "colored people live comfortably and be self-governing, and become a mighty nation to diffuse the blessings of civilization and Christianity over the innumerable peoples of the immense African peninsula."[45] Ralston thus recommended that "agriculturists and employers of laborers, cultivators of coffee, sugar, cotton, and other staple products, with their families, should now be selected and aided to remove to Liberia" and called for the establishment of "a special fund of thirty thousand dollars" for the proper colonization of three hundred such persons.[46]

---

[40] See R. J. M. Blackett, "Anglo-American Opposition to Liberian Colonization, 1831–1833." *The Historian*, Vol. 41, No. 2 (1979): 276–294; "Martin Delaney and Robert Campbell: Black Americans in search of an African Colony, *The Journal of Negro History*, Vol. 62, No. 1 (1977): 1–25; "Return to the Motherland: Robert Campbell, a Jamaican in Early Colonial Lagos," *Phylon*, Vol. 40, No. 4 (1979): 375–386.

[41] Ousmane Power-Greene, *Against Wind and Tide: The African American Struggle against the Colonization Movement* (New York: New York University Press, 2014), 149.

[42] *The African Repository*, Vol. 40 (1864): 368.

[43] Ibid. Also, for discussions about emigration to Haiti, see "The Free People Colored Convention," *The Baltimore Sun*, August 13, 1852.

[44] Ibid.

[45] Ibid.

[46] Ibid.

In Ralston's mind, of all the possible sites of settlement, "Liberia held out the best hope."[47] He pointed to a Charles Williamson, who visited "Canada twice; in the West Indies three times, and, under the British government in Trinidad five years," Ralston saw Williamson as an unbiased sixty seven-year-old man who had little to gain from spreading misinformation.[48] During his visit, Williamson had examined the countries with the intention of ascertaining "which was the best for the colored people." Ralston got a sense of the core dilemmas of Caribbean post-emancipation from Williamson's experience. He surmised that "in the West Indies capital ruled the people – the government recognizes you, but the planters, who had been accustomed to drive on slaves, knew you not."[49] Williamson had also complained that "in the West Indies he had to take his hat around to get the dead out of the way of the turkey-buzzards – that showed their sympathy."[50]

As far as Ralston understood, Afro-Barbadians would also not better their condition if they emigrated to Canada. Ralston himself had lived there for seventeen months. He explained that "it costs money to get to Canada" as it did to get to other West Indian territories. Moreover, in Canada, "the leading men were principally Yankees."[51] Ralston argued that the Barbadians would have no political representation. According to him, "in Canada, you cannot be recognized in office – in the West Indies it is better, and some colored persons get into office. In the Canadas, he never heard of but one colored man being in office." As for staying in the United States, "they did not want the colored people anymore, they had got the use of them, and now in this state, the new constitution did not recognize them at all." He concluded that while "the Canadas are a fine country," but there could be no permanent home for blacks except in Africa. From his estimation, and this would resonate with the Barbadians, it was Liberia "where their children could enjoy all the blessings of liberty."[52]

Ralston also sought to win over the Barbadians by outlining the advances Liberia had made. He told them that the nation had previously formed "treaties with many of the nations of Europe and America and social and commercial relations with all the neighboring tribes, and

[47] Ibid.
[48] Ibid., 369.
[49] Ibid., 368.
[50] Ibid.
[51] Ibid.
[52] Ibid.

[Liberians] are enjoying a successful progressive career." Ralston outlined the ways in which Barclay's crew could contribute, noting that "we wish to accelerate and render more expansive by an increase of well-disposed, intelligent, and enterprising immigrants from Barbados." Ralston's descriptions suggested a confidence in the Barbadians' success: "good conduct and industry can turn the manifold advantages of a most fertile country and genial climate (for blacks, though unsuitable for whites) to the best account." He communicated all the possibilities that awaited free blacks in Liberia while also enticing the Barbadians with compliments on their intelligence and industriousness. What's even more interesting is how Ralston, a white colonizationist, saw Barbadians' fate as bound up with that of African Americans in a united pan-African brotherhood. Ralston praised the "enterprising black pioneers from the United States" who had settled in Liberia and tried to convince the Barbadians that the newly independent country was their only hope if they wanted to advance politically and economically. He reassured them of "the reception of and the comfortable residence of a large and constantly increasing number of immigrants of colored people from all parts of the Western Hemisphere." Ralston pointed out that advancing the diaspora was at the central concern: "the desire [is] to construct a vigorous nation from the Americo-African portion of the race, who will enjoy all the blessing of free and constitutional government with all the privileges which Protestantism, laws, customs, manners, language and other peculiarities of the Anglo-Saxons can alone bestow."[53]

AFRO-AMERICAN AND CARIBBEAN COMMUNICATION

Barbadian emigration straddled two distinct periods of large-scale African diasporic freedom achieved through different means. As the Afro-Barbadian middle class wrestled with the growing failures of emancipation in the 1860s, African Americans were engulfed by a civil war struggle to end slavery in the United States. Because African Americans and West Indians did not lead insular lives, Afro-Barbadians would have been able to weigh Ralston's glowing letter about Liberia against African Americans' deliberations over the scheme. The two groups had long communicated with each other through the movement and circulation of news by dock workers and sailors.[54] As a leading member of the BCL,

[53] Ibid.
[54] Scott, "The Common Wind," 4.

Joseph Attwell's admission to the Institute for Colored Youths in Philadelphia had placed him in a favorable position, enabling him not only to reach out to the ACS but also to develop relationships with African Americans. Thus, rather than developing in isolation, their investments in black nationalist and pan-African ideas transcended spatial boundaries and became an extension of each other.

The two diasporic groups engaged each other primarily through mediums that framed and constructed racial meaning. In the mid-nineteenth century, several black-owned papers, edited and led by black authors, forged a connection between Barbados and the United States. In Bridgetown, The *Barbadian, The Liberal,* and *The West Indian* emerged as semi-weekly publications that focused on lobbying for racial equality in Barbados.[55] As the first editor of the *New Times,* a weekly, Samuel Prescod devoted his "interests chiefly to the colored community." Recounting their visit to the Caribbean after slavery, the abolitionists James Thome and Thomas Kimball noted that the *New Times* "was the first periodical and the only one which advocated the rights of the colored people ... It boldly exposed oppression, whether emanating from the government house or originating in the colonial assembly."[56]

Barbadians looked to the United States, where sociopolitical issues in the early nineteenth century had shaped the formation and subsequent rise of an African American press that had become an important voice in the antebellum politics. African Americans debated migration and pan-Africanism through a prolific black press that also emerged during this era and enjoyed wide circulation in the Caribbean. Editorials in *Freedom's Journal,* the first weekly periodical to circulate widely, included refutations of slavery and biographies of prominent African Americans. Likewise, the *Colored American,* edited by Samuel Cornish, sought to "maintain [our] well-known sentiments on the subjects of abolition and colonization; emancipation without expatriation – the extirpation of prejudice – the enactment of equal laws, and a full and free investiture of [our] rights as men and citizens."[57] Frederick Douglass and Martin Delany, who edited the antislavery newspaper *The North Star,* leveraged its popularity into black leadership platforms. Other prominent nineteenth-

---

[55] Lowell J. Ragatz, *The Fall of the Planter Class in the British Caribbean, 1763–1833: A Study in Social and Economic History* (New York: Century, 1928), 391.

[56] Thomas and Kimball, "Emancipation in the West Indies," 74.

[57] Benjamin Fagan, "Americans as they Really Are: The 'Colored American' and the Illustration of National Identity," *American Periodicals,* Vol. 21, No. 2 (2011): 99.

century African American newspapers, including the *National Era*, *Frederick Douglass Paper, Douglass Monthly,* and *Christian Recorder* connected with groups of blacks across diasporic lines of differences.

Through newspaper articles, stories, and editorials, Barbadians created an atlas of their world, relationships to others, and an image of their possible destinations. As Barbadians searched for their place in the world, deciding where they wanted to go, newspapers functioned sometimes as mirrors and sometimes as maps. Through this form of communicative medium that Barclay, and other middle-class Barbadian potential migrants could read, they discursively created an image of Liberia and other possible emigration destinations. Newspaper communication allowed Barbadians to weigh their experiences of freedom against those elsewhere, thus creating an imaginary within which to consider the pros and cons of emigrating to Liberia. The cartography of freedom created by the types of literature generated by African Americans gave those Barbadians who desired a more expansive post-emancipation a broader landscape upon which to dream.

People in the United States increasingly became aware of the Barbadians' frustrations as newspapers circulated reports of the failures of Caribbean post-emancipation. On July 7, 1851, the editor of the *Baltimore Sun* republished a note from a West Indian native: "Can we not ... say [that the] Americans are successfully planting free Negroes on the coast of Africa, a greater event, probably in its consequences, than any that has occurred since Columbus set sail for the New World." The writer made it known that "the West Indians will emigrate to Liberia." In clarifying their interest in Liberia, the West Indian native described "the various burdens and vexations still imposed upon the Africans in the West Indies." Because of this "thousands of families are sighing for the vastly superior privileges of the young Republic of Western Africa."[58] In his concluding remarks, he promised, "They will crowd your steamers. They will take with them intelligence, wealth, and a perfect knowledge at once of the agriculture of the country. They will clothe the hillside and the vale with fields upon fields of sugar cane, a plant indigenous to Africa, and where it grows most luxuriantly."[59]

When Barclay and other members of FUBES began to stake their post-emancipation hopes on Liberia, newspapers circulated their interests to the United States. On June 15, 1857, the *Springfield Republican* reported:

[58] *The Baltimore Sun*, July 7, 1851.
[59] Ibid.

"A desire is expressed on the part of some of the more intelligent emancipated Negroes on the island of Barbados to emigrate to Africa. They have addressed a letter to President Roberts of Liberia on the subject, and ask that the veoools of the colonization society may touch at Barbados for emigrant passengers."[60] The *Republican's* story drew on reports from an itinerant minister, Reverend Hooker, who had traveled to Barbados in the period immediately following the apprenticeship program. Hooker reported that Barbadians were well on their way to progress but that "the lands [are] mostly in the hands of whites, and [are] held at prices beyond the reach of colored men who are generally poor." Education, Hooker noted, only compounded the Barbadians' plight. Given their general dissatisfaction, Hooker noted, some Barbadians wanted to establish a settlement in Africa, where they would be able to "sell and reap the fruit of their own industry and enterprise."[61]

As a medium of communication, newspapers became a conduit and forum for considering the issues of colonization, assimilation, and emigration and for bending and framing the issues of pan-Africanism and black nationalism. Whether emigration was a practical solution for ending slavery and the outlooks of various emigration destinations, these formed the points of contention between the different presses and distinguished the views of various editors. While many African Americans supported Liberian colonization, many prominent blacks loudly opposed it by branding the movement as the hypocritical plan of slaveholders and their dupes. These and other criticisms burdened Liberia and the legacy of the ACS with controversies. West Indian newspapers reprinted many articles from African American newspapers. Barbadian newspapers such as The *Liberal* regularly printed articles about Haiti and Sierra Leone, holding these societies up as symbols of black autonomy and racial equality. Toasts to "infant Haiti were a regular feature in the antislavery dinners at the St. Mary's School" in Barbados.[62] The *Liberal* often reprinted articles from African American newspapers. In one letter to William Coppinger, secretary of the ACS, the secretary of the BCL reported that "the editor of The *West Indian* newspaper has sent us two *African Repositories* from your society, and we are in daily communication with him."[63]

---

[60] *Springfield Republican*, June 15, 1857.
[61] Ibid.
[62] Newton, *The Children of Africa*, 204.
[63] ACS Reel 96, Domestic Letters, Letter No. 32. Folder 63367. Svend Holsoe Collection, accessed at the Barbados Museum and Historical Society, Barbados.

Long before the crisis leading to the Civil War, African Americans skewered the ACS's Liberian focus. On March 24, 1848, nearly one year after Liberia achieved independence, Frederick Douglass, through his newspaper the *North Star*, reminded his readers to continue being mindful of the motives of colonizationists.

"Be careful," warned Douglass,

of the alluring charms of nationality, independence, wealth, dignity and station, to induce the free colored man to emigrate to Liberia; they "threaten as well as coax," – they appeal to our "fears as well as our hopes," – they point to our degradation here, as well as our elevation in Liberia, and teach us to believe, that our condition here must become not better but worse, the longer we remain.[64]

Douglass further explained: "They tell us, that, now we may emigrate with our own free will; but that the time must come, when we shall have no option in the matter – that we shall be compelled under the arm of stern necessity, to quit this and seek another country." Referencing the publication of the thirty-first annual report of the ACS, Douglass mockingly called the ACS the "Negro-hating Society." He depicted colonizationists as "long-faced, smooth-tongued, mischievous hypocrites" who were still in the business of trying to get free Negroes out of this country to their home in Africa.[65] Douglass explained that his articles were meant to inform the colored people about those "who were operating against their hearths, homes, and happiness."[66] His focus on the ACS was not so much for the "benefit of our white as our colored readers; though it may be profitable to both." [67] African American authors like Douglass were addressing not only blacks in the continental United States but also those in other areas who read their papers.

Douglass was not alone in his condemnation of Liberia. Delany, who later migrated to Liberia, had initially criticized the ACS's Liberia project as "a burlesque on government" and as a "charnel house where black migrants went to die."[68] Other blacks also questioned colonization's "separate but equal" assurance. On August 21, 1859, a Philadelphian, J. G. Steward, wrote a letter to the editor of the *Christian Recorder* to warn blacks against the enticements of colonizationists and their true

---

[64] *The North Star*, March 24, 1848.
[65] Ibid.
[66] Ibid.
[67] Ibid.
[68] Richard Blackett, "Martin R. Delany and Robert Campbell: Black Americans in Search of an African," *The Journal of Negro History*, Vol. 62, No. 1 (Jan. 1977): 4.

motives. Steward wrote: "These dear colonizationists clothed in the hypo-critical garb of a mawkish philanthropy, are here to remove him to his own dear native land – the golden land of Liberia."[69] He questioned the reasons driving their interests: "First the ostensible purpose was to sup-press the slave trade, but the real purpose was, no doubt, to quiet agitation on the subject of slavery, and to allow the breeding process to go on." Steward ridiculed the idea that Liberia was "the bright prospect of a great country after the model of the United States. The ostensible object now," he observed, "is to induce emigration for the purpose of Christianizing Africa." For Steward, the real purpose was "to maintain the supremacy of the white race and justify themselves in history for their past treatment of the Negro."[70]

William Lloyd Garrison, one of the leading abolitionists of the time, also criticized colonizationists, depicting them as the enemy rather than as a friend of blacks. Garrison's position is particularly interesting for what it reveals about the changing opinions on the scheme. Up until the publica-tion of his book *Thoughts on African Colonization* (1832), Garrison had been part of a group of whites who had initially viewed removing free blacks from the United States to colonies in Africa as the best way to effect abolition. However, James Forten, a prominent African American Philadelphian, helped change Garrison's resolve by explaining that many African Americans fundamentally opposed colonization. Garrison's opposition to and subsequent lambasting of colonization hinged on the belief that it denied blacks the right to a better life in the United States, their native land, and took them away from their responsi-bilities to free those still in bondage. The publication of Garrison's work in his newspaper, the *Liberator,* and in *Thoughts on African Colonization,* which exposed those interested in colonization to the opinions of the black masses in the United States, created a significant turning point in the abolitionist and colonization movement, causing wealthy supporters to stop funding the scheme.[71]

Though many of the issues leading up to the Civil War that shaped the opinions on Liberia were not of immediate concern for West Indians, they empathized with their African American counterparts through letters that

[69] *The Christian Recorder,* August 21, 1859.
[70] Ibid.
[71] William Lloyd Garrison, *Thoughts on African Colonization* (New York: Arno Press, 1968); William Lloyd Garrison and Truman Nelson, *Documents of Upheaval; Selections from William Lloyd Garrison's the Liberator, 1831–1865* (New York: Hill and Wang, 1966).

would be reprinted in numerous publications. In 1840, the *Colored American* printed a letter from the Anti-Slavery Society of Brown's Town, Jamaica, declaring that "the day is not far distance when America will be brought to repentance and will be induced to restore to the Negro his long with-held birthright."[72] On April 10, 1851, the *Pennsylvania Freeman* reported on a meeting in Bridgetown, Barbados, likely attended by the Liberia-minded Barclay and Harris, in which "West Indians expressed their solidarity with African Americans against the 1850 Fugitive Slave Law and announced their intention to collect funds to aid fugitives in their escape."[73] As African Americans in their struggle to end slavery were being scared by events in places like Kansas, West Indians lacked those critical experiences that had helped to define the subjectivities of African American slavery and their particular meanings of race. Yet, the reprinting of articles focused on these issues from other parts of the black world in African American newspapers revealed their interest in the experiences of other blacks.

Some African American writers highlighted the ways in which they viewed their fates as bound up with one another by openly declaring their affections for West Indians. In outlining his choice to start a black newspaper in Canada, Samuel Ward defined it as a promoter for the advancement of freedmen, so as to raise them "to the proud position of the blacks in other parts of our glorious empire."[74] In an article in the *Colored American,* reprinted in the *African Repository,* one author noted, "If we could suppose that the American citizen cared nothing for the wrongs and sufferings of the Negroes in the West Indies, there is another point of view, in which it cannot be denied that the subject has an intense interest in this country." The author was particularly concerned about the effect of the abolition of slavery across the Caribbean on African Americans in the southern slave states.[75]

Encounters with West Indians also provided fuel for the American abolitionist movement. For those who doubted that blacks could handle the experiences of freedom, African Americans turned directly to the West

---

[72] *Colored American*, June 20, 1840.

[73] *Pennsylvania Freeman*, April 10, 1851. For further explorations of West Indian celebrations see Jeffrey Kerr-Ritchie, *Rites of August First: Emancipation Day in the Black Atlantic World* (Baton Rouge: Louisiana State University Press, 2007); Edward Bartlett Rugemer, *The Problem of Emancipation: The Caribbean Roots of the American Civil War* (Baton Rouge: Louisiana State University Press, 2008).

[74] *Frederick Douglass Paper*, March 18, 1853. The newspaper in question is *The Provincial Freeman*, which Ward founded in early 1853.

[75] *The African Repository and Colonial Journal*, Vol. 7 (1831): 247.

Indies to point to a peaceful transition and provide a context for the experiences of black freedom. It was for these reasons that in 1836 the executive committee of the American Anti-Slavery Society had sent James Thome and Thomas Kimball on a "Six Months Tour in Antigua, Barbadoes, and Jamaica to make proper investigations into the great experiment of freedom." When Kimball and Thome reported the absence of the kinds of violent disruptions the proslavery advocates had expected to follow abolition in the West Indies, it challenged a belief about race that had been used to keep African Americans in slavery. Still deeply entrenched in slavery, North America watched in vain for rebellion and riots. One writer, in a letter to the editor of the *Colored American* titled "Satan Out-generaled," remarked at the West Indian post-emancipation transition and examples of peaceful demands for wages: "Throats cut? No. Towns in conflagration? No. Plantations plundered? No. What then? On several plantations, the laborers would not work till they were satisfied that they should receive fair wages! Prodigious! What will sensible men at the South infer from such news?"[76]

African Americans openly joined in celebrations of West Indian freedom as a way of resisting American slavery. Frederick Douglass reported that "people of colour in New York turned out in full force to celebrate another return of the day that brought the Emancipation Act into full force in the West India."[77] From Douglass's perspective, this gave "impetus to the anti-slavery cause of which it stands greatly in need."[78] A writer to the *African Repository* noted that "the colored population of New York has always felt a deep and cordial connection with the condition of the West Indies. They aim at being put to in public law in the same condition in which their brethren in those islands are found."[79] By leveraging good characterizations of black freedom in the West Indies, African Americans furthered their cause.

African Americans also engaged West Indians in more direct ways. Numerous black Loyalists had emigrated to the West Indies after the Revolutionary War.[80] In the 1830s, African Americans became even

---

[76] *The Colored American*, September 22, 1838. Also see Thomas Holt, *The Problem of Freedom: Race, Labor and Politics in Jamaica and Britain 1832–1938* (Baltimore: John Hopkins University Press, 1992), 55.
[77] Ibid.
[78] Ibid.
[79] Ibid.
[80] See Danyelle Valentine, "Embarking on Revolutionary Migrations: The Black Loyalists' Southern Campaign for Freedom during the Revolutionary Era, 1775–1862," PhD thesis in progress (Nashville: Vanderbilt University, in progress).

more interested in migration to the West Indies after emancipation in 1834. William Wells Brown, a former slave, author, and abolitionist, in a letter from England to Douglass on the fugitive slave issue argued, "Owing to the great influx of fugitives into this country within the past and present year, and the comparative destitution that many are in ... many of these people might be induced by an offer of fair compensation, to go to the West Indies and become tillers of the soil, instead of wandering about the streets of London, looking in vain for work."[81] Another writer, however, cautioned African Americans that they should be aware that the state of things in the West Indies was not as they imagined. He noted that if African Americans realized that a "Christianized human nature was far from being gained in the West Indies," they would come to a conclusion that "whatever can in the present circumstances of the world, elevate their race, may be looked for in Africa more readily than in other places."[82] For African Americans, Caribbean emancipation served as an example of negative freedom, whereby blacks were only free of restraints. Interest in proselytizing in Africa eventually further directed African Americans' attention away from West Indian emigration.

In the same way that African American abolitionists, antislavery activists, and free-labor advocates took their cues about emancipation from "the great experiment of freedom," West Indians took cues about Liberian migration from African Americans and their tales of nation building, progress, and civilizing the continent. African American emigration to Liberia served as an example of positive freedom. Information around African American emigration to Liberia thus tempered West Indians' interest in Africa and sense of duty to their race, and informed their relationship to the ACS. Based on these developments, Barbadians sought to assist the cause of African American freedom in more direct ways. On February 24, 1834, a Barbadian newspaper reported that "when a ship of African American emigrants bound for Liberia stopped to provision in the Bridgetown port, the coloured portion of our community donated thirty dollars in provisions to the Liberian colonists."[83]

---

[81] *Frederick Douglass Paper*, September 25, 1851.
[82] Ibid.
[83] *The Barbadian*, February 24, 1834 reprinted in Newton, *The Children of Africa*, 201.

THE 1860S TIPPING POINT

The 1860s proved significant in drawing West Indians, African Americans, and Liberian officials closer together. Much had changed since West Indian emancipation in 1834 and the emergence of the BCL in the 1840s. The Pennsylvania Colonization Society (PCS) had promised the BCL assistance. Their corresponding secretary, Reverend Thomas J. Malcolm, had become determined to fulfill the desires of those he referred to as "some of the most respectable inhabitants of all classes in this Island" who "impel us forward."[84] The reverberations of the events of the American Civil War in the 1860s, however, transformed some of the very terms under which African Americans and West Indians considered freedom in Liberia as well as the ACS's receptiveness to helping non-American groups of black migrants. The long shadow cast by events in the United States largely helped to determine the possibilities of Barbadians' Liberian aspirations as the ACS promised to aid them.

The plans for development and nation building that accompanied Liberian independence reshaped the objectives of the emigration committee of the ACS. They vowed "to increase the number of emigrants for the reason that they are needed for the development of the physical resources of the country and for promoting the interests of Liberia generally."[85] By the 1860s, the growing need for skilled and educated blacks to assist in this national endeavor compelled Liberian officials to appeal to prospective emigrants to "come over and help us."[86] These requests included signs of fear of the indigenous African population, which far outnumbered the African American migrants. The very recognition of Liberia's modernity depended on increasing the number of its civilized and industrious migrants to offset its demographic imbalance. President James Payne, in his annual message to the Liberian Legislature, noted: "I consider it important to recommend to you for consideration the subject of immigration to this government. I am of the opinion that the circumstances of a country in which the proportion of the civilized populace bears so small a ratio to the uncivilized, make necessary that the government should not omit to use any means within its power to increase its enlightened population."[87]

---

[84] Anthony Barclay to His Excellency James Walker Esq. C.B 14th of December 1864 in the Svend Holsoe Collection, University of Indiana at Bloomington.

[85] "Report of the Committee on Emigration." *The African Repository*, Vol. 41 (1865): 72.

[86] Ibid.

[87] James Spriggs Payne Annual Message to the Legislature December 11, 1865 in Elwood D. Dunn, ed, *The Annual Messages of the Presidents of Liberia 1848–2010: State of the*

The end of the Civil War sparked new debate about the ACS's original colonization plans and Liberia's needs. Toward the end of the American Civil War, the Liberian President, J. J. Roberts, wrote a letter to a friend in the United States.[88] Roberts inquired: "What is to become of the large number of colored people who are now employed in the Federal Service when the war shall have ended? Is it contemplated to locate these people somewhere?"[89] Like most who had considered the answers to these kinds of questions, Roberts surmised, "I presume this is going to be a subject of no little importance to your government by and by."[90] Roberts's supposition proved accurate. Even before issuing the Emancipation Proclamation, Abraham Lincoln had reflected on Roberts's concerns. On August 14, 1862, Lincoln invited "a group of colored men" to the White House to inform them that "a sum of money had been appropriated by Congress and placed at his discretion for the purpose of aiding their colonization in some country of their people."[91] Pointing out, "You and we are different races ... [and] we suffer from each other," Lincoln urged them to "go where you are treated the best."[92]

Around the same period, as the ACS commemorated its forty-sixth anniversary, the celebration occurred amid complaints that the Civil War had "not only diminished our receipts, but it has deprived us of our usual supply of emigrants. Many who would have sought to improve their fortunes in Liberia have been diverted to the army."[93] With this growing reality, the ACS focused the agenda of its anniversary meeting on reasons why African American emigration to Liberia must be increased, and the ways to do so. John Latrobe, the president of the ACS, in an address to the members, outlined the critical factors that would boost African American emigration. "What are the causes that lead to emigration," he asked his audience during a presentation.[94] He noted that "two powerful causes

---

Nation Addresses to the National Legislature: from Joseph Jenkins Roberts to Ellen Johnson Sirleaf (Berlin: De Gruyter, 2011), 217.

[88] For early African American emigrants to Liberia see Marie Tyler-McGraw, *An African Republic: Black & White Virginians in the Making of Liberia* (Chapel Hill: University of North Carolina Press, 2007).

[89] *The African Repository*, Vol. 41 (1865): 249–250.

[90] Ibid.

[91] "Colonization of the Negroes Views of the President," *National Intelligencer*, Washington. Vol. LXIII, No. 9 (Saturday August 16, 1862): 364. Reprinted in *The Christian Recorder*, August 23, 1862.

[92] Ibid.

[93] *The African Repository*, Vol. 47 (1871): 56.

[94] Ibid.

always lead to emigration: the repulsions of the old home and the attractions of the new." He added that "moral causes operate as surely as physical causes." The religious impulse and missionary motives that brought the pilgrims to Plymouth Rock, Massachusetts, stood as a shining example. Latrobe concluded that, likewise, the "missionary motive in the Christian Negroes will carry them by thousands to their own nationality ... as sure as the relation of cause and effect."[95]

Despite the seeming universalism of Latrobe's idea, push-and-pull forces could not be divorced from the specificities of the conditions within which they operated. The direction that particular groups of migrants undertook critically depended on the constellation of sociopolitical and institutional factors that shaped their prevailing conditions. The sway of push-and-pull forces was contingent upon prospective migrants' perceptions of what they would acquire through migration as opposed to remaining in their homeland. For their part, African Americans, in weighing the possibilities, ultimately rejected Lincoln's offer. Rather than turning to either Lincoln's colonization proposal or the ACS's long-established Liberian scheme, African Americans began to look forward to the prospects of freedom in a post-Civil War United States. In the midst of African Americans' declining colonization interest, the ACS observed, "[emigrants] who could go have high anticipations that an important change will be wrought by it in their favor, and that their political and social condition will be so improved as to relieve them from the necessity of seeking a home elsewhere."[96] At the same time, Liberia became a new frontier for Barbadians. Decisions about pursuing a transatlantic path to freedom oscillated between staying in familiar surroundings or venturing into the unknown. The suppression of their rights in Barbados and the promise of a greater freedom inclusive of nationhood, citizenship, and political access was critical enough for them to consider the risk of crossing the Atlantic as favorable.

What merely appeared as isolated events within the Atlantic were indeed linked by the American Civil War. The effect of the war on emigration proved even more troubling to a Liberian government fraught with issues since independence in 1847. William C. Burke, an African American migrant in Liberia, in a letter to an acquaintance, complained that the effects of the war "must be the severest affliction that have visited the people of the United States and must be a sorce [*sic*] of great

<hr>

[95] Ibid.
[96] *The African Repository*, Vol. 41 (1864): 36.

inconvenience and suffering and although we are separated from the seane [*sic*] by the Atlantic yet we feel sadly the effects of it in this country."[97] The war had affected shipping across the Atlantic world. "The *Steavens* not coming out, as usual," Burke complained, "was a great disappointment and loss to this country."[98] Having stemmed the flow of emigrant ships, the war had created a transatlantic dilemma for Liberian emigrants and American politicians alike. By 1862, when the United States joined the throng of countries that had officially recognized Liberia's sovereignty, growing problems would irrevocably change the course of the ACS's emigration policies.

In a letter to Governor Walker, Barclay informed him that several other factors spurred Barbadian interest. They had first received an invitation from the government and people of Liberia in 1862, then the proclamation of the president in 1863, and, finally, the reply of Edward Blyden, the secretary of state, who had received an address from some people in the parish of Christ Church. Barclay noted that he had been convinced by "the excellent record the result of personal observation, received from truth telling visitors and others who have settled there, and the letters and published statements of distinguished individuals high in office."[99] Persistent concerns about demography in Liberia, exacerbated by the impact of the American Civil War, led to the usurpation of the ACS's main aim only to colonize African Americans living in the United States. Though the ACS had been formed exclusively to aid African Americans, the latter's declining interest in emigration and Liberia's political goals had created an opening for the interested Barbadian migrants. It opened up the ACS to assisting other black migrants. This was a significant change, but few colonizationists expected it to have a practical effect. In 1862, Edward Blyden, Liberia's secretary of state, recommended that then President Daniel Warner recruit migrants from the West Indies. As a migrant from the Virgin Islands, Blyden personified the identity that the Barbadians would later embrace. After taking on the position of emigration Commissioner, Blyden published a notice to circulate "to the Descendants of Africa throughout the West Indian Islands."[100]

---

[97] Bell I. Wiley, ed., *Slaves No More: Letters from Liberia 1833–1869* (Lexington: University Press of Kentucky: 1980), 211.

[98] Ibid.

[99] American Colonization Society Records, Reel 196, Domestic Letters, Letter no.163. Folio 63559. Svend Holsoe Collection. Accessed at the Barbados Museum and Historical Society, Barbados.

[100] Ibid.

On July 5, 1864, Edward Blyden, then secretary of state of Liberia, wrote a letter to the ACS expressing his satisfaction at "the willingness of the American Colonization Society to co-operate in this work to encourage new immigrants." He noted, however, "[w]e do not propose that your Society should 'colonize' West Indians in Liberia for we know that your operations are limited by your constitution to the United States; but we only wish to effect a kind of charter of the [ship] 'Stevens' to carry out a project of this Government for which the Society will be in no way responsible."[101] In requesting that the ACS's roving emigrant ship – the Stevens – call at Barbados at least twice per year, Blyden not only recognized that the ACS was politically beholden to their African American constituents but understood the ethnic differences within blackness. Nonetheless, the opening up of the ACS's Liberia emigration scheme to West Indians essentially made this period the turning point and the pivotal moment in the Barbadians' quest to emigrate to Liberia. Sociopolitical, economic, and ideological push-and-pull factors combined to breathe new life into Latrobe's idea of the repulsion–attraction dynamic. The synergy of the ACS's need for emigrants to develop Liberia with Barbadians' desires to emigrate was making the emigration of the 346 Barbadians a reality.

Blyden returned to his native St. Thomas to launch an appeal for Liberian emigration throughout the West Indies. Blyden's circular promoting emigration became especially popular in Barbados, where it was reprinted numerous times. On March 1, 1864, following the warm reception of Blyden's circular in Barbados, the Liberian president, Daniel Warner, reported receiving hundreds of letters inquiring about Liberia. The Liberian state department subsequently wrote to inform the BCL that their letters had caused "the president considerable gratification. Entertaining ardent desire that the exiled sons of Africa from all parts of the world should return and unite their efforts in building upon this benighted shore a home for themselves and their posterity, it occasions him real pleasure to notice the enthusiasm."[102] Whatever the enormities of their struggles, one of the few things migrants had in their favor was the claim to imperial identity. In considering the particular interest of the Barbadians, the Liberian government lingered on the point that "these emigrants have enjoyed personal liberty for thirty years in one of the most beautiful West India Islands, under the colonial government of Great

---

[101] Letter from Edward Blyden to the American Colonization Society, July 5, 1864, in the Svend Holsoe Collection, Barbados Historical and Museum Society.
[102] Ibid.

Britain."[103] The Barbadians had been "represented on respectable authority as industrious, moral and intelligent." Altogether, their desires for self-
improvement, their work ethic, and their discipline conveyed core values
that suggested to Warner that they "would be justly considered as
a desirable accession to that country."[104]

The length of time that blacks had experienced in freedom held currency for Liberian officials, who regularly referenced it. Using it to point to
the Barbadians' civilization, it projected them as a rare type of black
people. The ACS used the language of abolitionism and Afro-West
Indians' progress after emancipation to raise their status and thereby
justify the suitableness for black colonization of Africa. The Barbadians
were seen as coming of age in a British civilized post-emancipation era that
endowed them with unique understandings of living in a free society.
Given their new obligations as social subjects, the republic's officials
inferred that the Barbadians "longed for a higher theatre of action, and
had made up their minds that Liberia, the black man's Republic on the
black man's native continent, above all other places, could satisfy their
desire."[105] This to them was also indicative of "the final judgment of the
multitudes of the African race recently emancipated." They concluded
that "when a clearer view of the claims of humanity and Christianity
prevail, thousands of them will call upon us to aid them to plant colonies
and spread Christian civilization and freedom along the whole African
coast." The officials conceded that Liberia held different prospects
according to the class of the emigrant: "If of the better class they can
rise in Liberia at once to social equality and usefulness. They can enjoy the
dignity of true self-respect beyond anything they can attain in our midst."
They, however, decided, "If of the lower sort, they will have open doors
and more inducements to successful activity than they can have here.
Whatever their condition in any part of the United States, they will have
good reason to be thankful for encouragement and aid in securing an
asylum in the Liberian Republic."[106] Liberian officials, like Latrobe, thus
opined: "Repulsions here and attractions there will lead the colored
population to seek a nationality of their own, with actual homes, real
title to the soil and active dominion of the country where they reside."[107]

---

[103] Ibid.
[104] Ibid.
[105] Ibid.
[106] Ibid.
[107] *The African Repository,* Vol. 42 (1863): 41.

When President Warner issued his proclamation to "the descendants of Africa throughout the West Indies who may be desirous to return to their fatherland and assist in the building up of an African nationality," he established a clear link between the goals and objectives of Liberia and those of the Barbadians.[108] Warner told the Barbadians that "the government and people of this Republic are anxious to welcome them to these shores."[109] The Liberian Legislature had recently enacted a law that revised the initial land grants for migrants. It provided that "each family emigrating from those islands to that Republic shall receive, instead of ten acres of land, as heretofore, twenty-five acres, and each single or unmarried individual ten acres instead of five."[110] Liberian officials proceeded to entice the Barbadians further. "Brethren of the Antilles," they addressed the Barbadians, "we are one in origin and destiny. We have the same history of centuries of suffering, of tribulation and woe."[111] Using the language of shared fate, they encouraged the exiles to come back to the fatherland. "The time seems to have come in the Providence of God," Warner noted, "when this oppressed people, wherever they may be found in their exile, should seek together and co-operate for the establishing in the land of their fathers a home and a nationality."[112]

Warner keenly pointed out why Liberia was the best choice among all the emerging black republics. For one, its independence was acknowledged by all the leading nations of the world, and this made it "the most suitable starting point from which the returning exiles may begin to take possession of and [civilize] this long-neglected land and thus aid in restoring to this ancient cradle of [civilization] her pristine glory."[113] In areas where post-emancipation had failed the Barbadians, the Liberian government pandered to their desires by offering them direct incentives. Though "persons of all classes and pursuits are invited," the Liberian government repeatedly noted that families and individuals would receive twenty-five- and ten-acre grants of fresh, fertile land, respectively.[114] These particular provisions enticed the Barbadians, providing a direct counter to the issue of expensive and unavailable land they had dealt with in Barbados.

---

[108] Quoted in Karch Brathwaite, "London Bourne of Barbados," 31.
[109] Ibid.
[110] Burleigh Holder, "A History of Crozierville," A Speech Given at the Crozierville Centenary, 1965, reprinted in the *Liberian Studies Journal III: 1* (1970–1971): 23–24.
[111] Ibid.
[112] Ibid.
[113] Ibid
[114] Ibid.

As a growing country, Liberia especially demanded unlimited numbers of "persons skilled in all the professions and in every branch of industry."[115] The demand for skilled persons also directly addressed the Barbadians' desire to improve themselves "by diligent labor." The timely coincidence of these transatlantic issues brought together the once disconnected desires of the Barbadians, Liberia, and the ACS.

Pushed by the crises of Caribbean post-emancipation, the desire to civilize Africa, and an embrace of pan-African and black nationalist ideologies, Barclay followed incentive rather than instinct. On July 9, 1864, Barclay reached out to William Coppinger, the corresponding and recording secretary of the ACS in Philadelphia.[116] He acknowledged that he was writing "on behalf of the company of tradesmen and others of African descent in this island ... respectable but poor."[117] The letter informed Coppinger that they had taken steps "to accept the very liberal offer of which the government of the Republic of Liberia so reasonably set forth, and would request of you such facilities as may enable us to obtain an easy passage to that great and growing republic."[118] Newspapers indeed had proven critical in forging their connections to the ACS. As Barclay noted, "The committee notice with pleasure in a recent local paper here, a communication from Mr. Geo. L. Armstrong, a colonizationist, in which it is stated that the colonization society is about to equip and send a vessel to Barbados for the purpose of conveying respectable colored persons to the shores of Liberia."[119] In the political and social lexicon of Liberian nation building, respectability and diasporic responsibility had become a part of the expected ethics and morals of immigrants.

Ten days later, Anthony Barclay wrote to Armstrong again that he had heard the ACS would be sending a ship to Barbados "for the purpose of conveying any, and all well-behaved coloured people who are desirous of emigrating to the shore of Liberia."[120] Barclay clearly shared and embraced the ACS's sentiments about diasporic ethics. Rather than clarifying what the

---

[115] Ibid.
[116] Domestic Letters, letter no.32, folder 63367. American Colonization Society, Washington. DC, reel 96. Svend Holsoe Collection. Accessed at the Barbados Museum and Historical Society.
[117] Holder, "A History of Crozierville," 25.
[118] Ibid.
[119] Ibid.
[120] ACS, Reel 96, Domestic Letters, Letter no. 50, folder 63389. Svend Holsoe Collection. Accessed at the Barbados Museum and Historical Society.

ACS meant by "well-behaved," Barclay requested information such as the name of the vessel, the merchant to whom it belonged, what time it was expected to arrive in Barbados, and the number of persons it would be able to accommodate. He pointed out that he was "personally interested in this movement, my greatest desire being to leave Barbados with my whole family being very large and settle in Liberia."[121] Upon hearing the news of a possible ACS vessel arriving in Barbados, other migrants began securing affidavits of their character from neighbors. Jacob Padmore secured two, one of them from an H. Thomas of Lodge Hill in the parish of St. Michael, who affirmed, "I have known Jacob Padmore for several years. He is the owner of a piece of lands in my neighbourhood and a good carpenter, and I believe a steady and industrious man. He tells me he is going to Liberia. I wish him all prosperity and success in his new home." The other came from Thomas Ellis of Canefield in the parish of St. Thomas, who noted, "I have known the bearer Mr. Jacob Padmore for several years. I believe him to be a very good man as I've never heard anything ill of him. He is a carpenter by trade." John Hoad, who knew John Frances Marshall for ten years and once employed him, certified, "I believe he has been struggling to get an honest living in this Island but has failed to do so. He has expressed himself wishful to go to Liberia where I believe that he will do well .... I believe him to be sober, steady, and honest."[122]

Barclay's FUBES members were not the only Barbadians who desired to quit Barbados for Liberia.[123] Other emigrants in Barbados had expressed interest in Liberia but had changed their minds, opting to go elsewhere. Barclay, at a meeting of the Fatherland Union Society, reported that "some of the people from Christ Church, being impatient, have gone to Jamaica, but the great majority of our people who are disposed to move, are in favor of settling in Africa, their fatherland."[124] Barclay and his colleagues, in communicating with Coppinger, keenly distinguished the others from their own Fatherland Union.[125] In one letter, Barclay noted, "The Barbados Company for Liberia is not identical with the people of Christ Church who have corresponded with the Secretary of State of the Republic of Liberia and are in possession of his reply."[126] He noted,

[121] Ibid.
[122] Reel 97 in Svend Holsoe Collection. University of Indiana, Bloomington. Liberia Collections.
[123] *The Times*, Friday July 7, 1865.
[124] Ibid.
[125] Ibid.
[126] Ibid.

"Those persons have changed their minds and have turned their attention to another land, viz Jamaica." He identified his group as consisting "chiefly of coloured men of the city of Bridgetown, chiefly artisans who nevertheless have the ambition of advancing themselves both in the social and political scale." It was for these reasons that Barclay noted that they "do therefore gladly hail the liberal invitation offered them by the government of the Republic of Liberia – to return to their fatherland and assist in building up a nationality for their own good, as also for the elevation of degraded Africa."[127]

The Barbadians had reason to believe that the ACS would prioritize their emigration. News circulated that the ACS would be dispatching the ship *Mary C. Stevens* to Barbados. Emotions ran high as the Barbadians made every sacrifice to be ready to embark.[128] On November 9, 1864, Barclay, perhaps out of the frustrations of preparing for their migration only to be disappointed, sent a long letter to the ACS in which he declared himself to be: "A humble individual surrounded by a few friends who desires to settle down quickly on the western coast of Africa, in the Republic of Liberia, on a session of peace, industry, and civilization to our favor." Many persons from the Barbados Company for Liberia, who were mostly from the parish of Christ Church, were disappointed as they were led to believe that the vessel would arrive on December 11 to take them to Liberia, free of all charge for three hundred persons to settle there. Barclay repeatedly distanced himself from the BCL, pointing out, "I am not a member of that company nor am I aware of their general mode of action therefore under what assurance this opinion [was] obtained I know not." Barclay worried that the miscommunication would affect his group by hindering their emigration to Liberia. Barclay blamed the misinformation on unqualified people who were "less interested in West India[n's] interest than those whom their instructions and directions and whose advice they readily took to go to Jamaica, after having to leave [emigrating to] Liberia as a home." Though those who had gone to Jamaica explained it as a necessity, Barclay condemned their choice as lacking discipline. He hoped the ACS understood the distinctions of his group. "But be that as it may, they are not at all to be regarded as the leaders of a movement of exact great importance, they were only an isolated few in a Country District whose governments were not known to the Townsfolk until it

[127] Ibid.
[128] J. T. Worrell to George L. Armstrong, November 1st, 1864, in the Svend Holsoe Collection, Barbados Museum and Historical Society.

was too late to avert the evil, and as much as their failure ought not in Justice to be visited in another and mine steady people who long have labored for, and desired to emigrate to Africa and nowhere else.[129]

Both the PUBES and the BCL had been corresponding with the ACS in an attempt to obtain space within a packet ship. They had received information from one or two favorable people from the society and had begun to make every preparation necessary for transit. They had received a response in which the ACS expressed "discouragement in the hope of witnessing an emigration from hence to Liberia, at least this fall." Much of the problem between the different groups of interested Barbadians and the ACS had to do with determining the exact number of migrants who could be funded. On October 10, 1864, the emigration committee of the Pennsylvania Colonization Society reported that it had recently received letters from Barbados applying for passages to Liberia for about "two hundred and fifty persons, and credible statements that one thousand persons are desirous of emigrating to Liberia." The committee felt the call important enough to recommend the collection of donations for "the specific purposes of aiding this enterprise so full of promise, and at this time furnishing the only known opening for furthering emigration to Liberia."[130] The ACS was now hesitant as fear lingered that the failure of the Christ Church emigration group, "from their broken faith with the authorities of the Liberian Republic," would again prove disruptive. Other Barbadians interested in Liberian migration worried that their example would be followed: "Having no guarantee that in the event of your vessel arriving here, whether certain circumstances peculiar to this country might not influence a different insult from the one anticipation and also the amount of means necessary to colonize 300 souls, say 30,000 dollars." The ACS noted that their committee would not be likely to assume the weight of financing all of the interested emigrants and "that the success of the movement to be [effective] depended widely on themselves."[131]

At an earlier meeting with the board of directors, ACS members had murmured about the impending cost of the Barbadian voyage. They determined that "the whole trip [would] cost ... a hefty portion of

---

[129] Anthony Barclay to William Coppinger, American Colonization Society, November 9, 1864, in the Svend Holsoe Collection, Indiana University, Bloomington.

[130] Minutes of the Pennsylvania Colonization Society, October 10, 1864. Pennsylvania Abolition Society Papers, 1751–1992. Accessed at the Historical Society of Pennsylvania.

[131] Ibid.

a declining treasury."[132] The funds the ACS managed to put together necessarily meant quality over quantity and only selecting from the best of the prospective emigrants. With this, the ACS tirelessly sought information about Barbadians from "merchants engaged in trade in Barbados as well as those who had visited the island." Bearing the larger goals for Liberia in mind, it was probably only natural that they would have inquired about the Barbadians' religious orientation, industriousness, manners, civility, and intelligence. On one occasion, the ACS mused:

The Bearer J.W. Blackman belongs to the Fatherhood Society of persons going to go to Liberia. He has been for about seven years employed in their office as Pressman. He could read and write. He is fond of reading and is of a religious time. I think he is going to get on in Liberia, being a person of intelligence and robust in health. He is indeed of the idea of promoting as far as in the prosperity considers their fatherhood. I believe [they are] free [with] good and manners.[133]

The Barbadians also had cause to believe that the ACS had been misled regarding the BCL and had provided unfavorable information about them. James Wiles wrote to George Armstrong, whom he had previously met in Barbados, with the worry that:

fearing lest from your long absence from this island you may have forgotten me. I may pardon your memory by telling you that I am the reputed colored son of your old and esteemed friend R.J. Wiles Esquire and to confirm any assertion I have requested my Brother to affix his signature, and he has also given him a letter to you.[134]

Wiles was convinced, from their early acquaintance, that Armstrong's liberal mind would lead him to sympathize with them. The colonization society asked for a further guarantee. On October 31, 1864, John Worrell and V. Lawrence also wrote to Coppinger to clear up some miscommunications that had caused the ship, supposedly sent by the ACS for the migrants, not to turn up as planned in Barbados. As he noted, "From the letter we last received of you under date 12th September, we fear that our situation have been misrepresented by our governor who it appears – have been misinformed when he represented us as 'actuated by very different view than those of labor.'" The BCL sent Attwell as a delegate to reason with the ACS.

---

[132] *The African Repository*, Vol. 42 (1866): 35.

[133] James Barclay to the American Colonization Society, in the Svend Holsoe Collection. University of Indiana at Bloomington.

[134] Letter from James Wiles to George L. Armstrong, November 1, 1864. Svend Holsoe Collection. Accessed at the Barbados Museum and Historical Society. St. Michaels, Barbados.

Even with their limited means, the BCL had begun to make arrangements to help obtain a vessel and finance their voyage. They begged the ACS to do all in their power to effect Attwell's mission as well as do "more to grant him that hospitality which is so desirable to a stranger in a strange land."[135] Worrell and Lawrence hoped that, in personal conversations with Attwell, his intuitions, principles, and "views will be better made known to you and a much further explanation given [because our] preparation [was] in vain, by depending on your crew, sending their vessel to transport us to Liberia by the first day of December."[136]

The organization had high hopes for the Barbadians, but there were persistent lingering doubts and an air of suspicion hanging over them. On March 16, 1865, an anonymous person wrote a letter to the ACS disparaging the Barbadian emigrants. "With reference to your peasant business that you came to the Island about and as a one-timed watchman I have forward you this precaution against the Barbadian rebels that you will have in hand for they are a lot of mules who will require bridle and whip in the process of time." Another wrote, "Most of the young men that are about to leave, they are comfortably, some is working for $6 per week and some for 4$ per week and they have given [th]is up saying that they going to live [like how] gentlemen lived." He suggested that "most of them have taken advantage of poor young females by seducing them and trying to make their escape to Liberia because they shall not act honorable." He concluded that "if they should go on in company with you in the vessel, I think the vessel it will sink with you as the prayers of the poor seduced females is all way upon them."[137]

This person had special advice about Anthony Barclay, who, he noted, was:

like a beast out of harness for he once had a situation having the poor men in his case and he robbed and inflicted severe stripes on their poor hides and all the food he kept it for himself and family and starve the poor. The committees then had to meet and take it away and give it to the peasant keeper ... [W]hen he is go to Liberia you will soon have to make him Governor.

The writer further noted that Franklin, the secretary, was middle class and might be inclined in those ways too. As for "Mr. Worrell, he went into the court house and told our Peasant Governor that he was an emigrant. I read

---

[135] John Worrell and V. Lawrence to Coppinger Esq. October 31, 1864. Svend Holsoe Collection. Barbados Museum and Historical Society.
[136] Ibid.
[137] Reel 15. Svend Holsoe Collection. University of Indiana. Bloomington.

how insulting he was and what the governor has written about them it is all truth for they are all black girds [*sic*]." The writer concluded with prophecy that the ACS would have to deal with "whirlwind generals and earthquake lawyers" and some who desired to be president in a relatively short time, "three years after leaving Barbados."[138]

Other Barbadians continued to write to the ACS in support of the colonization effort. William McClain, the financial secretary of ACS, responded: "The people (African) have insist[ed] upon it that I am getting another vessel ready here and I am continually receiving applications for passages. I could doubtless fill a vessel of five hundred capacity in a month [sic] time." His concerns were about whether "they have the people they want." On this count McClain had strong opinions about which groups would make better migrants: "My opinion is that our American Africans rank higher than the Barbadians in fitness for Liberia."[139] Joseph Tracy, secretary of the Massachusetts Colonization Society, in a letter to William Coppinger, secretary and treasurer of the ACS, shared his concern: "I shall be rather sorry if the Barbadoes expedition fails, but we must not risk too much. You and the committee will be able to judge whether it is safe. I have always had some doubts."[140] McClain vowed to patiently wait for some kind of development, which he hoped would be good. Given that the number of interested Barbadians had risen to 333, he mused that "they may as well prosper beyond expectations."[141] Given that the Barbadians were their last hope, the ACS proceeded to raise over $10,000.

The ACS was successful in their mission. The president of the Pennsylvania Colonization Society (PCS), John P. Crozer, who was the brother of the well-known pioneer of Liberia, Dr. Samuel A. Crozer, who many defined as "unpretentious, wealthy, universally known, and respected and beloved for his many most admirable traits of character, and for his never ceasing words and deeds of kindness and charity," contributed the larger percentage of the money. The ACS subsequently sent Reverend John Seys, who had been a superintendent of a large plantation in Trinidad prominently connected with the Missions of the Methodist Church in Africa and who acted as an agent for recaptured Africans for the government at Monrovia, to Barbados on a fact-finding

---

[138] Ibid.
[139] Joseph Tracy to William Coppinger, ACS reel 96, Domestic Letters No.166. Folio 63563. Liberia Collections. Accessed at the University of Indiana, Bloomington.
[140] Ibid.
[141] Mr. McLain, 21 April, 1865. Svend Holsoe Collection. University of Indiana at Bloomington.

mission. Seys reported, "Emigration to Liberia will essentially benefit the colored people of Barbados." Seys conveyed the plight of the Barbadians, noting, "In that Island, as in all others in the Carribbean Sea [*sic*], the Negro is a kind of serf or at most, an alien, and may earn a mere living, but no more." Whites, he surmised, "will forever keep him down, and he can expect nothing but to remain as a servile portion of the community."[142] Seys believed Liberia was the natural home of black Barbadians because they would be "eligible to the highest place in the gift of an independent and sovereign nation of [their] own complexion, origin, tastes, and habits." Seys was confident that they would be successful should they emigrate to "a climate perfectly congenial to [their] constitution, where the temperature, productions, soil, and everything else, are precisely like those of [their] native Island."[143]

Seys was also certain the ACS would ultimately benefit from the emigration of persons of color from Barbados to Liberia. He told the story of a Mr. Tait, a Barbadian migrant who had emigrated to the republic, taking his wife and seven children with him. He had financed nearly all of his voyage to Sierra Leone alone and after he arrived sacrificed his "last dollar in hiring an open boat to take him to the promised land." Arriving during the rainy season and experiencing the most inclement weather, they "arrived at Monrovia, wet, wearied, hungry, and everything in the shape of clothes, books, and furniture utterly spoiled." However, because the Liberians largely sympathized with him, "donations poured in from every quarter." They were provided with accommodations, money, clothes, food, in the receptacle provided Mr. Dennis, the ACS's agent. After recovering, they "went to work on the soil, and the Legislature gave Mr. Tait $100, and fifty acres of land on the St. Paul's river." Seys concluded that "Liberia fully appreciates the West India emigrant and invites him to her shores."[144]

According to Seys, if the interest from the Barbadians proposing to go to Liberia consisted of "cultivators of the soil, no greater boon can be bestowed on the negro Republic. They want just such men – tillers of the ground." Having witnessed life on the West African coast, he confirmed that the republic was interested in men experienced in the cultivation and manufacturing of the sugar-cane, arrow-root, ginger, and other kinds of tropical products. Seys upon learning of the offer of

---

[142] *The African Repository*, Vol. 42 (1865): 119.
[143] Ibid.
[144] Ibid.

land the Liberian government had made to the Barbadians, saw it as a reflection of their value. "And here it may be said that the Government of Liberia fully realizes this. They offer more of actual real estate – land in fee-simple – to these Barbadians, than to any other class of emigrants – twenty-five acres to every family and ten to every single adult."[145]

Seys was keen to highlight that the Barbadians would be adding to an established foundation. According to him, the great Liberian experiment in nationhood being undertaken by the ACS who created the republic in front of the "whole civilized world" was a monument to African freedom. Because of this, there should be enough room "for all the despised children of Ham to gather themselves from all parts of the world, and there become a people challenging the respect and admiration of all nations." Liberia was to be the "Ark of Safety for the black race." As Liberia progressed in "wealth, population, revenue, commerce, literature, or moral worth, in the eyes of mankind," it would add in Sey's estimation "so much renown and honor to that Society." In the same regard, "Whatever detracts from, or depreciates Liberia in any wise, or causes even a pause in her glorious career, detracts in just so much proportion from the renown and honor, nay from the usefulness of that Society."[146] Seys predicted that the emigration of the group of Barbadians was only the beginning of a massive exodus of migrants from the Caribbean. In greatly adding to the "wealth, revenue, and moral status of Liberia," they would also prop up the status of the ACS in the eyes of "all true philanthropists." Furthermore, he concluded that "the emigration of blacks from Barbados to the Republic of Liberia, will have a reflex action of the happiest character, on the colored population of the United States."[147]

Following these lengthy back-and-forth communications between the Barbadians, African Americans, the ACS, and Liberian officials and diplomats, President Warner instructed Blyden to write to the ACS to provide its ships for two to three years to bring emigrants from the West Indies. When at long last Warner learned that the ACS would assist Barbadian migrants, he promptly responded that "the government of this republic feels very grateful to the Society for the great interest it has taken in its West Indian emigration enterprise, both as it regards the pecuniary means it has furnished and the happy selection of the emigrants sent out." As much as Barbadians had considered Liberia to be "a more auspicious

---

[145] *The African Repository*, Vol. 41 (1865): 118–122.
[146] Ibid.
[147] Ibid.

shore," Liberian officials thought just as much, hailing the Barbadians "as highly auspicious for the future welfare of Liberia and the civilization of Africa."[148] By 1865, when McLain wrote to the Barbadians to offer financial support for their emigration, Barclay relayed the news that "so desirous were many of these people to remove to Africa that before intelligence of the action of the ACS could reach the island" several members of the emigration society, including its chairman, vice president, secretary, and several of its members, numbering in all sixteen persons, embarked on a small vessel chartered by the British government to transport recaptured Africans from her colonies in the West Indies to Sierra Leone. He noted that "they regretted they could wait no longer."[149] The trying nature of Barbados post-emancipation had been compounding for years. Now at a tipping point, these men could no longer tarry.

Given the push-and-pull forces that migrants had to negotiate, the pressures of Barbadian post-emancipation could not be regionally contained. Setting their sites across the Atlantic, the Barbadians confronted their postemancipation anxieties. The possibility of crossing the Atlantic increasingly looked amenable, fitting with Barbadians' desires and demands of postemancipation. Holding possibilities for economic as well as political advancement, migration to Liberia offered a more substantive experience of freedom. They envisioned an improvement of their condition as they helped to build Liberian nationality. While they were excluded and denied civil and political rights in Barbados, Liberia had offered inclusion in the nation-building effort, citizenship, and land. With these possibilities on the horizon, British postemancipation breached its Caribbean shores and spilled across the Atlantic.

Changing dynamics brought about by an extension into Barbados gave life to the ACS's efforts to craft an image of philanthropy and goodwill that they hoped would color emigrants' views of Liberian colonization. Barbadian emigration to Liberia expands the scope of colonization to the post-1865 period, a time when some scholars had viewed the ACS as defunct. That the ACS went beyond the boundaries of the United States warrants a revisiting of the persistent racism–benevolence debate. Some scholars, such as Catherine Reef, have suggested that the organization was taken over by a group of colonizationists who were interested in building an American Empire in Africa.[150] While the ACS was largely defined by its

---

[148] *The African Repository*, Vol. 42 (1866): 38.
[149] Ibid., 36.
[150] See Catherine Reef, *This Our Dark Country: The American Settlers of Liberia.* (New York: Clarion Books, 2002).

relationship with African Americans, its expansion into the West Indies seems to support Reef's contention. The ACS's effort to save the Empire from failure brings into view the newer interests they attempted to explore and the practical transformations they made to the organization. With growing divisions, insufficient funding, and a host of other problems that led many to view the society as a "nullity," the organization's expansion into Barbados could also be seen as a move to improve its image in the United States. Their extension of support to the Barbadians must have cast an image of benevolence on the scheme. Regardless of their motivation to extend assistance to blacks outside of the United States, this shift unequivocally changed the lives of the Barbadian migrants and Liberia's historical trajectory.

More importantly, however, viewing colonization through the motivations of its supporters often obscures what the establishment of Liberia meant to the different black migrants who went there. The inclusion of the Barbadians thus adds to the work of those scholars who have sought to examine Liberian migrants rather than the leaders of ACS. Comparing African American attitudes toward colonization and the ACS to Barbadians' views of Liberia and their relationship with the ACS highlights not only how emigration functioned for different streams of migrants, but also how the colonization movement evolved. Exclusive focus on the efforts of the ACS in the United States centers questions about colonizationists' motives around racism or benevolence. Considered in isolation, the poles of racism and benevolence do not tell us nearly enough about either the ways in which blacks struggled to define their freedom, or about how they sought to remake the world to meet their needs. The limited focus on the black migrants themselves rather negates the instances in which Liberia became a place that attended to the needs of blacks whose desires for freedom were not being met. Rather than ask the value-laden question of how racist or benevolent colonizationists were, it might be more useful to ask, how did blacks make use of colonization? How did it meet their needs?

Thus, the insertion of the Barbadians into Liberia's colonization story builds on traditional African American colonization and emigration historiography and transforms some of its traditional arguments. Scholars have tended to look to different waves of African American emigration to Liberia to explain social, cultural, and political transformations in the republic. The inclusion of Barbadians offers an opportunity to look at Liberian emigration from a comparative perspective that shows the similarities and differences in the factors that motivated emigrants, their experiences, and their social, cultural, and political contributions to the nation-building efforts. Barbadians' experiences alongside African Americans thus illustrate the significance of the unique circumstances from which they came, the ways in which their paths sometimes intersected and overlapped, and their roles in shaping Liberia's cultural, social, and political landscape.

PART II

THE MIDDLE PASSAGE

4

Middle Passage Baggage

On March 11, 1865, William McClain traveled to Barbados to oversee the emigration efforts. After calling a meeting of the prospective emigrants, McClain struggled to select from the large number of interested Barbadians. This created difficulties in finding an appropriate ship. After several days, the colonization secretary approached the captain of the *Brigantine Cora*, anchored in the harbor, to negotiate a reasonable chartering rate. In the early days of April, McLain chartered and attempted to dispatch the *Brig Cora* with about three hundred Barbadian emigrants. Before they could depart, however, orders came from Government House that the boat could not leave until a commission ordered by the governor surveyed it and the harbor master and comptroller of customs completed an inspection. Given that the colonial administration had made earlier attempts to inhibit Barbadian emigration, this new hindrance likely stemmed from a similar case of unease couched under the same guise of concern. McLain, who was oblivious to this contentious history, simply noted in his report to the American Colonization Society (ACS) that the governor of the island delayed the ship's departure "until the following day to allow a commission ordered by the governor of the island to survey her and for the English Admiral commanding on that station to enable his first executive officer to make an examination of how the Queen's subjects were provided for."[1]

On April 5, as the wharf thronged with spectators, Captain William Henderson again prepared for embarkation to Liberia, the *Brig Cora*, having been "finely fitted out, and bountifully supplied with medicines, food,

---

[1] *The African Repository*, Vol. 42 (1866): 37.

water, fuel, cooking utensils, and all things requisite for the voyage."
The emigrants, with much excitement, filled the lighters and went on
board. By 4 pm, as the farewell service commenced on board, every available
crevice of the *Cora* became crowded with visitors. At one point, the crowd
became so rowdy that McClain was unable to account for the migrants on
the ship's manifest (see Figure 4.1). McLain had recorded the names, ages,
occupations, and religions of the over fifty large families. The *Cora*'s pas-
sengers had recognizable Barbadian surnames: Adamson, Alleyne, Austin,
Barclay, Bignall, Blackett, Bourne, Braithwaite, Briggs, Broome, Brown,
Cadell, Clarke, Collier, Cox, Dayrell, Denny, Devonish, Doldron,
Douglas, Earl, Eastmond, Forbes, Francis, Gall, Gibson, Gittens,
Goodridge, Greaves, Highland, Hinds, Holder, Hunte, Inniss, Jackman,
Jones, Jordan, King, Layne, Marshall, McLean, Moore, Murray, Nelson,
Pollard, Porte, Simmonds, Skeete, Taylor, Tull, Ward, Wharton, Wiles,
Williams, and Worrell. In the confusing attempts to identify those whose
names were being called, many passengers who were refused a passage
threatened to stowaway. After the departure clearance the next day,
McClain discovered that there were more passengers than the 320 available
berths on the ship. At final roll call, in addition to those 15 who had left
before he arrived, there were 333 passengers on board. Overriding the
captain's protest of the overcrowding, McClain gave his blessing. Finally,
on April 8, 1865, the *Brig Cora* set sail, departing Carlisle Bay, Barbados, on
its momentous voyage to Liberia.

The *Brig Cora* encapsulated all that enabled its journey and that of its
Afro-Barbadian passengers. Had the *Cora* embarked in an earlier period,
it would have likely been transporting enslaved Africans or recaptives, or
perhaps even taking the Barbadians to Sierra Leone. The abolitionist
and colonizationist efforts that curtailed the flow of enslaved Africans
and drove the ship's transformation had also shaped the convictions and
imaginary of its new passengers. Likely a repurposed slave ship, the *Cora*
had exchanged shackled, enslaved Africans for freedmen embracing the
weighty demands of African civilization in Liberia. As the Barbadians
envisioned their journey across the Atlantic to be another transforma-
tional experience, the Atlantic Ocean became a crossroad, separating
what laid behind and before them—two separate poles of freedom, one
of Caribbean emancipation and the other of African liberation.[2]

---

[2] See Caree Banton, "Who is Black in a Black Republic," in *Race and Nation in the Age of
Emancipations*, Whitney Nell Stewart and John Garrison Marks, eds. (Athens: University
of Georgia Press, 2017).

EMIGRANTS FROM BARBADOS.

LIST OF EMIGRANTS BY THE BRIG CORY FOR LIBERIA,
From Barbados, W. I., April 6, 1865.

No.	NAME.	AGE.	OCCUPATION.	RELIGION.
1	Samuel Primus Skeete............	39	Trader.............	Protestant.
2	Sarah Jane Skeete....................	39	.. ..	do
3	Catharine Thomas Skeete........	18	....	do
4	Sarah Frances Skeete...............	15	....	do
5	Joseph Evans Skeete...............	14	....	do
6	John Bishop Skeete.......	14	....	do
7	Jane Judith Skeete..................	11	....	do
8	Samuel Skeete........................	10	....	do
9	Letitia Evans Skeete...............	8	....	do
10	Elizabeth Skeete.....................	6	....	do
11	Edward Wordworth Skeete......	4	....	do
12	Charles Stewart Skeete...........	4	....	do
13	Primus Samuel Skeete.............	19 mos	....	do
14	James William Austin	40	Planter.............	do
15	Frances Maria Austin...............	45	....	do
16	James Jeremiah Austin............	17	....	do
17	Francis Austin	16	....	do
18	Ernest Adolphus Austin	15	....	do
19	Philip Devonish......................	57	Planter.............	do
20	Dorothy Devonish....................	30	....	do
21	Joseph Clarke Devonish..........	4	....	do
22	Frederick A. W. R. Devonish...	4	....	do
23	James Thomas Wiles.......	34	Smith	do
24	Mary E. Wiles......	28	....	do
25	Laura Editha Wiles.................	12	....	do
26	Florence Irene Wiles...............	10	....	do
27	William Stanley Wiles.............	8	....	do
28	Richard Jones Wiles...............	6	....	do
29	Blanche Henrietta E. Wiles......	3	....	do
30	Ellen Alberto Wiles.................	6 wks.	....	do
31	Helen Beatrice Wiles..............	"	....	do
32	Henry Thornhill Cadogan.......	56	Farmer............	do
33	Sarah Christian Cadogan.........	56	....	do
34	Jerome Dessaline Cadogan.......	17	....	do
35	Cordelia Cleopatra C. Cadogan..	14	....	do
36	Robert Valery Cadogan	12	....	do
37	Arviza Eloise Cadogan............	11	....	do
38	John Robert Padmore.............	39	Planter.............	do
39	Mary Susan Padmore...............	28	....	do
40	Christiana Hinds Padmore.......	9	....	do
41	Mrs. Elizabeth Ann Worrell.....	25	....	do
42	Mrs. Edward Nelson	25	Pastry Maker....	do
43	John Francis Marshall.............	40	Baker.............	do
44	John Weeks Padmore..............	25	Mason.............	do
45	Elizabeth Frances Padmore......	22	....	do
46	Peter Stapleton Padmore..........	4	....	do
47	Jacob Padmore......................	45	Farmer............	do
48	Lucretia Padmore.....................	45	....	do
49	Caroline Padmore...................	19	....	do

FIGURE 4.1: Ship Manifest List of Barbados Emigrants to Liberia
Source: *The African Repository*, Vol. 41, April (1865): 242

EMIGRANTS FROM BARBADOS.

No.	NAME.	AGE.	OCCUPATION.	RELIGION.
50	James Padmore	19		Protestant.
51	Mary Evans Padmore	16		do
52	George Stanley Padmore	14		do
53	Frances Augustus Padmore	11		do
54	Ruth Padmore	9		do
55	Joseph Alonzo Padmore	6		do
56	Alfred Ernest Padmore	3		do
57	William Earl	30	Farmer	do
58	Sarah Elizabeth Earl	24		do
59	Letitia Earl	8		do
60	Joseph Thomas Gibson	28	Cooper	do
61	Isaac William Denny	29	Planter	do
62	John Richard Pollard	35	do	do
63	James Bignail	40	Shipwright	do
64	Mary Jane Scott Bignail	30		do
65	Joseph Abraham Douglas	33	Farmer	do
66	Caroline Douglas	33		do
67	John Frederick A. Douglas	13		do
68	Angelina Theresa Douglas	8		do
69	Irene Josephine Douglas	4		do
70	Elvira Jane Douglas	2		do
71	Holborn Jessamy	65		do
72	Frances Rebecca King	38	Seamstress	do
73	John Isaac Thorpe	35	Farmer	do
74	Elizabeth Maria Thorpe	34		do
75	Elizabeth Rachel Ann Thorpe	14		do
76	Adriana Alberta Louisa Thorpe	12		do
77	Nathaniel Theophilus A. Thorpe	10		do
78	Thirza Ezelia Dorindo Thorpe	8		do
79	Laura Hannah A. Thorpe	7		do
80	Charlotte Evangelina F. Thorpe	5		do
81	John Isaac A. F. G. Thorpe	1		do
82	Edward Hunte	27	Farmer	do
83	James Alexader Dayrell	36	Cooper	do
84	Margaret Ann Dayrell	28		do
85	Theresa Dayrell	11		do
86	Matilda Fitz Gerald Dayrell	9		do
87	Mathaniel Evans Dayrell	8		do
88	Julia Lee Dayrell	5		do
89	James Alexander Dayrell	2		do
90	Jane Benson Dayrell	2 mos.		do
91	Thomas Henry Eastmond	23	Sugar Boiler	do
92	Rebecca Ann Eastmond	22		do
93	Laura Matilda Eastmond	4		do
94	Ruth Ann Eastmond	1		do
95	Edward Thomas Holder	28	Sugar Boiler	do
96	Ellen Holder	27		do
97	Samuel Hall Holder	21		do
98	James Daniel Holder	5		do
99	Thomas Albert Holder	2		do
100	Robert Jackman	40	Sugar Boiler	do
101	Eleanor Jackman	40		do
102	Margaret Jane Jackman	18		do

FIGURE 4.1: (Cont.)

EMIGRANTS FROM BARBADOS.

No.	NAME.	AGE.	OCCUPATION.	RELIGION.
103	Mary Elizabeth Jackman........	14	....	Protestant.
104	Statira Jane Jackman.............	12	....	do
105	Joseph Nathaniel Jackman	11	....	do
106	David Nathaniel Jackman........	8	....	do
107	Samuel Jackman	18 mos	....	do
108	John Abraham Cox.................	23	Plumber	do
109	Mary Ann Cox.......................	23	....	do
110	Josiah Cox...........................	15 mos	....	do
111	Guy Brown...........................	40	Planter	do
112	Delia Brown..........................	38	....	do
113	Albert Augustus Brown..........	13	....	do
114	Nathaniel Brown....................	10	....	do
115	Ernest Horatio Brown.............	3	....	do
116	Frederick Augustus Brown......	2	....	do
117	John Worrell Hinds................	25	Millwright.......,	do
118	Thomasin Ann Hinds..............	23	....	do
119	Sarah Elizabeth Hinds...........	6	....	do
120	Desdemona Alicia Hinds.........	3	....	do
121	Reginald Wesley Hinds...........	5 mos.	....	do
122	Thomas Cadell......................	30	Planter	do
123	Elizabeth Cadell	27	....	do
124	James Cadell	12	....	do
125	Jane Ann Cadell....................	9	....	do
126	Elizabeth Cadell	6	....	do
127	William Cadell......................	4	....	do
128	Samuel Cadell.......................	1	....	do
129	Francis King.........................	34	Carpenter........	do
130	Frances Ann King..................	30	....	do
131	George Francis King..............	8	....	do
132	Sarah Henrietta King.............	7	....	do
133	Henry Parey King	8 mos.	....	do
134	Francis Bourne......................	52	Trader............	do
135	Susan Bourne........	33	....	do
136	Martha Jane Bourne...............	15	....	do
137	Mary Elizabeth Bourne...........	14	....	do
138	Sarah Christian Bourne...........	11	....	do
139	Frances Eliza Bourne.........	9	....	do
140	James Francis Bourne	6	....	do
141	Eleanor Lucretia Bourne.........	4	....	do
142	David Gibson.........................	24	Cooper	do
143	Simon Peter Broome...............	31	Planter............	do
144	Ellen Rose Broome.................	24	....	do
145	Mary Dinah Broome	12	....	do
146	Albert Barclay Broome...........	9	....	do
147	Georgiana Effalanda Broome....	5	....	do
148	Roselia Adriana Broome..........	2	....	do
149	Ernest Augustine F. B. Broome	4 mos.	....	do
150	William Edward Inniss............	25	Smith.............	do
151	Harriet Henery Inniss.............	22	....	do
152	Mary Anna Inniss...................	12	....	do
153	Thomas Hunte.......................	35	Planter............	do
154	Elizabeth Jane Hunte.............	31	....	do
155	Martha Hunte........................	15	....	do

FIGURE 4.1: (Cont.)

EMIGRANTS FROM BARBADOS.

No.	NAME.	AGE.	OCCUPATION.	RELIGION.
156	Dorathy Ann Hunte	19		Protestant
157	Eveline Hunte	8		do
158	Simon Edgar Adolphus Hunte	5		do
159	James Thos. Crichlow Hunte	2		do
160	William Edward Tull	44	Planter	do
161	Sarah Ann Tull	40		do
162	Joshua Tull	13		do
163	Esther Tull	12		do
164	Catharine Herdle Tull	10		do
165	Henry Herdle Tull	7		do
166	Vashti Tull	1		do
167	Edward Blackett	29	Smith	do
168	Mary Elizabeth Blackett	25		do
169	Catharine Jackman Blackett	6		do
170	Alonzo Horatio F. H. Blackett	5		do
171	Alfred Eleazer F. G. Blackett	3		do
172	Alberto Lavinia Blackett	1		do
173	Joseph Applewhaite	24	Planter	do
174	Anna Lewis Applewhaite	22		do
175	Mary Jane Applewhaite	7		do
176	John Brathwaite Weeks	40	Planter	do
177	Joseph Weeks	12		do
178	James Dial Weeks	5		do
179	Jacob Holder	28	Planter	do
180	Joshua Holder	15		do
181	John Brathwaite	20	Planter	do
182	Samuel Tappin Holder	26	Distiller	do
183	Susannah Jane Holder	24		do
184	Nathaniel Holder	2		do
185	Margaret Ann Holder	1		do
186	John Benjamin Adamson	22	Planter	do
187	Cornelia Amelia Goodridge	30	Mantua Maker	do
188	Judith Ann Goodridge	26	do	do
189	Mary John Goodridge	24	do	do
190	William Henry Goodridge	16	Carpenter	do
191	James Abel Goodridge	15	Tailor	do
192	John Richard Francis	49		do
193	Triphena Francis	14		do
194	James Edward Francis	14		do
195	Abijah Francis	13		do
196	Jason Francis	12		do
197	Henry King Jones	45	Carpenter	do
198	Nancy Ann Jones	38		do
199	Elista Harewood Jones	6		do
200	Joseph Highland	28	Millwright	do
201	Florence Adelisha Highland	19 mos		do
202	James Taylor	36	Trader	do
203	Sarah Ann Taylor	34		do
204	Henry King Taylor	10		do
205	Sarah Jane Taylor	6		do
206	James Taylor	2		do
207	Robert Clarke	35	Carpenter	do
208	Caroline Cecilia Clarke	31		do

FIGURE 4.1: (Cont.)

EMIGRANTS FROM BARBADOS.

No.	NAME.	AGE.	OCCUPATION.	RELIGION.
209	Samuel Christopher Clarke......	10	....	Protestant.
210	Joseph Emmanuel Clarke.........	7	....	do
211	Abraham Orion Clarke............	6 mos.	....	do
212	Francis Thome	20	Mason	do
213	John Prince Porte....................	50	Farmer	do
214	Ellen Ann Porte............	20	....	do
215	John Edward Porte	15	....	do
216	Joseph Porte,...................... ...	13	....	do
217	Samuel Thomas Porte............	12	....	do
218	Nathaniel Porte......................	4	....	do
219	John Marshall Nightingale.......	26	Reporter	do
220	Thomas H. Greaves	45	Tailor.............	do
221	Adelaide Greaves....................	38	....	do
222	Susan Thomas Greaves	18	....	do
223	Joshua Greaves	16	....	do
224	Mergiana Greaves	14	....	do
225	Morrington Greaves................	11	....	do
226	Henry Greaves	8	....	do
227	Eliza Ann Hinds	38	Trader.............	do
228	Rebecca Went Senhouse Hinds.	16	....	do
229	Emily Went Senhouse Hinds....	11	....	do
230	Frances Alice Hinds...............	7	....	do
231	John William Hinds	40	Painter	do
232	Rebecca Ann Hinds............	42	....	do
233	Catharine Ann Hinds	18	....	do
234	Rebecca Ursula Hinds............	16	....	do
235	Elizabeth Lavina Hinds...........	14	....	do
236	Joseph Egerton Hinds.............	9	....	do
237	Emanuel Woodville Hinds.......	4	....	do
238	Virginia Alice Hinds...............	9 mos.	....	do
239	Catharine McLean......	60	....	do
240	Benjamin I. Forbes	37	Tailor	do
241	James E. C. Forbes	14	....	do
242	—— Adams........................	24	Printer	do
243	Anthony Barclay......................	55	Penman	Episcopalian.
244	Sarah Ann Barclay	48	Confectioner....	do
245	Antoinette Hope Barclay.........	28	School Mistress	do
246	Mary Augusta Barclay............	27	Confectioner....	Wesleyan.
247	Elizabeth Ann Barclay............	25	School Teacher	do
248	Malvina Barclay.	24	Fancy Worker..	Episcopalian.
249	Anthony Barclay	22	Merchant's Clrk	do
250	Sarah Helena Barclay.............	20	Music Teacher..	do
251	Ernest Barclay......................	18	Coppersmith....	do
252	Laura Barclay	12	....	do
253	Arthur Barclay..........	10	....	do
254	Florence Barclay....................	10	....	do
255	Ellen Mai Barclay...................	8	....	do
256	Nathaniel Doldron......	48	Carpenter	Wesleyan.
257	Phillis A. Doldron..................	48	....	do
258	Nathaniel Doldron..................	20	Joiner	do
259	Lydia J. Doldron	18	....	do
260	Rosina Doldron	15	....	do
261	Jane Collier	23	....	do

FIGURE 4.1: (Cont.)

EMIGRANTS FROM BARBADOS.

No.	Name.	Age.	Occupation.	Religion.
262	Samuel Inniss	29	Boot Maker	Wesleyan.
263	Charles Inniss	23	Cabinet Maker	do
264	Augustus Gall	37	Cultivator	do
265	Cornelia Gall	35	Seamstress	do
266	Miriam Gall	5		do
267	Ruth Gall	3		do
268	Edward Alleyne	38	Sugar Boiler	Episcopalian.
269	Andrew Campbell	31	do	do
270	Edward H. Williams	49	Mason	do
271	James W. Blackman	27	Printer	do
272	Isaac Graves	39	Sugar Boiler	Wesleyan.
273	Rebecca Graves	20	Seamstress	do
274	George Francis Graves	18		do
275	Mary Elizabeth Graves	14		do
276	Sarah Jane Graves	12		do
277	Edward Nathaniel Graves	10		do
278	Charles Graves	7		do
279	William Herbert Graves	5		do
280	Mary Emily Graves	4		do
281	Thomas Wharton	50	Sugar Boiler	Episcopalian.
282	Ann Wharton	47		do
283	Thomas H. Wharton	15	Sugar Clarifier.	do
284	Edward Wharton	12		do
285	Elizabeth Wharton	11		do
286	David Wharton	5		do
287	Josephine Wharton	2		do
288	Edward Moore	53	Sugar Boiler	do
289	Molly Moore	50		do
290	John Edward Moore	17		do
291	Molly Moore	15		do
292	Jane Moore	13		do
293	James Edward Moore	10		do
294	Amelia Moore	7		do
295	James H. Briggs	33	Planter	do
296	Margaret Briggs	37		do
297	Lucretia Briggs	5		do
298	Mary Augusta Briggs	4 mos.		do
299	Elizabeth Moore	19		do
300	Charles Simmonds	14		do
301	James E. Murray	34	Tanner	do
302	Sarah B. Murray	24	Seamstress	do
303	James E. Murray	8		do
304	Edward H. Murray	6 mos.		do
305	Samuel Collier	37	Baker	Moravian.
306	Jacob Collier	13		do
307	Samuel Collier	11		do
308	Henry P. Collier	8		do
309	Ernest Collier	6		do
310	Elvina D Collier	2		do
311	Thomas B. Layne	31	Butcher	do
312	Sarah B. Layne	37		do
313	John Bell Layne	11		do
314	Mary Eliza Layne	10		do

FIGURE 4.1: (Cont.)

THE BARBADOS EXPEDITION.

No.	NAME	AGE.	OCCUPATION.	RELIGION.
315	Samuel Solomon Layne............	8	....	Moravian.
316	Paul Layne................................	7	....	do
317	John H. Nurse..........................	35	Planter............	do
318	Elizabeth Nurse........................	36	....	do
319	Nathaniel Nurse........................	15	....	do
320	Alberta Nurse...........................	2	....	do
321	John W. Jordan.........................	34	Seaman	Episcopalian.
322	Dorothy Jordan	32	Seamstress......	do
323	Sarah Elizabeth Jordan............	10	.. ..	do
324	Benjamin Gittens......................	18	....	do
325	James C. Gittens.......................	60	Tailor	do
326	Ann Gittens..............................	....	....	do
327	James Gittens...........................	35	....	do
328	Joseph Gittens..........................	12	....	do
329	Joshua Gittens.....	10	....	do
330	James Gittens	5	....	do
331	John Warde..............................	40	Carpenter........	do
332	John T. Worrell........................	59	Joiner.............	do
333	Angel W. Worrell......................	35	....	do
334	John E. Worrell..	21	....	do
335	Robert Alfred Worrell...............	14	....	do
336	Edward Ashworth Worrell	10	....	do
337	Henry Albert Worrell................	4	....	do
338	Albert Gittens..........................	27	Cabinet Maker..	do
339	Martha A. Gittens....................	26	....	do
340	Edward Gittens	3	....	do
341	Bristowe Armstrong.................	51	Sugar Boiler....	
342	Nanny Armstrong	42	Cultivator.......	
343	Emily Armstrong......................	23	....	
344	Mary Catharine Armstrong......	15	....	
345	Alexander Armstrong	4	....	
346	Benjamin Brathwaite	30	Tailor	

————ooo————

FIGURE 4.1: (Cont.)

Creating an additional dimension of emancipation, the vast sea further signified blacks being made free in the Caribbean but aiming to claim their own freedom in Liberia, and being "civilized" in the Caribbean but becoming civilizing agents in Africa.

The emigration of the Barbadians to Liberia brings together post-emancipation British efforts to civilize Africa and nineteenth-century pan-Africanist movements. The ideological elements undergirding the Barbadians' sojourn—the drive for African civilization and the cultural demands of black nationalism—served as additional push factors for emigrants who were already suffering under the economic and political pressures of emancipation. Put together, these factors focused the

emigrants' discontents into efforts to emigrate to Liberia. British subjectivity shaped the ways in which West Indians imagined their lives; the
Afro-Barbadian emigrants and their views on African civilization and
pan-Africanism emanated from a distinctly British colonial perspective.
Misrepresenting the lived experiences of West Indian post-emancipation
as a replica of extant African American views effaces the manifestations of
Afro-Barbadians' pan-African ideologies as the outcome of their efforts to
negotiate different push-and-pull migration forces to create a freedom
that was to their liking. Afro-Barbadian emigrants proposed an additional
path to Liberian modernity, and their identity further revealed the ways in
which they embodied seemingly contradictory viewpoints.

In the host of factors that influenced them, the personal and ideological
views reflected who the emigrants were, their ambitions, and who they
strived to be as Liberian citizens. The heavy weight of the Afro-
Barbadians' "racial, nationalist, and political ideologies" shaped their
identity and views of Africa. Their colonial and diasporic sense of duty
and obligation created a peculiar baggage that they would contemplate in
the travel days ahead.[3] Such viewpoints were the logical outcome of Afro-
Barbadians who had arrived at black nationalism after rationalizing about
their future from their oppressed positions in British colonial society.
Capturing the zeitgeist of the time, black racial nationalism appeared to
West Indians in an oppressing post-emancipation society as the only route
through which they might be able to claim the full breadth of a freedom
inclusive of nationhood and citizenship. There was an unspoken assumption that a modern black nation-building project might subvert the norms
of race and empire but reinforce the values of class and patriarchy. As they
prepared for the confrontation with the African coast, the Barbadians'
plan facilitated their support of British efforts in Africa and created the
kinds of imperial association that provided cover, protection, support,
and leverage. The Barbadians' strategies to civilize Africa and eradicate
the slave trade not only presented a new vision of black nationalism and
pan-Africanism, but also disrupted the dynamics of African American
plans for Liberia. In addition to the Republican principles on which
Liberia was founded, the royalist political ideologies that the Barbadian
emigrants carried with them not only impacted Liberia's nation-building
project but further added to the tensions. These ideas further serve as the
background against which the migrants' perplexing social, cultural, and
political decisions in Liberia can be understood and contextualized.

---

[3] Sandiford, *Theorizing a Colonial Caribbean-Atlantic Imaginary*, 55.

The Afro-Barbadians' conflicting identity crystallized a set of the ideological impulses and ethics that shaped the African diaspora through the lens of pan-Africanism and black nationalism as well as colonization and imperialism. The Barbadian emigrants' intents came from an attitude of good faith. Thinking of themselves as beleaguered superheroes, they were going back to Africa to construct a respectable republic that would exude blacks' capacity for civilization and self-improvement. However, fitting together a sense of imperial duty with diasporic obligations created an unanticipated set of ideological conflicts that overshadowed their journey. The usual consequences of colonization and nationalism plagued blacks. Moreover, black nationalism sometimes meant commitment to Western ideas, and its manifestation only served to shelter a different group of elites' political benefits in a different manner. Consequently, the plans to civilize other blacks in Africa and create a black nation-building project established the dynamics for confrontation and struggle. Even as the Barbadians' journey was about destroying the hierarchical systems that controlled their lives, they were oblivious to those they held within themselves.

As a consequence, despite the outward appearances of the Barbadians' civilizationist agenda, Liberia became a "more auspicious shore" because the ideology provided direct solutions to their post-emancipation imperial dilemmas. As such, focusing on the Barbadian migrants as only philanthropic abolitionists with Africa's best interests at heart would be to miss the ways in which imperialism was also wrapped up in their African civilization and black nation-building packages. Afro-Barbadian creole elites who had strong loyalties to empire embraced options for post-emancipation reforms through pan-Africanist rather than separatist black nationalist movements. In the same way that they used millenarianism and religious symbolism in their decisions to emigrate, middle-class Afro-Barbadian migrants also enveloped ideas of British royalism within the purview of pan-Africanism to promote their cause as just. Afro-Barbadians attempted to cope with their diminishing and untenable positions in the post-emancipation Caribbean by harnessing a similar power through Liberian colonization. Their emigration represented a post-emancipation denunciation of the loss of secure status over enslaved Africans and being cast into the market with the laboring class. Middle-class Afro-Barbadians desired to use the tools of colonialism to attain the kinds of power they had been denied in Barbados: the power to determine who failed and succeeded in the post-emancipation era. Though they resented racial subjugation in Barbados, middle-class Afro-Barbadians

were ready to be part of the British imperial arrangement if it had
a hierarchical colonial structure that offered them respectability, preserved their position of privilege, and gave them an enviable entry into
the capitalist market and the ability to take advantage of those below
them.[4] Their loss of power was simultaneously recouped and concealed as
Afro-Barbadians created a sense of racial identification with Africans, but
as model civilizers. Couched within the perceived selflessness and courage
of their interest in African civilization were also the kinds of upward
mobility, respectability, and power the emigrants had expected to accompany post-emancipation. Indeed, the Afro-Barbadian civilizing and
nation-building ideology was not in tension with their self-interest as
a class; it existed to protect their self-interests and to justify themselves
to the different power brokers.

The axes on which Afro-Barbadians built their politics were numerous.
The fragile dynamics linking Barbadians' civil, religious, and political
ambitions to their economic and ideological ambitions rendered their pan-
Africanist ideals problematic from the outset. As harbingers of the troubling dynamic that influenced the course of nation-building in Liberia, the
Barbadian contradictions raise questions about imperialism and colonization as a starkly white racist phenomenon. The ambiguities, conflicts, and
philosophical tensions that manifested in the ways Barbadians imagined
themselves as actors in Liberia begs questions that transcend the over-
simplified ideas of black nationalism, pan-Africanism, imperialism, and
colonization. Whether Barbadians were black British imperialists or pan-
Africanists obscures the ways in which their actions as imperial surrogates
and colonial bedfellows enabled and maintained these systems. Thus, it
might be more generative to consider the nature of the intersecting relational structures to which Afro-Barbadians subscribed. How do these
overlaps disrupt imperial or anti-imperial as well as pan-Africanist and
black nationalist narratives? If Afro-Barbadians were somehow trapped
within an imperial identity, were they engaging with colonialism and
black nationalism to devise an ideological escape?

THE BORDERLAND OF BARBADIAN COLONIAL BLACK IDENTITY

The *Brig Cora* carried much more than met the naked eye. Its Barbadian
travelers must have felt the historical weight of their mission as soon as

---

[4] See Imani Perry, *More Beautiful and More Terrible: The Embrace and Transcendence of
Racial Inequality in the United States* (New York: New York University Press, 2011).

they boarded the ship. In addition to the Afro-Barbadian emigrants and their meager supplies, the boat lugged the complexities of their identity to their Liberian destination. Afro-Barbadians' identity and relationship to Africa manifested through transatlantic slavery, British abolitionists, civilizing, Christianizing, imperialist efforts, and emergent nineteenth-century black nationalist and pan-African movements. Out of the unique "ecology of belonging" produced from their experiences as British colonial subjects and members of the African diaspora, Afro-Barbadians embodied the duality of Africa and Europe within their migrant identity. This divided Afro-Barbadian identity revealed what it meant not only to be a colonial subject but also to be impaired by racial thinking. Through an identity that enabled them to simultaneously work within and against the British Empire, the Barbadian emigrants found themselves in a position of liminality.[5] With that, their agenda was aimed in multiple directions. Through the industrious habits and religious beliefs gained through association with the West, they intended to reproduce the Western civilized world for native Africans through their presence. As the beneficiaries of emancipation, the Afro-Barbadian emigrants' royalist appeals to white Britons through the prism of African civilization endeared them to the Empire. Beyond any simple expression of gratitude, such attitudes attracted the kinds of respectability they desired. Finally, it was also geared toward Liberia's religious elite, whom the Barbadians needed to woo in their quest for social acceptance within the hierarchies of the Christian Negro Republic.

The leadership of the emigration organizations in Barbados included an all-male cast of prominent Afro-Barbadians who self-identified as middle class. Barclay, the chairman of the Fatherland Union, was a well-known ambitious politician. John Blackman, the vice chairman, was also politically inclined and financially prosperous. Like Barclay, Blackman was also a signatory of the Belgreave Counter Address, a movement that emerged after free coloreds denounced the Bussa Uprising and sought to distance themselves from enslaved Africans. Still, Blackman raised several questions about Barbadians and their dual identities. Blackman, in his will, left "six slaves to be sold and the balance of the estate to be divided among children; one child received £30 less than others because that is what he paid to have them manumitted."[6] Blackman was possibly not

---

[5] Paul Gilroy, *The Black Atlantic: Modernity and Double Consciousness* (Boston, MA: Harvard University Press, 1993), 3.

[6] Handler et al., *Freedmen of Barbados*, 6.

a traditional slaveholder but someone who had bought slaves who were likely family members.

Another member, Charles Phipps, had also been free before 1834 and signed the Belgreave Counter Address alongside Anthony Barclay Sr. Not only was Phipps secretary of the BCL, he was noted as being "the first teacher at the Colonial Charity School for Boys that started in 1819 or 1820 and taught at the school until at least August 1831 and perhaps longer."[7] In October 1829, Phipps and Joseph Kennedy were noted as being secretaries of the Barbados Auxiliary Bible Society. In March 1831, Phipps along with Thomas Cummins, another leader in the BCL, were the secretaries of the Colonial Charity School. Phipps, like several other Afro-Barbadians, had expressed an interest in a career as an imperial official. When it was not realized, Phipps and others had joined the Society for the Extinction of the Slave Trade along with John Sheafe, Samuel Sandiford, and John S. Gaskin. They were also a part of the leadership of the BCL, which also included Samuel Donokan, treasurer, and five other members, including Conrad Reeves and Henry Dayrell, who seconded a motion at a public meeting of freedmen.

British colonial Afro-Barbadians often expressed ideas about themselves through an antagonistic relationship with African retentions in the colonies.[8] Before migrating, Afro-Barbadians viewed themselves within and outside of their relationship to Africa. Under slavery and colonialism, Afro-Barbadians internalized ideas of blackness filtered through its all-encompassing relationship to Africa. As Melanie Newton explains, "Some of the prominent pre-1834 free men of color who sought to promote racial solidarity and pride in their African origins also exhibited a profound sense of shame about cultural practices associated with Africa."[9] She described how James Thorne, "a prominent free man of color," aggressively dispersed a gathering of apprentices who were attempting to conduct an "African inspired slave burial." Newton read Thorne's reaction as "rooted in a deeper sense of personal shame at his own origins in a community that indulged in such forms of cultural expressions." Newton concludes that Thorne's later political career and that of other middle-class Afro-Barbadians reflected an internal identity conflict that guided their behavior towards former slaves and their own

---

[7] Ibid., 42.
[8] James Sidbury, *Becoming African in America: Race and Nation in the Early Black Atlantic* (New York: Oxford University Press, 2007), 14.
[9] Newton, *The Children of Africa in the Colonies*, 219–220.

perceptions of their African heritage.[10] As it turned out, these views shaped how Afro-Barbadians would come to see themselves in their relationship with Africa as civilizers.

In the Afro-Barbadian community, class and color proved to be a reliable predictor of status and loyalty. Between free coloreds, who were mixed race and could acquire education, property, and status based on color and kinship relations, and free blacks, who often acquired their freedom through self-purchase, it would be the latter group who expressed solidarity with slaves, revered Haiti, and eventually expressed interest in Liberia. Scholars tend to think that skin color politics was not as significant in Barbados as other islands. But like other societies forged in slavery, skin color emanating from race played a significant role in Afro-Barbadians' ideas about shared identity.[11] In Barbados, while lighter complexions were celebrated and could be a source of admittance into respectability, blackness was often derided. Though lighter-skinned Afro-Barbadians held up whiteness as an ideal, a mixed-race background did not always serve free blacks in Barbados because the stigma associated with Africa also followed blacks in a multiplicity of negative ways.

London Bourne, who had been a slave before finding an enterprising career as a Bridgetown merchant, exemplified the shame and scourge of blackness in Barbados. Bourne, known to be of dark complexion, was often described as "a man of unmixed African blood."[12] Though he identified as one of those who exhibited a strong sense of African consciousness and identity, Bourne experienced the effects of color politics in Barbados. At one point, after he accused his store assistant John Piper, a light-complexed man, of theft, a large group of free coloreds attacked him. The large crowd allegedly stoned Bourne's house and made threats to kill his son, who had testified in the case. The crowd referred to London Bourne as a "Barbadian Congo" and his son as "the Congo son."[13] The pejorative use of "Congo" in Barbados denoted the pure and unadulterated African. Used to assign an African identity to blackness, it also came with an additional assumption of low standards of living, uneducated manners of speaking, ignorance, and, ultimately, stupidity.[14]

[10] Ibid.
[11] Quoted in Newton, *The Children of Africa*, 220.
[12] Karch, "A Man for All Seasons," 19.
[13] *The Liberal*, September 3, 1842. *The Barbadian*, August 20 and 27, 1842. Quoted in Newton, *The Children of Africa*, 220.
[14] Richard Allsopp, *Dictionary of Caribbean English Usage* (New York: Oxford University Press, 1996), 167.

Bourne's ordeal served as an example of how "the whole colonial racialized system" lived traumatically "in the interior of the family and in the collapses of [the] mind." For Bourne's family and class in Barbados, the psychological legacy of the power held by slave owners had left a color line drawn within them.[15] Bourne, who had supported numerous missionary and civilizing endeavors in Africa, also illuminated the problematic embrace of ideas of race. Through their experiences, West Indians like Bourne came to understand race not as any illusion but as essential and natural. For them, race was not only a way to be in the world but also a way to be embraced by it if they were able to invert their subordinate places. Consequently, Afro-Barbadians' interest in civilizing Africa was about blacks throwing other blacks under the bus so that they would be spared the same fate, exemplifying arguments about victims who were willing accomplices in their own victimization and who turned victimizers.

Blacks in the Caribbean represented the dividing line in the colonial world, which was bureaucratically and architecturally structured to have notable go-betweens to represent the oppressed voice.[16] In their movement between private and public currents of colonial subjectivity, the Afro-Barbadians enacted their mediating status.[17] When two American abolitionists, James Thome and Thomas Kimball, went on a six-month tour of the West Indian experiment of freedom, they were entertained by several members of the Afro-Barbadian middle class.[18] To assess Afro-Barbadian standards of living and advances towards civilization and culture, the abolitionists used consumption patterns and the tendencies of the middle class to overcompensate for black depravity. At the home of Thomas Harris, they ate "an epicurean variety of meats, flesh, fowl, fish, vegetables, pastries, fruits and nuts, and that invariable accompaniment of a West Indian dinner wine." They described Joseph Thorne, once enslaved at the Belle Plantation until about twenty years of age, as "a dark mulatto with Negro features and curly hair" who had a "large library of religious, historical and literary works." Sturge and Harvey and his generation of abolitionists regarded objects such as "costly and elegant" furniture as the standard by which members of the Afro-Barbadian middle class were admitted into a realm of "civilized" society to which black peasants

---

[15] Stuart Hall, *Familiar Stranger: A Life Between Two Islands* (Durham, NC: Duke University Press, 2017).

[16] Ibid., 14.

[17] Sandiford, *Theorizing a Colonial Caribbean-Atlantic Imaginary*, 54.

[18] See Pedro L. V. Welch and Richard A. Goodridge, *"Red" and Black Over White*, (Bridgetown, Barbados: Carib Research and Publications, 2000).

were not privy.[19] The Barbadians' claim to these material experiences marked the kinds of civilization by which they considered themselves fit to regenerate Africa.

Thus, in their positions in Barbadian society, the middle class acted as a bulwark against and managers of the unruly and uncivilized Afro-Barbadians' base instincts. The notion that Afro-Barbadians, by their very nature, could not become productive citizens without white supervision pervaded the Afro-Barbadian consciousness. Instead of white supervision, middle-class Afro-Barbadians, by their racial, social, and cultural proximity to whiteness, often played this role. In straddling free and unfree, and sometimes black and white, the Afro-Barbadian middle class acted as a buffer zone between whiteness and unadulterated blackness. In post-emancipation, slavery's presence remained in the hierarchy it had created. Domination itself was unimportant; it was the act of dominance that mattered. By placing themselves in this position of controlling the black underclass, the middle class assumed the role of whiteness and Empire. Middle-class Afro-Barbadians, having been elevated above enslaved Africans through their proximity to whiteness, occupied an in-between status that allowed them to serve in those capacities from slavery and freedom. Given their positions, they were viewed as more civilized than Africans because of the proximity to the whiteness and thus were allowed to speak for them.[20] Afro-Barbadians' in-betweenness thus existed as a borderland.

A case in point was Bourne's responses to a questionnaire distributed by the abolitionist Charles Tappan during a visit to Barbados in 1858. Bourne's views provide further insights into the nature of the Afro-Barbadian middle-class subaltern consciousness aboard the *Cora*.[21] The questionnaire that sought to elicit "the Results of Emancipation in Barbados" featured thirteen questions geared towards gauging if freedom had bettered the lives of ex-slaves, in particular, and Barbadian society, in general. When Tappan asked, "Do laborers usually take a greater interest in estates than under slavery," though not a laborer himself, London Bourne responded, "Yes, where there are good feelings between employers, laborers, that is, where wages are fairly established fairly paid, there is no dissatisfaction of the slightest nature exists." Tappan concluded by asking, "On the whole, have former slaves benefited otherwise by

---

[19] Thome and Kimball, *Emancipation in the West Indies*, 72–73.
[20] Frantz Fanon, *White Skin, Black Masks* (New York: Grove Press, 1967), 26.
[21] Karch Braithwaite, "A Man for All Seasons: London Bourne."

emancipation and in what respects?" To this Bourne replied, "They have all the rights of men and all those attributes which providence in his goodness has destined for men."[22]

In 1858, the Victorian-era novelist Anthony Trollope reflected on his observations of the workings of the Afro-Barbadian middle-class consciousness. After sailing to the West Indies to inspect the land and negotiate treaties for the English government, Trollope wrote *The West Indies and the Spanish Main* (1860). In a recounting of his experiences on the islands visited and the people encountered, Trollope observed, "The West Indian Negro knows nothing of Africa except that it is a term of reproach. If African immigrants are put to work on the same estates with him, he will not eat with them or drink with them or walk with them. He will hardly work beside them and regards himself as a creature immeasurably the superior of the newcomer. But yet he made no approach to the civilization of his white fellow-creature, whom he imitates as a monkey does a man."[23] The large body of creole slaves born in Barbados looked at new incoming enslaved Africans, who were largely from Congo, Angola, with derision, seeing them as savages bereft of civilization. Trollope's observations and reports further captured a spirit of truth about color, ethnicity, and racial oppression in the Afro-Barbadian community. The more assimilated Afro-Barbadians came to detest in the newly arrived Africans what they hated in themselves. In one now-famous passage of the book, reflecting upon West Indians' biracial-ness, Trollope referred to them as "creole negroes." He observed: "But how strange is the race of creole negroes—of Negroes, that is, born out of Africa. They have no country of their own, yet they have hitherto no country for their adoption; for whether as slaves in Cuba or free laborers in the British Isles, they are in each case a servile people in a foreign land."[24] That Trollope was most intrigued by the West Indians' creolization suggests its visible embrace.

What Trollope considered creole behavior, other observers had long observed about the Barbadians before they were halfway across the Atlantic Ocean. A Mr. Sain repeatedly wrote damning letters as a way of discrediting and bad-mouthing the Barbadians to the ACS. Sain depicted the Barbadians as having similar hang-ups about race as whites, which they acted out in religious and social gatherings. "But there are too

[22] *The Liberal*, February 9, 1859.
[23] Anthony Trollope, *The West Indies and the Spanish Main* (Cambridge: Cambridge University Press, 1860), 56.
[24] Ibid., 55.

[those that] belong to the colored race who [have] just as much a prejudice existing among them against the black race, as there is between the high aristocratic white race. And about these cases, the prejudices are as a great as in the rest of country between the whites and the Africans." Sain observed that these attitudes prevailed in churches. He recalled that if a church where the majority of the congregation was colored people were to invite a preacher "who is too black to preach for [them], a third of the congregation would get up and march out of the house." He grimaced as he demanded, "What do you think of that?" He also observed the ways in which these behaviors filtered out into other domains as blacks strived to treat those they considered their racial superiors with great respect. In his letter, Sain noted, "I think I have not told Jon that a colored man half-soled my shoes. They were not the real squares toes but moderately so. Nell said he took great pains to cut off the corners to make them round, because he could not bear the thought that 'the Reverend' shan't wear shoes so out of fashion."[25]

As a group that was also oppressed and denied rights they deserved, middle-class Afro-Barbadians harbored secret desires to become like the privileged. Membership entailed being in a dominant position, acquiring the same resources as the privileged, and claiming and appropriating an imperial genealogy to prop themselves up in power. Being in a colonial society, the Afro-Barbadian middle class regularly engaged with some aspects of the privileges of British colonialism. Indeed, there was an acceptance on the part of the Afro-Barbadian middle class of a hierarchy that established whiteness as the standard. When the Afro-Barbadian middle class became the vanguard of black post-emancipation activism, it was because of the specific kinds of civil and social privileges that it afforded them. As the influential group leading the revolution, the Afro-Barbadian middle class were usually ones who profited from the cultural benefits of the arrangement they criticized.[26]

The twinning of African diaspora with British colonialism haunted Afro-Barbadians' future as much as it had done their past. Living under British colonialism in the Caribbean, Barbadians walked a tightrope, navigating an inherited tension between ideas of blackness and tenets of modernity that drew on the social, economic, and political premises of

---

[25] Mr. N. Sain, Barbados, April, 24, 1865. Svend Holsoe Collection. University of Indiana at Bloomington.

[26] C. L. R. James, *The Black Jacobins; Toussaint L'Ouverture and the San Domingo Revolution* (New York: Vintage Books, 1963).

imperialism. Afro-Barbadians' leadership proved critical to their sense of place in the rank and order of Barbadian society. Their demonstrated commitment to social and political reform reflected a post-emancipation climate that threatened their positions. The middle class's assumption of leadership over the larger Afro-Barbadian community mirrored their recognition that in the absence of slavery's class restrictions of free and unfree, race linked together their collective social, civil, and political fates. In some sense, the desire for the dominance inherent to slavery was on par with their love of power and profit.

Given their position, Afro-Barbadians held both slavish and monarchial views in the same body. As Anglo-centric royalists, Afro-Barbadians did not disagree philosophically with the monarchy. People who prostrated themselves before the monarchy desired to be a part of the monarchy. As British colonial subjects, Barbadians held particular ideas about dominance that were largely scripted and shackled by their historical experiences of a colonial order left intact after emancipation and coopted by the demands of mid-nineteenth-century racial capitalism. Despite their migratory protest of imperial racial subjugation, Afro-Barbadians failed to break radically from its inherently oppressive ideas. And as a consequence, they would remain entangled in the patented realities of colonialism in Liberia. Barbadians' journey away from British Empire led them down a path of African liberation and redemption, and they were unaware of how the invisible tentacles of colonial imperialism were spurring them toward contradictory ends. By imbibing the attitudes as well as the rules, social organization, and machinations of white supremacy, colonial Afro-Barbadians had learned to express power through settlement, exploitation, and ideologies that valorized whiteness.

Middle-class Afro-Barbadians used colonial subjectivity to leverage their importance to the African civilization project. The West Indies' liminal position in the Atlantic constituted a sort of grounding for Afro-Barbadian middle-class ethics that featured ideas about nature versus nurture theories of being not Africa but not Europe: somewhere else, mini-Africa and not yet Europe.[27] At no point did the Barbadians' black diasporic experience yield a political ideology radical in its future redistribution of social, political, and economic power. Instead, the Afro-Barbadian middle class imitated the West, absorbing an image of themselves created to keep them subordinate in the first place but now

[27] Belinda Edmondson, *Making Men: Gender; Literary Authority, and Women's Writing in Caribbean Narrative* (Durham, NC: Duke University Press, 1999), 29.

refashioned to create a worldview that equally subordinated indigenous Africans.

Part and parcel to the Afro-Barbadian colonial inheritance and their steadfast subscription to British sensibilities was a superior attitude towards continental Africans. In a logic structured by colonialism was a pre-figured social hierarchy that placed Afro-Barbadians above native Africans. Imperialist images wedged within the minds of colonial subjects were sustained by Western imperial power. When Afro-Barbadians highlighted their identity as colonial West Indians, it called on Britain's far-reaching existence as "an imperial totality."[28] It pulled with it all the imperial connotations—the authority and strength commanded through vast amounts of acquired territory. They could also claim the "manners, habits and the positioning of the English gentlemen class through the acquisition of Victorian models of intellectual authority and knowledge."[29] Though transformed by their experiences of diaspora, as part of their creole sensibilities, West Indians embraced "English gentlemen archetypes and a conflictual investment in English modes of masculinity."[30]

Much of these attitudes were absorbed through institutions such as churches and through books. Edward Blyden, the West Indian migrant from the Virgin Islands who became an educator in Liberia, "wrote letters to Prime Minister Gladstone requesting that he be sent English literature classics." The extent to which Blyden found this to be a vital part of his "development as an African leader" highlights the ways in which English modes of thinking shaped West Indians.[31] These epistemic sources shaped West Indian imagination. In the context of their post-emancipation deprivation of things that were needed to flourish, the Barbadians' views betrayed an underlying optimism and hope. Tempered as it was by notions of British superiority, the problematic nature of Barbadians' view of their relationship to Africa and Africans foreshadowed future problems.

For Barclay and other middle-class members of the Barbadian emigration societies, Africa served as a backdrop of not only the fantasies of the diaspora but also their sense of heroism. A detoxification of the sum of their positive and negative experiences in Empire allowed Barbadians to create meanings that supported their desires in Africa. Their larger-than-

---

[28] Van Gosse, "'As a Nation, the English Are Our Friends': The Emergence of African American Politics in the British Atlantic World, 1772–1861," *American Historical Review*, Vol. 113, No. 4 (2008): 1005.

[29] Edmondson, *Making Men*, 30.

[30] Ibid.

[31] Ibid.

life ambition for Liberia was as much a flight into ideological escapist fantasies as it was a willful pragmatic strategy aimed at finding land, economic security, social mobility, and power. Unveiling the historical, spatial, and relational contingencies of Afro-Barbadian identity shows the diversity of interests and events that shaped their ambitions. This configuration also illustrates historical, temporal, and spatially specific subjectivity of their ideas. Their rootedness in specific historical processes illuminates "the roads not taken and the limits of contemporaneous imaginations."[32] Within an ideological quagmire molded by the entanglements of race, imperialism, and modernity, Barbadians conceived of their relationship to Africa in general, and Liberia, in particular. This reflected the complex identity formation at the core of British imperial subjectivity in the Caribbean.

Afro-Barbadians projected their anxieties, ambitions, narcissistic and sadist impulses, and the masculine desires for dominance into messianic visions across the Atlantic with the same force that post-emancipation frustrations pushed them out of the Caribbean. In structuring their colonial project for Liberia, middle-class Afro-Barbadians increasingly modeled a novel form of bourgeoisie development that reproduced the conventional assumptions of British liberal subjecthood within the political practices of black nationalism.[33] As "children of Africa in the colonies," the West Indians saw themselves at the nexus of an Afro-European oppositional narrative that often defined encounters between the two continents. Driven by a sense of duty to British civilizing efforts and a racial obligation to African development, Afro-Barbadians on their journey found themselves being forced to divide their loyalty between building a respectable black nationality and aiding British imperial activities. On the journey across the Atlantic, the collective sum of all the practices the Afro-Barbadians had learned was far greater than any one part. The Afro-Barbadians' middle class imitated the behaviors of white colonialism and its patriarchal order. By embracing this logic of white supremacy and colonialism, Afro-Barbadians viewed themselves as the core of the future of African development and black racial advancement. Armed with the Western knowledge they deemed necessary to guide Africa into the new world order, Barbadians positioned themselves as the vanguard of modern Africa. They envisioned

---

[32] Holt, Thomas. "Marking: Race, Race-making, and the Writing of History." American Historical Review, Vol. 100, No. 1 (1995): 10.

[33] Ho, *Nation and Citizenship*, 22.

using their in-between status to secure more freedom and to create opportunities for the kinds of upward mobility that evaded them in the Caribbean via the debilitating constraints of racial prejudices. In these instances, the memory of slavery, racism, and colonialism worked to re-inscribe rather than ameliorate Afro-Barbadians' understanding of inequality and also shaped their intentions for a Liberian modernity constantly under the white gaze. Viewed from this vantage point, it was no wonder that Barbadians remained in a relationship with the British Empire or that they tried to resolve their unspoken issues by acting out the same patterns in their relationships to Africans, hoping that it would be different. The ensuing fragility of the Liberian colonization project rested on the complex ideas emanating from the various vantage points of the migrants who ended up there.

THE CHALLENGES OF AN IMAGINED BLACK COMMUNITY

Insofar as Barclay and the Barbadian migrants identified themselves with the class interests of the colonial elite, their ideology was detectible in ideals and principles visible within a broader sociocultural imaginary.[34] Barclay and other migrants obscured their efforts under a cover of black racial solidarity, while discounting their part as negotiators of political power who readily worked in a political landscape intended to oppress blacks. Yet, a most important aspect of the Barbadians' political vision was their commitment to black nationalism and pan-Africanism. Not only did they make emigration decisions from this vantage point, it further gave them social, religious, and political leverage. The formation and emergence of the emigration societies in Barbados intersected with the formative beginnings of a black nationalist and pan-Africanist movement.

The interest of Barbadian emigrants emerged out of interrelated ideas about the moral, social, and cultural development of African people. By their ontology and aesthetics, black nationalism and pan-Africanism as black liberation ideologies were responses to Western racism, discrimination, and subordination. At the time of Barbadian interest in Liberia, the concept of black nationalism, still very much in its infancy, drew the African diaspora together through the commonalities of oppression and strategies of liberation into a socio-political and economic contract. The ideologies grew to encapsulate the shared historical chain of oppressive experiences as well as a belief in the common destiny of African

[34] Ibid.

peoples wherever they happened to reside.[35] As sociopolitical worldviews, both were grounded in ideas of racial solidarity, self-determination, and cohesion with goals of social, economic, and political equality. As the ideology evolved, racial, political, and economic progress became its driving tenets.

Afro-Barbadians aboard the *Cora* were on a journey that would unite them with other members of the diaspora. Though emerging from different colonial projects, a shared Christian civilizing vision that they viewed as essential to the growth and modernity to Africa brought them together within pan-Africanism to Sierra Leone and Liberia. Though Barbadians empathized with African Americans, they could never quite fully appreciate their desires to flee the United States. The politics of location that differentially shaped their race, class, and gender identities through these forms of domination also separated them. Unlike African American loyalists in Nova Scotia, deported maroons in Sierra Leone, and slaves manumitted and sent to Liberia, Barclay, Wiles, and other Afro-Barbadians in the FUBES and BCL had experienced over thirty years of freedom prior to their emigration.

Though reasons driving emigration among different segments of the diaspora were not always the same, differences within black life were overlooked in the interest of a broader vision of racial uplift. The unspoken considerations, mutual cultural traditions, a shared sense of heritage and destiny, and a common language of racial similarity resonated between West Indians and African Americans.[36] Ideas about a common African heritage that routinely united African Americans and Barbadians in the diaspora served to create essentialized meanings of blackness. Over time, their complementary experiences morphed into their own language and created a sort of code that allowed both groups to view their life experiences as related. Indeed, the fight against slavery and the pursuit of freedom brought Barbadians, other West Indians, and African Americans together in a mutual cause. In 1829, in his "Appeal to the Colored Citizens of the World," David Walker linked pan-African impulses and a black ethos to form the ideological foundation of black nationalism in the nineteenth century.[37] Through his widely circulated

---

[35] Immanuel Geiss, "Pan-Africanism" *Journal of Contemporary History*, Vol. 4, No. 1 (1969): 187–200.

[36] Higginbotham, "African-American Women's History and The Metalanguage of Race," 274.

[37] Sterling Stuckey, *The Ideological Origins of Black Nationalism* (Boston, MA: Beacon Press, 1972); Sterling Stuckey, *Slave Culture: Nationalist Theory and the Foundations of Black America* (New York: Oxford University Press, 1987).

proclamation, Walker engaged not only African Americans but also the wider African diaspora. These kinds of relationships between different parts of the African diaspora that shaped their ideologies about freedom produced what Richard Blackett calls the "Hamic connection."[38] As ideas of black nationalism and pan-Africanism flowed through these channels of communication, they helped to rewrite concepts of belonging against the particularities of structural racism by expanding citizenship to a larger black community.[39]

Between the geographical divide, newspapers and other forms of communication that functioned as double-faced mirrors through which West Indians and African Americans examined themselves and other blacks created a degree of connectedness. In circulating a black Atlantic agenda, Afro-Barbadian newspapers participated within a larger public sphere to foster the appearance of a common goal and, as a consequence, often papered over differences between West Indians and African Americans. West Indian and African American "print culture" created an "imagined community" by generalizing issues to target a larger global black audience.[40] By using similar images and vernacular, the diasporic readership came to identify aspects of their life as a part of a larger collective. This allowed members of the African diaspora to develop a bond between their disparate communities and to plot a way forward collectively as well as forge a visible public voice. The editors used authorship discursively to forge a larger diasporic citizenship by establishing themselves as protagonists representative of the larger collective and by recasting blacks as parts of a larger visible unit.[41] Prescod and Douglass, who both played significant roles in the abolitionist and racial justice movements, came to represent the rise of individual authors who worked through these channels and acted as representations for a collective vessel of stories about racial oppression.[42]

The connections between different instantiations of black nationalism and pan-Africanism highlight ideological divisions that would find a place

---

[38] Richard J. M. Blackett, "The Hamic Connection: African Americans and the Caribbean, 1820–1865," in Brian L. Moore and Swithin R. Wilomot, eds., *Before and After 1865: Education, Politics and Regionalism in the Caribbean* (Kingston, Jamaica: Ian Randle, 1998), 318.

[39] Ibid.

[40] Benedict Anderson, *Imagined Communities. Reflections on the Origin and Spread of Nationalism* (Ithaca, NY: Cornell University Press, 1972).

[41] Ho, *Nation and Citizenship*, 22.

[42] Ibid.

in Liberia. The early black press conveyed the issues surrounding class conflicts within the black community.[43] In serving as "an instrument of social interpretation and caste domination," the press represented an elite class of people who translated issues in terms its black audiences could understand.[44] Along with the question of color, class responsibility to lead and instruct the race out of its social degradation became a leading attitude. Newspapers circulated the idea of Christianizing heathen Africans as part and parcel of a reductionist approach to black uplift. Economic aspects of the issues of assimilation, emigration, and colonization divided the different editors. Assimilationists believed that blacks would be considered citizens once they were able to build and acquire financial wealth. There was also an argument between Christian morality versus economic and political gains as the leading contributor to national development. Given their increasing significance, the divergent opinions of the press houses playing out in the public sphere fractured attempts at an alliance between different black communities.

Afro-Barbadians and African Americans shared other commonalities. Enslaved Africans in both places developed a profound but complicated relationship with Africa.[45] The connection between the diaspora and Africa had entered a slow fade after the Atlantic crossing but, other than the edifying currents created by detachment, no real breaks occurred between the diaspora and the continent. In the golden haze of distance, the sense of connection to Africa remained alive and real, figuring in the diaspora's efforts to sustain their humanity to survive. Africa came to occupy an ever-shifting place in the lives of different members of its diaspora. Against the strictures of their subjectivity, Barbadians, like African Americans and other West Indians, looked to Africa for a kinder form of belonging. Memory of the "homeland" inspired the emergence of a variegated political, cultural, and religious consciousness.[46]

Africa figured significantly in perceptions of black identity individually and collectively and in how different groups imagined their place in the world. Yet the particularities of African Americans and Caribbeans and their connections held history and consequence. With this, conflating African American and Caribbean identity within blackness would be

---

[43] Kinshasa, *Emigration Versus Assimilation*, 3.
[44] Ibid.
[45] See Claude Clegg, *Africa and the African American Imagination* (Chapel Hill: University of North Carolina Press, 2006).
[46] Ibid.

problematic. Pernicious forms of racism created by racial capitalism shaped both African Americans and West Indians as enslaved Africans. African Americans experienced slavery in particular systemic ways that shaped their ideas about Africa. Though oppressed, the differences in codes of operation differed from one place to the other and dictated the kinds of strategies that different sectors of the diaspora deployed to attain freedom. Thus, individual group determination forged through the constraints and particularities of place, different silos of information, and possibilities structured by the politics of race all shaped the ways in which ideas of Africa loomed in the imaginaries of different sectors of the diaspora as well as how it inhabited their different black identities.

The nature and configurations of power and culture in local diasporic sites disentangle the characteristics of subjectivity as an analytic separate from racial identity. The differences across societies and individuals outline the dissimilar ways in which racism functioned as both an aspect of structural dynamics and a source of meaning. The particular development and articulation of historical consciousness that were sometimes expressed in political demands, identity formation, and tactics across different spaces within the African diaspora also defined their subjectivity. Sociologists Michael Omi and Howard Winant use the term "racialization" to denote the projection of "racial meaning to a previously unclassified relationship, social practice or group." In many cases, the decision to either accept or contest meanings of race depended upon the ways those views were defined and who defined them. For Omi and Winant, the creation of racial identity develops from the ideas and struggles of contending political schemes and their desires to express parallel features inversely. As an unsteady and fragmented series of social meanings that frequently underwent transformation through political struggle, the uniqueness of social, economic, and political forces served to control the substance and significance of racial identities.[47] These are consistently reconstructed, repeated, and reassigned in connection to new systems of accumulation. Understanding the diaspora from their points of subjectivity reveals its numerous groups operating at different levels of "blackness."

The outlines and layers that created the resultant trans-local cumulative blackness that converged in Liberia were forged in the dialectic between inside and outside forces that diverged across diasporic

---

[47] Michael Omi and Howard Winant, *Racial Formation in the United States*, 3rd ed. (New York: Routledge, 2015), 13–19.

communities. The development of cultural belonging by exchanging symbolic or material meanings created identities and memories through specific traditions and rituals. In the creation of these dynamics, Barbados, in many ways, functioned as an exception to the Caribbean rule.[48] From its very inception, as the launching point for British imperial efforts in the Americas, Barbados boasted a substantial population of whites who exercised violent forms of prejudices. By contrast, the establishment of the United States as a white settler society relied on ideology, law, and social relations to assert dominance over blacks. Though the British launched the basis of controlling slaves from Barbados, the island lacked equitable amounts of white settlers to necessitate the kinds of laws that secured status. Still, the realities of the significant enslaved populations in Barbados and Virginia necessitated comprehensive slave codes. In South Carolina, a black majority and vested white settler interests meant draconian slave codes. Thus, in the Caribbean, enslaved Africans were said to be "cogs in the machine," whereas in the United States they were the productive and reproductive machine.[49]

Through laws across different states, blackness in the United States came to be defined by the one-drop rule. For instance, a 1662 act noted that "some doubts have arisen whether children got by any Englishmen upon a Negro shall be slave or Free" and so "be it therefore enacted ... that all children born in this country shall be held bond or free only according to the condition of the mother."[50] Thus, an African American black identity was experienced within the compounding effects of being property, the rejection of political rights, slavery, and violent extermination that did the work of creating white supremacy, leaving little room on the hierarchy for other types of blackness.[51] While Barbados circulated racial codes through its white population to other areas in the British Empire, the kinds of absenteeism that prevailed in West Indian colonies buffered the effects of the racialization process that created a black identity there.[52] In many places across the Caribbean and in US states such as

---

[48] See Jenny Shaw, *Everyday Life in the Early English Caribbean: Irish, Africans, and the Construction of Difference* (Athens: University of Georgia Press, 2013).

[49] See Richard S. Dunn, *A Tale of two Plantations: Slave Life and Labor in Jamaica and Virginia* (Cambridge, MA: Harvard University Press, 2014), 324.

[50] "Laws on Slavery," *Virtual Jamestown*, www.virtualjamestown.org/laws1.html#4.

[51] Dunn, *A Tale of Two Plantations*, 13.

[52] Keith Mason, "The Absentee Planter and the Key Slave: Privilege, Patriarchalism, and Exploitation in the Early Eighteenth-Century Caribbean," *The William and Mary Quarterly*, Vol. 70, No. 1 (2013): 79–102.

Louisiana, free coloreds and blacks were given special privileges. Indeed, many came to occupy a separate and cherished rung on the white supremacist hierarchy.

Similarly, the machinations of racial exclusion worked differently across Caribbean societies for other reasons. The making of imperial English subjects differed in terms of how the nation-state as a body politic was constituted and the ways in which rights and responsibilities of citizenship were claimed. The governing rules in the British Empire rendered anyone born within the lands and territories as a crown subject. In the British nationality, subjecthood created a personal vertical link between the subject and the monarch through rights and duties. The natural-born subject came to owe loyalty and fidelity to the king or queen.[53] Though enslaved Africans were subjects, they were largely excluded from rights by race. Though free Afro-Barbadians could claim the rights of subjecthood by appealing to the monarchy for protection and reprieve, they often were treated as third-class citizens.[54] Contrarily, following the Revolutionary War with Britain, the United States severed ties with British forms of belonging. By moving from the idea of natural allegiance to naturalization, the United States shifted from subjecthood to citizenship. Naturalized individuals became members of the body politic through their will as well as an expressed consent to the rule of the government.[55] After the revolution, the United States moved to deprive Africans, enslaved and free, of the very same equality and rights they had gone to war for by rooting their conception of citizenship in republican ideology. The Naturalization Act of 1790 that served as a key feature in constructing the US nationality excluded blacks of all classes. The horizontal definition of citizenship in the United States depended on communities of shared loyalties and commitments. This dependence on recognition from fellow citizens who held pre-determined ideas about race created a constant daily assault on African Americans with little outlets for reprieve. Thus, while the Dred Scott ruling rendered African Americans non-citizens, imperial views, policies, and techniques of

---

[53] Thomas Hennessy, *Dividing Ireland: World War One and Partition* (London: Routledge, 1998), xv.
[54] Trevor O'Reggio, *Between Alienation and Citizenship: The Evolution of Black West Indian Society in Panama, 1914–1964* (Lanham, MD: University Press of America, 2006), 34.
[55] Rieko Karatani, *Defining British Citizenship: Empire, Commonwealth and Modern Britain* (Abingdon: Routledge, 2002), 17.

government that informed the political development of the Caribbean shaped the ways in which Barbadians experienced the key pillars of modernity.

As West Indians and African Americans negotiated the problems of race in efforts to find solutions to the problems of freedom, the particularities of diasporic experience shaped what each group desired from freedom and their subsequent approach. The divergent institutional, ideological, and economic factors within their sociopolitical contexts mediated the push-and-pull factors that drove African American and Barbadian emigration to Liberia. The differing forms of subjectivity inevitably produced differing motives, visions of freedom, and emigration trajectories. In addition to their different socioeconomic, political, and cultural factors, the Afro-Barbadians interested in Liberia, unlike their African American counterparts, were not emigrating from a slave society. A desire to escape slavery, attempts to flee violence, and racial discrimination drove African American emigration and pan-African and black nationalist interests. On the other hand, Barbadian Anglophile pan-Africanists were seeking respectability and an elevation in their status as well as that of the race.

Not only had Barbadians experienced freedom for almost thirty years before the abolition of slavery in the United States, but their emigration to Liberia was largely a self-generated, voluntary initiative that emerged in a British imperial, post-emancipation context. This placed post-emancipation circumstances surrounding labor, material freedom, and respectability at the forefront of Barbadians' pan-African considerations and decisions to emigrate. In Barbados, both the universalistic and particularistic impulses in black nationalism combined to create motivations for emigration to Liberia, resulting in similar kinds of contradictions. The imperialist framework in which Barbadians combined religious virtues with their political and economic ambitions complicated their pan-Africanist visions. Balancing the tension between the two often proved difficult. Barbadians came to an understanding of freedom and free labor as defined by Whig liberalism, which figured in their visions of Liberian nation building as well as their efforts to reconstitute themselves as self-owning beings. The effects of British racial subjectivity and colonialism on their ideology were already evident in their consciousness as middle-class Afro-Barbadians. These underlying differences in motive and purpose distinguished Afro-Barbadian reasons to emigrate from those of African Americans, and marked their ideological locations within pan-Africanism and black nationalism.

African American and West Indian interests in Liberia underscore the incoherence in Black nationalism and pan-Africanism. While African Americans had been seared in ways that drove them to black nationalism and an interest in Liberia, West Indians' understanding remained around the vagaries and vagueness of racial identity. As Stuart Hall notes, "the problem of ideology is to give an account, within materialistic theory, of how social ideas arise."[56] These details within Black nationalism and pan-Africanism and their outlines and meanings were neglected for a veneer, reduced to forge collective racial power. That emigration meant different things to African Americans and West Indians and was used to fulfill different needs speaks to the complexities within black nationalism and pan-Africanism. When embraced by different sectors of the diaspora, pan-African and black nationalist ideologies did not amount to a contract between equals as believed. There was much imbalance between the parties involved because the economic systems of colonialism and imperialism in their societies had oppressed them by placing them into social classes.

Different groups developed their own consciousness regarding their racial location that conformed to or rejected their colonial and slaveholder expectations. As such, groups across the African diaspora did not have the same understandings of black nationalism and pan-Africanism or even the means to negotiate their relationship to Africa or blackness on equal terms. While some groups had an ability to forge their own path, others did not. This would shape perceptions of civilization, structure migrants' place in the republic's hierarchy, and play a role in determining the groups' coexistence in Liberia and how outsiders, especially missionaries and colonizationists, would view them. Black nationalist and pan-African ideologies assiduously glossed over the imbalances in bargaining power, knowledge, and influence of different sectors of Africa and the diaspora. They developed a flexibility by adjusting to the different sectors of black life, choosing parts of the ideology to suit their needs. An inability to balance racial communalism with discrete motives rendered these ideologies unable to move from theory to praxis. Whether lofty pan-Africanist ideals could stand up to the realities of life in Liberia depended on a willingness to adjust. Resolving these kinds of tensions would be necessary to achieve more functionality.

[56] Stuart Hall, "The Problem of Ideology: Marxism without Guarantees," in David Morley and Kuan-Hsing Chen, eds., *Stuart Hall: Critical Dialogues in Cultural Studies* (Abingdon: Routledge: 1986), 27–46.

The Barbadians' political and socio-economic drive shaped their divergent visions for Africa. Many migrants to Liberia identified themselves with the petite bourgeoisie group of quasi-capitalist pan-Africanists. The British imperial heritage which undercut Barbadians' sense of diasporic identification with Africa meant that in addition to developing connections to Africa in ways similar to African Americans, Barbadians also embraced and asserted racial ideologies as long as they supported their ends or served their meanings of achieving freedom. In addition to viewing Africa through British imperialism, Afro-Barbadian pan-Africanism was also a realpolitik that emerged from the push-and-pull of post-emancipation. More importantly, however, as stated in letters to the ACS, the emigration societies placed themselves within a variety of black self-help respectability capitalism.

NEARLY THERE

On the Caribbean coast, more than three thousand miles separated the Barbadians from their destination. The implications of their arrival in Liberia raised questions among those on the other side. Many wondered whether the Barbadians would do well and show themselves as valuable to the republic as African Americans. The ACS considered the possible impact of the Barbadian emigrants on account of their perceptions of the level of civilization of the families and individuals in the group. In these assessments, their experiences as British subjects, which served to distinguish them from other Liberian emigrants, forecasted the kinds of fractious issues that would later prove ruinous to the nation-building project.[57] As the ship inched forward towards the Atlantic's edge, it brought the Barbadians closer to their missionary objectives. Had Afro-Barbadians turned to look back at the Caribbean, they might have been reminded of the closer regional destinations that aligned with their understandings of post-slavery free labor and afforded economic and social opportunities. That they managed to keep their gaze focused on the African landscape ahead of them displayed their dogged sense of determination.

The sentimentality of the journey and enormity of the task ahead loomed large aboard the *Brig Cora*. Positioned within a liminal Atlantic space, the middle passage became symbolic of a fractured Afro-Barbadian identity but also laid bare the heaviness of their metaphysical baggage on

[57] *The African Repository*, Vol. 41 (1865): 118–122.

the open sea. The willingness to forgo life in the Caribbean and to risk the disease and death of an Atlantic crossing illustrated the Barbadians' lack of confidence in a Caribbean future but also the sense of duty to both the British Empire and Africa. Though the Barbadians had faith in their civilizing abilities, some still fretted about the perils of going to Africa. Africanus, himself, shrugged off this concern, reasoning that "if some of us perish through the blissful influence of climate in our attempts to build for ourselves a temple of liberty, we will die with the consoling reflection that our race will reap the benefits of our martyrdom in their cause."[58] In a journey to Liberia that transmuted "old discourses of filiation that were fraught with contents of the British colonial baggage," it also created an outlet that magnified the longings and suppressed voices of Afro-Barbadian colonial subjects.[59] That British imperialistic designs for blacks on both sides of the Atlantic would, in a sense, be derailed, mattered less. Like with other nationalist undertakings, they viewed the cause of African restoration as worthy of the noble act of self-sacrifice. Afro-Barbadians' efforts to find freedom, albeit under British imperial auspices, ultimately restructured post-slavery plans and brought uniformity to the transatlantic abolitionist campaign. Their presence in the African civilization project meant blacks would be at the center of orchestrating their freedom.

[58] Ibid.
[59] Sandiford, *Theorizing a Colonial Caribbean-Atlantic Imaginary*, 54–55.

PART III

AFRICAN LIBERATION

5

Barbadian Arrival and Social Integration in Liberia

After thirty-four days of travel, sighting the African coast gave the Barbadian migrants some reason to look towards their future. As the shoreline of the Liberian coast rose to meet the arrival of the *Brig Cora*'s Barbadian passengers, the seemingly irredeemably conflict-ridden Caribbean fell away as they looked forward to the new frontiers of freedom and their desires for a better life. One passenger, John Padmore bitterly complained that "we would have reached here sooner, but we met with nearly eight days' calm." On May 10, 1865, one Liberian reporter celebrated the successful journey of *Brig Cora*, noting "All who left Barbados in her reached Africa alive; there was not a single death on board during the passage!"[1] (See Figure 5.2)

The movement of ships on the Atlantic and their successful arrival remained critical to Liberia's existence. They played a significant role in replenishing the migrants necessary for the colony's survival amid hostile indigenes, a persisting transatlantic slave trade, and European colonial speculators. By bringing people from different places of origin, ships persistently orchestrated changes in Liberia's demography, altered its social and political landscape, and transformed the nation into a multi-ethnic space.[2] Ships also became important social markers in other ways. The type of ship on which migrants arrived and their time of arrival significantly determined their subsequent place in the republic's socio-political order (See Figure 5.1). Liberia had been accustomed to the

---

[1] *The African Repository*, Vol. 42 (1865): 37.
[2] Jehudi Ashmun, ed., *The African Intelligencer*, Vol. 1, No. 1, July 1820. Rare Books and Special Collections Division. Library of Congress.

VESSELS.	SAILED FROM.	TIME OF SAIL-ING.	NUMBER OF EMIGRANTS.
Barque Greyhound........	New York	January 16, '65.	1
Brig M. A. Benson........	Boston	February 9, '65.	1
Brig Cora	Barbados	April 6, 1865.	346
Barque Thomas Pope.....	New York..........	June 3, 1865.	7
Schooner H. P. Russell..	Baltimore............	November 4,'65.	172
			527

FIGURE 5.1: *The African Repository*'s Record of Migrant Ships to Liberia in 1865
Source: *The African Repository*, Vol. 42 (1866): 35

arrivals of African American mainlanders. As such, the coming of the Barbadians took on a spirit of uncertainty.

Nonetheless, upon arrival, Barclay and the other Barbadians joined a broad cross section of black migrants who had arrived in Liberia under varying conditions of un-freedom as a result of overlapping, yet different socio-political and economic forces within an Atlantic world.[3] This included Africans Americans and African recaptives who were Africans liberated from slave ships (hereafter liberated Africans or African recaptives). African indigenes of various ethnicities were themselves migrants but had long lived in the area, before European arrival, to trade grains and, later, slaves. With the Barbadians' arrival, four groups – with different experiences of oppression and brutality shaping their paths to Liberia – met to envision a common future. West Indians, African Americans, African recaptives, and indigenes collided in the Liberian nation-building project, making the West African coast a black multicultural space with multiple voices and visions.

A spirit of pan-Africanism and black nationalist solidarity and the common experience of racial oppression in the diaspora had been the unifying forces for African Americans and West Indians. Yet the migrants' embrace of Liberia as a black nation and its much-heralded end to the artificial borders imposed by slavery, imperialism, and diaspora led to unintended consequences. Whereas the struggle in the diaspora was between races, the arrival of the various migrant streams in Liberia

---

[3] See Alexander Byrd, *Captives and Voyagers: Black Migrants Across the Eighteenth-Century British Atlantic World* (Baton Rouge: Louisiana State University Press, 2008).

FIGURE 5.2: Memorial of the Barbadians' Arrival
Source: Photograph by Matthew C. Reilly

created a new milieu that nurtured intra-racial rivalry among ethnic identities. As disparate strangers gathered under the umbrella of the nation state, Liberia both dissolved the issues of diaspora and magnified them. Distance had created a mirage of simple unity. The real differences became pronounced only upon arrival when experience replaced rhetoric, thus challenging the process that shaped racial identities. After settling, each group tended to operate within their networks and traditions, or opportunistically allied with others. This created dynamics that reinforced the processes of designation and difference.

West Indians and African Americans who had endured similar experiences of slavery, emancipation, and diaspora allied with each other on the basis of various ideological and socio-religious beliefs. As a part of the African diasporas from similar areas, they shared language, traditions, and culture. Within these practices, a selective kind of black typology that was preferred emerged. What also unified African Americans and West Indians in Liberia was a shared culture of blackness. Both Caribbeans and African Americans could find a place in the language of blackness that the Liberian nation state mobilized to their benefit. Such narrow racially tribal groups of migrants and their myopic political vision had no place for uncivilized and unrespectable Negroes. While understandings of blackness were created on the backs of Africans, civilized blackness emerged from the initiatives of diasporic migrants. The architecture of the hierarchy within blackness was built in such a way that Africans were permanently at the bottom to act as a platform for not only whites but also the diaspora. Through the process of valorization, each group of black migrants was assigned a value based on other races. By virtue of the cemented status of Africans on the bottom of the hierarchy, diasporic migrants were evaluated against them as well as from their relative position to whites. These practices of making blackness deployed methods to achieve hegemony over recaptives and indigenes who had not gone through the full experiences of slavery and life in Western society.

Although migration to Liberia linked the fates of similarly oppressed black people, it did not automatically forge collective bonds of solidarity. The way in which labor rendered certain migrants visible in Liberia suggests that it being broadly defined played an important role in constituting the cultural meaning of migrant identities, in particular, and of blackness, in general. An invisible screen of "civilization" separated migrants of the diaspora from indigenes and recaptives. Experiences of enslavement pointed to the affluence of black immigrant life in Liberia. This new ethic resulted in the emergence of social ascriptions and nomenclature that would be politicized and mobilized in establishing intergroup relationships as well as relationships with the state. Both practices are important for what they reveal about who fell outside the bounds of "civilized" modern blackness. The social segregation of the different communities, reinforced by geographic lines and nomenclature within the social system, created a self-perpetuating, privileged group. Increased distinctiveness in the social sphere ultimately crushed abolitionist, colonizationist, black nationalist, and pan-Africanist expectations that Liberian nation building would help blacks overcome the inter-ethnic hostilities that had served the slave trade and black oppression.

MIGRANTS AND THE TRANSFORMATION OF LIBERIA

The Barbadians' arrival was a generative but also destabilizing moment. Liberian officials struggled to make sense of what to do with them. As the Barbadians were not the customary African American migrants, Liberian officials marked their arrival differently. More Barbadians arrived aboard the *Cora* on May 10, 1865, than were initially anticipated. They reported that rather than the expected 333, the ship's captain arrived with 346 healthy people. This was 46 more than the FUBES and BCL representatives had arranged for with the ACS and 13 more than answered to their names when called prior to the sailing of the vessel. The extra Barbadians, numbering 26 more than the berths provided for on board, had made for crowded conditions on the ship.[4] On May 13, President Daniel Warner wrote a letter acknowledging the arrival of "Captain William Henderson of the *brig Cora* ... bringing to us a company of emigrants from the Island of Barbados."[5] Though the ACS had debated its constitutional provisions in extending Liberian emigration to the Caribbean, differences of history and origins still hung over the heads of the arriving Barbadians. Warner noted that "they were sent under the auspices of the ACS, but owing to the people being from a country not included in the constitutional provisions of the Society, but more particularly on account of the high prices of provisions, the usual six months of supplies were not furnished them."[6] Because they were not African Americans, the Barbadians were viewed and treated differently. In spite of the unequal treatment, Barclay and the other Barbadians who had experienced an uncomfortable Atlantic crossing were now determined to find and realize their post-emancipation aspirations.

---

[4] *The African Repository*, Vol. 42 (1866): 37.
[5] Ibid.
[6] Daniel Warner Annual Message to the Legislature December 11, 1865 in Dunn, ed., *The Annual Messages of the Presidents of Liberia 1848–2010*, 190.

The Barbadians' arrival made for much spectacle and fanfare on the Monrovia docks. Even as the Afro-Barbadian migrants had considered Liberia to be "a more auspicious shore," Liberian officials were equally enthusiastic in hailing the Barbadians' arrival "as highly auspicious for the future welfare of Liberia and the civilization of Africa."[7] Such enthusiasm was, however, tempered. After their arrival, President Warner observed: "My opinion of the Barbadians is that they will do well, and will prove as valuable an acquisition to the country as the same number of the American population that have come into it have done. On this question, there is amongst us a variety of opinion – some favoring the American side of the question; others the West Indian side."[8] For Warner, this moment of uncertainty signaled concerns about potential national instability. Arrival erased previous ways of knowing blackness. Warner's speech signified efforts to identify distinctions between African Americans and West Indians and inscribed ethnicity as a new frame of reference. To more fully understand the competitive logics that framed Warner's perception of the relationship between African Americans and West Indians, it is helpful to outline the ways in which such perceptions held meaning for not only experiences of citizenship and nationhood but also meanings of blackness.

Indeed, the story of Liberian colonization changed dramatically as other groups of blacks, racialized in ways that converged as well as diverged from the African American experience, joined in the nation-building process. A period of seasoning after arrival that often resulted in death featured strongly in the stories of the different migrants, regardless of origin. During this seasoning period, the different groups assembled ad hoc materials to survive. Their encounters with climate and disease created an additional "middle passage" that shaped their collective experiences, served to alienate them from their former identities, thus preparing them for their new Liberian identity. This process of seasoning and settling, however, involved a new racial logic that excluded natives and recaptives. Given the horrors that often haunted these kinds of transatlantic journeys, Warner celebrated the Barbadians' successful crossing of the Atlantic. "They are all landed, three hundred and forty-six in number, not one having died on the passage out." But having survived the terror of the sea, Barbadians now faced the difficult period of seasoning and adjustment. One observer noted: "They had to pass through as severe an ordeal of acclimation in the fever as any

---

[7] *The African Repository*, Vol. 41(1865): 247.
[8] *The African Repository*, Vol. 42 (1866): 38.

company that ever came from the United States. As they came from the tropics, we cannot account for this fact." Luckily, by the time of their arrival, new methods of receiving and settling migrants saved them from the mass fatalities caused by overexposure to the rainy season and the accompanying mosquito swarms that the African American pioneers had to endure.[9] The Barbadians would later be "consigned to Mr. Henry W. Dennis, the Society's Agent at Monrovia who was instructed to transfer them to the authorities of Liberia."[10]

The former president J. J. Roberts's letter to the colonization society reflecting on the Barbadians' arrival showed the changing concerns of Liberian officials. Roberts noted, "Mr. Dennis will, of course, write you fully all about the Barbadians; how they have been, and are now getting on; the numbers of deaths, etc." Having observed the social and material conditions of the new West Indian migrants, he pointed out: "A large majority of these people arrived here wholly destitute – except the limited supplies furnished them by American Colonization Society – much less, as you are doubtless aware, than the support usually allowed to emigrants from the United States." Roberts assigned the blame to the Barbadians: "as I understand they persisted and prevailed upon Mr. McClain though he cautioned them against it, to permit a much larger number to embark than he had the means of amply providing for." As such, "[t]he consequence is that when they were taken down with fever, nearly the whole of their supplies had been expended; and the government was not able to afford them adequate relief." African Americans reached out to help the West Indian newcomers as the common illnesses of settling set upon them, filling in spaces where the government failed. Roberts reported that many Liberian citizens "have done what they could to relieve their most pressing necessities. I am told that those who are settled at Harrisburg, and in the neighborhood of Careysburg, are well pleased with the country, and [with] the prospect of making themselves comfortable."[11]

The four other migrant ships the ACS sent to Liberia that same year showed the bold outlines of the diversity among Liberia migrants. On January 16, Nicholas Augustus, a blacksmith from the Caribbean island

[9] See Claude Clegg, *The Price of Liberty: African Americans and the Making of Liberia* (Chapel Hill: University of North Carolina Press, 2004); Mark Harrison, "'The Tender Frame of Man': Disease, Climate, and Racial Difference in India and the West Indies, 1760–1860." *Bulletin of the History of Medicine*, Vol. 70, No. 1 (1996): 68–93.

[10] *The African Repository*, Vol. 41 (1865): 37.

[11] J. J. Roberts to the Colonization Society, August 19, 1865. Svend Holsoe Collection. Accessed at the Barbados Museum and Historical Society, Barbados.

of St. Thomas who had "worked his passage to New York on the ship *Theresa*," traveled to Liberia on the *Barque Greyhound*.[12] The following month, John Blyden, a steam-engine boilermaker (and brother of Edward Blyden, Liberia's secretary of state), noted for his experience of having "survived ten months as a fireman in the U.S. Navy," sailed from Boston to Liberia in the *Brig M.A. Benson*.[13] John Blyden and Nicholas Augustus were friends, both being from the same Caribbean Island. Their relationship points to the web of social, familial, and political connections that defined nineteenth-century transatlantic migratory networks and relationships in Liberia. Having paid their way to New York, the ACS assisted with their voyage to Liberia. In a Liberian colonization movement previously dominated by African Americans, the migration of the two islanders was as atypical as the arrival of the 346 Barbadians.[14]

Given earlier trends, the migration in May of 172 African Americans from the Baltimore port on the schooner *H.P. Russell* was unsurprising. Legislation in the 1860s had made life unbearable for free blacks in Maryland and Virginia. They left under the auspices of the Lynchburg Emigration Society (LES), which had been founded in 1825 as a chapter of the larger ACS. The LES publicized their goals as "aiding and promoting ... the amelioration of the conditions of free persons of colour in the United States by resettling them in Liberia."[15] Mostly Baptists, the emigrants had been a part of a class of freedmen from Lynchburg, Virginia, who were known to be "agriculturalists and mechanics of experience and business character."[16] John McNuckles, the leader of their emigration movement, was described by colonizationists as "a man of unusual shrewdness and practical good sense, a master plasterer and bricklayer, possessing the confidence and regard of the entire community in which he lived, and from which he removed to Africa."[17] The circumstances under which these emigrants departed Maryland, and their experiences and practical skills, projected some sense of the future they expected to find in Liberia and also marked them as much different than the Barbadians.

---

[12] *The African Repository*, Vol. 42 (1865): 35.

[13] John Tracy to William McLain, September 26, 1864, in the Svend Holsoe Collection, Blue Folder: University of Indiana, Bloomington.

[14] See Caree Banton, "Who is Black in a Black Republic," in *Race and Nation in the Age of Emancipations*, Whitney Nell Stewart and John Garrison Marks, eds. (Athens: University of Georgia Press, 2017).

[15] *The African Repository*, Vol. 42 (1865): 35.

[16] Ted Delaney and Phillip Wayne Rhodes, *Free Blacks of Lynchburg, Virginia, 1805–1865* (Lynchburg, VA: Warwick House Pub, 2001), 24.

[17] *The African Repository*, Vol. 42 (1866): 35.

The other states that served as points of departure for African Americans fostered a more abstract imagination about life in Liberia. On June 3, 1865, seven emigrants left New York on the ship *Greyhound*. Among them was Daniel Walker from Carbondale, Pennsylvania, and Henry W. Johnson, his mixed-race wife, Patience, and their children, who were from New York.[18] Johnson was born in Vermont but moved to Canandaigua, New York, where he resided for over twenty years.[19] He had been a barber for many years, but according to the ACS, "in the face of obstacles such as would turn back a man of more ordinary perseverance, Mr. Johnson acquired a knowledge of law, and was admitted to practice in the Supreme Court of New York."[20] In clarifying what motivated individuals like Johnson to emigrate, colonizationists pointed out that "Mr. Johnson removed to Liberia, believing that in that field he can accomplish more for the political and social equality of his race than in America." New African American migrants, especially the skilled and professional, were always a welcome sight in Liberia. In a letter to Alexander Crummell, who had at one time served as the governor of Maryland in Liberia, one settler announced the arrival of the Johnsons.[21] Johnson himself spoke glowingly of his "pleasant voyage of thirty-six days" in a letter to a relative. Having to grapple with sickness and disease, migrants' imagination and expectations about life in Liberia did not always match their experiences on arrival, but an African American identity often predetermined social acceptance. As Johnson pointed out, "no incident happened during the journey, and we have been kindly treated by all the prominent citizens of Monrovia."[22]

In 1865, as the five ships arrived in the Monrovia harbor filled with different migrants hoping for all the rights and privileges of citizenship, efforts to counteract the "Second Slavery" had been transforming Liberia.[23] British and American ships routinely deposited African recaptives rescued

---

[18] Pennsylvania Colonization Society. Meeting Minutes from October 10, 1864 to March 13, 1877, http://www.lincoln.edu/library/specialcollections/society/1864-1877.pdf.

[19] See Preston E. Pierce, *Liberian Dreams, West African Nightmare: The Life of Henry W. Johnson, Part Two* (Rochester, NY: Office of the City Historian, 2005), 8.

[20] *The African Repository*, Vol. 42 (1866): 35.

[21] H. D Brown to Alexander Crummell, Monrovia August 20, 1865. Alexander Crummell Letters. Schomburg Collection, New York Public Library. New York.

[22] Ibid.

[23] For more on the "Second Slavery," the resurgence of the slave trade in the 1840s, and the campaign to abolish the Atlantic slave trade, see: Dale Tomich and Michael Zueske, eds., "The Second Slavery: Mass Slavery, World-Economy, and Comparative Microhistories, Part II." *Special Issue. Review: A Journal of the Fernand Braudel Center*, Vol. 31, No. 3 (2008): 251–437.

from the Atlantic slave trade onto Liberia's shores in the 1860s, making African recaptives yet another dimension of Liberian immigration. One report from Liberia, marveling at the alarming rate at which recaptives poured into the republic, noted: "Several years since there were nearly 5,000 Congoes rescued from slave ships by American men-of-war who were landed at Liberia." Unlike African American and West Indian emigrants, recaptives were not always a welcome addition. An African America Liberian official frowned at "the alarming influx of savages landed from American cruisers in our midst within a few weeks or months," who would have to be "civilized and [make] a profession of religion."[24] The identification of recaptives as the "other" from the outset became one of the several discursive exercises in ethnic identity-making and social stratification in Liberia.

LIBERIAN COLONIZATION AND INDIGENOUS ERASURE

As they had done at every other turn in their lives thus far, the Barbadians were going to have to learn to adjust. In Liberia, this began with the establishment of their settlement, a ritual of arrival and encounter that every migrant had to endure. The prospects of land on which to build their homes, to better themselves, and to help forge a successful black nation had partly enticed Barbadians to migrate to Liberia. As was customary, rather than becoming a part of the established migrant communities, Barbadians were allotted land on which to create their own distinct community. In a letter to relatives back home, John Padmore outlined that "the president has directed that our lands of twenty-five acres shall be laid off on Monday 16th on Carysburg road, which is the best locality for us."[25] The Barbadians now had land, a commodity that had been scarce and beyond their reach in post-emancipation Barbados. Liberian officials knew that land would give the Barbadians a stake in the nation and that it would be an important link to their freedom and citizenship. By acquiring their land and fulfilling one of their dreams of emancipation, the Barbadians began to fashion themselves as Liberians, building their homes and remaking themselves into commercial and subsistence farmers. The ACS exercised an essential feature of colonialism by naming the Barbadian settlement Crozierville after Samuel and John P. Crozer, Philadelphian colonizationists who had accompanied the first group of

---

[24] *The African Repository*, Vol. 41 (1865): 355.
[25] Ibid., 243.

African American emigrants to Liberia in 1820 and had contributed significantly to the Barbadians' migratory efforts.[26]

Once they had settled in, Barbadians upon arrival were quickly given what they sought in Liberia. John R. Padmore (born in 1826), a planter at the time the *Cora* left Barbados, wrote to a Mr. B. (possibly London Bourne) to note his family's arrival in Monrovia. Padmore recalled the kind reception during the Barbadian contingent meeting with the Liberian president, and that they even had the honor of having a glass of wine with him in the State Hall. Of the Barbadians who had departed before the *Cora*, driven by the same migratory impulse, Padmore noted that "Mr. W[orrel] and wife and Mr. and Mrs. G arrived three days before us; all the others are at Sierra Leone. We are very comfortable; and except a slight cold, all are quite well."[27] Padmore had no regrets. In fact, he noted, "Liberia is a great place." He promised to write soon again with more details about the African continent.

The *Brig Cora*'s arrival from Barbados in 1865 was another in a long line of arrivals that, over time, had given the republic shape and form and established a different sense of place. In 1821, the first ship, *Elizabeth*, arrived on the Liberia coast with some eighty-six African American emigrants, three white officials, and supplies to plant a settlement at Sherbo Island in Sierra Leone.[28] A voyage born simultaneously out of benevolence and racism, it represented a kind of perverse logic, circumscribed by the colonial sentiments of the white savior shining a light on the uncivilized. The new black migrants' inherited a Western social identity, inscribed in their skin, their religion, and their labor, which would be passed on to Africans through the civilization learned in the West.[29] Slave trading, representing the very creation of the returning diaspora, lingered along the coastline. Legend has it that as the *Elizabeth*, hailed as "the Mayflower of Liberia," off-loaded the pioneers to their new land of liberty, slave ships could be seen loading their human cargo.[30] With the slave trade still flourishing, the emigrants had not entirely escaped its traumas, physically or psychologically.

That Liberian society had long been entrenched in migration before the arrival of the various diasporic groups under nineteenth-century

---

[26] "Crozierville Past and Present," *The Crozierville Observer*, September 10, 1903.
[27] Ibid.
[28] See Bronwen Everill, *Abolition and Empire in Sierra Leone and Liberia* (Palgrave Macmillan, New York, 2013).
[29] Morgan, *American Slavery, American Freedom*, 56.
[30] Ibid.

colonization, abolition, and pan-Africanist projects, highlights the kinds of migration that would be seen as critical in making the new civilized blackness.[31] To be sure, African Americans, West Indians, and recaptives had arrived in a migrant society long established by a multiplicity of African ethnicities on the western African coastline.[32] Migrants from the Mande, Kwa, and Mel linguistic groups occupied the area around the Grain Coast following the breakdown of a number of Empires on the continent.[33] The Mande group, from the interior of what is now Ivory Coast and Ghana, was one of the first African ethnic groups to settle in the area. Overcrowding drove migrants from north-central Africa, who had initially settled in the hinterlands, to the coast. The Vais also came to the area after the collapse of the Mali Empire and the disruption in the salt trade.[34] The Kru, who were a seafaring people, were also present in the area and quickly mounted an attack against the encroaching newcomers.[35] Prominent among incoming groups were the Vai people, who had invented an alphabet and spoke Arabic and English. Kwa-speaking ethnic groups who occupied the southern half of present-day Liberia included the Bassa, who would become the largest group of ethnic Liberians in Monrovia. Other groups included the Grebo, De Belleh, and Krahn, who all partitioned the area into several kingdoms. They vested political power in chieftaincies, which made citizenship horizontally defined through kinship groups. Altogether, these ethnic groups spoke more than a dozen languages. That English eventually became the official language of Liberia was thus a testament to imperial power dynamics rather than demography.

Predating the arrival of the diaspora, state formation among different ethnic groups in the area had established an indigenous way of being with which the new migrants would have to contend. The different ethnic groups lived in the area between the Lofa and

---

[31] See Frederick Starr, *Liberia: Description, History, Problems* (Chicago, 1913), 7.

[32] See Harry Hamilton Johnston and Otto Stapf, *Liberia* (London: Hutchinson, 1906).

[33] Very little historical material exists on the various ethnic groups that inhabited Liberia in the early nineteenth century. Though the records of the colonizing organizations are problematic, they remain as some of the only sources of this scarce archive. See Bai T. Moore, *Liberian Culture at a Glance: A Review of the Culture and Customs of the Different Ethnic Groups in the Republic of Liberia* (Monrovia: Ministry of Information, Cultural Affairs & Tourism, 1979).

[34] *The Lagos Weekly Record*, November 9, 1896.

[35] Jane Martin, "Kru men 'Down the Coast': Liberian Migrants on the West African Coast in the 19th and early 20th centuries," *International Journal of African Historical Studies*, Vol. 18 (1995): 401–423.

St. Paul Rivers. In 1819, walking along the coast as far as Grand Bassa, J. B. Coates, a member of the Church Missionary Society (CMS) from Sierra Leone, observed that the Dei were concentrated in the coastal areas, living in small huts where they engaged in boiling salt. Just above the Lofa River was a state headed by "Zolu Duma, also called King Peter and Peter Careful by Europeans." It was alleged that King Peter's power extended over most of the Southwestern Gola people to the north of the river, possibly some of the Gola to the south and the Vai in the Gawula and Tombe areas. The settlement of various African ethnic groups that came to inhabit Liberia was in many ways dictated by the geography. European observers noted that King Peter also seemed to have some control over the Dei area.[36] The Lofa River appeared, to J. B. Coates, to have formed an important line of demarcation, separating the Vai ethnic territory ruled by King Peter from the area belonging to the Dei ethnic group.[37] Crossing this river had ostensibly brought Coates into a supposedly friendlier territory ruled by the Dei chief King George.[38]

Like in many other Atlantic coastal areas in Africa, the transatlantic slave trade had transformed the area in the sixteenth century.[39] African ethnic groups that had established themselves on the coast became active participants in the Atlantic slave trade. Native ethnic groups occupied various positions in the slave trade. The Vais took on roles as middlemen between Africans in the interior and the Dutch traders and slavers on the coast. The Kru, largely employed on slave ships, also became active participants in the trade – a move that simultaneously rewarded them and exposed them to its vulnerabilities. Amos Beyan argues that although Kru involvement in the slave trade provided them material rewards that often led to social and political mobility, it also affected their institutional development by restructuring their traditional ethnic

---

[36] Ephraim Bacon visited Liberia in March, 1820. Ephraim Bacon, *Abstract of a Journal Containing an Account of the First Negotiations for the Purchase of Lands for the American Colony* (Philadelphia, 1824); *Abstract of a Journal Kept by E. Bacon, Assistant Agent of the United States, to Africa: with an Appendix, Containing Extracts from the North American Review, on the Subject of Africa. Containing Cuts, Showing a Contrast between Two Native Towns* (Philadelphia, 1824), 9.

[37] J. B. Coates, "Journal of a Journey by J.B. Coates," C.A. 1/E7A, 75-76. Church Missionary Society Archives (London) quoted in Svend Holsoe, "Chiefdom and Clan Maps of Western Liberia," *Liberian Studies Journal*, Vol. I, No. 2 (1969): 23–39.

[38] Ibid.

[39] See Toyin Falola and Paul E. Lovejoy, *Pawnship in Africa: Debt Bondage in Historical Perspective* (Boulder, CO: Westview Press, 1994), 19.

hierarchies.[40] The anthropologist Svend Holsoe, however, insists that the Kru only enjoyed the material rewards of the slave trade.[41]

Attempts to erect a temple of pan-African liberty on a coast where ethnic indigenes profited from the bondage of other groups symbolically represented the most glaring contradiction in the Liberian nation-building efforts. Much to the chagrin of early black nationalist like Blyden, plans to build a nation did not include becoming a part of the traditional African social and political systems. To create a new respectable society in Africa, the African American pioneers sought to escape identification with Africans. Still, the cooperation of some native groups proved invaluable to the new settlers. Having worked on British merchant vessels and American naval ships, the Kru ethnic group, for example, had learned a kind of Pidgin English that allowed some of them to serve as guides and interpreters for the new settlers. The Kru were also some of the first to provide labor for the colony, helping immigrants to clear lands for their settlement. They also supplied fish, rice, palm oil, and other local goods that proved critical to the migrants' survival during the first years of the settlement. Indeed, throughout the nineteenth century, the Kru fished and worked as laborers for African American settlers and European trading firms, loading and unloading passengers and goods on ships docked in Cape Mesurado.[42]

The ACS sponsored its initial voyage in 1820. The ACS later transported an estimated sixteen thousand migrants to Liberia. All the time, as increasing migration created the need for more land, new comers were constantly fomenting designs to further overpower their neighbors. This generated an additional dimension to the kinds of aggressive actions that created strife between the different groups in Liberia. The ACS sent Eli Ayres and Robert Stockton, two white colonizationists, to retain an area for the settlement. Envisioning Liberia as an American empire in Africa, they were prepared to use force to extend the colony's territory. As the legend goes, Stockton persuaded King Peter, the chief of the Dei and Bassa ethnic groups, to sell Cape Mesurado by pointing a pistol at his head. In the treaty of May 1825, King Peter and other native kings agreed to sell Cape Mesurado, totaling 130 square miles of land stretching from the Atlantic Ocean deep into the hinterlands, in return for "500 bars of

---

[40] Amos Jones Beyan, *The American Colonization Society and the Creation of the Liberian State: A Historical Perspective, 1822-1900* (Lanham, MD: University Press of America, 1991), 35.

[41] Svend Holsoe, "A Study of Relations between Settlers and Indigenous Peoples in Western Liberia, 1821-1847," *African Historical Studies*, Vol. 4, No. 2 (1971): 341.

[42] *The African Repository and Colonial Journal*, Vol. 15, June (1839): 157.

tobacco, three barrels of rum, five casks of powder, five umbrellas, ten iron posts, and ten pairs of shoes, among other items."[43] Between 1825 and 1826, Jehudi Ashmun, a white colonial agent, took steps to further lease, annex, or buy tribal lands along the coast and on major rivers, including the St. Paul River that led inland where the Barbadians settled.[44]

Through cultural and social interactions with indigenes, moments of contestation over land, and resistance to their increasing hostility, African Americans began to revise and define their identity. War over seemingly worthless ground imbued meanings that helped to draw lines around blackness in the area. Reports noted that when the agents and colonists tried to take possession of their newly acquired land, the chiefs, particularly Peter, refused to acknowledge the society's rights and tried to return the payment made in the treaty. The settlers were forced to retreat to Darzoe Island, a small islet located in the Cape, where they commenced building their homes. After the work had started, a British cruiser, with thirty African recaptives on board, was blown off course near the cape, near chief King George's Town. King George's people tried to take possession of the ship, assuming it was theirs since it was on their land. Once attacked, British seamen returned fire, and the new African American colonists came to their aid. The settlers' intrusion failed to endear them to King George and his people, who responded by blockading the island and burning the houses of the settlers on the cape. Other settlers who ventured off the island to fetch freshwater from nearby streams were also attacked and killed.[45]

The dreams of a Liberian nationality were essentially one of Africa without Africans. Indigenes only became visible on the African landscape through violent encounters and in missionary projects; they were seen as savages to be civilized and as laborers for migrant farms. Otherwise, they were essentially erased in the discourse of citizenship and nationhood. Diasporic Africans seeking a progressive identity for themselves erased indigenes in Liberia through their domination. Migrants' views of indigenes reflected an identity constructed in opposition to African nativity. Just as American imperialism was predicated on pushing indigenes off the

---

[43] *The African Repository and Colonial Journal*, Vol. 1, August (1825): 129.

[44] Ralph R. Gurley, *The Life of Jehudi Ashmun, Late Colonial Agent in Liberia* (Washington, DC: J.C. Dunn, 1839), 186.

[45] Jehudi Ashmun, Memoir, printed in *The African Repository and Colonial Journal*, Vol. 1 (1826), 116–119.

lands of North America, African Americans wanted to remove indigenes in their own imperial endeavor. Liberian migrants became "mediocre citizens, a member of a colonizing community, who unrecognized, and or marginalized by his society, assumes a position of power over a colonized subject. His relationship to the colonized becomes a means to erase the truth of his previous status in his mother country."[46]

In attempts to uphold a superficial peace, tension and unease enveloped the area as both the migrants and the natives prepared for possible attacks. In October 1822, the kings of various native groups in the area secretly met to discuss a strategy of attack on the migrants' settlement. It appears that Kings Peter, Bristol, and Getumbe stood against the attack. They likely felt some sense of kinship with the settlers and thought them to be "their countrymen, as proven by their skin color."[47] It is also likely that they proposed peace because they feared the military strength of the colonists.[48] But the natives also feared the expansion, destruction of their way of life, and loss of power to a colony of settlers they perceived as strangers. King George and the other chiefs felt that the colonists were strangers who had forgotten their attachment to their fatherland, reasoning that if they had not, they would have placed themselves under the protection of the indigenous kings rather than the white men in the ACS.[49]

BARBADIAN SETTLEMENT IN CROZIERVILLE

The Crozierville landscape was a character in itself. Located upcountry and toward the hinterlands, Crozierville sat near approximately two thousand ethnic native villages in central Liberia, in the northwest, and in the coastal region near Monrovia.[50] In that area, they also joined a group of illiterate and

---

[46] E. Anthony Hurley, Renée Brenda Larrier, and Joseph McLaren, eds., *Migrating Words and Worlds: Pan-Africanism Updated* (Trenton, NJ: Africa World Press, 1999), 157.

[47] Holsoe, "A Study of Relations between Settlers and Indigenous Peoples in Western Liberia, 1821-1847," 336.

[48] Jehudi Ashmun, "History of the American Colony in Liberia from December 1821-1823," (Washington, 1826), 24, as recorded in Svend Holsoe's "A Study of Relations between Settlers and Indigenous Peoples in Western Liberia, 1821–1847," *African Historical Studies*, Vol. 4. No. 2 (1971), 331–362.

[49] Ibid.

[50] *An Address Delivered by Rev. J. I. A. Weeks On the Occasion of the Eighty-Second Anniversary of the Landing of the West Indian Immigration to Liberia, at the Methodist Church, Crozierville, May 11th, 1947.* Liberia Collections, accessed at Indiana University, Bloomington.

semi-skilled African American settlers who had been freed on the expressed condition that they would be repatriated to Liberia. Many African recaptives were also settled nearby in the Clay-Ashland settlement. Altogether, those who lived in settlements up alongside the St Paul's River engaged in farming, supplying food to the urban coastal settlements. Other migrants used their location to engage in missionary activities. Located in the space between Native African and African American settlements, Barbadians in Crozierville helped to mark the patterns that reflected the spatial, social, and political segmentation of Liberia. Their settlement did much to interrupt the coexisting rural–urban and traditional–modern divides that ordered Liberian society. African American settlements in a few interior and coastal areas featured large plantations and mining activities. The location of the Barbadians in the middle may have softened the sharpness of the spatial divide, but it also outlined the complexity of new dynamics and the uncertainty about their place in the Liberian social order. Barbadian settlement that buffered the indigenes and the migrants functioned as an intermediate borderland between the "civilized" and the "uncivilized," representing their continued in-between identity now actualized as "civilizers." The rural nature of the Crozierville location shaped Barbadians' Liberian identity in other crucial ways (See Figure 5.3A and 5.3B).

The introduction of the Barbadian settlers created a racial cascade that radically changed the social as much as the physical landscape of Liberia. The imprints of the diaspora were everywhere in Liberian life: in how Monrovia was configured, the social geography of the settlements, the epistemology of racial identity, and views about labor could not avoid its reach. Settlement, labor, and religiosity formed key sites of regulation of behavior that conferred legitimacy to some actions while disallowing others. As values from the old world manifested in new venues, Liberia became a new platform for longstanding problems. Settlement patterns became one of the best opportunities for imputing Western values into the nation order. The imitation of European-style buildings in the black republic sustained European culture and civilization and invoked a proximity to whiteness as well as empire and higher social status.[51] In the early years, settlement patterns reproduced the socially segregated plantation societies typical of the United States and the Caribbean. Even as migrants boasted of building up a black nation, they were creating second-class citizens through their settlement decisions. The establishment of this and other migrant settlements

---

[51] See Svend E. Holsoe and Bernard L. Herman, *A Land and Life Remembered: Americo-Liberian Folk Architecture* (Athens: University of Georgia Press, 1988).

FIGURE 5.3A: Sign Memorializing the Crozierville Settlement
Source: Photograph by Matthew C. Reilly

created social and economic networks of collaboration among distinct groups that in many ways reinforced their sense of Barbadian-ness as an ethnic identity rather than a black racial identity. This further served to fracture the notion of a collective black identity.

The settlement of the Barbadians away from the urban area in Crozierville critically served to shape the development of their identity apart from other migrant groups. Located upcountry along the St. Paul's River in Monserrado County, Crozierville was about twenty miles from the capital of Monrovia, where the majority of African American emigrants had settled. In 1868, H. W. Johnson Jr., writing from Lower Caldwell after visiting the Barbadian settlement in Crozierville, observed, "It is a beautiful section of the country. It may be called a 'hilly region.' The air is very pure, the water clear and cool, and the prospect very fine."[52] He added: "On every side we see a succession of valleys and hills, very much resembling the finest sections of Western New York. For romantic beauty, I have never seen anything in America to excel it. The further you go towards Carysburg the more magnificent

[52] Harry Hamilton Johnston and Otto Stapf, *Liberia* (London: Hutchinson, 1906), 23.

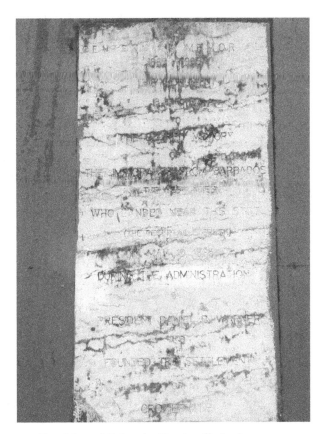

FIGURE 5.3 B: Sign Memorializing the Crozierville Settlement
Source: Photograph by Matthew C. Reilly

the scenery."[53] Johnson's observations of the environment reflected the constant efforts to compare Liberia to the United States. But the fact that the Barbadian occupants of Crozierville had previously lived on some of the flattest land in the Caribbean rendered such comparisons futile.

Survival remained the largest hurdle for the emigrants. Migration opened a way for a greater experience of freedom, but it equally exposed migrants to graver problems such as the experiences of death. Some Barbadians quickly changed their minds about life in Liberia. Untimely

[53] See James Washington Lugenbell, *Sketches of Liberia: Comprising a Brief Account of the Geography, Climate, Productions, and Diseases of the Republic of Liberia* (Washington, DC, 1850).

early death was a fortune that would befall many of the Liberian migrants, and diseases further haunted the dreams of freedom. Most of the Barbadian children arrived in Liberia with the agility of youth. Many other migrants, however, would not be able to circumvent the barriers and death traps that usually plagued other Liberian settlers. Like many other migrants, the Barbadians had to endure an environment of new diseases. Some of the Barbadians were immediately attacked by one of the seasonal fevers even before they could be removed from Monrovia, but they were soon sent to their settlement to sufficiently recover from "the fatigue of traveling." H. D. Brown, in a letter written to Alexander Crummell just a few months after the Barbadians had arrived, pointed out that some of the Barbadians had fallen sick. Four of the 346 had died by the time of his writing.[54] Among the dead was one of the prominent patriarchs, Samuel Skeete. Brown explained that since this death, "his family have concluded to return to Barbados."[55] Crummell in turn, in relaying this information in a letter to the PCS, noted that the coast had experienced the most extreme rains it had seen over the past few years, which greatly aggravated and exposed the sufferings of the Barbadian emigrants in Liberia.[56]

Worse yet, for the Barclay family who had led the charge to leave Barbados, life upon arrival would also be quickly disrupted by death. The leader of the Barbadian Emigration Society, Anthony Barclay, became one of the first casualties, dying just within a year of his arrival in Monrovia on January 16, 1866, at the age of fifty-six years. Four months later, Elizabeth Ann, Barclay's third child, died at twenty-six.[57] The death of the patriarch and daughter left the widowed Sarah Barclay with the responsibility of raising the family and leading the immigrants.[58] Struggles against disease and for survival leveled out the otherwise growing divide within the Liberian society. That the Liberian environment was impartial to all, regardless of social station, brought migrants into a community that approximated, if only harshly and for fleeting moments, some semblance of egalitarianism. Barbadian mortality rates were comparable to those of earlier African American settlers but seemed excessive for the 1860s. Pioneering African American settlers had encountered

---

[54] H. D. Brown to Crummell, Alexander Crummell Letters. Accessed at the Schomburg Center for Research in Black Culture, Harlem, New York.

[55] Ibid.

[56] Pennsylvania Colonization Society, *Meeting Minutes*, Sept. 11, 1865.

[57] Mary Antoinette Brown Sherman, "Barclay Women in Liberia: Two Generations: A Biographical Dictionary," *Liberian Studies Journal*, Vol. 30, No. 1 (2005): 28–38.

[58] Ibid.

hardships and successes during their first few years in their new home and became martyrs for white bourgeois guilt. Whatever presumed biological inoculations the migrants possessed were no match for the perils of the African environment or for a wet season that exposed them to yellow fever and malaria.[59] Those who arrived during the disastrous wet season had to clear swampland for their settlement.

In the constant struggle to survive, migrants' once energetic imagination of a future of freedom on the western shores of the Atlantic gave way to disillusionment and dismay. The new Liberians had to contend with inadequate food and shelter, conflicts with natives, various diseases, and overgrown land that was difficult to clear and cultivate, while they struggled to establish schools and churches.[60] Their letters often mentioned illness and deaths, crops, home building, newcomers, and the many other difficulties that surfaced once emigrants confronted the on-the-ground realities. Almost all requested supplies and sent regards to family members left behind. The fatal costs of migration, loss of liberties, property, family, and life itself led many migrants to question whether the liberty and freedom they sought were worth the costs.[61] As the novelty wore off and disease began to take its toll, disillusionment and homesickness became the prevalent pattern of reaction, replacing the initial enthusiasm for the new land and the new life.[62]

Despite their initial struggles, migrants succeeded in achieving a tolerable existence. As some migrants' letters demonstrated, they were able also to find some degree of success and happiness exceeding anything known by their black friends and relatives in America. After Confederate General Robert E. Lee freed William and Rosabella Burke in 1853, they migrated with their children to Liberia. On arrival, William joined the seminary in Monrovia, becoming a Presbyterian minister in 1857. The words of Lee's former slaves would be encouraging for those who came after them. A year after his arrival, William wrote a friend: "Persons coming to Africa should expect to go through many hardships, such as are common to the first settlement in any new country. I expected it and was not disappointed or discouraged at anything that I met with; and so far from being dissatisfied with the country, I bless the Lord that ever my lot

[59] For views on climate and racial differentiation, see Mark Harrison, "The Tender Frame of Man: Disease, Climate, and Racial Difference in India and the West Indies, 1760–1860." *Bulletin of the History of Medicine*, Vol. 70, No. 1 (1996): 899–935.

[60] Wiley, *Slaves No More*, 5–7.

[61] Clegg, *The Price of Liberty*, 7.

[62] Ibid.

was cast in this part of the earth." In a letter to Mary Curtis Lee, Rosabella Burke noted, "I love Africa and would not exchange it for America."[63]

The New Yorker Henry Johnson, who arrived in Liberia on August 10, 1865, wrote a letter to satisfy the curiosity of those who were waiting to hear how he was adjusting to Africa. Indeed, he had been really pleased with Liberia, viewing it "a noble country" as well as being delighted by his fellow people. But Johnson was "disappointed with the progress and present state of this infant republic," which the American Civil War had greatly affected by stalling black migration. Still, he found "many evidences of prosperity, industry, and enterprise" among those he saw as "high-minded and intelligent freemen! They look and act like men who know and have no superior but their maker." Together with other migrants, they were "successfully solving the great problem in regard to the capacity of the black man for self-government; they are working out their own destiny in the land of their forefathers. With the help of God, they will succeed in spite of all opposition." For Johnson, "the Republic of Liberia is no longer a myth, existing only in the brain of the enthusiast. It is a sober reality – a solemn fact." But he too was aware of the demands of life in Liberia: "The only question is, shall it, for want of aid and emigration from abroad remain for sometime weak and feeble, or shall it speedily become great and powerful?" Johnson closed his letter by appealing to those blacks who chose to remain in the United States and who did not imagine Liberia and Africa to be their rightful home: "Black men of America! What a shame that you do not come here and aid the young republic; eternal disgrace to you if this government is allowed to languish and die for want of your aid."[64]

MIGRANT SETTLEMENTS AND SOCIAL PLURALITY IN LIBERIA

The mass of the early African American migrants to Liberia came from mid-Atlantic states such as Virginia, Maryland, and Pennsylvania. In the early decades emigrants came largely from northern states, whereas by mid-century the majority would hail from southern states, including North Carolina, Arkansas, Tennessee, and Georgia.[65] Many of the southern

---

[63] *Slavery Pamphlet Collection.* 1857. Drew University.

[64] *The African Repository*, Vol. 41 (1865): 37.

[65] In the late 1800s, more African-Americans left the state of Arkansas for Liberia than from any other state in the United States. Kenneth C. Barnes, *Journey of Hope: The Back-to-Africa Movement in Arkansas in the Late 1800s* (Chapel Hill: University of North Carolina Press, 2004).

migrants were born free, but a large number had been freed on the express condition that they leave the United States. These state divisions surfaced in disputes among migrants. Barbadians entered Liberia with enormous cultural capital and credibility, but Liberian officials pondered upon the implications of their settlement. Before their arrival, Liberian officials had often referenced the Barbadians' experience of over thirty years of freedom, their industriousness, and their widely acclaimed religious character. Their religiosity further confirmed their pedigree and connections with their African American counterparts as a good number of the Barbadians were noted to be "the professed followers of Christ," mainly Episcopalians, Wesleyans, and Moravians, with Episcopalians being the most numerous.[66] This review of Barbadians' skillfulness and religion led the African American officials in Liberia to determine that the West Indians were indeed like them because they too had come to Liberia "prompted by the love of souls as well as the desire to improve their temporal condition."[67]

With increasing tension and a growing lack of confidence in the ACS, state colonization societies sought to establish their own colonial settlements in Liberia. Maryland colonizationist Benjamin Latrobe proposed that Maryland develop a colony. In 1832, following an incident with the ship *Lafayette* in Cape Mesurado, Maryland ceased operating under the auspices of the ACS and established the "Maryland in Liberia" settlement at Cape Palmas with John Russwurm as the governor.[68] Other settlements soon followed suit. Located on the left bank of the St. Paul River, on the ridge formed by Cape Mesurado, Monrovia, the oldest settlement, became the focal point of political, economic, and cultural activities. Other settlements included Buchanan, Edina, Greenville, Harper, Robertsport, and Marshal, which all boasted newly constructed or improved roads.[69] The ascribed names, rather than the landscape, were proof of a more subtle distance between the Liberian migrants.

In the Liberian settlements, demarcation of the landscape not only reflected the ways in which material cultures moved within the Atlantic World but also their relationship to social hierarchy. The inscriptions of settlements further represented new identities emerging in another form. Against a backdrop of clay huts, migrants constructed one- or two-

---

[66] *The African Repository*, Vol. 42 (1866): 37.
[67] *The African Repository*, Vol. 41 (1865): 243.
[68] Penelope Campbell, *Maryland in Africa: The Maryland State Colonization Society, 1831–1857* (Urbana: University of Illinois Press, 1971), 8.
[69] Jo Mary Sullivan and Camille Mirepoix, *Liberia in Pictures* (Minneapolis: Lerner Publications, 1988).

storied, stone-and brick-porticoed houses in their settlements, resembling antebellum American plantations.[70] "Symbolizing Western ways in an African setting," settler architecture encoded new ethnicities right into the Liberian landscape.[71] Visitors to the area noted that the immigrants wore Western modes of dress to which they had been accustomed in America, however unsuitable these were to Liberia's tropical weather: "a black silk topper and a long, black frock coat for men, and a 'Victorian' silk gown for women." African Americans also preferred to eat American foods such as flour, cornmeal, butter, lard, pickled beef, bacon, and American-grown rice, large quantities of which they imported annually – and not African foodstuffs such as cassava, plantains, yams, palm oil, sweet potatoes, and country rice grown by Africans in the Liberian hinterlands.[72]

Barbadians' arrival in Liberia revealed the enduring ties of Empire. Even as Afro-Barbadians sought to resist the British Empire through migration, their fight was problematized by their own embodiment and internalization of ideas of colonial dominance. Barbadians marched forward into a hazy unknown future aiming to transition into life in the West African republic but all the while glancing backwards. But "you can never cross the ocean until you have the courage to lose sight of the shore."[73] Upon arrival in Liberia, Barbadians masked their sociopolitical and economic interests behind the honor and innocence of pan-African and black nationalist ideals and leveraged the yoke of British imperialism to fulfill what they considered to be diasporic obligations. The black Nationalist Alexander Crummell told a group during a sermon:

We must not forget that we have a multitudinous emigrant population here at hand, indigenous to the soil, homogenous in race and blood; a people "to the manor born," fitted to all the needs, of this infant state, wanting only in the elements of civilization, and the training of the Christian life. It is our duty to supply this deficiency. We were sent here, in God's providence, to stimulate, by government.[74]

Acting through old forms of power in new guises, Barbadians secured political and economic privileges in the republic above other blacks. Embracing an English imperial identity by acting as agents of African civilization, Barbadian migrants deployed the unpleasant memory of

---

[70] *The African Repository and Colonial Journal*, Vol. 6 (1830): 47.
[71] Holsoe and Herman, *A Life Remembered: Americo-Liberian Folk Architecture*, x.
[72] *The African Repository and Colonial Journal*, Vol. 3 (1828): 16.
[73] Andre Gide, *The Counterfeiters* (France, Alfred K. Knopf, 1925).
[74] *The African Repository*, Vol. 47 (1871): 233.

colonialism not through the usual dynamics of racism in the diaspora but in reassigning labels of "savage" and "civilized" to other groups of blacks. By using these means to secure power in Liberia, the former colonial subjects found themselves reproducing the economic and political ideas bound up in imperialism. The resurgence of colonial ideology in Liberia to sustain exclusionary practices mirrored hierarchical arrangements against which the emigrants had previously struggled.[75] African diasporic migrants civilized through their proximity to whiteness in slavery were allowed not only to prosper but also "to acquire social, psychological, and political advantages that turned the thrust of exploitation away from them and aligned them with their exploiters."[76] The specter of white racism that united black migrants in a common fight also made it possible for them to discretely colonize and subjugate Liberian indigenes and recaptive Africans.

Perceptions of racial homogeneity in Liberia that created an illusion of equality shrouded the creation of new hierarchies that were based on labor, civilization, and other Western means of differentiating status.[77] A collective sense of blackness hid the fact that for some in Liberia, the road to a fuller freedom was marked by rough patches and detours; and, in some important respects, freedom remained an incomplete journey for others. Yet, to dismiss the Barbadians as hypocrites who moved from being victims on one side of the Atlantic to victimizers on the other side would be to ignore the itinerancy, power, and psychological impact of colonialism. It also overlooks what Stuart Hall calls "the two moments of diasporic identification."[78] The Barbadians' second moment comes through confronting their new challenges, thus revealing colonialism and imperialism as evolving projects, moving across time and space and manifesting in Barbados and Liberia in different ways.

In seeking respite from civil, political, and economic oppression, migrants found common ground with their contemporaries, but this did not mean social equality. Indeed, the social sphere created numerous battle lines that predated the Barbadians' arrival. According to an American physician who toured the settlements in 1858, "one source of friction was the assumption of an air of superiority on the part of

---

[75] Tomas Almaguer, *Racial Fault Lines: The Historical Origins of White Supremacy in California* (Berkeley: University of California Press, 1994), 1.

[76] Edmund Morgan, *American Slavery, American Freedom: The Ordeal of Colonial Virginia* (New York: Norton, 1975), 344.

[77] McGraw, *The Work of Recognition*, 5.

[78] Stuart Hall, "Old and New Identities." In *Culture, Globalization, and the World-System*, edited by Anthony D. King (Binghamton: State University of New York Press, 1991), 27.

emigrants from Virginia." Migrants from Virginia who were mostly mulattoes drew cultural capital from their mixed-race origins. He further noted that some of the colonists "complained of caste and say that the Virginians are mostly too high-headed and are all the time claiming that they are the quality of Liberia."[79] J. J. Roberts, who became the first president of Liberia, was one such migrant from Virginia; he was largely viewed as nearly white and parlayed his social status into economic and political prosperity. Conversely, "pure blacks," who often came from other states, were not viewed in the same way. On June 2, 1834, a Samson Ceasar noted in his letter: "There have come a great many from North Carolina who are dregs in this place." Seasoned migrants like John Brown Russwurm noted that new migrants were refusing to earn their stay.[80] Like "saltwater" slaves and creoles on American plantations, conflicts again developed between established migrants and new arrivals.[81]

RECAPTIVES IN LIBERIA

That some in the Barbadian migrant group were recaptive Africans from the areas around Sierra Leone and Liberia illustrates the distinctiveness with which the migrants would be received. John Padmore, who had landed in Sierra Leone, met some of those recaptives from Barbados who also had arrived in a vessel in Freetown, Sierra Leone, from Barbados before the *Brig Cora* reached Liberia with the other emigrants. Of those who had arrived in Sierra Leone, six proceeded to Monrovia before Padmore himself had even left. Another migrant to Liberia on the *M. A. Benson* stopped over in Freetown and became acquainted with the group of recaptives. On the same day Padmore had arrived in Freetown, one of them had sailed for Monrovia. Others, however, were sick and were unable to go. They requested that the Liberian government allow Mr. Worrell to choose the land allotted for them until they would be able to get passage to Liberia.

Of the six recaptives who had arrived in Sierra Leone, one was a minister from Demerara, who reflected the desire of the black Demerarans to get back to the area. He had previously traveled to Sierra

---

[79] Wiley, *Slaves No More*, 6.
[80] Ibid.
[81] Ira Berlin, *The Making of African America: The Four Great Migrations* (New York: Viking, 2010), 8.

Leone three years prior, likely after Blyden had traveled throughout the Caribbean distributing circulars encouraging migration to Liberia. At the time, about thirty or forty persons who belonged to the Akoo ethnicity and had been residing in Demerara had gone with him. He had gone down to Grand Bassa, where his grandparents were born and where they were taken as slaves, and had a desire to get to Liberia but was unlucky. Still, he had returned to his home, satisfied with the reports he had heard from Liberia. Having returned with intentions to get to Liberia, he had brought his wife and a young "black man" who served as his assistant.

In the search for home, recaptives and Barbadians showed the stark differences in the circuitous route that defined diaspora. The Akoo ethnic group, who were often hired labor in Sierra Leone, had come back to the area from Barbados via Demerara with intentions to settle in Liberia. Also noted as present among the recaptives was "a native Bassa man who went to Freetown several years ago, enlisted in the British Army, went to Demerara and served several years as a soldier," who was said to be "a kinsman of Boyer." To reconnect these groups, President Warner had "sent him down to Bassa in company with Mr. Ulcans and his party."[82] In this case, return to their "homeland" completed the circle of diaspora.

African recaptives had been a part of the Liberian republic since its inception, but the movements to counteract the "second slavery" dramatically increased in number after the 1840s. In the 1860s, one Liberian official bitterly complained that "during the present week two prizes were brought in within eighteen hours of each other; the first, a brig, supposed to be the Storm King of New York, the San Jacinto with 615–620 recaptives; the Ship Erie of New York with 897 – making over 1,500; both vessels were captured near Congo." As Liberian officials observed, most slaves captured in this era were from Central Africa. Recaptives brought to Liberia were often taken from other points, even as far as Cuba. One official recorded that:

several other prizes are expected up from the south coast momentarily; so that I doubt not at all – taking those that will likely be captured on the coast of Cuba, with those that will be captured on this coast – that the number of recaptives that will be brought to this Republic by American cruisers, to be landed, will, within the next three months, reach as high as ten or twelve thousand.[83]

The official further noted, "Those we now have here, with those now on their way from the United States, and expected momentarily, will

[82] *The African Repository*, Vol. 41 (1865): 279–280.
[83] "Meeting of the Board of Directors," *The African Repository*, Vol. 36 (1860): 356.

constitute a number over 3,000, which number cannot possibly be controlled and trained but under the exclusive authority and supervision of the Government of Liberia."[84] By all accounts, receptives outnumbered their African American and West Indians counterparts in Liberia. This served to create anxiety and a degree of unease about what the republic would look like.

As these various groups of blacks entered the evolving cosmopolitan black society, they transformed Liberia demographically, culturally, and socially. By bringing issues, visions, and demands different from those of African Americans, migrants created tensions around claims to freedom, citizenship, and nationhood in the republic. Given the nature of their Atlantic experiences that often lacked the kind of sustained historical breadth in the diasporic circuit, recaptives were not as welcomed in the Liberian republic as other migrants. As such, after arrival, the recaptives did not seem to have the full measure of citizenship that others enjoyed. Thrust into the forefront with every increase in number, their presence incurred whispers of the damage they would cause to the unfolding national image. In the 1850s and 1860s, during which they arrived in Liberia in critical masses, they not only began to rival African Americans in numbers but also changed the complexion of Liberian society. Compared to the early mixed-raced Virginians and Marylanders, African recaptives were darker in complexion, spoke a different language, were not Christians, and often could not read and write. Reports circulated about the "great alarm and consternation of the people of this community in particular, and of the Republic in general."[85] Stratifying Liberian society, the new racial caste created with color politics separated the diasporic migrants from the recaptives as well as the native ethnic groups.

A "perception of linked fate" had drawn together different members of the African diaspora. As evident in the migrants' complaints about the high-headedness of the Virginians, this question of "color" increasingly complicated national identity even as it structured power dynamics.[86] Holding the reigns of politics and color, Americo-Liberians wielded each in the service of the other to exclude recaptives from full citizenship. With the fight against racial hierarchy requiring their main loyalty, many chose

---

[84] *The African Repository* (1865): 157.
[85] *The African Repository*, Vol. 45 (1869): 182.
[86] See Evelyn M. Simien, "Race, Gender, and Linked Fate," *Journal of Black Studies*, Vol. 35, No. 5 (2005): 529–550.

not to express alarm about the internal hierarchies. The lack of an outlet for expressing the harm inflicted within these structures created a black nationalist paradox. Under this logic, white supremacy became a zero-sum fight between whites and blacks. Acknowledging these kinds of power and privilege in Africa and the diaspora threatened a powerful, singular narrative and sense of cohesion. In this way, the capaciousness of white supremacy directly fed the persistence of intra-racial issues.

Imperialism brought the necessity of examining the other in order to provide a rationale for maintaining dominance over them. Fragile new black states like Liberia attempted to police and regulate the social practices of those citizens whose very existence threatened the stability and viability of these newly independent nations. The treatment of recaptives in Liberia and efforts to civilize and uplift them became a way of re-enacting diasporic subaltern consciousness. For recaptives, Liberia retreated from the full promises of emancipation. Institutional arrangements and structures shaped the ways in which different groups negotiated their daily routines. The nature of the relationship between the state and the recaptives would be quite different from that between the state and the African Americans and Barbadians. African American and Barbadian immigrants were all given parcels of land, the very act of ownership accruing to them certain rights. Contrarily, recaptives with no access to land would not hold similar rights and privileges. As author Richard Stivers explains in *The Illusion of Freedom and Equality*, "[w]ith the disappearance of a common morality, and the ascendancy of the group over the individual, equality becomes an equality of power."[87]

Claims about recaptives' lack of civilization were supported by Atlantic world practices surrounding recaptive settlement and labor arrangements. Unlike their Barbadian counterparts, recaptives' relationship to the state would be in the form of arranged housing and planned labor. Given the kinds of demographic pressures that guaranteed low wages in Barbados, few Barbadians would have had interaction with recaptives, but their experiences in post-emancipation would have familiarized them with post-slavery labor control. To control recaptives, the Liberian government proposed a plan "to lay off a sufficient area of land at some suitable place in each county, say of several hundred acres of land each; to build one or more large suitable houses on them, and to settle the recaptives thereon, under good teachers, mechanics, and agriculturists,

---

[87] Richard Stivers, *The Illusion of Freedom and Equality* (New York: New York Press, 2008), 84.

employed by and amenable to this government."[88] The politics of patronage started by the ACS evolved into a modified form of paternalism
exercised by the migrants over the recaptive Africans.

Diasporic migrants used control over recaptives' labor as a veneer of help
and upliftment when their position over them was indeed essential to their
identity. The migrant groups determined recaptives' labor organization and
supervised their lives. Old forms of discrimination emerged and were made
legal through governmental provisions. It became standard to victimize
recaptives in Liberia, in the same way that whites discriminated against
Barbadians in the Caribbean and blacks in the United States. This bears
a resemblance to the immediate post-emancipation period in the West
Indies. Thus, free labor on the African side of the Atlantic did not mean
the end of coercive and restrictive labor regimes. This attitude toward
recaptives was in part a reaction to the quest for a national image that
would be acceptable to whites and legitimize Liberia's treaty-worthiness.
The fear of white perceptions of Liberia's lack of civilization overrode the
pan-Africanist rhetoric that had driven many of the emigrants to Liberia.
Recaptives, having just been taken off slave ships, were perceived as an
uncultured, socially disruptive element for a Liberian society aiming to
project black humanity and civility to the broader white world.

The juxtaposition of Barbadians to their black counterparts in Liberia
reveals how labor functioned differently in experiences of citizenship from
place to place. In the Caribbean, labor's proximity to racial slavery mal-
igned Barbadians as British subjects. Across the Atlantic, however,
Barbadians touted their proximity to racial slavery as a mark of civilization. Liberian officials who received them in that light therefore gave them
access to citizenship. Discourses around the productivity of Barbadians'
labor not only redefined prior forms of Liberian citizenship but also
became a place from which to exhibit the republic's modernity. Thrust
into the national spotlight, "civilized" Barbadians and their perceived
productive labor further helped to redefine blackness.

The premise of a black essence was based on a perceived similarity that
had not been given to all before arrival in Liberia.[89] For Africa and the
diaspora, the Atlantic became a powerful force of genealogy that further
served ethnic distinctions within a cosmopolitan landscape of black
migrants. White supremacy rendered race an imprint of power that
could open and retract in different places as meanings of blackness

---

[88] Ibid.
[89] Achille Membe, *On the Postcolony* (Berkeley: University of California Press, 2001), 248.

expanded and contracted with different migrants. Implicit in the civilizationist doctrine was the assumption of a dichotomy between the diaspora
and Africa. The Atlantic, like the Cartesian mind/body split, fragmented
meanings of blackness. The black identity that was reduced to the body
through slavery overcomes subjectivity through proximity to whiteness,
while ethnic Africans' access to modernity was presumed to be foreclosed,
remaining in a state of suspended animation without the Atlantic crossing's access to whiteness and civilization.

Modes of emancipation and migration also affected migrants' reception into the Liberian nation. New ideas of blackness in Liberia were
correlated with one's ability to dissimulate "African-ness," believed to
be embodied in certain cultural practices, such as superstitions, witchcraft, and polygamy. Black migrants came to be seen as the immutable
voice of progress and civilization. The diaspora blacks presented themselves in Liberia as demonstrative of Africans' capacity to overcome their
Africanisms or recast them in ways that appeared civilized. A certain
baseline "black demeanor" that included Christianity, civilization, and
modernity was prescribed and required for the attainment of modern
blackness and agency in the Liberian nation. In spite of its African location, Liberia routed blacks' sense of civilization, modernity, and progress
through European behavior.

The migration of the various groups of blacks, each with different points
of entry into the Atlantic, signals the limits of frameworks often used to
address black cosmopolitan spaces like Liberia. Recaptives in Liberia –
often hailing from West Central Africa, particularly Congo and Angola –
had, in many cases, not crossed the Atlantic and therefore had not experienced the middle passage and slavery that were seen as central to diasporic
identities. These migrants defied the traditional definitions and identifica-
tions of diaspora in Liberia. For them, diasporic identity was never the
controlling identity but rather the subordinate. Generalizations made about
recaptives in the context of identity politics played a disciplinary function
within the group, not just describing but also dictating the self-
understanding that its members held. Thus, the supposedly liberatory new
identity inhibited autonomy – as Anthony Appiah puts it, replacing "one
kind of tyranny with another."[90] In the same way that dominant cultural
groups insisted on integrating the marginalized to their norms through
assimilation, migrants also imposed their visions of black identity on others.

[90] Kwame Appiah, *Identity against Culture: Understandings of Multiculturalism.*
Occasional Paper Series (Berkeley: University of California Press, 1994), 28.

With the presence of the West Indians, Liberia's political culture entered into a complex political entanglement with English, American, and African cultures. The British background of the West Indians had inculcated a certain identity that influenced understandings of politics, citizenship, and nationhood. British imperialism was such that questions of citizenship trumped race.[91] All belonging to the empire were considered citizens, though race figured in that question to various degrees. Culture, practice, loyalty, and allegiance, which developed conterminously with the creation of the British Empire, determined belonging and citizenship. Contrarily, race lay at the very foundation of the question of citizenship in the United States. Beyond the vision of a unifying national sentiment, these differences highlighted the on-the-ground realities that fractured notions of a collective black and pan-African identity.

NOMENCLATURE AND IDENTITY

In the post-migration Liberian landscape, racial rules became slippery and social and demographic pressures from the new groups of migrants resulted in the creation of new administrative categories. By pushing and pulling against the boundaries of the nation in these ways, Liberia's different migrants re-inscribed it with the content of their ethnicity. The shared codes of reference in diaspora gave way as its shifting divisions boldly manifested in the tensions of settlement. As migrants politically strategized, individually and as communities, the tensions surrounding settlement, encounters, and sociocultural formation – creating new group identities, social ascriptions, and nomenclature – became a way of establishing relationships with diaspora and the state and to demarcate new identities. The unconditional distinctions between West Indians, African Americans, natives, and liberated Africans that emerged represented an essential method of organizing Liberian society and structuring experiences of citizenship. Distinctions were conceived through ideas of labor and civilization and consolidated through racialization, cultural discourse, legal practices, social conventions, and official and unofficial documents referring to the natives and liberated Africans pejoratively as "congoes and savages."[92]

---

[91] See Linda Colley, *Britons: Forging the Nation, 1707-1837* (New Haven, CT: Yale University Press, 1992).

[92] Jemima Pierre, *The Predicament of Blackness: Postcolonial Ghana and the Politics of Race*, (Chicago: University of Chicago Press, 2013), 14.

Diasporic positioning had practical implications for experiences in Liberia. Ethnic labels loomed large in the migrants' daily lives in various levels of social and political organization.[93] Ethnicity has been a function not of birth but of juridical power. New ethnicities emerged when blacks held power. In the same way, power gave the capacity to define and create others while not also being defined. The diaspora was the ethnicity that was not an ethnicity. This staked out an epistemic position from which to intercede. The diaspora's ethnic perspective held the privilege of envisioning themselves as the standard in opposition to what was being defined as different. These maneuvers were more than just about making subjects to rule over. As Jemima Pierre has argued, "it was a distinction of ethnological proportions" that linked views about the different groups' "physiological, emotional, mental character, the capacity to rule and citizenship."[94] The migrants marked the relevant details associated with nomenclature alongside Liberia's nation-building agenda. Skin color, language, and religion formed frameworks of categorization. "Congo," the name used to refer to liberated Africans, was as political a language as "indigenes," used to refer to native Liberians. "Americo-Liberian" was used to refer to African Americans, and "Islander" referred to West Indians. The appellation of West Indian became a casual extension of the British Empire as Americo-Liberian America. Nomenclature became a mindful distortion of a persisting tradition. In this fashioning of nomenclature, the historical connections between black migrants and racialized savages, however re-channeled, influenced the appeal as migrants behaved as if they were different from the white predecessors even as they acted like them. Migrants did not so much abandon the basic tenets of the life they had left behind. They merely subsumed them into behaviors spatially unbounded by Western white racism. Recall that it was darker-skinned West Indians who used to be called Congoes and the diaspora, in general, who were thought of as being too savage to remain among whites. Thus the migration and circulation of the pejorative terms are telling in the ways they expose anxieties within the nation.

In those moments of civilizing and hierarchy, white supremacy formed a dark spectral presence and Liberia became a veritable economy of symbols, on which the nation worked out its racial anxieties. Caged in their immigrant aspirations, with a knowing, haughty attitude toward

---

[93] Stephanie Smallwood, *Saltwater Slavery: A Middle Passage from Africa to American Diaspora* (Cambridge, MA: Harvard University Press, 2007), 107.

[94] Pierre, *The Predicament of Blackness*, 14.

Africans, the diasporic migrants could become European.[95] As J. Bernard Blamo observed, "the American Colonization Society instilled a sense of community among the diverse Negro migrant population. This often evolved from common involvement, shared interests and goals, the similarity of social experiences, and problems and external threats. A common culture is developed and nurtured through partaking in the meaning and the exchange of shared symbols by the constituent groups of the community."[96] Migrants were perhaps not cosigners for white supremacy, but merely allowed themselves to be swept along in its capacity for absorption. Nomenclatures solidified the invidious distinctions between the different groups of blacks in Liberia. They thus functioned as a type of ethnic designation, binding together and defining one's kinship group. With the African American pioneers, West Indians, liberated Africans, and the natives – pushed deeper and deeper into the interior and hidden in plain view – four different Liberias swirled around each other.

Nomenclature filled in political content by conjuring up attachment and distance from civilization. As the African diaspora and their offspring distinguished themselves from recaptives and natives. As such, those who had experienced slavery traveled a different path from those who had not. Immigrants adopted the prevailing racist sentiments of the global white supremacist power, which decidedly holds those religiously, socially, and politically closest to white in esteem and those farthest away in contempt. Observers deployed the terms Americo-Liberian, Congo, Islander, and indigene in different ways. As Paul Gilroy has argued, people mobilized nomenclature "often by default rather than design, as part of the distinctive hermeneutics of nation building."[97] Nomenclature, as a way of socially constructing ethnicity, also mapped the relations of power and patterns of contestations and reflected the struggle out of which it emerged. Thus, in Liberia, the fact of collective experiences of slavery did not imply equal citizenship, but rather parallel lines of activity originating from different cultural and political spaces.[98] A collective "we" based on race was disregarded for

---

[95] Richard Cohen, "Rethinking 'Babylon': Iconoclastic Conceptions of the Diasporic Experience." *Journal of Ethnic and Migration Studies*, Vol. 21, No. 1 (1995): 5–18.

[96] J. Bernard Blamo, "Nation-Building in Liberia: The Use of Symbolism in National Integration," *Liberia Studies Journal*, Vol. 4, No. 1 (1971): 21–30.

[97] Gilroy, *The Black Atlantic*, 5.

[98] Anne C. Bailey, *African Voices of the Atlantic Slave Trade: Beyond the Silence and the Shame* (Boston, MA: Beacon Press, 2005), 65.

a particularized experience of freedom and experience in Western civilization denoted by nomenclature.[99]

The differences between black and African, between Congo, native, and Americo Liberian, further mapped the boundaries of estrangement between the diaspora and Africa. The terms Americo-Liberian and savage functioned in a sectarian context. Congo not only denoted blackness but also implicitly acknowledged an intra-racial hierarchy (in which, it goes without saying, Africans were on the bottom because of perceived retrograde cultural practices). It followed the classic American Horatio Alger rags to riches story, extolling the virtues of African culture while simultaneously scolding it for its flaws. Blamo notes: "When a community adopts a set of self-referent symbols, it becomes a separate entity. Each time the agent cited a self-referent symbol, he unwittingly or wittingly defined the boundaries between Liberians and the indigenous population."[100] Identifiers such as African or black were used to reinforce solidarity and to integrate conflicting interests. Liberia struggled as migrants tried to sort through this muddled ethnic topography. The ability of race and blackness in Liberia to encompass many different meanings made it difficult to portray a stable, civilized identity. The sheer breadth undermined its utility for Liberian identity.[101] The dissonance between the different social groups – for example, perceiving African Americans as "enlightened" while expressing a dismissive attitude toward continental Africans and recaptives – begs the question of whether this was due mostly to ordinary classism or to a more complicated kind of Western racialism.

RELIGIOUS AND SOCIAL INTERACTIONS WITHIN THE NATION

National belonging was not only politically conceived but also religiously determined. Colonizationists had sought to establish "a separate, black Christian empire in Africa which they would ultimately parallel the white Christian Empire in America – twin beacons of a sort."[102] Liberia had been built on American religious foundations with Baptist and

---

[99] McGraw, *The Work of Recognition*, 2.
[100] Blamo, "The Use of Symbolism in National Integration," 4.
[101] Kathleen Brown, *Good Wives, Nasty Wenches, Anxious Patriarchs Gender, Race, and Power in Colonial Virginia* (Chapel Hill: University of North Carolina Press, 1996), 19.
[102] Frankie Hutton, "Economic Considerations in the American Colonization Society's Early Effort to Emigrate Free Blacks to Liberia, 1816–36." *The Journal of Negro History*, Vol. 68, No. 4 (Autumn, 1983): 377.

Methodism as the predominant denominational practices. Given this, Barbadians' Anglican religious orientation further unsettled the question of citizenship while also adding to the complexity of the multi-directional power struggle. Padmore, in his first letter to a friend in Barbados, noted, "A special service was called for us on Sunday the 14th at the parish church by Prof. Crummell, which was handsomely responded to." In his sermon to the Barbadians at the Trinity Church in Monrovia, Alexander Crummell chose a passage from Deuteronomy that summed up the exodus of the Israelites out of Egypt and their final settlement in the land of Canaan.[103] Crummell infused the Barbadians' journey with the same notion of providence. He called on persons of African ancestry around the world to be actively engaged in the religious, economic, and social development of the African continent. In these kinds of performances, the larger black populace coalesced and fragmented along religious lines. Sharp lines of demarcation were drawn between Western and African religion. In these instances, race was muted as other lines of identity became available as religion was accorded specific duties in the African diaspora. Crummell pointed out: "Our mission is evidently to organize the native labor all around us; to introduce regulating and controlling law among them; to gather their children into schools in order to train their intellects; to make these people civilized and Christian people; and to incorporate them into our Republic as citizens, and into the church of God as Brethren."[104] By these means, Crummell and other migrants propagated a black civilizationist and nationalist vision.[105]

Barbadians had many deferred dreams they hoped to revitalize in Liberia. The social and cultural experiences and values they sought to transplant said much about the dreams they had for Liberia. Among the first sociocultural aspects of a life they sought to leave behind, the Barbadians sought to transplant them through church and other institutions in Liberia. Indeed, religious life became an important register of how they identified and set themselves apart from newly arriving recaptives and the natives. A mere ten days after their arrival, the Barbadians commenced the building of Christ Church in their settlement of Crozierville (See Figure 5.4A and 5.4B). Reports confirmed that the

---

[103] *The African Repository*, Vol. 41 (1865): 243. *The Times*, June 6, 1865.

[104] Alexander Crummell, *Africa and America: Addresses and Discourses* (New York: Negro University Press, 1969); Blackett, "Martin R. Delany and Robert Campbell," 8.

[105] See Wilson Jeremiah Moses, *Alexander Crummell: A Study of Civilization and Discontent* (New York: Oxford University Press, 1989), 3.

Barbadians "have an Episcopal church in this settlement, of which Rev. A. F. Russell is the industrious and energetic pastor, and like all other Liberian people they profess to be very religious." The rich indigenous religious practices in the area were soon ignored. Still, attempts to transplant British colonial social, religious, and political institutions in Liberia waxed and waned because the political traditions needed to maintain them did not exist in totality. These institutions were supported by a political system that permitted a narrow group of citizens to guide political choices, thus ensuring that their interest would reign supreme. With its patriarchal and capitalistic structure, institutions like the church encouraged elites to distort it in ways that would enrich themselves and their political allies. This, in turn, functioned to tighten their control even more.

As one of the first West Indian migrants, Edward Blyden favored non-Western and African forms of social organizations. Blyden remained keen on the Muslim religious traditions and what they could mean for regenerating the continent. In "Mohammedanism and the Negro Race," the first chapter of book exploring blacks' relationship with different religions, Blyden showed his high regard for Islam as a political and civilizing force: "Mohammedanism in Africa has left the native master of himself and of his home; but wherever Christianity has been able to establish itself ... foreigners have taken possession of the country, and, in some places, rule the natives with oppressive rigour."[106] Blyden viewed Islam as a better civilizing force than Christianity. Drawing from his observations, he pointed out, "No one can travel any distance in the interior of West Africa without being struck with the different aspects of society in different localities, according as the population is Pagan or Mohammedan." Not only is there "a difference in methods of government, but in the general regulations of society, and even in the amusements of the people." He pointed out that "the love of noisy torpischorean performances, so noticeable in the Pagan communities, disappears as people come under the influence of Mohammedanism."[107] The implicit Christian imperatives in the idea of civilizing Africa meant that Blyden would not find much support for this Islamic vision for Liberia, which often put him at odds with Americo-Liberians.

[106] See Edward Wilmot Blyden, *Christianity, Islam and the Negro Race* (Edinburgh: Edinburgh University Press, 1967), 309.
[107] Blyden, *Christianity, Islam, and the Negro Race*, 27.

FIGURE 5.4A: Christ Church Episcopal, Named after the Parish of Christ Church in Barbados
Source: Photograph by Matthew C. Reilly

The social and religious sphere defined various relationships that fostered horizontal and communal cross-cultural interactions. Naturally, these communities overlapped, but primary social networks formed among those living within the same spaces who also came from similar backgrounds. In these early years, intra-black fragmentation was more palpable than ever. The social landscape created identity politics, which posed challenges to ideas about blackness and raised questions about the social stability of the nation. The ensuing relationships became a litmus test on which other forms of black solidarity and advancement would be measured. Intermarriage, cross-religious interactions, and labor relations brought together African Americans, West Indians, recaptives, and indigenes. Many sought social advancement in Liberia through marriages. As a site for reconstituting new familial relationships, networks of new non-biological relationships and new members, marriages became the means by which many Barbadians rose to elite social standing in Liberia. Different migrants had arrived in Liberia, often with established family and kinship networks, but marriages and other social activities became an arena in which social and cultural lines would be crossed.

Although the Barbadians, to a large extent, married each other, they also married into indigenous and Americo-Liberian groups. The *African Times* reported one such marriage, on an evening in May, "at the

FIGURE 5.4B: Christ Church Episcopal, Named after the Parish of Christ Church in Barbados
Source: Photograph by Matthew C. Reilly

commodious dwelling house of the bride's father in Ashmun Street by the Rev. C. A. Pitman, pastor of the Methodist Church, Monrovia, Florence Irene, eldest child and only daughter of the Hon. J. T. Wiles, Secretary of the Treasury, Republic of Liberia and Jesse Randolph, eldest son of the Hon. Henry Cooper, merchant, of Monrovia." The Coopers were a prominent Americo-Liberian family in Liberia, among the first colonists arriving on the *Elizabeth*. Some of the most prominent Liberians witnessed the marital union of these two families. Their wedding guests included "President James S. Payne and wife, the Secretary of State and wife, and the Hon. C. B. Dunbar, M. D. and wife." The *Observer* further reported: "The early part of the evening was most agreeably spent; music and song, and the manifest care, forethought, and solicitude of the host and hostess for the perfect enjoyment and gratification of their guests, rendering everything delightful." This account of a wedding further provides a view into the lives of prominent Liberians:

The nuptial rites being ended and followed by a sumptuous and more substantial repast than the preceding varied and delicious dainties during the evening, dancing under the graceful leading of the bride and bridegroom and bridal suite, succeeded and was continued with refreshing intervals throughout the lovely moonlight night long after the youthful bride had departed to her new-made home, and the bright morning star sparklingly pellucid in rapt serenity bespoke the approach of day.[108]

The Barbadians' course of life through the late nineteenth century evolved through their social relationships. By facilitating the formation of kinship and other forms of solidarities, marriages produced and consolidated the cultural and social hierarchy in Liberia. Other West Indians who settled in Liberia in the early twentieth century joined the Barbadian community. The Trinidadian George Stanfield Best, who settled in Liberia after the First World War, married Lillian Porte, the daughter of the Barbadian Conrad Porte. John Blyden, the youngest brother of Edward Blyden, who had emigrated the same year as the Barbadian group, married Sarah Barclay. In 1873, Sarah served as the assistant to W. M. Richards, who was the principal of Trinity P. Episcopal Church School in Monrovia. One advertisement that year noted that the school was now open for accommodation for pupils from all parts of the country, particularly noting that the "interior and river settlements will do well to avail themselves of the advantages it affords."[109]

Also within the Barclay family, Mary Augusta Barclay married James Padmore. Sarah Helena Barclay married Joseph Blyden at Grand Bassa on May 17, 1873.[110] Ella Mai Barclay married the attorney general, H. W. Grimes, the father of Louis Arthur Grimes, who later became chief justice. Though Antoinette Barclay never married or had children, she "had a strong impact on her nephews and nieces by teaching them through elementary school in a private institution in Monrovia."[111] Death also mediated familial relationships. Arthur Barclay first married Miss Mary Marshall, by whom he had five children, three boys and two girls – Sarah Elizabeth, Augustas, Mary Antoinette, Gerald, and a baby boy who died a few days after birth along with his mother. Following his first wife's passing, Barclay married Jane Lomax, who had previously been married to the attorney general, William Davis. The couple had two children, both of whom died in infancy. Upon the death of Jane Lomax, Arthur Barclay married Mrs. Florence Cooper, widow of the late Senator A. B. King. After her death, he married Mrs. Sarah Cooper-Barclay, widow of the late Jesse

[108] " Marriage at Monrovia." Reprinted in *The African Repository*, Vols. 51–53 (1877): 30.
[109] *The African Repository*, Vol. 49 (1876): 45.
[110] See "A Brief Life Sketch of the Malvina Barclay," 8.
[111] See Mary Antoinette Brown Sherman, *Barclay Women in Liberia*.

Cooper.[112] Within two generations, the Wiles and Barclay families, having moved into the elite class through politics, education, work, and marriage, became the leaders of the Barbadian dynasty in Liberia.

Most suggestive of the migrants' cultural conceit was perhaps their lack of intermarriage with the indigenes. This did not necessarily mean the absence of relationships, just their lack of legal recognition. In 1836, the acting colonial governor, Reverend B. R. Skinner, had observed that "the marriage of a colonist with anyone [from] the neighboring tribes was considered exceedingly disreputable and subjected the individual to the contempt of his fellow citizens."[113] As late as 1879, Liberia's Daniel Warner – who advocated intermarriage as a panacea to the cultural and social cleavages between the migrants and natives – nevertheless noted that "it would require on the part of the man of the least culture, strong moral courage to break through the strong prejudice against the inter-marriage of the colonists and natives which prevail here among the Americo-Liberians."[114] In the few cases when settlers intermarried with indigenes, it was often with the coastal Vai and Grebo ethnic groups, who often lived with settler communities and were the beneficiaries of educa-tion and "civilization." Two examples are that of Euphemia Mary Davis, daughter of William McCall Davis of Americo-Liberian descent, and Jane Seton Davis of the Grebo ethnic group, who was born in Monrovia, Liberia, on July 19, 1884. Davis grew up and was educated in Monrovia, graduating with a Bachelor of Arts degree from Liberia College in 1905. She married Edwin James Barclay, secretary of state (1920–1930) and president of the nation (1930–1944). Although she never had children, she was said to have fostered many.

The different groups, although they had been spatially cordoned off, were mutually interactive in a variety of ways. The indigenes entered migrants' lives as laborers, traders, and household wards in much the same way that Native Americans interacted with European settlers. Much of the Barbadians' acts of civilizing would be achieved through wardships, guardianships, and foster-parenting. The Barclay women were especially known for this practice. Mary Antoinette Brown Sherman, a descendant of the Barclays, noted in her work *Barclay Women in Liberia* that many of the Barclay women had no children and resorted to fostering native

---

[112] See "A Brief Life Sketch of the Life of Malvina Barclay."
[113] A. Archibald, *A History of Colonization on the Western Coast of Africa* (Negro Universities Press, 1969), 511.
[114] *The African Repository and Colonial Journal*, Vol. 10 (1834): 316–318.

children. Born in Jondu, Cape Mount, Liberia, in February 1889, Victoria
Elizabeth Jelloh Cheeseman – the daughter of Ambollai Fahnbulleh and
Jarsie Fahnbulleh of the Vai ethnic group – spent the first six years of her
life in Jondu but then became the foster daughter of President Joseph
James Cheeseman and Mary Ann Crusoe Cheeseman, and moved with
them into their executive mansion. She later married Louis Arthur Grimes.
Ella Mai Gilbert Barclay, who married Henry Waldron Grimes, had two
children, Louis Arthur and Florence Mai Isabel, and one foster son, Frank
Tarr Grimes. Georgia Ann Barclay, the daughter of Anthony Barclay Jr.,
never married or had children but was said to have fostered several
children.[115]

A doctor visiting Liberia in the 1830s noted other oppressive ways in
which the migrants interacted with the indigenes. He highlighted that it
was the Bassas that "the colonists were most acquainted with, having
daily and hourly intercourse with them, with nearly all of the resident
natives living in the settlements being members of this large tribe."[116]
The report noted that "Many Bassa children lived in the settler homes and
attended Sunday school and school with the settlers." The children were
often wards or servants who relieved the settlers of the most difficult work
in the households and on the farms and who learned particular skills in
settler workshops. In many of these cases, there were charges and admis-
sions that some of the children were beaten because they were "lazy or
scoundrels."[117] Still, friendships and other relationships would be established. It was within this social context that the English language, civilization, and Christianity were most effectively transmitted.

While the Atlantic had opened the way for the Barbadians to
experience greater freedom, citizenship, and nationhood, it was also
a revolving door through which old mechanisms of exploitation and
subordination made their way to Africa. In their transition to citizenship in Liberia, Barbadians imbibed British imperial notions as
a liberatory mechanism. As the portable vessels of imperialism,
migrants were able to act out these claims in their relationships and
their efforts to subordinate other groups. By their acquisition of
Western culture and possession of some knowledge of the modern
political organization, the Barbadians regarded their culture as superior to that of the African population. Their very experiences as

[115] Sherman, *Barclay Women in Liberia*.
[116] *The African Repository and Colonial Journal*, Vol. 14 (1838): 336.
[117] Ibid.

imperial subjects made Barbadians the agents of the imperialism that
they had disavowed. It was observed that they too "disapproved of the
scanty dress worn by many of the African peoples, whom they
regarded as semi nude, untutored savages "[118] They despised African
forms of religion as paganism, heathenism, and idolatry, and they
looked contemptuously at African social and political formations.
Natives had active institutions such as *poro,* a secret society for men,
and *sande,* for women.[119] While the Freemasonry quickly became an
influential organization in the political life of the country, natives
continued to maintain their cross-ethnic solidarities by retaining their
institutions and keeping their secrets from the migrant populace.[120]

Many observers also believed that the Africans themselves were
culturally prejudiced against the settlers. They, too, disapproved of
and despised many aspects of the settlers' way of life. In particular,
many of them sneered at the slave ancestry of the settlers and regarded
them as socially inferior. An American visitor to Liberia observed
in March 1844 that, on one hand, the colonists "would never recognize the natives otherwise than as heathens;" while on the other hand,
"many of the natives look with contempt on the colonists and do not
hesitate to tell them that they are merely liberated slaves."[121] Africans
were said also to have loathed the permissive sexual standards among
the settlers, some of whom carried on irregular sexual relations with
African women, particularly African girls apprenticed to settler
families.[122]

Other differences created divisions among the black populace.
The experiences of the various emigrant streams were also used as
a source of differentiation. The weight of history and the migrants'
past were politicized and used to make social and political claims.

---

[118] J. J. Roberts, Annual Message in *The African Repository,* Vol. 27 (1851): 117, in
H. A. Jones, "The Struggle for Political and Cultural Unification in Liberia
1847–1930." PhD thesis (Evanston, IL: Northwestern University, 1962), 151.

[119] Benjamin J. K. Anderson, *Narrative of Journey to Musardu. The Capital of the Western
Mandingoes* (S. W. Green, Printer, 1870), 68–69.

[120] See Beryl Larry Bellman, *The Language of Secrecy: Symbols & Metaphors in Poro Ritual*
(New Brunswick, NJ: Rutgers University Press, 1984), 8.

[121] M. B. Akpan, "Black Imperialism: Americo-Liberian Imperialism, 1841–1964,"
Canadian Journal of African Studies, Vol. 7, No. 2 (1973): 225.

[122] U.S.M. 5, "Complaint of the Cape Palmas Tribe," Big Town, Cape Palmas,
30 July 1875, reprinted in M. B. Akpan, "Black Imperialism: Americo-Liberian Rule
over the African Peoples of Liberia, 1841–1964," *Canadian Journal of African Studies /
Revue Canadienne des Études Africaines.* Vol. 7, No. 2 (1973): 217–236.

A particular significance was accorded not only to place of birth but also to the number of years of freedom a migrant had experienced. The length of freedom featured largely in these differences and became a status symbol that drove access to citizenship in Liberia. Recaptives who had received freedom on the Atlantic could make little claim on the republic. Natives were seen as even farther removed because of their involvement with the slave trade and other activities that marked them as heathens. The fact that, unlike African Americans, Barbadians had not emigrated from a slave society and had experienced thirty years or more of freedom distinguished them from African Americans and accrued enormous social capital to them. Pre-existing notions of community and family undoubtedly also contributed to intra-black differences, which further complicated efforts to create administrative, bureaucratic, and legal structures that would register across the different groups of migrants.

Barbadian migration to Liberia fostered legally egalitarian relationships within the family and across genders. In Liberia, Barbadian women openly challenged their male counterparts in court. In 1904, for example, Florence Wiles challenged her brother, Richard Jones Wiles over the will of their father, James Thomas Wiles (who was still living), for property he had left behind. Florence, obviously aware of the law (specifically, the Homestead Act), was able to retain half of the property. That she was able to appeal and be legally recognized suggests the degree to which migration had enhanced the lives of the Barbadian migrant women. Correspondence related to this case is revealing in other ways as well.

J. T. Wiles had been thirty-four years old when he emigrated to Liberia, but he later returned to Barbados. As he was described in the *African Repository*, "Mr. J.T. Wiles one of their best men and first class mechanic, engaged in mercantile pursuits, for which his superior business education and urbanity of manners seems to have well qualified him. He bids fair to be a successful merchant."[123] Writing from Barbados, Wiles sent a power of attorney to his son, Richard, and Mr. Grimes, empowering them to act on his behalf in the disposal of property in Monrovia and the renting of other premises. He gave his son instructions related to property business and indicated that he did not expect to live much longer. Deprived of the common beverage that he had drunk often, he asked his son to get some Liberian coffee "from

[123] *The African Repository*, Vol. 49 (1876): 274.

those Arthington people and send for me. I long to taste a little Liberian coffee. You could ship to Edward Bros. or your own agent asking them to ship to my address, and it would come safe. You will have to double bag it so as to save it better." He also asked his son to remember to send him postage stamps: "I have been asking for them for four years." He then chided him on his command of English and encouraged him to improve himself: "I understand from Mr. Grimes that both of you and himself have [come] together and gone to housekeeping in the cottage. This gives me much pleasure. You will be in good company by which you can immensely improve yourself," Wiles advised his son, "Get a dictionary and an English grammar and get him [Grimes] to instruct you. I believe he will take pleasure in so doing. Your spelling is very bad, try to improve it now."[124]

Wiles also drew on the experiences of past president J. J. Roberts to motivate his son:

Mr. Roberts said that when he was conferring degrees on some of the students of Liberia College that he was thirty-five years of age before he really began to study anything; and said that it was never too late to begin to improve the mind and in keeping with that it is just your time to begin – go on my son and try to make yourself a pillar of the State.

Wiles was coming to the end of his life but remained fully committed to the idea of upward mobility, telling his son: "I may not live to see that, but my spirit will hover around you and your brother until the trumpet will sound. I have mentioned to Mr. Grimes my wishes and doubt not that he will give you his attention if you show any willingness."[125] J. T. Wiles died in Barbados at the age of sixty-six on February 6, 1897, and was buried in Westbury Cemetery.[126]

GROUP IDENTITY IN LIBERIA

On occasions, notions of civilization served as a means of bringing together Americo-Liberians and West Indians as the country's elites while it relegated the natives to the bottom. The struggle to maintain and elevate one's status, at the cost of racial solidarity, contributed to conflicts between migrants and the natives. Pan-Africanism did not make an easy Atlantic crossing. The quest for liberty and emancipation

[124] Ibid.
[125] Ibid.
[126] Ibid.

for blacks from the diaspora became less of an advocacy of racial equality and fragmented into group solidarities. Geographical, socio-economic, and political separation produced a rift between the indigenes and later settlers long before the civil wars of the twentieth century. With its various African ethnicities, Liberia had always been a heterogeneous society. These were further subdivided into roughly sixteen ethnic groups who sometimes cohered and were other times divided by differing cultural, social, and religious practices. Africans exhibited group consciousness on occasions, which was often in opposition to African American settlers. The African Americans were divided by the states from which they had migrated. Such divisions, exacerbated by skin color, were reflected in society and politics. African recaptives formed another societal group. Coming from Congo-Angola, they held a different set of religious beliefs that separated them from the indigenous African ethnicities as well as from the African American and Barbadian settlers.

Barbadians further added to the complexity of the Liberian mosaic with their backgrounds as West Indians and British imperial subjects. Afro-Barbadians fashioned their identities as Liberians in ways which played upon and against existing logics of race, all the while enacting forms of affective insurgency which would critically influence future iterations of black identity and culture. In the public and private spheres, they fashioned distinct modes of colonial West Indian practices and cultural expressions that were grounded in and altered through their identities as black migrants, yet also reacted to internal and global figurations of blacks in the global imaginary. Reflective of their diasporic identity, the West Indians' British colonial identity and their common referential use of the title "West Indians," was used to test and predict the existing opportunities for the emancipated people of African descent affiliated with the British empire. While "black" and "African" had been the predominant mode of identification in the diaspora, in Liberia the increasing visibility of the image of the indigenes served to fragment this collective sense of blackness and cement efforts by the migrants to distinguish themselves. Being distinguished as British in Liberia did not automatically lead to a recognition of British subjecthood. By the late nineteenth century, by fashioning themselves as industrious British emancipated subjects deserving of imperial protection and privileges, Barbadian migrants began to keenly solicit the British support.

As a result, different nodes of identification emerged. Loathing to leave behind the prestige that their connections to America afforded, African Americans saw themselves as Americo-Liberians, a moniker that sustained their American past as it demarcated the distinctiveness of their identity. Americo-Liberians stood apart from African recaptives, who were labeled "Congoes," and even further still from the "heathen and uncivilized" natives. Barbadians seemingly remained a floating group, sometimes associated with the "Congoes" and at other times regarded as the "West Indians" or "Islanders." These kinds of designations not only determined one's place in society but also served as a marker of differentiation. On the one hand, the designation of "West Indian" rooted them within imperial belonging and sealed them in a racially exploitative relationship to the empire. On the other hand, it also broadened the racial boundaries of colonialism.

Despite constitutionally opening up citizenships to blacks, migration alone proved inadequate for certain groups to fully make such claims in Liberia. As the various groups of blacks demonstrated their different impulses toward citizenship, Liberia's connection to each of them was manifested in various ways to credit or discredit their claims. Distinctions were conceived of in absolute ideas about labor and civilization and were consolidated through racialization, cultural discourse, legal practices, social conventions, and official and unofficial documents referencing the natives and liberated Africans pejoratively as "congoes and savages." Ultimately, Liberia's fear of portraying an uncivilized front to whites overrode the pan-Africanist rhetoric that had accorded the extension of citizenship to blacks, drawing them to the republic.

African Americans' and West Indians' citizenship was identified and strengthened by their relationship to the "others" they created by racializing themselves as blacks and native Liberians, and liberated Africans as tribes. Savage and inferior identities were placed on native ethnic Liberians and liberated Africans, who were defined regarding their capacity to labor and their ability to do appropriate productive labor toward projecting the republic's modernity. West Indians and African Americans could claim citizenship concessions gained through long-standing historical negotiations, while ethnic Africans and liberated Africans, by having not experienced slavery or crossing the Atlantic, were dislocated from the arena in which both groups had negotiated the terms of their citizenship. Class status, skills, and education all added to emigrants' sense of place in the republic, prefiguring a hierarchy that called for an unequal relationship between the different cohorts of blacks even before their arrival. By not allowing these "others" to occupy the same "proper" citizenship spaces, and by judging them by a rubric of savagery, racialized native and liberated Africans provided a mirror through which to articulate shifting perceptions of themselves as civilized and superior. The diaspora's achievement of citizenship in Liberia structured new relationships of dominance.

6

Making Citizenship and Blackness in Liberia

Barbadians' arrival in Liberia proved momentous. But if they found their unusual social environment to be worrisome, their ambiguous political status created even more alarm. The Barbadian cohort arrived in a Liberian republic where African American migrants turned Americo-Liberians controlled the politics. The Americo-Liberian Joseph Jenkins Roberts, a migrant from Virginia who had served as Liberia's first president, anxiously observed the 1865 arrival of the 346 Barbadians: "Heretofore we have had now and then a family or two to arrive from the British West Indies; but nearly all, after a while, make a visit to Sierra Leone, and in most cases finally settle there, where the manners and customs of the people are more English, and, of course, more adapted to their early habits and taste."[1]

With an acute awareness of the political implications of the Barbadians' presence, the former president set aside his fears as he attempted to remain optimistic. Roberts hoped that, as the largest group of West Indians to have settled in the republic, "perhaps this company, being a large number and forming themselves a neighborhood, as I understand they propose settling pretty much together between the St. Paul's and Carysburg," would keep them in Liberia. But Roberts also sensed the Barbadians' political dislocation in republican Liberia and understood the implications for the migrants and the state. As such, he prayed that they would "gradually slide into our republican feelings and sentiments, and soon find themselves entirely identified with this country. If so, as I think most likely, these people, with the blessings of providence, will doubtless prove a great acquisition to

[1] *The African Repository*, Vol. 41(1865): 249–250.

Liberia."[2] Perhaps Roberts's conscious hostility to the migrants' non-Republican political ideology was rooted in the agitation of British encroachment evoked by the West Indians' presence. Migrant British colonial Barbadians were in many ways similar to the African Americans, reflecting the overlapping layers of identity-making in Liberia. Yet, as royalist imperial subjects, Barbadians provided a counterweight to African American republicanism. By politically distinguishing the West Indians from their African American counterparts, Roberts admitted that their different political legacy would disrupt the communalism that Liberia had forged through a black racial identity.

Roberts's remarks upon the arrival of the group of Barbadians highlighted the different markers of blackness that underlined the veneer of an ostensibly homogeneous black populous in Liberia. Placing the West Indian migrants' success on their assimilation to Americo-Liberian republicanism revealed the practicalities of decisions that had been made on the basis of reductive ideas of blackness as well as forecasted the difficulties that laid ahead of rendering diasporic theories feasible. Roberts's comments about the Barbadians might have left the already vulnerable migrants feeling even more lonely, and made the otherwise familiar racial environment of Liberia appear stranger. In this moment, the Barbadians perhaps came to regret not emigrating to Sierra Leone. Whether Barbadians would find Liberia "more auspicious" depended on their own political calculations and Liberia's adjustments to the palpable sentiments their presence raised: How would Barbadians, as British subjects, adjust to life in an American-styled republic? What elements of their colonial black identity would the Barbadians project in their new homes? What aspects of their identity would the other groups of blacks embrace? Which would they shun?

In the nineteenth century, after the ACS set Liberia up as a colony for formerly free and enslaved African Americans, Liberia took on a broader symbolism in the African diaspora. Liberia evolved from a bastion of freedom into the "black man's republic." From its national vantage point, Liberia projected ideas of a common racial identity and visions of a shared fate. Roberts's initial observations thus contradicted Afro-Barbadians and other black migrants who, before coming to Liberia, had participated in a print culture that enabled them to claim de facto citizenship by allowing them to join in the ideological narrative of the republic. Unlike the indigenes and recaptives, and supposedly who had little

---

[2] Ibid.

ideological stakes in the ideas of a Liberian nationality, African Americans and Barbadians anticipated sharing in Liberian citizenship through their similar historical experiences and goals to improve themselves and civilize the natives. In spite of the many points of diasporic cohesion, the coming together of disparate experiences and dynamics challenged the Liberian nation-building process in ways uncharacteristic of other post-emancipation societies, and shaped blacks' experiences of citizenship and nationhood in critical ways.

Whereas the collectivizing experiences of the migrants functioned to repair the rupture and fragmentation of diaspora, the political dynamics of nation building allowed blacks to recognize their points of difference with searing clarity. Differences in the migrants' political heritage produced fault lines that affected their integration into the Liberian nation. The elimination of the magical haze of distance overshadowed opportunities to unite under a singular identity and ideological vision without conceding the fractures, ruptures, and discontinuities that constituted the particularities of the subjectivities involved. As the lives of different groups of blacks banged against each other, revealing blackness in ways yet unknown, it brought about a realization that the ideas surrounding blackness were in many ways fictional. By prompting a reflection on what it meant to be black and who was included, differences that initially appeared small and imperceptible later grew, with the advent of the Barbadians, increasingly large, visible, and troubling. Indeed, upon their meeting in Liberia, migrants realized that their identities were not already fixed and could not transcend place, time, history, and culture. Migrants further realized that their identities were shaped by the dissimilar ways in which they were positioned as well as by how they positioned themselves in narratives of the past and present.[3] Migration to Liberia cemented Stuart Hall's argument that cultural identities are "without fixity and essentialism, undergoing constant conversion."[4] As blackness in Liberia remained synonymous with African Americans' identity, its meaning remained unclear. Acting as a force against assimilation, the migrants' differences prolonged the act of diaspora and created the foundations for new forms of ethnic identity formations.

By entertaining a multiplicity of views projected from all angles, the Liberian nation became a highly contested political space. If, as David

---

[3] Stuart Hall, "Cultural Identity and Diaspora," in Jonathan Rutherford, ed., *Identity: Community, Culture, Difference* (London: Lawrence and Wishart, 1990).

[4] Ibid., 225.

Lambert argues, the ideological war over representations of black freedom took place in sites such as Sierra Leone, Liberia, by comparison,
became the controversial site in the war over black citizenship and nationhood. This was largely because of the lack of cohesion around meanings of
blackness wrought by the different migrants and stakeholders.[5] Liberia
was conflated as an abolitionist, colonizationist, and black nationalist
project. As such, its visions of black citizenship were often at odds with
its other obligations. Americo-Liberians in Liberia, too, understood the
limits of their political community and justified expanding or contracting
the boundaries of the nation at certain moments to include some blacks,
while excluding some at other times. The Liberian nation-building project
thus lingered in uncertainty in much the same way that the meaning of
freedom remained undefined in both the Abolition Act of 1833 and the
Emancipation Proclamation of 1863.

With the influx of the Barbadians that disrupted the creation and
unfolding of Liberia's black nationalist fiction, the 1860s proved
a transformative moment for the migrants and republic alike. Barclay
and other Barbadian migrants soon realized that what, indeed, would
determine how they would become a part of the body politic as citizens
was not their racial sameness but their utility to Liberia's nation-building
endeavor. Barbadian cleavages manifested not only in racial identity but
also political style. Whereas early African American pioneers linked
Liberia as a nationality to a certain ethnic orientation and cultural particularity, the new Barbadian migrants ushered Liberian citizenship into
a political era that went beyond the bounds of those kinds of narrow
affiliation.

By the late nineteenth century, as the Barbadians helped to create the
True Whig Party (TWP), they successfully challenged African Americans'
ability to wield political power in the republic through the force of the
Republican Party. The ascendancy of the TWP, formed by Barbadian
migrant farmers in 1869, marked the decline of early Americo-Liberian
Republican leadership.[6] It also reflected Afro-Barbadians' exploitation of
their in-between spatial position to carve out political positions (as they
had done in Barbados) and build political support. What ultimately made

---

[5] David Lambert, "Sierra Leone and Other Sites in the War of Representation over Slavery,"
History Workshop Journal, Vol. 64. No. 1 (2007): 103–132.

[6] Carl Patrick Burrowes, *Power and Press Freedom in Liberia, 1830–1970: The Impact of
Globalization and Civil Society on Media-Government Relations* (Trenton, NJ: Africa
World Press, 2004), 88.

the TWP successful was the intercultural community founded along the St. Paul's River, to which the Barbadians belonged. In this space, culture passed back and forth between the different groups of Barbadians, recaptives, and natives in interesting ways. The evolution of Afro-Barbadian politics in Liberia from 1870 to the turn of the century saw the development of their own positions on issues such as the Scramble for Africa in 1884, Liberia's territorial boundaries, and its image on the world stage during this era. Having lived under a monarchy, Afro-Barbadians had a different view of democracy and republicanism that the experience of living in Liberia shaped and changed over time. Political alignment reflected Americo-Liberians and Afro-Barbadians. According to Carl Burrowes, the "TWP comprised new personalities with new interests."[7] Burrowes identified the West Indian political style of government as emphasizing education, critical journalism through social commentary in the form of broadsides, and a belief in service to the government. These cultural practices were necessary for a Barbadian community that was too small and thus did not have the electoral base to elect their own into government as African Americans could. They thus came to office after long years in service and government bureaucracy rather than through national elections.

Barbadians further revised African American visions of Liberian identity and citizenship. Barbadians carved out new forms of Liberian citizenship that derived their meanings through actions that served Liberia's modernizing goals. While the Liberian nation had been formed to derive its identity from some "common ethnic and cultural properties," the post-independence exigencies of diplomacy and modernity moved the definition to one of the "praxis of citizens who actively exercised their civil rights."[8] By serving the demands for a civilized and productive workforce, Barbadians' aspiration for citizenship ushered in a different mode of migrant absorption unencumbered by ethnic identity. Barbadians found refuge in the universal recognition of the utility of productive labor and Liberia's own desire to project a modern and civilized image. Productive labor served to control and transform an individual's mind, body, and soul. In serving as acts of recognition that affirmed them, discursive exchanges, missionary observations, government regulations and practices, and press stories came together to not only re-racialize the different migrants but also prescribe and affirm ideas of labor productivity as

---

[7] Ibid.
[8] Ho, *Nation and Citizenship in the Twentieth-Century British Novel*, 7.

grounds for qualification for citizenship. By showing that they understood the complicated responsibilities of freedom through attentiveness to work discipline, religion, and capital, blacks could demonstrate their ability to develop a black nation.

THE POLITICAL CONSTRUCTION OF LIBERIA

Following their long-standing discomfort in the Caribbean, the Barbadians arrived into a new and complicated political situation in Liberia. They were forced to navigate a political system of power that took its inspiration from a series of unfamiliar tenets. Before its establishment and throughout its existence, Liberia's multiple inhabitants and different interest groups contested its meaning. In the early nineteenth century, the ACS held up Liberia as "the hope for the Negro." President James Monroe, a slaveholder who had successfully petitioned Congress for funds to repatriate blacks, predicted that Liberia would be "little America, destined to shine gem-like in the heart of darkness of Africa."[9] For benevolent colonizationists who reasoned that racial prejudices, labor competition, and rivalry over wealth would not advance blacks in America, solutions called for blacks to be "placed beyond this prejudice – whereas the weaker class, he will not be depressed and overshadowed by the stronger – he should be removed to the home of his ancestors where he may elevate himself."[10] Thus the creation of Liberia aimed to provide a "fair field, an equal chance, and a free fight" necessary for "developing all the elements of [blacks'] latent and long obscured manhood."[11] Informed by these viewpoints, the Liberian nation-building project served as a barometer of blacks' potential for progress and modernity. On this basis, blacks would receive white recognition and respect.

If abolition had been a daunting task, building a black nation, no less on a coast overrun by slavery, proved even more formidable. Symbolically straddling the past and future by ending up in Liberia, African Americans, West Indians, and recaptives represented the unfinished work of emancipation in the Atlantic world. At the core of Liberia's formation were desires of transforming the inhumanities of slavery and slave trading by creating a modern black nation. As a site that brought together disparate

---

[9] See Eric Burin, *Slavery and the Peculiar Solution: A History of the American Colonization Society* (Gainesville: University Press of Florida, 2005), 16.

[10] Staudenraus, *African Colonization*, 123.

[11] *The Christian Mirror*, September, 29, 1863.

visions into the discipline and order of a black nation-state, Liberia embodied a significant part of the unfolding emancipation project. Like the Caribbean, where freedmen, British officials, and white plantation owners struggled over the meaning of freedom, Liberia produced multiple political and ideological contestations among whites, African indigenes, and diasporic groups over the meanings of freedom, citizenship, and nationhood. Such an image of "returning Africans" was functional for a classical liberalism that constituted itself by inscribing itself in the continuing presence of slavery and slave trading. It posed the emigrants returning to build the republic as the inheritors of its freedom, albeit achieved only in a minimal form. Migrants' presence in Liberia produced a cartography of freedom minimally defined by what states do. Rather, freedom in Liberia appeared as the spatial negation of slave trading and slavery and redemption wrought by Western civilization.

Liberia's creation reflected colonial efforts to create a racially bound republic in the United States. British colonial ventures, like Liberia, had started with aims of achieving a clear sense of the liberty and equality in the United States. But colonies imagined in the crucible of other British American colonies ultimately adopted the paradoxical twin practices of freedom and slavery.[12] American colonizationists thus demonstrated an early idea of liberty that made freedom and liberty contingent on enslaving others. As such, "they can't give it up without becoming slaves."[13] This became the driving force for land ownership and the basis for expanding political participation in early America. Migrant equality never worked out in the Americas, as Europeans who brought religion to the Americas had created differences based on race. Despite their proclaimed belief in black abilities, the white leaders of ACS had keenly held onto the leadership and control of Liberia. The ACS made the rules and laws they saw fit for the government of the settlement and vowed to leave only when the migrants could govern themselves.[14] The ACS gave their agents authority in Liberia and granted legislative powers to the various state colonies but made them subject to change by their board of managers. They made common law applicable though it was not African-inspired. For instance, an early digest

[12] Jack P. Greene, *Imperatives, Behaviors, and Identities: Essays in Early American Cultural History* (Charlottesville: University Press of Virginia, 1992), 141.

[13] Jasper Mauduit, "Agent in London for the Province of Massachusetts-Bay, 1762–1765." Massachusetts Historical Society Collections. Volume 74 (Boston, 1918), 39–54, reprinted in Craig Yirush, ed., *Settlers, Liberty, and Empire: The Roots of Early American Political Theory, 1675–1775* (New York: Cambridge University Press, 2011), 2.

[14] *The African Repository and Colonial Journal*, Vol. 11 (1835): 21.

of laws stated that "quarreling, rioting, drunkenness, Sabbath-breaking, profaneness, and lewdness are infractions of the public peace."[15] In many ways, the American background of Liberia's early black colonists and the United States' development as a nation foretold the republic's fate. Though the migrants had ostensibly crossed the Atlantic to escape white racism and patriarchy, the presence of ACS officials in Liberia created a black and white racial dynamic that played out in politics.

By the 1840s, economic and diplomatic difficulties made Liberia a financial burden to the ACS. The increasing interests of the emerging settler merchant class also played a crucial role in inciting independence.[16] Consequently, discussions emerged about making Liberia independent.[17] On the eve of independence, while the ACS continued to hold a perverse influence over the colony, debates over a future constitution emerged. When Simon Greenleaf, a white colonizationist jurist from Massachusetts, first offered his assistance and services to draft the new state constitution, he ensured that the new political body would continue to be inspired by American ideas of race. In June 1846, the ACS sent Greenleaf's proposal inclusive of all the clauses of the constitution to the delegates who were about to gather for a convention. Though they were only intended as a guide to the impending deliberations of the constitutional convention, there were clear tensions. The colonists in Liberia found much of Greenleaf's "proposals inappropriate" and the document altogether underwhelming.[18]

On July 5, 1847, long before Barclay and the other Barbadians arrived, twelve African American representatives from the various states in Liberia met in Monrovia to draft the constitution.[19] The conveners chose Hilary Teage, a Virginia migrant who served as the editor of the *Liberian Herald*,

---

[15] Eleventh Annual Report of the American Society for Colonizing the Free People of Color of the United States, 1828, 41, Hathi Trust Digital Library.

[16] Robert Smith, *Deeds Not Words: A History of the True Whig Party* (Monrovia: University of Liberia, 1970).

[17] The U.S. Congress consistently refused to support the movement. Daring attempts were made by Henry Clay with his distribution bill to use the money from the sale of lands for the colonization enterprise, much to the chagrin of those who opposed the scheme. For more, see Frankie Hutton, "Economic Considerations in the American Colonization Society's Early Effort to Emigrate Free Blacks to Liberia, 1816–36," *The Journal of Negro History*, Vol. 68, No. 4 (1983), 376–389.

[18] Robert T. Brown, "Simon Greenleaf and the Liberian Constitution." *Liberian Studies Journal*, Vol. IX, No. 2 (1980–1981): 51-60.

[19] The signers of the Declaration of Independence were: Samuel Benedict, Hilary Teage, Elijah Johnson, John Naustehlau Lewis, Beverly R. Wilson and J.B. Gripon (Montserrado County); John Day, Amos Herring, Anthony William Gardiner and Ephriam Titler (Grand Bassa County); and Jacob W. Prout and Richard E. Murray (Sinoe County).

and a Baptist preacher, as the chairman of the committee, to draft the preamble, bill of rights, and the declaration of independence. As the black colonists worked to draft various other parts of the constitution, they outlined their own political and ideological vision for what they considered to be not only an independent republic but even more so "a colored, Christian community." Three intellectual traditions undergirded their thinking: "Republicanism, Black nationalism, and Christianity."[20] While Teage and others desired to restrict ownership of property and citizenship rights to blacks only, the ACS and Greenleaf desired the exact opposite of no racial restriction. Further arguments regarding women's rights seemed to have appeared between the Americans, who were yet to have women's suffrage, and the Liberian colonists, who sought to carve out new avenues of liberty based on gender. On July 16, 1847, Liberia emerged from a series of disjointed states and became the first African colony to declare independence. Their new constitution, which represented a new contract for a racialized bourgeois political system – much like the one that emerged in the United States in 1787 – held similar kinds of problematic contradictions that went beyond engagement in slavery.

Thus, preceding the Barbadians' arrival, the idea of Liberia was collectively imagined in the minds of African America migrants. Even before their arrival, it was clear that the nation was insufficiently and artificially imagined. Unsurprisingly, under the guidance of the ACS, African Americans in the post-independence nation-building efforts relied on the American political traditions and precedents. Beyond the reasons of ideological, political, and civil understandings of citizenship, an impulse for eradicating the slave trade, and a rationalization over territorial control, the idea of a Republican state prevailed over Islamic, African, and other political forms. What it meant to be Liberian was imposed from the political expedience of white colonizationists, patrons, and immigrants who had grown up under the veil of white supremacy. As such, the instinctive ways of representing Liberianness still continued to rely on the idioms of the West.

AFRICAN AMERICANS AND THE REPUBLICAN PARTY

The insertion of the Barbadians into Liberian society brought other ideas and tools to the forging of the country's future. African Americans had always had their own interpretations of democracy but seldom had the

---

[20] Carl Patrick Burrowes, "Black Christian Republicanism: A Southern Ideology in Early Liberia, 1822 to 1847," *The Journal of Negro History*. Vol. 86, No. 1 (2001): 30.

power to define and impose it. They may not have been conscious of how deeply invested they were in the American racialized political structure from which they had "escaped." Within their efforts to re-imagine and define their freedom and to build a nation, the imprints of the lives presumed to have been left behind resurfaced. Through the constitution, the models of government they sought, and their political parties, it became evident that Western ideas informed the idea of the nation, citizenship, and freedom. The political tools sought in the making of Liberia reflected blacks' biases, undoubtedly shaped by their experiences of freedom, citizenship, and nationhood. Ultimately, in the choice of a Republican style of government, the settlers established a political system and standards for citizenship independent of and in opposition to the customs and interests of the local Africans, recaptives, and Barbadian migrants. This implicitly resolved the debate about which political system was most suitable. Transposing these ideas onto an African polity meant rewriting aspects of the script to meet on-the-ground demands. What came out during the transposition process reflected blacks' beliefs, expectations, and rejections of the social and political systems left behind.

African Americans in Liberia recreated a revised, American, racialized republicanism that profited a new merchant elite. The aftermath of the independence convention resulted in the formation of the True Liberian Party (TLP), also called the Administration Party and later renamed the Republican Party of Liberia. With a composition of mostly mixed race African American migrants who had been born free and were educated, the Republican Party was created as much along the lines of color as socio-economic divisions. In 1847, the light-skinned blacks of TLP won the first election and held onto power until 1869. J. J. Roberts, who had been governor of the commonwealth, became the nation's first president. His leadership of the Republic in its infancy invited occasional references and comparisons to George Washington.[21] Roberts, who had become a wealthy merchant, often loaned money to the Liberian government. For decades after independence, African American migrants in Liberia drew on their past experiences to articulate who would be Liberians. Their new form of racialized republicanism grounded ideas of natural rights and conflicting ideas of liberty in efforts that placed black men atop a new hierarchy. The Liberian government came to represent the narrow interests of a particular merchant class of Virginian migrants who had settled in Monrovia, not unlike those that had rallied against the British

[21] Tyler-McGraw, *An African Republic.*

monarchy or emerged in the aftermath of settler colonialism in the United States.[22]

Indeed, the conceit of the new Liberian nation starkly ran up against the indigenous nations in the area. Natives did not disappear with the coming of the black immigrants or with the legal statutes attaching the nation to African Americans. For them, their place and attachment to the land was through custom and kinship. They held by prescription and customary right the land on which they lived and on which their ancestors were buried.[23] The new Liberian state came to represent natives as opposed to any semblance of political rationality, and thus natives could only fall outside of the settlers' modernizing vision. As the settlers constructed Liberia's identity as a black republic, they located it not within the traditions of African empires to which some had aspired. In the newly contrived hierarchy, Liberian indigenes were excluded from citizenship. The ideals of democracy in the American constitution that emerged in the Liberian constitution embraced principles such as centralism. This shored up issues surrounding the nation's territorial integrity and addressed questions of citizenship. Power and authority in Liberia were now placed within an over-arching national governmental structure that was unlike African political forms. For those immigrants who had only imagined what freedom would be like, centralism and statehood meant sentiments became less self-defined and more institutionally based.

DEFINING LIBERIAN CITIZENSHIP

The citizenship status of everyone in Liberian society, from African Americans to West Indians, indigenes, and recaptives – their entitlements to civil liberties and privileges, their degree of boundedness to the law – depended on how African Americans enshrined these ideals into the new constitution. Through territorial acquisition and trade regulations, African Americans worked hard to create political symbols of the state that imposed new ideas of belonging on the diverse ethnic groups in the area. Through this means, there was a delicate balance of extending the constitution over the indigenes without including them as citizens of the state. All inhabitants in the area, whether political citizens

[22] See William A. Pettigrew, *Freedom's Debt: The Royal African Company and the Politics of the Atlantic Slave Trade, 1672–1752* (Chapel Hill: University of North Carolina Press, 2013).

[23] See Hendrik Hartog, "Pigs and Positivism," *Wisconsin Law Review*, Vol. 759, No. 4 (1985): 899–935.

or not, would have to accept the sovereignty of the Liberian government over their forms of governments. They would also have to acknowledge the laws of Liberia as binding onto themselves. Inter-clan and inter-ethnic disputes now referred to the national government for solution, and all offenders would be punishable under the new laws. Between the extremes of excluding and drawing in natives and recaptives, Liberian officials rendered citizenship contingent.

The Liberian nation-building project had grown out of a need to cement racial identity. However, the over-determined symbolic function of blackness changed in Liberia as racial identification failed to mean and do the same kinds of work it had done in the diaspora. The transference of a liberal democratic system to African soil ensured that access to citizenship would be made by predefined norms that straddled both the political and the social sphere. Slavery, abolition, and colonialism had hinged on the question of whether black and modern were mutually exclusive. Black independence and nation building responded to this question by showing the ways in which blacks could transcend the deprivations associated with African-ness. Viewing the stain of inferiority associated with blackness was something to be overcome, and diasporic blacks saw themselves as achieving this with abolition and emancipation in the Americas, migration to Africa, and Liberia's independence. The diasporic migrants to Liberia represented themselves as a group of blacks who had transcended the supposed inferiority of blackness by their suffering. Through their experiences, they had acquired a moral, cultural, and religious regeneration that further liberated them. Following independence, Liberia faced anew the question of how to define blackness in relationship to citizenship. Fashioned in the mold of American republicanism, fitness for citizenship also became contingent on the attributes of character, industry, and Western religiosity.

During the process to formally define the terms of citizenship, Americo-Liberians sought to transform assumptions implied within the broader black nationalist goals into a nationally recognizable legislative language. Liberia's social pluralism, evident through the multiplicity of practices and normative identities, values, and issues, would have to be brought under legal order. Liberia's constitution addressed African Americans' oppressive past when it made citizenship in the republic legally dependent on race. Article 5, Section 13 declared: "The great object of forming these Colonies, being to provide a home for the dispersed and oppressed children of Africa, and to regenerate and enlighten this benighted continent, none but Negroes or persons of Negro descent shall be eligible to citizenship in this Republic."[24] Reading race into political questions of citizenship reflected the persistence of republicanism across the Atlantic but with a new reinterpretation. Within the crucible of racially oppressive societies, African Americans had seen the racialized workings of citizenship in American democracy and experienced and tested the resolve of race as legally prescriptive. West Indians themselves, who had been excluded from the privileges of citizenship, would also have seen this clause as necessary. The principle of blood descent that had previously excluded them from citizenship and full participation in the body politic made this one of the legacies of the African American pioneers. In Liberia, however, African Americans inverted this practice to elevate themselves to the top, while relegating other races to a subordinate status. Under reversed blood-descent, having any amount of black "blood" or ancestry rendered an identity of blackness, with entitlement to citizenship and ownership of property.[25]

Certain constitutional provisions showed that Liberia's architects did not want to subject themselves to the uncertainties of customs where power was not expressly defined. To that end, Article 5, Section 12 stipulated: "No person shall be entitled to hold real estate in this republic unless he be [a] citizen of the same."[26] Though the architects were determined to establish their country as a model of racial equality based on laws that did not mandate racial discrimination, the article masked real patterns of social inequality and political stratification. Though it seemed inclusive and all-encompassing in its definition of citizenship, the article proved to be ambiguous when subjected to interpretation. This vague insistence on black national identity both opened up possibilities for inclusion as well as placed boundaries on the ways that participation could be thought about, claimed, and exercised. With this article, African American republicans ensured that state power in property and all other material aspects would legally be in the hands of the merchant class of blacks.

In spite of the sense of pan-Africanism that pervaded the nation-building process, some blacks came to believe that they had more claim to the nation than others. As the pioneers, African Americans saw themselves in the

---

[24] The constitution of Liberia recorded in Starr, *Liberia*, 256.
[25] Konia T. Kolllehlon, "On Race, Citizenship, and Property in Liberia: A Sociologist's Point of View." *The Perspective.* March 19, 2008, http://www.theperspective.org/2008/0319200803.html.
[26] Starr, *Liberia*, 256.

forefront and others as catching up. From the birth of the colony to the drafting of the constitution, the political sphere would be coded African American. In an effort to affirm their status and rights to retain access to public and religious offices, African Americans grafted their own historical genealogy into the national narrative. By citing their suffering in the United States and their inability to improve themselves under those conditions, African American migrants not only justified establishing a nation on the western coast of Africa but also expressed their claims to the Republic. They used this pretext to further rationalize their leadership in the new political order in the preamble of the 1847 constitution:

We the people of the Republic of Liberia were originally the inhabitants of the United States of North America. In some parts of that country, we were debarred by law from all the rights and privileges of men – in other parts, public sentiment, more powerful than law, frowned us down. We were everywhere shut out from all civil office. We were excluded from all participation in the government. We were taxed without our consent. We were compelled to contribute to the resources of a country, which gave us no protection. We were made a separate and distinct class, and against us, every avenue to improvement was effectually closed. Strangers from all lands of a color different from ours were preferred before us. We uttered our complaints, but they were unattended to, or only met by alleging the peculiar institutions of the country. All hope of a favorable change in our country was thus wholly extinguished in our bosoms, and we looked with anxiety abroad for some asylum from the deep degradation.[27]

As they excluded indigenes and recaptives from the nation, African American migrants legitimized their place in the republic and cemented their leadership of the new country.

As the identity and values of the new nation defaulted to the history and experiences of African Americans, it tied the definitions and cultural moorings of the new nation to their identity. The new architects of the polity used a variety of important codes to confirm their commitment to the republic's socio-political groundings as well as to buttress their policies and legitimize sporadic official adjustments to the political system. Public officials manipulated words such as "constitution, fundamental law, and declaration of independence" to stake out their claim to power. Ultimately, the migrants accepted these symbols with an understanding that they exemplified the goals and desires for not only themselves but global blacks.[28]

---

[27] Starr, *Liberia*, 259.
[28] Blamo, "The Use of Symbolism in National Integration," 2.

The outcome of the Liberian constitution also revealed it to be largely a masculine project that created exclusionary ideas of blackness based on gender. The architects of pan-African ideology had conflated freedom with nationhood, race, gender, and citizenship, but the nation state embraced the notion of citizenship as gendered. Following gendered norms only allowed for migrant men to transition from property-based franchise to universal black male suffrage. As the Liberian nation was wholly suffused with black masculinity, it allowed migrant men to claim political privileges as part of their identity. As constitutional provisions added a gender-specific language to the Liberian constitution, national identity became directly linked to the political actions of males who could vote.

Section 1st.   All men are born equally free and independent, and have certain natural, inherent and unalienable rights; among which, are the rights of enjoying and defending life and liberty, of acquiring, possessing and protecting property and of pursuing and obtaining safety and happiness.

Sec. 3rd.   All men have a natural and unalienable right to worship God, according to the dictates of their own consciences, without obstruction or molestation from others: all persons demeaning themselves peaceably, and not obstructing others in their religious worship, are entitled to the protection of law, in the free exercise of their own religion; and no sect of Christians shall have exclusive privileges or preference, over any other sect; but all shall be alike tolerated: and no religious test whatever shall be required as a qualification for civil office, or the exercise of any civil right.

Sec. 11th.   All elections shall be by ballot and every male citizen, of twenty-one years of age, possessing real estate, shall have the right of suffrage.[29]

By excluding indigenes and recaptives and providing that all men over the age of twenty-one who had property had the right to vote, the achievement of citizenship was transformed most rapidly for men.[30] The constitution functioned as the most important document and connected African American masculinity with "political privilege."[31] The gendered basis of political citizenship reflected the nature of relationships to the state and an additional tier of inequality that migrants experienced. Were other migrants to not fit these outlines stipulated in the constitution, they would essentially emasculate the nation. As gender became the single most important marker

---

[29] Constitution of the Republic of Liberia, 1847 in C.H. Huberich, *The Political and Legislative History of Liberia*, Vol II (New York: Central Book Company, Inc., 1947), 852–864.

[30] *The African Repository*, Vol. 41 (1865): 87.

[31] Laura Free, *Suffrage Reconsidered: Gender, Race, and Voting Rights in the Civil War Era* (Ithaca, NY: Cornell University Press), 155.

of rights, it not only developed as a vital instrument of claiming state political power but also set a precedence that institutions such as courts and churches sought to uphold.[32]

Liberian migration produced an interesting paradox that showed the limitations of diasporic citizenship constructs. Though Liberia's founding rested on a deeply penetrating belief that black and white racial dynamics were the basis for inequality, the nation's location on the African continent, supposedly "outside" the purview of white racism, did not mean the erasure of racial issues. The presence of the ACS and Europeans on the African coast ensured the persistence of struggles deeply intertwined with race. Black migrants entered Liberia with their various historical baggage colored by race that informed their competing interests. These views, as well as patriarchal ideas about the instrumentality of the nation-state, continued to bind black migrants in relationships of inequality. Liberia's pan-Africanist vision that intersected with white imperialism and colonizationism affected questions of citizenship and nationhood for some of the migrants.

The modern Liberian nation-state made citizenship an unmediated relationship between the individual and the state, contrary to kinship that informed African's collectivist sense of citizenship.[33] Over time, Americo-Liberian identity coalesced into a migrant genealogical and historical consciousness that asserted both linkage to the African nativity by blood and attachment to white civilization via diaspora. In the nation-building efforts to regenerate the continent, the diaspora created ways to separate Africa as a space from the inhabitants, a move that served to separate black diasporic identity from African identity. Both diasporic blacks and whites reached into the hinterlands for African indigenes to locate black inferiority. In the quest for a nationality and black modernity, blacks effectively set up a distinction between the idealized fatherland from which all blacks came and the depraved natives who had sold their "brothers" into slavery. The diasporic migrants were unwilling to take on some of the duty of leading their Negro charges. Profoundly persuaded, notwithstanding all visible opposing declarations that Africans were unqualified to preside over an enlightened state, black migrants dreaded the input of the indigenes in the Liberian government.[34] As a consequence,

---

[32] Brown, *Good Wives, Nasty Wenches*, 14.

[33] Elwood D. Dunn, Amos J. Beyan, and Carl Patrick Burrowes, *Historical Dictionary of Liberia*. 2nd ed. (Lanham, MD: Scarecrow Press, 2001), 84–86.

[34] Blamo, "The Use of Symbolism in National Integration," 2.

the nation became invisible in the presence of native ethnic Liberians who were seen as participants in the slave trade but were nonetheless a part of their immediate African environment.

The return Atlantic crossing served to further complicate blacks' racial identity. From a vantage point on the African continent, the extent of residence in diaspora proved critical. The Atlantic mediated the new genealogical fictions that were needed to produce new identity categories of black descent. In its ability to draw lines of distinction around civilization and proximity to whiteness, the Atlantic served as a new logic to fill racial space. Diasporic identities' proximity to power functioned to erase African ness. Liberia's ideological boundaries around what it meant to be Liberian came through methods that were not unlike those that emerged during the period of European colonization of Africa. It produced citizenship by way of a black racial identity created in diaspora through slavery and proximity to whiteness and also created subject-hood and native identity in its African ethnicities through an association to slave trading and distance from whiteness.[35] Implicit in these drawn lines was an assumption of a dichotomy between the diaspora and Africa, where the Atlantic functioned to fragment meanings of race and blackness. As different groups vied to wield the power of the state, national identity became increasingly narrow and unsettled. As other intra-black issues came to the fore, the question of race, shoved in the shadows, became opaque.

Though Liberia was assumed to be a black nation, and presumably all blacks could be citizens, the presence of slave trading in the area added the first source of national conflict that complicated understandings and experiences of citizenship. Indeed, ending the slave trade had been among the first order of business for blacks in Liberia and received even more prominence with independence. The diaspora, themselves victims of the slave trade, had direct reasons to try to criminalize slavery and slave trading. In the diaspora, blacks had had a long track record of attempts to restrain, limit, and even eliminate the ideologies supporting slavery as well as slave-trading practices. Before their arrival in Liberia, much of this debate and confrontation was with whites. In Liberia, the culpability of Africans in the slave trade became more obvious with their increasing visibility. The migrants had come to show Africans the errors of slave trading. Thus, among the first set

---

[35] See Mahmood Mamdani, *Citizen and Subject: Contemporary Africa and the Legacy of Late Colonialism* (Princeton, NJ: Princeton University Press, 1996); Jemima Pierre, *The Predicament of Blackness*.

of laws in the constitution were those that strictly prohibited the "dealing in slaves by any citizen of the Commonwealth, either within or beyond the limits of the same."[36] This law, meant to completely divorce connections of slavery and the slave trade with blacks and the Republic, reinforced natives' exclusion. The haunting history of slavery and slave trading created a disguised ethnic hostility that would take the place of race as known in America as a signifier of difference. The migrants' mission to civilize the natives registered an awareness of meaningful differences between themselves and Africans. The presence of slave trading made indigenes the target of the national government and justified the necessity of a missionary strategy for their conversion. Thus, Liberia's institutions hardly saw themselves as serving natives and recaptives outside of civilizing and labor. By applying the logics of production and labor to the natives, the Liberian officials could sell the state as the bastion of black civilization.

Questions around slavery and the slave trade became one way of rejecting indigenous citizenship and skirting the issue of inequality within the Republic. Natives were forced to overcome the presumption that they were dealing in the slave trade to become citizens. Migrants viewed these clauses as morally and ethically justified. Africans could by no means make a claim for their customary practices, let alone slavery. Such a claim conflicted with the social and political commitments of the members of the new nation. And there were legitimate authorities, including abolitionists, colonizationists, organizations, and nations, to which the settlers could appeal to confirm the morality of these actions. But the impetus for this law was also thinly veiled justification for furthering Liberia's expansionist agenda. Smaller ethnic groups in Liberia such as the Deys and the Queahs were anxious to secure Liberia's protection against powerful slave-raiding chiefs further inland such as the Golahs and Condos. On this basis, they signed formal treaties of cession with the Liberian government.[37] Many of these native chiefs also signed agreements with the central government hoping to profit from trade with the new merchant class and so that their children could benefit from the establishment of missionary schools in their territories.[38] Thus, to survive, many indigenous Liberians adopted the new systems of government and values of the migrants.

---

[36] *The Anti-Slavery Reporter*, October 1, 1858, 233.
[37] *The African Repository and Colonial Journal*, Vol. 19 (1843): 169.
[38] D. T. B Buchanan to Wilkerson, Monrovia, 13 December 1880, as quoted in Akpan, "Black Imperialism: Americo-Liberian Imperialism," 217–236.

The ways in which the settlers sought to reduce further the power of certain indigenous groups framed the nature of the conflicts the Barbadians would encounter. Although the cooperation of the Kru ethnic group had been initially appreciated, the government enacted a number of measures to reduce their economic and political influence. In the pre-independence decades, the ACS forced the Krus to renounce their role in the slave trade. Failure on their part provided the ACS with justification to absorb their lands.[39] The government further threatened Kru fishermen and other natives with manual labor and jail if they ran foul of the law.[40] By the mid-1840s, having abolished their connections to slave traders in the area and with the introduction of "legitimate trade" through the mechanisms of the state, settlers also replaced the Kru as coastal middlemen in other forms of commercial trade. The Common Council of Monrovia further intervened in the political affairs of Kru Town by allowing the mayor of Monrovia to appoint a headman with limited magisterial powers to settle disputes and maintain law and order among the natives.[41] The establishment of the nation-state in many ways meant that the indigenous sense of identity as a group and their efforts to pursue their own goals would be routinely erased and denied.

Liberian officials' deliberations over the native question created a loophole for Barbadian citizenship. The question of native citizenship and status in the Republic had far-reaching implications beyond the question of Liberia's modernity. In 1869, President James Payne addressed the question of the indigene's affiliation with the Republic by proposing a "passports for natives" legislation.[42] Payne pointed out: "If you Senators and Representatives should entertain my recommendation with regard to an

---

[39] See Lawrence Breitborde, "City, Countryside and Kru Ethnicity." *Africa: Journal of the International African Institute*, Vol. 61–62 (1991): 186–201; George Brooks, *The Kru Mariner in the Nineteenth Century: An Historical Compendium* (Newark, DE: Liberian Studies Association of America, 1972); Robert Burroughs, "[T]rue Sailors of Western Africa: Kru Seafaring Identity in British Traveler's Accounts of the 1830s and 40s." *Journal for Maritime Research*, Vol. 11 (2009): 51–67.

[40] See Charles Henry Huberich, *The Political and Legislative History of Liberia; A Documentary History of the Constitutions, Laws and Treaties of Liberia from the Earliest Settlements to the Establishment of the Republic, a Sketch of the Activities of the American Colonization Societies, a Commentary on the Constitution of the Republic and a Survey of the Political and Social Legislation from 1847 to 1944; with Appendices Containing the Laws of the Colony of Liberia, 1820–1839, and Acts of the Governor and Council, 1839–1847* (New York: Central Book Company, 1947), 506.

[41] See Lawrence Breitborde, *Speaking and Social Identity: English in the Lives of Urban Africans* (Berlin: Mouton de Gruyter, 1998).

[42] *The African Repository*, Vol. 45 (1869): 50.

act by which Aborigines shall be formally acknowledged, then an additional act requiring masters of vessels, supercargoes, and agents taking them out of the jurisdiction of the Republic to obtain a passport for everyone, will become imperatively necessary."[43] Natives became visible invisible beings, subject to the "representation" and "re-presentation" of larger oppressive social institutions.[44] Native affiliation complicated not only practical matters of movement and jurisdiction, but also issues surrounding trade and foreign relations with the Republic. As civilized diasporic migrants who could carry out missionary work, Barbadians could earn citizenship by civilizing and Christianizing natives, thus serving to draw them closer to the ideals of the state.

The more Liberia expanded, the more the government came into contact and conflict with different ethnic groups in the outlying areas. Though excluded from being citizens, land and commerce routinely drew natives into the nation. Scholars such as M. B. Akpan have argued that "the African peoples came into a protectorate relationship with the Liberian government, just as later in the nineteenth century African territories elsewhere became protectorates of European colonial powers."[45] Americo-Liberians' presence in Liberia was also an impetus to establish "legitimate trade," and to enact this meant putting up barriers between the hinterlands and the coast where natives traded. To further curtail British and French merchant trade with the indigenes living along the coast, the Liberian government sought to make currency the only legal means of exchange for goods. In retaliation, the local traders stopped trading with the settlers and devised a secret system of trading with foreign merchants. Under the national structure, settlers sought to stymie these efforts by passing a law prohibiting natives who had not first secured permission from the government from trading with foreigners. Furthermore, while they were not citizens, they would have to pay excise duties.[46] Thus, the making of the nation-state deeply affected the natives economically.

As accommodation of their "brothers" in the nation-building efforts continuously pushed natives deeper inland, land became an arena of persistent conflict. The state reinforced these conflicts by using land to lure and attract more migrants. The indigenous forms of being that were

[43] Ibid.
[44] Rosalind C. Morris, ed., *Can the Subaltern Speak? Reflections on the History of an Idea.* (New York: Columbia University Press, 2010), 28–29.
[45] Akpan, "Americo-Liberian Imperialism," 222.
[46] Warren L. d'Azevedo, "A Tribal Reaction to Nationalism," *Liberian Studies Journal* (1969) *Liberia Studies Journal,* Vol III, No. 1, 1970–1971, 1–21.

deemed uncivilized and un-Christian were caricatured through threat and fear. The natives' relationship with the much-coveted land and their apparent lack of utility of it, were used to authorize its taming and colonization. This exposed the differences between Western and African views of land. As with many African ethnicities, kinship groups defined ownership of land, and it mediated the relationship between individuals, both the dead and the living. Conversely, Americans and Europeans viewed land as personal property. This drove the settlers' efforts to control land as well as other means of production. Ownership of land broadly meant that individuals, peasants and yeomanry included, could reap the benefits of their labor. In the United States, land ownership was believed to unshackle individuals from dependent and corrupting relationships. Because of the level of independence that land provided, it acted as a measure of equality. The literal and figurative displacement of native Africans from land and their denial of citizenship in the new nation exposed the unevenness of nation building and the complexities of lived pan-Africanism. While "Americo-Liberians" achieved political and economic prosperity, the natives who constituted the majority of the nation's population became a dubious appendage to the state, enjoying neither citizenship nor the franchise.

BARBADIANS, LABOR, AND NEW MODES OF LIBERIAN CITIZENSHIP

With independence, the relationship with the ACS became invisible but did not disappear. Relationship dynamics, however, would transition with the appearance of the different black migrants. By migrating to Liberia, especially in this post-independence period, blacks – having moved ostensibly beyond the strictures of a race-conscious society – were viewed as finally receiving some measure of freedom. Codifying categories of citizenship as new migrants entered the state remained integral to the creation of Liberian nationhood.[47] In joining other migrant blacks in Liberia, Barbadians brought about a different challenge and new conceptual understandings of citizenship and nationality in Liberia. Differentiating citizenship (a political status to which rights and obligations were attached) from nationality (an ethnocultural form of identity) outlines the ways in which Liberian colonization relied upon notions of

---

[47] Ricard Marback and Mark Kruman, eds., *The Meaning of Citizenship* (Detroit: Wayne State University Press, 2015), 28.

racial capital that read the norms of blackness through African American ex-slaves. This exclusive concern with African Americans has occluded alternative frames through which the constitution of the nation-state and the incorporation of its members might be understood. Barbadian emigration both eroded and created new possibilities for citizenship in Liberia. Their motive was to go to Liberia to build a nationality, "a prepolitical unit community linked by ethnic descent, tribal allegiances and common cultures that had not yet organized themselves into larger political associations which could transcend these particularities."[48] On the other hand, citizenship demarcated a political status to which rights and obligations were attached, from nationality, an ethnocultural form of identity.[49] On the one hand, a lack of transatlantic mobility, the experiences of diaspora, and access to whiteness systematically undermined rights of citizenship and animated social exclusions. On the other hand, progressively joining together national identity with citizenship, by linking the status of those included, and allowing citizenship in the nation with rights and obligations whilst excluding those who were viewed as harmful to the image, served to usher the nation into modernity.

The Barbadians had been written out of the original social compact of the constitution of a Liberian nation-building project imagined for African Americans. As the ACS declared in their constitution: "The object to which its attention is to be exclusively directed, is to promote and execute a plan for colonizing (with their consent) the free people of color residing in our country in Africa, or such other place as Congress shall deem most expedient."[50] Out of their own nationalistic fervor, Barbadians had responded to African Americans' calls for blacks to "come over and help us," citing their interest in emigrating to Liberia as being a "noble desire of assisting to elevate their fatherland, or building up a nationality, without which they consider their race can never attain their proper position in the family of nations."[51] They counted their "advantages gained in slavery" towards their "special duties and glorious privileges" to teach the African indigenes. Barbadians ascribed their significance to the African civilization project to their historical connection to both Africa and Europe. Placing this dual heritage at the core of African modernization efforts, they believed that they were especially valuable to the quest to recover Africa's past and

[48] Ho, *Nation and Citizenship*, 8.
[49] Ibid.
[50] *The African Repository and Colonial Journal*, Vol. 11 (1835): 150.
[51] *The African Repository*, Vol. 41 (1865): 37.

unlock its great destiny.[52] This sense of nationalism had been resonant in other nation-building efforts, thus undergirding the sensibility that "nationalism is not the awakening of nations to self-consciousness: it invents nations where they do not exist."[53] As Benedict Anderson has argued, "it is the magic of nationalism to turn chance into destiny;" nations "loom out of an immemorial past" and "glide into a limitless future."[54]

Barbadian citizenship in Liberia might have been a forgone conclusion because of the Republic's need for productive labor. Upon arrival in Liberia, they were made citizens in a variety of ways. Receiving property, however, implied that citizenship had been granted upon their landing on Liberian soil. The presence of other blacks in Liberia not only marked important social and demographic changes but also created ideological and political tension. On December 10, 1868, three years after the Barbadians' arrival, the sitting president, James Payne, explored the issue of naturalization in his annual message to the Legislature: "There is good reason to apprehend that the oath of allegiance to this government is being considered in the light of a custom-house oath, sometimes regarded as allowing any amount of reservation; and to prevent the advantages which are taken of it, that a special act of the Legislature is necessary." Payne further pointed out that of those persons "coming from distant climes into Liberia and taking this oath, there can be no apprehension; but it is an acknowledged fact that those who come from the colonies on the Western Coast of Africa, come principally for the purpose of trading." On this account, Payne argued for the making of special provisions: "We have no objection whatever to their residing for this or any other legitimate purpose among us; but if they wish to assume the relations of citizens, they should be required to take an oath, make registry of themselves, and procure a uniform certificate by which their allegiance to any other government shall be rendered to their admission to citizenship in this republic."[55]

Even if the Barbadians could exercise both British and Liberian citizenship, British trade and diplomatic disputes with Liberia made it necessary for them to cast off one for the other. British efforts to increase their territory and trade with the natives steadily put territory that was assumed

---

[52] *The Liberal*, February 17, 1841.
[53] Ernest Gellner, *Nations and Nationalism* (Ithaca, NY: Cornell University Press, 1983), 141.
[54] Anderson, *Imagined Communities*, 4.
[55] James Spriggs Payne, "Annual Message to the Legislature December 11, 1865," in Dunn, *Annual Messages of the Presidents of Liberia 1848–2010*, 217.

to belong to Liberia into dispute. This put the Barbadians' British background in question and resulted in increasing tensions along the Sierra Leone border. With this reality, Liberians viewed Barbadians' old imperial relationship with suspicion. Being British subjects probably increased the necessity for the Barbadians to swear the oath of loyalty as a condition for citizenship. Though republicanism and liberalism could inhabit the same political institutions, the political assumptions underlying each differed markedly, a contrast captured in placing the politics of interests and the politics of citizenship against one another. Simply becoming republican would not suffice to mitigate the danger contained in the differences. Thus, Liberian officials' strategy for coping with the Barbadians' difference necessitated them to swear an oath that would register institutionally.

Many onlookers were curious to see if the Barbadians would take the oath. To symbolize their movement from one authority to another, the Barbadian newcomers did indeed take the requisite oath of allegiance required for citizenship. In a letter to the ACS on August 20, 1865, Mr. M. Davis pointed out that within the first week of their arrival, hordes of Barbadians had gone down to the State Department to take an oath of allegiance. He marveled that "sometimes a dozen men a day inquire where they should go to take the oath, and where they could get copies of our Statute Laws." Davis admired the gesture as he had "not known a dozen emigrants from the U[nited] S[tates] to make any efforts to acquaint himself with the laws under which he had come to live, until after he had been here for months and probably had gone through the fever."[56] Oath-bound incorporation of outsiders into the nation countered the pervading discourse of homogeneity even as it also served to reconstitute the community. Having taken the oath, Barbadians moved from one form of allegiance to another. The oath ceremony might have also served to usher the Barbadians into another political order governed by freemasonry, which had started to establish itself as a source of power in Liberia. The oath, in that sense, might have recognized the Barbadians as worthy to participate in the benefits of the society.

Davis's observations of the different way that the Barbadians inhabited experiences of citizenship relative to their African American counterparts were telling. Davis noticed that the Barbadians seemed to be accustomed to acquainting themselves with the laws that governed them so as to be

---

[56] M. Davis, August 20, 1865. Svend Holsoe Collection. Barbados Historical Society and Liberia Collections at University of Indiana, Bloomington.

able to tell how to follow them. He pointed out that Barbadians seemed to "have a better idea of the severance and respect that was due to the law and to Magistrates."[57] Davis observed that, unlike the Barbadians, African Americans held different ideas about citizenship. He noted that they tended to obey the laws not from a point of understanding but from a "habit of imitating their White neighbors," a priori attributing rightness to white behaviors. He thought another good trait of the Barbadians to be that everyone seemed inclined to follow the family business, which raised the possibilities of them prospering. Contrarily, he witnessed that:

many of the emigrants from the U[nited] S[tates] when they come here, give up the trade or business, at which they have been working all their lives and go into trading with the natives, or keeping store, or some return businesses with which they are wholly unacquainted, and the consequence is that instead of being healthy and prosperous mechanics or laborers they soon become diseased and reduced in health and means and die, paupers.[58]

Yet to him "the emigrants from the U[nited] S[tates] in general, appear[ed] to be more enlightened and refined; and more clear in thinking habits and mode of living than the Barbadians." He concluded that the government should welcome all the immigrants it could muster as they would undoubtedly add to Liberia's prosperity. While being able to get migrants to come in larger numbers remained a problem, Davis had a further warning for the Liberian Government. He pointed out that they should not create separate migrant communities as they had done with the Barbadian expedition as that would serve to not only "keep the knowledge of agriculture in which they excel us, from the search of the citizens" but also further "create sectional prejudices arising [between] the people from the U[nited] S[tates] and those from the West Indies."[59]

As Liberian officials viewed the Barbadians as a first-class addition to the country, their labor created an alternative form of accessing citizenship. Barbadians' skillfulness was declared the "most important part of the whole sojourn for a nation desperate for a healthy and productive population." Colonizationists as well as Liberian officials saw Barbadians as possessing the kinds of agricultural and artisanal skills and experiences that were imperative for the future development of the country. President Warner, in a check of the Barbadians' professions, affirmed their value to the young republic, observing: "Among them were coopers, carpenters,

[57] Ibid.
[58] Ibid.
[59] Ibid.

shoemakers, a wheelwright, printer and teachers, with several who thoroughly understood the cultivation of the cane and manufacture of sugar, and the culture and preparation of all kinds of tropical products."[60] One onlooker noted: "As far as my observations have gone, the people just landed seem, upon the whole, to be a well-selected company, and may be regarded as a valuable acquisition to our young Republic."[61]

Liberian government officials valued the Barbadians as additional bodies but were even more ecstatic about the utility of their skills. The persistent recognition of the need for the Barbadians' labor by Liberian officials elevated them into a realm of importance in the republic that was on par with African Americans. The Liberian government thus extended citizenship to Barbadians by virtue of the fact that they were perceived as important stakeholders in the Republic's priorities. Writing to the Colonization Society, J. J. Roberts noted: "They appear, from what I have seen of them, an interesting company. Most of the male adults, I am told are mechanics and practical farmers, and seem to have correct ideas about the circumstances and capabilities of the country – so far greatly pleased." The migrants impressed Roberts in other ways: "We have long needed men here who thoroughly understand the cultivation of the canes and the manufacture of the sugar and indeed the culture and preparation of all kinds of tropical products."[62] For this, government officials praised the ACS for selecting those who possessed the wherewithal necessary for building Liberia: "To your large experience in the kind of materials required here for the up-building of this offspring of American philanthropy, and the further development of the country and the character of the people in it, and your sagacity in selecting those materials, is due the very respectable and promising immigration with which we have just been favored." Officials further expressed their appreciation, noting that "the government of this republic feels very grateful to the Society for the great interest it has taken in its West Indian emigration enterprise, both as it regards the pecuniary means it has furnished and the happy selection of the emigrants sent out."[63] The central Liberian government perceived the Barbadians as a group of skilled, educated, and professional migrants, and saw them as a valuable addition to the Republic.[64]

---

[60] "Letter from Ex-President Roberts," *The African Repository*, Vol. 41 (1865): 249.
[61] Ibid.
[62] *The African Repository*, Vol. 41 (1865): 249–250.
[63] Ibid.
[64] Ibid.

While working for wages had defined economic life and their relationship to the land in Barbados, Liberia reversed those dynamics so that Barbadians could fulfill their desires of building themselves up through their labor. Acquisition of land and the power to actually dig into the landscape in Liberia gave Barbadians further stakes in the nation and additional means of acquiring citizenship. Liberia's national development prerogatives progressively drew Barbadian immigrants into a relationship with the land, other migrants, and the nation. A later letter written by Padmore, dated May 27, 1871, noted, "The young crops look promising. We have sold about fifty thousand pounds of arrow-root and eight thousand pounds of ginger."[65] Linking their body and labor to the Liberian nation enabled Barbadian migrants to claim Liberian citizenship in more direct ways, allowing them to move from the discursive sphere of claim to its very embodiment.

Class hierarchy that was built on the narrative of productive labor in Liberia re-imagined earlier relationships in the United States and the British colonies that were structured on race. A rethinking of earlier discourse of "races" gave credence to emerging class identities. In the West race had determined labor, but in Liberia labor would determine a "civilized race." Race and labor in the United States and the colonies laid the foundation for black migrant bourgeoisie self-definition in Liberia. The role of colonial experiences in shaping the black identity provided a framework for the relationship between race, ethnicity, and power in the Liberian nation-building project. Race acted as a mechanism that enabled elites to retain class privilege during the transition from a vertical model of subjecthood to a horizontal model of citizenship. Nation building in Liberia depended on the republic's ability to yoke itself to the everyday power relationships that directed people's lives. In this milieu, labor resonated with Afro-Caribbean and African American migrants because it drew and innovated upon the earlier discourse of race that had determined the migrants' prior societal position. Race and labor were not artificial addendums to the modern Liberian state; they were common tactics for harnessing the power of earlier discourse to the service of the new nation-state. By reconfiguring the pre-existing discourse of race and labor into the new discourse of race and labor, in which being civilized governed the eligibility for citizenship, emerging modern states legitimated their claim to authority over how people lived.[66]

---

[65] *The African Repository*, Vol. 45 (1871): 278.
[66] See Laura Stoler, *Race and the Education of Desire: Foucault's* History of Sexuality *and the Colonial Order of Things* (Durham, NC: Duke University Press, 1995).

In 1873, nearly twenty years after their arrival, Barbadians grappled with several issues that would redefine their new lives in Liberia. The exigencies of nation building necessitated that central government make new demands upon them. Issues regarding labor, law enforcement, education, and Christianizing defined their structured role in the civilizing project. The politicization of Barbadians' work as agriculturalists and artisans made sites of contestations over citizenship. In the ways that it reflected American ideals of virtuous citizenship, the Liberian government used Barbadian labor for civic education on citizenship. The newspaper *New Era* began as a publication with the purpose of visiting all the agricultural districts to evaluate what their "chances [were] for success in this department of industry." The publication's title highlighted the import of labor and the new migrants to Liberia's Renaissance period. The newspaper went on a campaign "to lecture to the citizens of the several districts on the importance of educating their children and native boys, improving themselves, and sustaining their families by an economical and judicious system of farming." In 1873, after a tour of the Barbadian settlement in Crozierville, the *New Era* reported: "This district is made up of small farmers. ... Many of these people were first-class mechanics, some farmers, some teachers, and some small traders. The Barbadians are known to be the most intelligent and best-educated company of emigrants that ever came to Liberia, and equally industrious."[67] In this performative sphere, it was not only the civilized discourse of the diaspora that counted but also the recognizable signs of their laboring bodies that projected the modernity of the race.

The *New Era*'s depiction of labor relations in Liberia became a reflection of how Barbadians accrued discursive power in both mainstream Liberian culture and black freedom struggles after 1865. Late nineteenth-century mass media formulated popular understandings of appropriate use of space and the connection between labor and meaningful citizenship. The symbolic associations that these narratives took on encouraged popular constructs of citizenship. As editors trafficked discourses that refracted national anxieties about nation building and modernity, newspapers enabled reporters to inform the public on appropriate forms of blackness and proper education about citizenship. Such focused attention raised the status of the Barbadians. The *New Era* transmitted ideas about acceptable forms of labor and held up Barbadians as the perfect example. During this time, labor emerged in the national lexicon

[67] *The New Era*, January 17, 1878.

to critically shape conversations around citizenship. The *New Era* journalist casted the Barbadians' citizens in one telling recommendation:

But if I had to recommend and be responsible for any class of our people their honor, I know of none more reliable than the Barbadians. They certainly are deserving encouragement and patronage. There is room in Liberia for ten thousand such people. They would soon make a mark for good upon the age and the country.[68]

Barbadians' agricultural labor was valued not only for national development but also for the image of the nation that it projected. The image of civilized blacks diligently laboring toward the mission for Liberian modernity thrust Barbadians to the forefront of the nation and into the gaze of observers, particularly white missionaries. With commentary often reflecting on the Barbadians' institutions, industry, character, and the infusion of their material cultures into Liberia, observers marked productive labor as the preserve of Barbadians. The exigencies of nation building and the larger civilizing project, in making new demands on Barbadian labor, fermented and recognized their citizenship. Missionary onlookers also reported elaborately in letters, "The small farms of the Barbadians are cultivated with great care. They keep down all the grass and noxious weeds, and thus produce from one acre twice the amount of product that is made by other farmers that we have noticed."[69] Observers viewed Barbadians as respectable custodians of the land, delineating this habit as a characteristic demonstrative of proper citizenship.

As these publications shifted the focus away from the ethos and language of Liberian nationality to one of locality, the fixity of Liberia's national identity would often be at odds with the ethnicities in its localities. Within two years of their arrival, the Barbadians in Crozierville had roused comments that signaled the nature of their presence and impact and the shifting sociopolitical power dynamics of Liberian society. On one occasion in 1867, an observant Episcopalian missionary hinted at the growing dialogue surrounding Barbadian presence in Liberia: "Who in the world raises those fine yams why we never saw any like them for the many years we have been here?" "The Barbadians up the river," a companion responded, hastening to add more details: "So too in Krootown, maybe seen as good a tailor cutting and finishing as neat work as any man of the shears and needle ever made in any community. He too is a Barbadian!" Pointing to another of the Liberian newcomers,

---

[68] *The African Repository*, Vol. 49 (1873): 275.
[69] *The African Repository*, Vol. 42 (1865): 47.

the friend further explained: "Go to that man's brother's shoe-shop in Monrovia and see him make as neat and nice a shoe or boot as ever came from the hand or from the last of any of his trade. He is a Barbadian!"[70] The boot-maker was probably Samuel Inniss, who practiced that profession in Barbados.

Moreover, the fact that Barbadians made use of Liberia's natural resources through their various skills exhibited their citizenship worth. The observant missionary further outlined this thought about the Barbadian newcomers: "Now and then we see beautiful pieces of furniture carried through our streets made of the unrivaled wood of the Liberian forests. These are made at Carysburg by a Barbadian, a first-rate cabinet maker [who] would shame a furniture warehouse in any city in the United States." The Barbadian cabinet-maker in question was Charles Inniss, the brother of the boot-maker, Samuel Inniss. Charles had been a cabinet-maker in Barbados. A circular advertising his work in Liberia mentioned his skills: "Charles Inniss: Cabinet Maker; Careysburg, near the residence of Mr. McDowell, all orders are entrusted to the care of the above named will be executed with neatness and dispatch and in the latest American and English style."[71] These kinds of reports relating to Barbadians' labor highlighted the connections between labor and citizenship and extolled American and English styles over African ones.

As the Barbadians' labor became a part of their civic duty, it also served efforts to remake the nation in their image to cast the Liberian republic in a civilized light. In the new Liberian image, West Indians claimed the purchase of empire through manners, habits, and Victorian models of political and intellectual authority. The influx of the different groups within the political sphere manifested similar mutually beneficial interactions as well as points of tension. As much as the political sphere was coded African American and the labor sphere was Barbadian, recaptives took over the religious and missionary sphere. Liberian officials delighted in the fact that recaptives who showed the most promise should be sent back as "missionaries to the Congo country whence they were taken by the slavers."[72] Recaptives proved essential in the efforts to Christianize natives as many of them in this period were from areas such as Central Africa where Christianity had long established

---

[70] *The African Repository*, Vol. 43 (1867): 269.
[71] Ibid.
[72] *The African Repository*, Vol. 53 (1877): 30.

a foothold.[73] Liberian officials concluded that "when it is considered that these heathen 'Congoes' numbered one-third as many as all the Liberians, it speaks well for the missionary spirit of the Liberian churches that such good results should have so speedily followed, Liberia deserves the name of 'the Missionary Republic.'"[74]

For the most part, Liberian policymakers agreed that they should move with all deliberate speed to prepare receptives and natives to join the labor force.[75] Through the labor department that required the civilized to train the uncivilized, the Barbadian migrants were called upon to take natives as apprentices. This placed the Barbadians in a position similar to that held by the white plantocracy in the Caribbean in the post-slavery period. Similar to what Barbadians had witnessed of the black masses in Barbados, as civilizers, they came to occupy that same space in a system designed for receptives in Liberia. Given the urgency and anxiety surrounding their influx into the Republic, apprentices became a new legal category for African receptives. This offered a tidy resolution to an identity and representation conflict, preventing their full entrance into citizenship and blackness.

Turning African receptives into civilized free laborers required multiple mechanisms, some coercive, others persuasive. The Liberian government, in order to create a relationship between the state and receptives, designed systems meant to instill the ideals of virtue, industry, and hard work. Starting in the 1860s, the Liberian government noted that "the receptives may, on the manual labor system, have a definite number of hours schooling each day, and a definite number of hours to work each day, at the various branches of industry, agriculture being the principal; and for them to be thus trained under the supervision of government, for their respective full terms of apprenticeship."[76] Instead of being small farmers, receptives would be landless laborers at the mercy of fellow blacks. One report noted, "The Executive Committee will, no doubt, at once agree with this government, that those receptives who may not be apprenticed out to

---

[73] For more on the religious backgrounds of West Central Africans, see Linda M. Heywood and John K. Thornton, *Central Africans, Atlantic Creoles, and the Foundation of the Americas, 1585–1660* (New York: Cambridge University Press, 2007); Beatriz Gallotti Mamigonian, *To Be a Liberated African in Brazil: Labour and Citizenship in the Nineteenth Century* (Waterloo, ON: University of Waterloo, 2002).

[74] *The African Repository*, Vol. 41 (1865): 345.

[75] Thomas Holt, *The Problem of Freedom: Race, Labor and Politics in Jamaica and Britain 1832–1938* (Baltimore: John Hopkins University Press, 1992), 18.

[76] *The African Repository*, Vol. 36 (1860): 356.

individuals immediately on their being landed, they should, without
a week's delay after being landed, be placed under the contemplated
systematic and authoritative plan of training."[77] According to the apprenticeship arrangements, a system of training and a labor agreement, where
a number were "bound out to reliable persons ... after the expiration of
the one year's support by the Society, [to] fall on the hands of government
to be supported and trained for terms of years, ranging from seven to
fourteen years, according to the laws of this Republic regulating the
apprenticeship of recaptured Africans."[78] The indentureship plan was
meant to socially, economically, religiously, and politically organize
recaptives. Their apprenticeship would not only render them useful to
themselves but also to the Republic. Paradoxically, this was meant to train
recaptives in the habits of free laborers such that they could fully enjoy
complete freedom.

The Liberian government used recaptives, together with natives, for
agricultural labor in practices akin to the systems of indentureship,
tenancy, and sharecropping that had existed in the West Indies and in
the US South after emancipation. The government noted that if recaptives
could not find individual masters or guardians to be bound to, the
Government of Liberia "would be obliged, for its own safety as well as
by the promptings of humanity, to take these people, thus unprovided for
and turned loose upon the mercy of the public, under apprenticeship to
herself, for the lawful term of their apprenticeship."[79] In Liberian society,
recaptives and natives became a part of a growing under-caste, a group
defined largely by color, religion, and culture, and relegated to a non-
citizenship status socially and legally.

The Barbadians seemed to approach this task of apprenticing the
natives and recaptives with some reluctance. One Liberian observer, presumably from the United States, worried that "they have no native
apprentice boys around them, except as by chance they hire them.
I think in this they are unwise." Perhaps unaware of the motivations of
land and labor that had driven Barbadian emigration to Liberia, they
reasoned that Barbadians should be more invested in apprenticing the
natives. As the observer pointed out, they "must get the good-will of the
natives, and induce them to bind their sons till of age, that they may be
taught to labor and educated to read and write, that both parties may be

---

[77] *The African Repository*, Vol. 36 (1860): 45.
[78] Ibid.
[79] *The African Repository*, Vol. 36 (1860): 12.

mutually benefited." Like Blyden and other West Indians in Liberia, the Barbadians chose to have a different relationship with natives than the Americo-Liberians. Onlookers continued to worry that without establishing an apprenticeship relationship with natives, Barbadians would not be able to "accomplish much beyond a bare subsistence by such a system of one-horse power as they now have. Besides, they need implements of agriculture and machinery, and then with their industrious habits and promptness, they will be sure to succeed."[80] Clearly, access to cheap native labor, which was an advantage of Liberian citizenship, ran contrary to the Barbadians' definition. For Barbadians, citizenship meant working their land and owning their labor so as to achieve the independent wealth they desired.

The transference to Liberia of apprenticeship as a labor arrangement shaped experiences of freedom, citizenship, and nationhood for these groups. The apprenticeship system inaugurated a form of "graduated sovereignty" that differentially located the various groups of blacks in the nation-state, thus affecting their abilities to claim rights and privileges. Dubbed Americo-Liberian imperialism, many attributed this brand of politics to the migrants' American and European sensibilities.[81] In many ways, however, the new post-slavery system, the evidence of coercion, and the persistence of various forms of un-freedom represented the recurrent system of caste in the Atlantic World. The inability to define freedom in clear terms often meant it would have to be made on the ground. Running contrary to ideas of liberty and free labor that had driven many migrants to Liberia, the implementation of these kinds of systems further showed the ways in which views about freedom and labor had transformed across space and time.[82]

Freedom in Liberia remained a historical and social construct with various competing definitions at work. In many post-emancipation and post-reconstruction societies, freedom for many would be politically constructed and legally defined. In some quarters freedom was viewed as an entitlement while others thought individuals needed to prove that they deserved their freedom through conduct, morals, and behavior. In post-Reconstruction United States, many viewed freedom as necessitating

[80] Ibid.
[81] M. B. Akpan, "Black Imperialism: Americo-Liberian Rule Over the African Peoples of Liberia, 1841–1964," *Canadian Journal of African Studies*, Vol. 1, No. 2 (1973), 217–236.
[82] For African American tenancy and share-cropping, see Walter Pannell, *King Cotton: The Share-Cropper and Tenant Farming in the United States* (Los Angeles: Thor's Book Service, 1943).

economic viability. This meant land was central to any material experiences of freedom and a militia was necessary to oversee this enforcement. With migration driving the unfolding of the Republic, freedom became a consistent process of contending with the normative order. These various contestations, exclusionary politics and hierarchical structures that blacks had previously struggled against drove the making of Liberia. Others viewed freedom as emerging from one's labor and work. Indeed, much of free labor ideology centered the principle of working for wages as the hallmark of freedom.

BARBADIANS AND THE TRUE WHIG PARTY

Not all of the Barbadians had chosen to settle in Crozierville. In a move that would prove shrewd and politically astute, others, including the Barclays, chose to settle in Grand Bassa, Monsterrado County, one of the fifteen political and administrative partitions located in the northwestern section of Liberia. The farmers who settled up-river were on the edge of the Liberian frontiers where they straddled the divide between African American settlements in the city of Monrovia, recaptives freed from slave ships, and natives in the hinterlands. The settlement of the skilled Barbadian artisans and planters ultimately changed the nature of the relationship between the rural interior settlements and those on the coast. As resource insecurity and its attendant power imbalance contributed to a certain kind of spatial menace, the Barbadians' position stood as a mitigating force in the social dynamics previously established between African Americans and the indigenes.

However, the Barbadians had found themselves in the middle of growing social, economic, and political tensions that were exacerbated by a color divide. Geographic boundaries that reflected ethnic belonging also highlighted the inequalities of political power. As a settlement, Monrovia represented lighter-skinned African Americans who dominated Liberia's social, economic, and political life. Though similar to African American families who migrated to Liberia in previous decades, Barbadians' color marked them as different. The Barbadians' settlement restructured politics of blackness on the basis of pigmentation rather than civilization. As members of the up-river communities began to form a shared sense of community and solidarity to combat Monrovia's social, economic, and political dominance, the Barbadians' dark pigment became a new political form of identification with recaptives. Such forms of unity held value as the up-river planters also increasingly began to form their own social groups and attracted many who had become weary of the color politics and elitism of the Americo-Liberian merchant class. Variations in skin color that correlated with class also influenced the experiences of Liberian citizenship and political power. Abayomi Karnga notes that Liberians evolved into a "hierarchical caste system with four distinct orders (or castes)." At the top were the mixed race Americo-Liberian political officials, followed by darker-skinned migrants who were predominantly laborers and small farmers. African recaptives and Liberian indigenes occupied the lowest rung of the hierarchy. Karnga notes, "The initial exclusion of indigenous Liberians from citizenship (and the franchise) may have been due to the simple fact that, as a subordinate group, they occupied the very bottom of this status hierarchy."[83] This grouse about who was to be included in the republic undergirded the beginnings of popular Whiggish politics in Liberia.

In the subsequent years in Liberia, the Barbadians continued to live up to their early reputation but began to direct their agricultural energy towards politics. As the new migrants added to the complexity of the black mosaic and the unfolding nation-building process, the republican foundation of Liberian politics, as well as its religious orientation, would come under threat from the West Indian migrants and the African recaptive groups on the frontier. Having embraced the ideals of agrarianism over industry, the up-river farmers had grown progressively independent and thus became sensitive to any encroachments by the merchant elites of the coast. The West Indians' labor that had been lauded by government officials, visitors, and missionary observers became central to their new political ideals.

In 1869, darker-skinned immigrants, driven by Edward Blyden, Alexander Crummell, and the Barbadian farmers in Crozierville, took the foundations of the Anti-Administration Party shaped by Samuel Benedict and created the Old Whig Party of Liberia. The party would later be renamed the True Black Man's Party before a final designation of the True Whig Party (TWP).[84] The True Whig party emerged through an opportunistic alliance and a consolidation of power between the Barbadian settlers along the St. Paul River, recaptives in the nearby

[83] Abayomi Karnga, *History of Liberia* (D.H. Tyte, 1926), 7.

[84] Julius Omozuanvbo Ihonvbere and John Mukum Mbaku, *Political Liberalization and Democratization in Africa Lessons from Country Experiences* (Westport, Conn: Praeger, 2003), 201; John Mukum Mbaku and Julius Omozuanvbo Ihonvbere, *The Transition to Democratic Governance in Africa: The Continuing Struggle* (Westport, Conn: Praeger, 2003).

settlement of Clay-Ashland, and natives. Driven in part by efforts to reconfigure Liberia, the Barbadians helped to consolidate the TWP against the Republican Party. According to Robert Smith:

The vital issue leading to the formation and development of the True Whig Party was whether the promoters and founders of Liberia had conceived it as a nation to be only for the advantage of the repatriated negroes from America, or was it to be a nation comprising of the returned exiles and aboriginal tribes, having negro nationality with its foundations rooted in Africa cultural institutions modified by western thoughts.[85]

Liberia was initially proposed as a community of small farmers, modeled after plantation style agriculture in the United States accompanied by its agrarian and republican ideology. Blacks had taken up these ideas as a way to secure their own visions of freedom. Migrants were to be given five acre plots that they would own once they cleared the land and built a house in two years. With efforts to turn blacks into property owners, the ownership of private property became the foundation of Liberia's political and economic system of self-determination. However, due to the favoritism that was shown to light-skinned blacks by white colonization agents, who also saw themselves as spiritual leaders in the drive toward African civilization, Liberia created a landed gentry that developed into an elite political class. Thus, the agenda for performing African civilization was shaped through ideas of property rights and labor overseen by black migrant administrators delegated by the ACS. Those who were for the ACS' administration were favored and those who railed against it argued that its paternalism undermined the migrants' freedom. For this reason, another concern emerged: was the government going to be "white or black?"[86] As a consequence, Roye, Blyden, and Crummell started the mantra, "true black men truly for Africa."[87] Under "deeds not words," the TWP's platform launched a campaign with promises of broadening of the Liberia political arena for the participation, thus making Liberia a space of freedom for all blacks without color and class distinction.

The disgruntled darker skinned African American migrants who were already anti-administration based on their hatred of the longstanding mulatto elitism, constituted a natural base for the TWP. However, as the party ideology came to represent farm interests and development of

---

[85] Robert Smith, *Deeds Not Words*, 2.
[86] Abayomi Karnga, *The History of Liberia* (Liverpool: D. Lyle, 1926), 47.
[87] Massala Reffell, *Echoes of Footsteps: Birth of a Negro Nation* (Bloomington, IN: Xlibris, 2012), 266.

the interior, it attracted more and more West Indians. Given the origins of "Whig" ideology in English radicalism and antislavery activism, it was no surprise that Barbadians became increasingly attracted to it. Like the indigenes and recaptives, the Barbadians might have also been concerned about whether they would be fully accepted into the Negro nationality. However, the new party's motto, "Deeds Not Words," cemented principles apart from those in Monrovia that were ratified in the constitution.

There were many points of cohesion between these groups. Coalitional members of the TWP opposed the political dominance of the urban African American merchant elites who they referred to as "mongrels, who were genetically unstable and unable to govern or even survive in Liberia."[88] For Barbadians, subscribing to the broader vision of what Liberia was intended to be would secure their place in the nation. This provided the basis on which they aligned with the recaptives and indigenes who were constitutionally written out of the vision of Liberia by the merchant class, who used the government for further empowerment. With the party, the grave discrepancies in power according to color became increasingly pronounced. This kind of color politics became the Afro-Barbadian approach to recaptives and indigenes. Indeed, it proved appealing to a large cross-section of Liberian society who had watched as the lighter-skinned African Americans like Roberts controlled every facet of Liberian life. At the crux of Whig ideology was a deep suspicion of political power that was concentrated and limited to the few. Whigs, with their emergence, sought to keep the government under close scrutiny from the corrupting forces of power. Together, the dark-skinned alliance of Barbadians and recaptives in the TWP ousted the Republicans. They were believed to be more liberal in their politics than the Americo-Liberian group. Indeed, after the 1870s, the Republican Party that established Liberia's political foundation was defunct.

By the late nineteenth into the twentieth century, there would be a triumph of Barbadian political ideals in Liberia's two-party system. How Afro-Barbadians deployed their politics earned them a reputation for service in education, journalism, and governmental service, creating further distinctions between the Americo-Liberians and West Indian migrants. For Barbadians, education became a means of acquiring the kinds of political mobility the emigrants had desired in Barbados, as well as inculcating the character and qualities necessary for first-class citizenship in Liberia. The Barbadians were noted for educating their children.

[88] Tyler-McGraw, *An African Republic*, 175.

Observers noted that "there were but few of their number that could not read, write, and cipher when they arrived in the country." Antoinette Hope Barclay, the first of twelve of Anthony and Sarah Barclay's children (See Figure 6.1), who was a schoolmistress before migrating, continued working in education in Liberia and was credited with being the first teacher of her brother, who many deemed one of Liberia's greatest statesmen. Bystanders noted, "They are more interested in the education of their children than any other community I have met with. They have one Episcopal school taught by Mr. I. J. Thorpe, in their chapel, and one of the so-called Government schools taught by Mr. Denny in a private house." These qualities were also being held up as a model of behavior for the larger populace.

Reports noted that the Barbadians were strictly temperance people. They often had little quarrels among themselves, "the nature of which I have never had time to understand. They seem to have been trained to promptness in the discharge of both public and private duties." Other viewers often commented, "These people are of industrious habits, pious, seemingly, withal. I learn that many of them have already fine gardens coming on just about their present temporary home – the Receptacle on the road." According to a report from the New York State Colonization Society, the Barbadians were to be seen as a lesson to future emigrants.[89] William H. Heard, who was minister in the African Methodist Episcopal Church (AME) and Consul General of the United States in Liberia, in his biography, *A Bright Side of Liberia* (1898), pointed out that S. E. F. Cadogan, who was born in Barbados in 1842, "was a clerk of the Supreme Court for ten years, and Register of Wills and Deeds for nine years." Cadogan was a soldier who rose from the rank of private to that of captain of the Johnson Volunteers, and then, on account of his bravery in war, was promoted to the rank of brigadier-major under General Sherman (See Figure 6.2). He concluded: "We present his intelligent face, and when you look upon it, you see a man who fully represents his race, and is a leader at the Liberian capital."[90]

Under the helm of the TWP, West Indians came to occupy some of the most important political positions in Liberia. By 1905, Arthur Barclay, ten years of age upon leaving Barbados, became the fifteenth president of Liberia; his brother Ernest Barclay became Chief Justice; four other emigrants held the office of Secretaries of State; two others were Associate Justices, and others served in various capacities in the government as well

[89] *The African Repository*, Vol. 46 (1870): 87.
[90] William H. Heard, *The Bright Side of African Life* (New York: Negro Universities Press, 1969), 59.

FIGURE 6.1: Sarah Ann Bourne Barclay and Daughter, Laura Ann Barclay
Source: Historical Preservation Society of Liberia

as in other institutions. In addition to occupying the seat of president, a Barbadian was also selected as the Pro Tempore of the Liberian senate. Along with Arthur Barclay, Ernest Barclay, Edwin Barclay, Louis Arthur Grimes, and Joseph Rudolph Grimes served as Secretaries of State while James T. Wiles became Secretary of the Treasury. Both Joseph and Louis Arthur Grimes became Attorneys General while Wiles was named the first Postmaster General of Liberia. George S. Padmore served as the Secretary of War and the Secretary of Education as did Edwin Barclay. Colonel James B. Padmore brought the Gola War in Crozierville to an end, and George S. Padmore, who twice fought in the Cape Palmas wars, resigned in 1910 as Secretary of War to head a military mission into the

HON. S. E. F. CADOGAN.
Attorney-at-Law, Monrovia, Liberia.

FIGURE 6.2: Hon. S. E. F. Cadogan, Barbadian Attorney in Liberia
Source: William H. Heard, *The Bright Side of African Life* (New York: Negro Universities Press, 1969), 65

hinterlands. Richard N. Holder was appointed Secretary of the Interior. Edwin Barclay became Secretary of National Public Health Services while James Milton Weeks became a director of the National Planning Agency. Everett Jonathon Goodridge served in the capacity of Administrative Assistant to the President. The Barbadians who served in the judiciary included Louis Arthur Grimes, who was Chief Justice of the Supreme Court. Richard S. Wiles became speaker of the House of Representatives. The first president of the University of Liberia was Dr. Rocheforte L. Weeks. Naturally, news of their successes in Liberia circulated back to Barbados and created more interest on the island in Liberian emigration. J. T. Wiles, for example, wrote to inform the ACS in 1870 that there "are thousands of people in Barbados that would be glad to go to Liberia, but have not the means to do so."[91]

[91] Ibid.

BARBADIAN [RE]PRESENTATIONS OF BLACKNESS IN LIBERIA

The colonization movement that facilitated the journeys of the migrants and their dreams, rhetoric, and expectations into what eventually became a cosmopolitan black space created a container that forced inflection points in race and ethnicity. Far from achieving a consolidation of black identity and aspirations, the Liberian nation-building process rather inspired crisis for both the migrants and the nation-state, as visions of race as a homogenizing force for nation building fractured. Coming together at an African point of the Atlantic, the tensions surrounding settlement, group identity, sociocultural formations, and social relationships between the Liberian migrant groups rewrote the theoretical formations around race and blackness along new lines. During the post-emancipation period, the arrival and settlement of the Barbadians alongside those of other migrants in Liberia and the genealogies of ideas that accompanied each group magnified the commonalities and particularities of the black experience. Liberia's cultural struggle to set the criteria for a modern, civilized black identity affected how the state related to the different migrant groups. As the various segments of the black population represented their identities in relation to the state and to one another, they bumped up against questions of black progress, modernity, and respectability. The challenges encountered in efforts to author a unified national vision that would be legible across the different contours of Liberia's black inhabitants exposed the differences of blacks' post-emancipation experiences, the complexity of defining blackness, and the uneven nature of nation building. The process also highlighted the difficult and fraught process of sustaining pan-African ideology, proving that it was far easier to talk theoretically about beliefs than to move from intentions to commitment.

Liberia was as much of an invention as blackness. Liberia reflected the different visions of blackness that coalesced and fractured along different lines as the different groups stood in tension with each other. The politics of blackness emerged at the intersection of several competing and contrasting interests. If the migrants ever fantasized about a black nationality, it was as an idea that was formed not so much by what they had experienced but what they fashioned from the alchemy of their imagination. Blackness as produced in Liberia became the outcome of various interests but also the imaginative work of black nationalists determined to come out from under white supremacy's tight grasp. In addition to African Americans' outsized role in defining blackness politically, debates about what blackness should look like continued through abolitionists, newspaper reports in the Caribbean, United States, and Liberia, and people inside and outside of Liberia. These various constituents in providing insight that affected the construction of blackness also complicated understandings of the roles of women, indigenes, recaptives, and indigenes in government, education, and social life. Black experiences of citizenship and nationhood and the making of a transnational black identity occurred through the dialectics of experiences and the political processes of nation building in Liberia.

The work of the nation-building project to define blackness with a new sense of heightened awareness emerged in stunning fashion with every migrant arrival. What materialized with the movement of African Americans, West Indians, and recaptives from the cultural economy of Caribbean post-emancipation to the African coast disputed the notion of a fixed, transcendent, and unchanged racial essence. Though, in the diaspora, blackness meant exemption from the susceptibility of the African environment, the scourge of migrant deaths during the period of seasoning invalidated those assumptions. Moreover, the presumed immunity of the indigenes to the environment designated them as the "other" in what appeared to be new efforts to widen the gap between Africans and diasporic blacks. In Liberia, the diaspora, marked by death and inability to survive, were situated inside the nation even as they positioned the presumably immune indigenes Africans outside. As a ritual that could be understood by those who ostensibly shared a lack of inoculation, the period of seasoning allowed the migrants to collectively share in the memory of diaspora.

The issue surrounding the making of blackness was particularly acute in Liberia because of its attachment to the national project. It was through the nation-building project that the question of who was black was communicated with the clearest outcomes. Race in Liberia came to shape the foundation for black bourgeoisie self-definition. The basis of race, religion, and culture on which blacks had been discriminated against in the West redeployed in Liberia through exclusionary practices and other social forms of stratification that created new power struggles. By reconfiguring the pre-existing discourse of races into the new discourse of blackness, in which diaspora governed eligibility for citizenship, Liberian migrants legitimated their claim to authority. With the ability to access and define blackness as a term at the rhetorical polemical level came different modes of claiming superiority. The volume of discourse was more prominent among English speakers whose conversations appeared and were articulated in spaces and moments of significance and whose voices registered more loudly in the archive of the different migrant voices.

Emancipation was understood as the promise of moral self-management, and many expected that blacks would fail; this provided all the more reasons for the need to inflict new regimes of power and control. Consequently, the late nineteenth century became a moment in the production of new realities for blackness. Space, both abstract and literal, figured not only in the construction of colonial power and authority but also in blackness. As Michel Foucault argued, the state or elites did not impose power through overarching state mechanisms. Instead, power emerged from a reciprocal web in which personal, private expressions of power attained resonance with societal and state mechanisms of power.[92]

One of the ways in which Liberia regulated blackness was through the natural landscape of rivers and forests that the environment provided. The ritual of encounter and settlement established the balance of power among the various groups. Liberian settlements' clustering of migrants who shared similar experiences, beliefs, and politics together created enclaves that fractured the black nationality (See Figure 6.3). After settlement, Liberians focused on development on the interior, becoming deeply involved in creating a capitalist system that connected their interior to the coast. In the era of the transatlantic slave trade, with power intricately linked to the coast, the displacement of the indigenes from the coastal area and the movement away from the slave trade to more "legitimate" forms of commerce symbolically marked the shift of power from natives to settlers. From the encouragement of commodity production to the construction of roads and bridges, the diaspora – who were the impetus for these creations – became the new signifiers of blackness. In its demand for liberal monetary policies, defense from native attacks, the creation of infrastructure, and the opening up of markets for agricultural and industrial goods, blackness also attached itself to new capitalist markets. Liberia's transformation from space to a place – through settlement patterns that displaced indigenes from the coastal areas and from points of contact with Europeans, locating "civilized" diasporic migrants there and in the cities – became a means of resolving the crisis of nationally representing a modernized black identity. Through these processes, blackness marked and redefined the environment, landscape, and emergent urban architecture in Liberia.

[92] See Michel Foucault, "The Subject and Power," *Critical Inquiry*, Vol. 8. No. 4 (Summer, 1982), 777–795.

In decoding the Liberian landscape on which blackness was staged, it became evident that the infrastructure was built to serve the political interest of the new black elite as well as an expanding white supremacy and colonialism that was meant to keep people in their proper social spaces. The migration of the different groups and the intimacy implied from their cohabitation with the indigenes interrupted efforts to properly show the republic's civilization. As a multi-ethnic space, Liberia maintained the emerging forms of segregation for specific reasons. Using the infrastructure of urban development to carve up the land, secured the durability of segregation. By ensuring that the civilized and the general population would not unnecessarily run into each other except through points of designated contact, infrastructure prevented other kinds of conflict. By controlling people's movement, modern, civilized infrastructure created a way of guaranteeing that populations would move in their own lanes based on the built environment. Yet, for West Indians and African Americans, who in essence became managerial figures and overseers for Liberian boundaries, infrastructure also functioned in ways that enabled the migrants to harvest much labor, power, and taxes from the confined populations of mostly indigenes.[93] The profitability and value of segregation property became related to the distance from indigenes in the hinterlands. In these circumstances in which land was always at issue, its deep political content not only constructed blackness but also continued to mire the republic in inequality.

Liberia increasingly moved away from the creation of blackness centered on African Americans. This became noticeable in the annual independence celebrations held on January 26. A public holiday throughout the settlement, it was commemorated each year by the processions of citizens. In celebrations held in Monrovia by the president, the mayor, and other officials, citizens marched from a designated place to the Public Hall, where religious services were conducted and an oration delivered. Amidst the reading of the declaration of independence and the singing of the national anthem, one of the most significant aspects of the celebration, was "a public oration by some qualified person chosen for that purpose."[94] The 1885 celebrations featured the Barbadians in a significant way. As the *Methodist Herald* reported, "there seem this year to have been a grand demonstration. The oration, said to be an able one, was delivered by Hon. H. W. Grimes."[95]

[93] See Nathan Connolly, *A World More Concrete: Real Estate and the Remaking of Jim Crow South Florida* (Chicago: University of Chicago Press, 2014).
[94] *The African Repository*, Vol. 61 (1885), 71.
[95] Ibid.

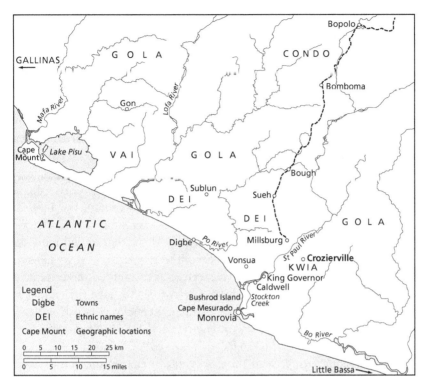

FIGURE 6.3: Map Showing African Polities and Migrant Settlements in Liberia
Source: Svend Holsoe Collection, Indiana University, Bloomington, Indiana

As one of the 1865 Barbadian migrants, Grimes had become the Attorney General. The Hon. C. T. O. King who presided over the occasion, proposed a toast to:

the health of the Orator of the Day, Henry W. Grimes, Esq. We must thank him for the able and intelligent manner he has entertained the audience today. He has given us enough to reflect on and profit by. I cannot but add in this connection that I think we need to cultivate more than anything else in Liberia, even more than the graces of literature – those qualities of sagacity, coolness, self-control and good sense, and at times magnanimity, which make men the successful leaders and guides of others.[96]

The Mayor then proposed a toast to "The Foreign Relations of Liberia," as a way of honoring E. J. Barclay, Esq., another of the Barbadian emigrants who had risen to the position of Acting Secretary of State.

[96] Ibid.

As Liberia made an attempt to present itself as civilized to the world, blackness was transnationally politicized to take on political valences. By the late nineteenth century, under the blinding light of the global stage, where the stakes were necessarily high and there was little room for confusion, observers increasingly kept the republic under their gaze. In 1893 at the Chicago World's Fair, Liberia crafted an image of itself and deliberately positioned itself under the world's gaze to announce its modernity to the world. The year before, in 1892, the Liberian government started making provisions – through a joint legislative resolution that had been passed the previous February – for an exhibit at the World's Columbian Exposition that was slated to be held in Chicago. Alfred B. King of the Clay-Ashland district in Monsterrado County and William E. Rothery, the Liberian consul at Philadelphia, were both appointed as commissioners, charged with the organization and execution of the exhibit that would represent the Liberian Republic at the exposition. The report of King to Liberian government highlighted what they conceived as the purpose and character of this exhibit: "The primary object in view was to have the exhibit so arranged at Chicago as to put the Liberian Republic in touch with the civilized world, to advance its commercial and industrial interests, and especially to attract attention to its unrivalled coffee."[97]

Commissioner King, who purchased and prepared the commodities and articles required for the purpose, had sent envoys to the kings and chiefs of the various ethnic groups in the interior. The Liberian government asked them to help the commission "by selling to it the many curious things at present and formerly used by them." It was proposed that "where the curio or relic was above a money value, the request was made that it be loaned to the commission for exhibition purposes, the commissioner promising to return whatever was entrusted as a loan." By the end of January 1893, the exhibit to be displayed in Chicago was secured. It consisted of nearly thirty tons of material, valued at over $5,000. Interestingly, the Liberian government also acquired an "ethnological portion of the exhibit" that it deemed "was not only curious, but particularly interesting to scientists. It showed most graphically the manners, customs, rites, and ceremonies of the primitive people of Liberia."[98] Many of the Barbadian migrants contributed to the construction of this new idea of blackness. Among them was Arthur Barclay, who served as the Postmaster-General of the Republic, Mrs. Florence A. King, and

---

[97] *The American Colonization Society*, Liberia, Issue 3, 66.
[98] Ibid.

W. H. King. They were joined by Mrs. Louisa Coleman, the wife of the Vice-President; Bishop Samuel Ferguson, M. T. De Coursey, Moses S. Boyle, H. Cooper and Son, Burgess Peal, Rix and Lomax, Williams Brothers, E. A. Snetter, J. H. Brooks, A. Woerrman and Co., R. H. Mitchell, and Hill and Moore, who all gave the commission significant support in shaping the exhibit.[99] The Liberian government noted that without the dynamic collaboration of the various participants, the pieces of the collection would not have been gathered soon enough.

On February 4, under the personal supervision of General R. A. Sherman, the 129 cases holding the pieces of the exhibit, "many of them large and unwieldy," were shipped from Monrovia in five boats. Sherman had sent his boats up the St. Paul's River to Clay-Ashland for the exhibit and later sent them from his wharf in Monrovia to the steamship that was to take them to Liverpool. The general took measures to ensure the safe transport of the exhibit while on board the British and African steamships. Without careful handling, many of the wrapped packages of the exhibit would otherwise have been useless for exhibition purposes at the end of a long journey. In England, the Liberian commission was met by the businesses of Elder, Dempster & Co., Edwards Brothers, Henry Hayman, and C. T. Johnson, who all regularly conducted trade with Liberia. By the time they arrived in Chicago, the Liberians had carefully constructed a display riddled with meaning:

The Liberian court was constructed entirely of native African woods, ropes, and tusks of elephants. A pyramid was built in the center of the court in three sections, 14 feet high. At each corner of every section was placed a tusk of ivory, and arranged on the shelves in neat glass jars were the different grades and qualities of coffee, cocoa, ginger, arrow-root, peanuts, palm oil, palm kernels, palm-kernel oil, vegetable butter, corn, rice, Calabar beans, locust beans, annito-seeds, Calabar pepper, alligator pepper, the whole decorated with native implements of war. A circular counter was made at the west side of the court, upon which was placed three flat and one upright glass show-cases to display curious exhibits to good effect. At the west entrance to the section there was an arch of pine, draped with native cloths of various tribes. The south entrance was constructed of mahogany, the columns being surmounted with the two largest tusks we had, the whole forming another archway. The main entrance was draped with French trimmings and with two Liberian flags. Each corner-post of the court was of mahogany, crowned with a tusk and draped with the star and stripes. The pyramid in the center was decorated with four flags. On three long tables made for the purpose were placed suitable showcases. On a show-board 12 by 12 were displayed photographs, a map of Liberia, a plan of Monrovia and of Clay-

[99] Ibid.

Ashland, the coin, currency, and stamps of Liberia, and some curios. The entire north wall was draped to the height of 29 feet with native cloths and skins. Two stands were erected, on which were placed models of an Americo-Liberian house and a primitive house in contrast. There were also four columns, 29 feet high, in the section. These were draped with native cloths, curios, and fibers. Our orchids and bulbs arrived in perfect condition.[100]

After the exhibits had been properly installed, the Liberians entered coffee, cocoa, palm oil, kernel oil, palm kernels, palm soap, arrow-root, hard-woods, dye-woods, seven kinds of fibers, ivory, rubber, minerals, and ethnology for competition and examination. It is alleged that approximately "1,000 to 12,000 persons daily thronged the Liberian court. Many came once, only to return again and bring their neighbors and friends." Of all the recognized and noted visitors who formally visited the exhibit were a deputation of the ACS that was comprised of Rev. Dr. Sunderland, Rev. Dr. Addison, and Secretary Thomas Wilson. The exhibit was also visited by "a number of distinguished Liberians," including "Hon. Arthur Barclay, Rev. David A. Day, Bishop H. M. Turner, Rev. Paulus Moort, M. D.; Prince Mommolu Massaquoi, Bishop Samuel D. Ferguson, and several of the Liberian consuls."[101]

The Liberian display at the Chicago World's Fair highlighted the advances the Liberian nation had made, and announced a shift that projected its posture as it advanced toward the turn of century. The display created an understanding of the migrants' association with the natives, who were present through their ethnology and objects. The display, even if it did not always enact it, marked migrants' desire to be contrary to natives. It aimed to depict not only the progress that had been made in civilizing the natives through the introduction of agricultural production, but also the migrants' advancement relative to natives' primitivism. The visual mosaic of Monrovia oriented people toward the kinds of products and iconography that projected the vistas and architecture of Monrovia, in contrast to the hinterlands, and represented the iconographies of capitalism and Christianity as opposed to primitivism. Liberians displayed native wares and architecturally complex buildings as testaments of their advancements. From the periphery, the city looked civilized and modern. Many of the exhibitions complicated accounts of migrants' interactions with natives represented in the broader social discourse. As they staged ideas of blackness alongside their views of

100 Ibid.
101 Ibid.

indigenes, black migrants projected meanings of race from the vantage point of the Liberia nation-building project.

Liberia represented blackness at the exposition. While blackness was linked to nation building and capitalist development, the diaspora could not account for the ways in which African indigenes represented blackness. Indeed, African Americans in diaspora such as Ida B. Wells and Frederick Douglass in an edited volume *The Reason Why the Colored American Is Not in the World's Columbian Exposition: the Afro-American Contribution to Columbian Literature* (1893), complained bitterly about their exclusion and highlighted the ways in which they would have used the opportunity to highlight black progress.[102] Liberians thus took on the ontological burdens of spectacle so that observers could look upon the modern civilized black identity. Yet, the ways in which Liberian migrants trafficked in the established norms, European notions made biological essences the fundamental ontology of deracialized indigenes even as they acknowledged their own non-whiteness. Even as diasporic migrants complicated the question of blackness, the kinds of blackness that fell outside of the spaces that tended to over-determine its meanings signaled its changing inflection points across space in relation to the questions of indigeneity and subalternity.

[102] Ida B. Wells, Frederick Douglass, Irvine Garland Penn and Ferdinand L. Barnett, *The Reason Why the Colored American Is Not in the World's Columbian Exposition: The Afro-American's Contribution to Columbian Literature* [1893], Robert W. Rydell, ed. (Urbana: University of Illinois Press, 1999).

A Changing of the Guards: Arthur Barclay and Barbadian Liberia Political Leadership

In January 1904, after winning the presidential bid of the TWP, Arthur Barclay was inaugurated as the fifteenth president of Liberia. The ever-observant schoolteacher J. A. Tuning sought to wrestle meaning from Barclay's migration experience in to his election: "Old man Barclay immigrated with a number of his countrymen and family to Liberia in May 1865. And again saw the familiar faces of Payne, Russell, and Roberts on these shores," all presidents of Liberia who had preceded Barclay.[1] In describing Anthony Barclay's reaction upon arriving in Liberia, Tuning noted: "His heart leaped within with indescribable joy as he placed young Barclay on these sunny shores."[2]

Arthur Barclay's West Indian-ness had proved critical in the election. Because no West Indian migrant had ever occupied the presidential position in Liberia, Barclay's election elicited much speculation. For Tuning, Barclay's presidential inauguration was more than historic. Tuning noted: "We are for the first time trying this experiment of an English-born subject." That a migrant of British heritage became the head of a nation established by the United States was evidently problematic. As Roberts earlier remarks suggested, the political traditions of British colonial Barbadians were incompatible with the dominant practices and traditions of the United States. Tuning, in pointing out these political implications, remarked: "The great American nation, the prototype of our constitution, would quake with fear to the risk."[3]

---

[1] *The Liberian Recorder*, December 1903. Liberia Collections. Accessed at Indiana University-Bloomington.
[2] Ibid.
[3] *The Liberian Recorder*, December 1903.

With the designation of "English-born subject" trailing them, it was evident that even at the turn of the century the Barbadian migrants had yet to be fully embraced under the Liberian identity. Indeed, Barclay had to "live down the charge of not qualifying as a true citizen and son of the soil" and was denounced as a black Englishman likely to betray the country to the British.[4] The new president, with his British West Indian political orientation, represented not only a changing of the political guard in Liberia but also a subversion of the established Americo-Liberian political power structure. The laser focus on the Barbadians was understandable; after all, for decades, Liberians had made natives and recaptives the prime existential threat to the greatest of Liberia's virtues: identity. By the turn of the twentieth century, the Barbadian migrants were perceived as equals who might usurp the republic's power dynamics. The anxieties surrounding the changing leadership were deeply shaped by the political changes the Barbadians wanted to help initiate on behalf of Liberia's marginalized. Tuning surmised that the coming changes that would accompany Barclay's presidency were merely "another national experiment." He insisted that Liberians were to be hopeful but should remain prayerful and watchful, in fact, "constantly watchful!"[5]

The vigilance necessary under the period of the national experiment held a double meaning for both the Barbadian migrants and Liberia. This was another national experiment for West Indians too, who were coming out of one experience of subordination across the Atlantic and entering into a new century at the same time. Additionally, for Liberia as a nation, this was a new experiment in a number of critical ways. The nation built on a coast previously dominated by the slave trade had become independent and was now heading into a new epoch. In a new age of legitimate trade and increasing European intrusion and challenge to national sovereignty, the more significant experiment that Liberia had to anticipate was the identity and allegiance of Barclay and other West Indians in Liberia. This had become especially significant as British intrusion on Liberian territory increased during the period of the Scramble for Africa. With the issues surrounding finance capital, debt in Liberia had become the new noose around the neck of the nation. What proved even more interesting was that, with this new European challenge, blacks had a superficial cloak

---

[4] B. K. Swartz and Raymond E. Dumett, *West African Culture Dynamics: Archaeological and Historical Perspectives* (The Hague: Mouton, 1980), 572.
[5] *The Liberian Recorder*, December 1903.

of sovereignty that was being tested by Europeans. How they fared would become a measure of how blacks and black countries would be viewed.

Liberia in its transition from the nineteenth to the twentieth century experienced a parallel change in political leadership from African Americans to West Indians. The Barclay presidency created a changing of the guard that was more significant than simply political change in leadership. Barbadian migrant political leaders in Liberia encountered a twentieth century born out of early nineteenth-century abolitionism, and an emerging new period of predatory European hyper-imperialism. Europeans in the years following the decline of the transatlantic slave trade, with growing budget deficits and shrinking continental markets for industrial goods, re-imagined their relationship to Africa.[6] In the mid to late nineteenth century, the African continent became a market for European trade surpluses, a source of raw materials, a site of cheap labor, and a place for capital investments.[7] New commodities and mechanisms to create capital outlined the new dynamics by which European dominance sought to operate. In 1884, the disputes that resulted from these renewed engagements with Africa led to the convening of European nations in the Berlin Conference to settle the terms of trade, treaties, and the establishment of protectorates in Africa.[8] In the aftermath of the conference, the delegates agreed that "in order for any nation to take possession or form a protectorate over territories on the African coast they had to inform the signatory powers of the Berlin Act and effectively occupy the space as proof of their authority to protect freedom of trade and transit."[9]

As the sovereignty of Liberia came into question so too did that of Barclay and other non-American descended migrants. Parodying the dilemmas of a nation caught in a critical turning point, J. A. Tuning observed: "The pessimist stands confronting the optimist in silent

---

[6] See George Neville Sanderson, *England, Europe & the Upper Nile, 1882–1899; A Study in the Partition of Africa* (Edinburgh: University Press, 1965), 4; Stig Förster, Wolfgang J. Mommsen, and Ronald Edward Robinson, *Bismarck, Europe, and Africa: The Berlin Africa Conference 1884–1885 and the Onset of Partition* (Oxford: Oxford University Press, 1988), 3.

[7] *Further Reports from Her Majesty's Diplomatic and Consular Agents Abroad Respecting the Condition of the Industrial Classes and the Purchase Power of Money in Foreign Countries* (London: Printed by Harrison & Sons, 1871), 17.

[8] See Thomas Pakenham, *The Scramble for Africa, 1876–1912* (New York: Random House, 1991).

[9] For acts of the Berlin Conference, see Bruce Fetter, *Colonial Rule in Africa: Readings from Primary Sources* (Madison: University of Wisconsin Press, 1979), 28–33.

consternation watching with deepest interest the issue of the auspicious event." Still, Tuning remained hopeful in reaching out to his compatriots: "Fellow citizens, to you I appeal, silen[ce] your fears and cease to despond. Let us as loyal and patriotic citizens be hopeful and leave the result to God. Know you not that there is divinity which shapes the end of every nation, rough hew them as you may. As it did in David's day?"[10] Barclay's election unearthed questions that had been raised in issues surrounding natives and European imperialism. But the gravity of this shift further affected meanings attached to blackness and its global signification. What is Liberia? Who is Liberian? What do the nation and its citizens represent? Who should have the power to represent the republic?

POST-INDEPENDENCE LIBERIAN LEADERSHIP

In the years following independence, the Liberian central government had only nominal authority that rendered the state weak. The first president, Joseph Roberts, had spent his first year as leader establishing Liberia's treaty worthiness in an attempt to garner recognition from European countries and the United States. Following Roberts, Stephen Allen Benson served as president for eight years, during which time he annexed Maryland country to the Republic of Liberia in 1857, thus bringing together the disparate colonial districts under national administration.[11] With the changing economies of the mid-nineteenth century, Liberia experienced marginal success in an early energetic merchant marine trade in coffee, palm oil, sugar cane, and other commodities that peaked in the period from the late 1840s leading up to the 1860s.

However, with the increasing native hostilities and various European trade rivalries along the coast, trade in Liberian commodities would later experience severe decline.[12] Given these trying issues, the main concern of Daniel Warner's presidency (1864–1868) was how the indigenous populations could be brought into Liberian society as cooperating subjects. Throughout the period, Liberia attempted to expand its territory through a series of expeditions into the hinterlands to establish treaties with local chiefs. Warner organized the first expedition led by J. K. Anderson into the

---

[10] *The Liberia Recorder*, July 23, 1904.
[11] Jesse N. Mongrue, *Liberia: America's Footprint in Africa: Making the Cultural, Social, and Political Connections* (Bloomington, IN: Universe, Inc, 2011), 11.
[12] See F. P. M. Van der Kraaij, *The Open Door Policy of Liberia: An Economic History of Modern Liberia* (Bremen: Im Selbstverlag des Museums, 1983).

interior to forge treaties with the local chieftaincies.[13] These moves created a gray area in race relations in the republic, effectively putting the black nation on similar colonizing footing with white European powers. In order to formalize the transitions from the slave trade to more legitimate forms of trade, Liberian leaders sought to establish laws for trading on the coast that had previously been free. Warner enacted the 1864 Ports of Entry Act aimed at controlling trade between the Kru ethnic group and Europeans, particularly the British.[14]

The 1860s carried with it a memory that probably held the Barbadians as former British subjects in a bad light. During that period, the British government began to put pressure on the government to settle the long-standing northwest boundary dispute between Liberia and neighboring Sierra Leone.[15] The British had made treaties with the indigenous population by offering them protection if they stopped the slave trade.[16] Being caught between the two colonial powers gave the natives enormous leverage. They could choose to go under the colonial control of either the Liberian central government or the British. However, the Port Act, having criminalized indigenous sources of livelihood, became problematic for those ethnic groups who were not in close proximity to the six trading ports to which trade was limited. The perceived antagonistic nature of the Liberian government pushed the coastal ethnic groups to be more receptive to the Europeans.

Following Warner, little had changed in the rivalry with the British. Some African Americans in the rural areas had even begun to embrace native antagonism toward Monrovia. James Spriggs Payne served as president from 1868 to 1870 and again from 1876 to 1878.[17] While important administrative policies were effected in these early periods, power resided with the small Americo-Liberian merchant class who jealously

---

[13] Benjamin Anderson, *Narrative of a Journey to Musardu the Capital of the Western Mandingoes Together with Narrative of the Expedition Dispatched to Musahdu by the Liberian Government under Benjamin J.K. Anderson in 1874* (London, 1971; first edition 1870, respectively 1912).

[14] See Robert Kappel, Werner Korte, and R. Friedegund Mascher, *Liberia: Underdevelopment and Political Rule in a Peripheral Society* (Hamburg: Institut für Afrika-Kunde, 1986), 151.

[15] Johann Büttikofer, Henk Dop, and Phillip T. Robinson, *Travel Sketches from Liberia: Johann Buttikofer's 19th Century Rainforest Explorations in West Africa:* Annotated English Edition (Leiden: Brill, 2013).

[16] Captain L. Wildman, Minutes of Evidence taken Before the Select Committee on Africa (Western Coast). House of Commons Papers, Volume 5, British Parliament. May 3, 1865.

[17] See Elwood Dunn and Svend E. Holsoe, *Historical Dictionary of Liberia* (Metuchen, NJ: Scarecrow Press, 1985).

protected their own interests rather than those of the state. According to Amos Sawyer: "Not only was the president not always the most influential individual in the political process, but even when such a person was the president, he was constrained in the exercise of authority."[18] Because of the self-interest of the merchant group, attention was not paid to how policies affected the indigenous population. In many cases, they were blatantly ignored. As a result, in the 1870s, encouraged by foreign traders, many of the Grebo chiefdoms, a subgroup of the Kru ethnicity, united to form a "kingdom" in a part of Maryland County and declared their independence from Liberia. They thereafter resumed trading on their own behalf with passing foreign ships. When war followed, the Liberian central government was almost overrun by the Grebos and they had to be assisted by an American warship that was in the harbor. This inability to control its own population and defend itself against domestic trouble-makers made Liberia particularly vulnerable to the machinations of European speculators.

With the decline of the economy under the Republicans and the backing of important leaders such as Blyden, many Liberians supported the leadership of Edwin J. Roye, who became the fifth president. As one of the wealthiest Liberians, Roye was not particularly popular. However, unlike the majority of his predecessors, his dark-skinned complexion not only became a source of unpopularity but also endeared him to those who were disgruntled about the dominance of the lighter-skinned merchant class.[19] His presidency, which marked the rise of the TWP, represented a direct affront to the racial, cultural, legal, and political norms that had become entrenched in Liberia. In an effort to consolidate power, Roye, in violation of the constitution, extended voting rights to the property-less, including African recaptives, and to a number of African ethnic groups.[20] He also began a program of reconstruction in Liberia with the intent of building new roads and schools. With these efforts, blacks such as Roye as well as the Liberian nation-state re-entered the geopolitical world and its new system of capital. In an effort to secure funds for his projects, Roye sailed to London in 1871, where he hoped to negotiate various lines of credit

[18] See Amos Sawyer, *Beyond Plunder: Toward Democratic Governance in Liberia* (Boulder, CO: Lynne Rienner Publishers, 2005); Amos Sawyer, *The Emergence of Autocracy in Liberia: Tragedy and Challenge* (San Francisco: Institute for Contemporary Studies, 1992).

[19] See J. Gus Liebenow, *Liberia: The Evolution of Privilege* (Ithaca, NY: Cornell University Press, 1969).

[20] Burrowes, *Power and Press Freedom in Liberia*, 86–87.

through bank loans. The results of this proved ruinous to him and Liberia. The terms of the loans were severe, among other things, carrying interest rates in excess of 7 percent.[21] Roye had hastily agreed to these terms without consulting the legislature. It is alleged that before Roye had even returned from London, approximately one hundred thousand dollars of the loan had been spent. Speculation included whether the subtracted amount was interest on the loan or money owed to Roye by the Liberian state.[22] Accusations of embezzlement resulted in widespread resentment and a dramatic loss of political capital.

When Roye further raised the chagrin of Liberians after trying to extend the two-year term of office for the president, his rule effectively ended. In October 1871, the Liberian legislature officially deposed Roye from office and summoned him to stand trial. In his bid to escape, Roye allegedly tried to swim to an English ship in the Monrovia harbour, where he drowned.[23] But even after his death, the loan from Britain continued to haunt Liberians.[24] In its efforts to meet payments on the loans, the country plunged further into debt and into greater economic dependency. By pushing the country into a cycle of debt, the loan sabotaged Liberia's efforts to negotiate other loans and attract the necessary and much needed investments. In 1874, the interest on the three-year term loan came due. As the country bargained with its creditors over the legality of the loan, its credit status continued to deteriorate. With no legal or economic loopholes to escape this commitment, Liberia lost credibility in diplomatic and economic negotiations, a move that promoted the stereotype that blacks could not govern themselves.

Whereas, in the early making of the nation, the indigenous had been the enemy, Europeans became the new enemies at the dawn of the twentieth century. To address these challenges, Barbadian leaders, unlike their early African American counterparts, sought to strengthen the central government through political and social consolidation. Through taxation measures, education policy, and territorial acquisitions, Barclay's government adopted a strategy of defensive imperialism to preserve the nation's sovereignty against European imperialistic designs. Barclay and other West

---

[21] Nathaniel C. Moak and John T. Cook, *Reports of Cases Decided by the English Courts [1870–1883]: With Notes and References to Kindred Cases and Authorities* (Albany, NY: W. Gould & Son, 1873), 45.

[22] Starr, *Liberia: Description, History, Problems*, 199.

[23] *The African Repository*, Vol. 48 (July 1872): 220–221; *African Times* (London), May 23, 1872.

[24] *African Times*, March 23, 1872.

Indian political leaders used approaches that starkly differed from their African American counterparts as they moved to modernize Liberia, negotiate European imperialism, and address the native question. The background, policies, and rhetoric of Arthur Barclay and other West Indian political leaders in Liberia, and reactions to their leadership during the era of the "scramble" highlight the ways in which Liberia's national identity was remade during the period. Despite intentions for greater native integration into the body politic as a way to stave off encroaching Europeans and save Liberia from colonization, these policies further abrogated the autonomy of indigenous cultural and political institutions by subordinating them to the will of the settler government. In many ways, efforts to consolidate the national government at the turn of the twentieth century only heightened institutionalized violence against the indigenes.

Barbadians' political leadership was challenged by the fact of Liberia's unusual position in Africa in the late nineteenth and early twentieth century. In the period of advancing European imperialism in Africa, Liberia's independence as an African state became a curious anachronism in the face of European hegemony. Before and following independence, Liberia, like European nations, had also mediated native trade and pursued national expansion along the coast and into the hinterlands, making treaties and laying claim to vast amounts of indigenous territory. Following the Berlin Conference, however, Liberia would be dragged unaware into a world economy dominated by outsiders and into a new international political system in which their claims to territories would be more sharply called into question. Thus, toward the end of the nineteenth century, Liberia was at the center of both domestic and international colonization dilemmas at the same time. The Scramble for Africa exposed Liberians as black colonists who also feared European colonization. Efforts to address the country's position relative to European dictates opened up larger questions about the relationship between race, colonialism, imperialism, and Liberian nationalism.

In June 1887, in an effort to define Liberia's position relative to European imperialists, Edwin Barclay – who had become Liberia's secretary of state – in a letter to Charles Henry Taylor, a black American minister in Monrovia, pointed out that "Liberia is neither a European power, nor a signatory of the decision of the Berlin Conference."[25]

[25] USNA, Dispatches of United States Ministers at Monrovia, Vol 10, diplomatic dispatch no. 12 enclosure. Barclay to Taylor, Monrovia 8, June 1887. Liberia Collections. University of Indiana-Bloomington.

Balking at Europeans' advances in Africa may have earned Liberia sympathy in the transnational black world, but it did not offer any real juridical protection from Europeans' efforts to enforce the Berlin Act. It had become particularly difficult for the Liberian central government to adhere to the "effective occupation" clause, with the decreasing migration of blacks from the diaspora and persisting native hostility. Seeking to find other loopholes through which Liberia's rights to territory would be acknowledged, Barclay de-legitimized the terms of the Berlin Act. He reasoned that Liberia "was not invited to assist in those deliberations and is therefore not bound by its decisions." Barclay further sought to differentiate Liberia's territorial acquisitions from those of the Europeans by adding that the Berlin Conference's "decisions refer to further acquisitions of African territory by European powers and not to present possessions or future acquisitions of an African state."[26] Evidently, for Barclay there was one set of rules for Europeans acquiring African territory from natives and another for the same actions carried out by the black settler government in Liberia.

In addition to Europeans, Liberia had other immediate adversaries lurking at the border. At a time when racial, cultural, and ethnic taxonomies were perhaps coalescing, the scramble re-opened gaps between the different groups of blacks in Liberia. African indigenes had been rejecting Liberia's claims to territories in the interior from the very beginning of the settlement and repeatedly contested them throughout the nation's unfolding.[27] That they had not become Liberian citizens with independence in 1847 had only cemented their sense of alienation, non-identification, and contempt for the Liberian central government. During the Scramble, natives who were once subordinated by Liberian settlers came to occupy an important bargaining position. Without their cooperation, the Liberian government would not be able to fulfill the effective occupation terms of the Berlin Act, and exposed the nation to European predations. At the same time, European speculators and merchants offered to trade and negotiate with them as well as settle their disputes with the Liberian central government. In the late nineteenth century, following the interactions of the government, Europeans, and indigenous groups, Liberia effectively lost the long-disputed Gallinhas territory in the northwest along the borders with Sierra Leone to the

---

[26] Ibid.
[27] See Raymond Leslie Buell, *The Native Problem in Africa* (New York: Macmillan, 1928), 705.

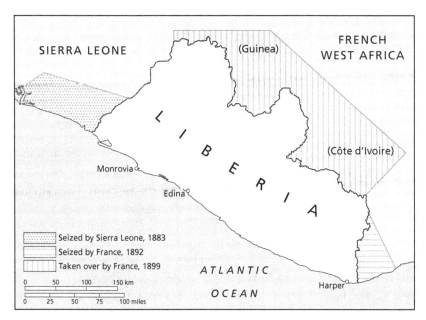

FIGURE 7.1: Liberian Territories Lost During the Scramble for Africa
Source: Svend Holsoe Collection, Indiana University, Bloomington, Indiana

British, and surrendered the Cavalla in the southeast to the French in Cote de I'voire and Guinea (Figure 7.1).

Hilary R. W. Johnson became the first Liberian-born president and served from 1884 to 1892. In an effort to renegotiate and revise the terms of Roye's loan, Johnson settled the boundary dispute with the British in the Gallinhas territory.[28] The West Indian Edward Blyden, who was then Secretary of State and Interior Secretary, was sent to negotiate with the British government.[29] Blyden, who had lived in Sierra Leone for a number of years, successfully negotiated and signed the Havelock-Blyden Treaty with Arthur Havelock, who had become governor of Sierra Leone in 1880. The treaty, which demarcated the boundaries between Liberia and Sierra Leone, also allowed the British to establish a rubber syndicate in those territories.[30] The treaty brought in much needed royalties to the Liberian government. With the

[28] Burrowes, *Modernization and the Decline of Press Freedom*, 94.
[29] Blyden to Coppinger, January 20, 1882, Papers of the American Colonization Society. Vol. 20. Accessed at Hathi Trust Digital Library, March 3, 2017.
[30] See *Liberia*, Vol. 19 (1882): 53 as quoted in Hollis Ralph Lynch, *Edward Wilmot Blyden: Pan-Negro Patriot 1832–1912* (London: Oxford University Press, 1967).

terms of the contract stipulating that the authorization of the Rubber Company was needed for other forms of trade, Liberia was again at the mercy of outside forces with little power to influence its own growth and development. West Indian identity in Liberia once again proved to be problematic as Americo-Liberians, who viewed Blyden as pro-British, opposed the treaty.

Blyden's decisions marked the kinds of issues that ultimately complicated the growing West Indian political power and leadership in Liberia.[31] Indeed, his perceived pro-Britishness became the lens through which future West Indian leadership would be viewed. Nonetheless, Americo-Liberians continued to rule until the turn of the century. Joseph James Cheeseman, who died in office in 1898, was replaced by William David Coleman, who took office with broad ideas of opening up the interior. He established Liberian influence in the interior northwest of the St. Paul River and conducted an unsuccessful expedition into Gola territory with the intent to subdue the ethnic group and their allies. This continued to be one of the biggest points of difference between Blyden and Americo-Liberians. Blyden believed that the migrants should have joined with the natives rather than attempt to subordinate them. These historical precedents haunted Liberia in a variety of ways. Indigenous hostility meant an inability to access resources, territory, and people needed to stave off continued European intrusion. Unfair loan agreements worsened inequalities that further contributed to Liberia's underdevelopment. At the end of the nineteenth century, Liberia found itself deeply entrenched in a world dominated by European outsiders: bankers in London, British traders in Sierra Leone, and French colonists in Cote d'Ivoire. How succeeding leaders like Barclay would address these problems was taken as an indication of Liberia's modernization, civilization, and progress.

ARTHUR BARCLAY AND TRANSATLANTIC POST-EMANCIPATION

As the first elected Barbadian migrant president, Arthur Barclay ushered in a new era in Liberia rooted in a British West Indian past not only in terms of identity but also through policies he implemented. The West Indies had been ground zero for the generation of leaders who emerged in Liberia at the turn of the century. Beginning with Arthur Barclay's father, Anthony Barclay, Barbadian political leadership in Liberia, seen

[31] Frank Sherman, *Liberia: The Land, Its People, History and Culture* (Dar es Salaam, Tanzania: New Africa Press, 2011), 205.

from a transatlantic and intergenerational perspective, served to fulfill Barbadian post-emancipation desires. Anthony Barclay had led the charge for migrating. Born in Bridgetown, Barbados, on July 31, 1854, he was the tenth of the twelve children of Anthony and Sarah Barclay.[32] From all accounts, Barclay's rise had confirmed the necessity for West Indian migration to Liberia. In keeping with the popular millenarian pan-African belief, Ethiopia had indeed stretched forth its hands to Africa. Barbadians, by responding to the call for the diaspora to migrate to Liberia, had brought with them the man who would become the nation's fifteenth president.

The twentieth century brought about experiences of nationhood to which the migrants had previously aspired. Whereas Barbadians aspired to leadership in Barbados, they could not have achieved those desires there. As people who had left Barbados under the duress of nineteenth-century post-emancipation, their migration to Liberia fostered the fulfill-ment of earlier aspirations. Achievements in Liberia thus became a culmination of previous Barbados post-emancipation aspirations. But though the twentieth century proved rewarding, it also became challen-ging in a different set of ways. In Liberia, the specter of West Indian-ness still hung over Barbadians. Spatial and temporal transformations for the Barbadians also meant changes in understandings of post-emancipation. Given that the immigrants had contributed to the efforts to build up a black republic, the next generation would turn their attention to main-taining the sovereignty and independence of the nation. In seeking to address the challenges of the new era, they would again have to confront Western hegemony as they had in Barbados.

While a West Indian heritage served Barclay at different points in his life, it also hindered him in many ways. After all, it was the assumed intelligence and industriousness of the West Indians that had driven the ACS to support their move to emigrate from Barbados in 1865. During the election of 1903, however, his West Indian background at times became a liability. While some saw his background and upbringing as an asset, others raised questions about his loyalty to Liberia in light of his "English" heritage. Contrary to the warm reception of Americo-Liberian migrants' arrival and views supporting their destiny to rule, the West Indians battled perceptions that challenged their legitimacy. As various newspapers reported during the election campaign, "the *Brig Cora* landed here in the administration of President Warner in the rainy

---

[32] "National Affairs," *The Literary Companion*, Monrovia, Liberia, July 31, 1938.

month of May an outlay of ten thousand dollars to the Colonization Society rendering them unable to provide them with sufficient food and comfort." The conditions under which the Barbadians landed were less than ideal. From the very beginning, however, it was noted that they were "hard pressed with hunger and woes but destined to rule."[33]

As if cautioning the newly elected president and other Barbadians to remember their initial experiences, the observer noted that it was the goodness of the Liberian settlers that helped them: "President Warner appealed to the charity and liberality of the citizens to come to the aid of these destitute emigrants [and] many of us contributed generously. He visited Palmas and brought their condition before the citizens generally with his old accustomed speech, 'If I can do no good, I will do no harm.'" Tuning recorded that J. T. Dimery, who was Warner's private secretary, said: "Now there is an opportunity to do good, if you scatter your seed in this direction, it may return to you a hundred fold. [Cape] Palmas boldly came to their relief in aiding them, she little knew that she was aiding her future president."[34] The early seeds sown by the Americo-Liberians had blossomed in the form of West Indian leadership and service to Liberia. Given the unfortunate nature of their arrival and the kindness rendered to them, questions from Americo-Liberians abounded now that they were in power: "Can Barclay forget all this and rashly cut from the body, the hand that thus administered to his wants and comforts? Brutus may slay Caesar, but will he like Judas betray Liberia?"[35] Behind these inquiries were more than fears about whether the Barbadians in power would return kindness to the Americo-Liberians. There were greater concerns about the future of the nation. Would Barclay forget the goodness of Liberia by betraying the nation to the British?

In 1894, Alexander Crummell had attempted to silence Barclay's detractors and critics as he contextualized and outlined the meaning of the Barbadians' ever increasing political leadership. He noted that Barclay was "one of the youngest members of a more than ordinary family, for no one could see and converse with the parents and with their sons and daughters, eleven in all, without being struck with both their character and their intelligence."[36] Crummell saw Barclay's family upbringing as

---

[33] *The Liberian Recorder*, 1904.
[34] Ibid.
[35] Ibid.
[36] Ibid.

critical and the son as reflective of the larger Barclay family values. He styled the Barclays as a group of "thoughtful, self-restrained, upright, and orderly people ... well-freighted with knowledge, acquirements and culture ... presented the unusual peculiarity of being heavily weighted with moral excellence as with the intelligent brightness of right-minded people."[37]

The great emphasis that was placed on education and the driving ambition to succeed traveled with the Barbadians to Liberia. Both the Wiles and Grimes families did well in this regard. By the time James Wiles left Liberia, he had purchased two houses in Monrovia and a number of other land properties. His son Richard Stanley Wiles, also born in Barbados, did well by becoming Speaker of the House in the Liberian government. Richard Wiles married Florence Mai Grimes, who along with Louis Grimes were the children of Ella Barclay, the sister of Arthur Barclay. Florence was among the first women to graduate from the University of Liberia in 1905. Her brother, Louis Arthur Grimes, served as Attorney General and Chief Justice of Liberia and was considered a renowned jurist and legal scholar. Based on their success, Crummell effusively praised the Barbadians' intellectual abilities. He saw their established precedence as a good predictor of Arthur Barclay's capacity to rule. In a nation concerned about the appearance of civilization and modernity, the Barclay family's much lauded moral fiber was also used to qualify Barclay's candidacy. In describing the family background and their belief system, Crummell stressed: "We put the word character first.[38] As a group, Crummell perceived the Barbadians "life and character during their long residence in Liberia have fulfilled the bright promise of their first coming."[39] He credited the success of the Barclay clan to the role played by the matriarch, Sarah Ann Bourne Barclay after the death of Anthony Barclay. He noted:

Such was the strength of the motherhood in the bereaved widow that his children, under her guidance and direction, have passed from youth into manhood and womanhood, honorable in character and useful and beneficent in life and conduct. They have risen, without any exceptions, to high positions in church and state, as teachers, merchants, lay readers, vestrymen, and statesmen.[40]

---

[37] Burrowes, *Power and Press Freedom*, 118.
[38] *The Liberian Recorder*, February 4, 1894.
[39] Ibid.
[40] Ibid.

With this storied and principled background, Crummell anticipated great things from the leadership of Arthur Barclay.

Arthur Barclay received his education in the schools of Monrovia with his oldest sister, Antoinette Barclay, serving as his first tutor.[41] Following this early education, Barclay reportedly sold salt on the streets of Monrovia before entering the Preparatory Department of Liberia College.[42] He was noted as scoring highly in his languages and mathematics classes. Having completed his courses, he matriculated into Liberia College and graduated with a Bachelor of Arts in the class of 1873. This kind of grit and perseverance led Crummell to conclude that these accomplishments, "coupled with his manifest uprightness, have made him a necessary factor in the public affairs of the young nation."[43] But as a minority group in Liberia, Barbadians' rise to office required more than educational training. It was also associated with extensive civil service and administrative experience. Barclay's own civil service position was seen as a qualifying factor in his presidential bid. In the years following his time at Liberia College, Barclay held several government positions. As Crummell noted, he always acquitted himself with "intelligence and honor."[44] He was appointed Principal of the Preparatory Department of Liberia College in 1877, a position he held for a number of years and served as Professor, Member of the Board of Trustees, and sometimes Acting President of the College in his later years. During vacations, Barclay served as Chief Clerk of the House of Representatives. In 1877, he was called to the Bar of Monserrado County and after practicing law for three years, attained the rank of Counselor of the Supreme Court.

Barclay's political career began to take shape when he served as the private secretary to J. J. Roberts, the first president of the Republic. In 1883, Alfred F. Russell, who had been the tenth president, appointed him as the second judge of the Court of Quarter Sessions and Common Pleas of Monsterrado County. He was appointed as sub-treasurer of Monsterrado County by H. R. W. Johnson in 1885, a post he held for

---

[41] Mary Antoinette Brown Sherman, "A Brief Sketch of the Life of Malvina Barclay," *Barclay Women in Liberia – Two Generations: A Biographical Dictionary*, The Archives of the University of Liberia.

[42] This was under the principalship of Anthony T. Ferguson. *The Crozierville Observer*, June 5, 1930.

[43] *The Liberian Recorder*, February 4, 1894.

[44] Ibid.

five years. During the administration of President J. J. Cheeseman, Barclay was elected to the cabinet as Post-Master General and afterwards became Secretary of State. He also served on several diplomatic missions and was sent as a commissioner to the World's Fair in Chicago in 1893. Four years later, through his association with Chief Justice Z. B. Roberts and Senator A. B. King, Barclay went on diplomatic missions to England and France. While in London, he arranged with the Council of Foreign Bondholders for the amortization of the 1870 loan contracted by President E. J. Roye, which had been in default for over twenty years. Upon the death of H. A. Williams in 1896, Barclay was appointed Secretary of the Treasury, a position he held until his election to the presidency in May 1903. In addition to his extensive civil service experience, Barclay served as the Chairman of the TWP. By 1903, he had civil service experience and practical knowledge of the functions of government and was the driving force in the workings of the TWP.[45] William Heard, who visited Liberia in 1898, noted alongside a photo of Barclay in his book, *A Bright Side of Liberia* that "Secretary of the Treasury, Arthur Barclay, is a clever scholar and has been connected with the government many years. He is therefore the one man that fits in any position. He is a lawyer by profession."[46] (See Figure 7.2)

Barclay was just one of a cohort of Barbadians to emerge as leaders in Liberia after the turn of the twentieth century, using their "unappropriated" status to climb the political ladder. Their West Indian-ness was critical to their political rise. Unlike African Americans whose relationships to whites was circumscribed by spatial restrictions and violence, the Barbadians' was framed by their belonging to a wide Empire. The Barbadians used this in-between-ness to simultaneously cushion the blows of racism as well as provide rungs for their climb. While Barbadians had used their education and civil service to serve in various capacities, none before Barclay had risen to the position of president. In a country dominated by Americo-Liberians, the implications of another group attaining power were still an issue at the turn of the twentieth century. This had nothing to do with legalities. As Tuning pointed out, "there is no provision in our constitution prohibiting any but a natural born from aspiring to that position." All blacks who were legally citizens of the Republic could qualify as president. But given that the world around

---

[45] Swartz and Dumett, *West African Culture Dynamics*, 572.
[46] Heard, *The Bright Side of Liberia*, 41.

Hon. ARTHUR BARCLAY,
Secretary of the Treasury of Liberia.

FIGURE 7.2: Photograph of Arthur Barclay as Secretary of the Treasury
Source: William H. Heard, *The Bright Side of African Life* (New York: Negro
Universities Press, 1969), 37

him recognized his English heritage, this made acquiring political power in
Liberia all the worse. After his election, a Newcastle newspaper keenly
pointed out: "The new president of Liberia is Mr. Arthur Barclay, who
was born in Bridgetown, Barbados and therefore is a former British
subject."[47] Such acknowledgments in the face of British imperialistic
aggression toward Liberia might have served to make Tuning and others
suspicious of the changing political leadership.

To many, Barclay's impending presidency depended on the track
record of the West Indians who had risen to some of the highest levels of
political leadership in Liberia. As Tuning noted: "we fondly hope that the
outcome will not be a duplicate of that Honorable Wiles who enjoyed the
full confidence of the nation in many of our important positions of trust,
but in the end foorsook us and fled to climates more congenial."

[47] FO 47/29. Foreign Office Correspondence. The National Archives. Kew Gardens. UK.

J. T. Wiles, one of the 1865 Barbadian migrants, chose to return to Barbados in the late nineteenth century, dying there in 1897. Tuning was also guarded because of prior experiences with migrants from the Caribbean who he saw as lacking the requisite patriotism and loyalty. It was the West Indian background and supposed pro-Britishness of other West Indian migrants that had led suspecting Americo-Liberians to that conclusion. Tuning was also not impressed with West Indians because, as he claimed, "the good old Dr. [Blyden] left us with the fifth chapter of Amos to read, after sharing our best gifts and blessings."[48] Blyden, who had migrated from the Caribbean Island of St. Thomas, had served in various political capacities in Liberia but had left the country after various political clashes, most notably about differences in racial attitudes and cultural understanding with Americo-Liberians. Blyden viewed Americo-Liberians as centering Liberia's development upon white supremacist ideas, which left him to lament that "all that will remain will be worthless as a bit of animal seized back from the predator."[49] He had settled in Sierra Leone after he was nearly tarred and feathered for allegedly fornicating with the wife of President Roye.

In spite of his initial skepticism, Tuning likened Barclay's ascendancy to the second coming, a tradition within pan-Africanism that imbued leadership with a sense of providence and the prophetic fulfillment of destiny. Tuning may have also been echoing a general skepticism, yet he sought to assuage these concerns by pointing to Barclay's background. In an address on the eve of Barclay's inauguration, he waxed poetic about the background of the leader: "The prophetic language which then tingled our fathers' ear quite eight years before young Barclay was born, and dangled a crowning laughing kid upon his mother's knees and heard the melodious strains of the nursery song, 'You are born to be the Negro ruler,' was the assertion made."[50] With this fanciful view of Barclay's presidency, Tuning mused: "Is this another reason why we should not doubt and despair? Should we not hope to see great things brought out for the salvation of our race in this child of promise, this son of providence? Does not God move in a mysterious way, his wonders to perform? Those fearful clouds we so much dread; Oft showers blessings on our head."[51] Tuning created an

---

[48] The prophet Amos had written a key chapter of the Bible where he railed against the privileged people of Israel who took advantage of the poor.
[49] Blyden, *Christianity, Islam, and the Negro Race*, 27.
[50] *The Liberian Recorder*, July 23, 1903.
[51] Ibid.

image of a leader who, like Liberia, had experienced great odds but had prevailed and who appeared strange but was a blessing. Through his background and migration experiences, Barclay became a metaphor for the Liberian nation.

ARTHUR BARCLAY AND CHANGING LIBERIAN PRESIDENTIAL POLICIES

Early political leadership in Liberia established precedents that persisted throughout the unfolding of the nation. The mistakes and false starts proved especially critical during the Scramble for Africa. White imperialist drive during the period threatened political sovereignty and reinforced black subjectivity through indebtedness. Unlike their predecessors, whose post-slavery challenges had been land, labor, and citizenship in Barbados, the issues for twentieth-century West Indians in Liberia proved to be debt, increasing European territorial encroachment, and challenges to national development. In a period characterized by African territorial divisions and where subordination was explicitly racialized, un-equalitarian terms of loans and increasing terms of interest became a disciplining factor for Liberians. To court and accommodate investors for development purposes and, in many cases, for their very survival, Barbadians in Liberia would have to escape the traps of debt, but also the internalized disciplinarian culture of Europeans and Americans. In this way, the flood of Barbadian leaders in Liberia at the turn of the century instantiated a contest between Empire and Republicanism and ideas of subjecthood versus those of natural rights. Barclay himself was conscious of the demands of the new times, telling Liberians that it was essential to keep their fingers on the pulse of international public opinion. In the past, Liberians' connections to Europeans and the outside world had been through church and missionaries, but this was a "material age," one in which the previous "philanthropic wave which moved and influenced the European world for over half a century seem[ed] for the present to have almost entirely ebbed."[52]

In a later assessment of the period that preceded his leadership, Barclay remarked that at the time of independence, Liberia had been formally recognized by the powers as a nation "*in posse* rather than *in esse*," as a possibility and with potential rather than a state in actual existence. In his political leadership, Barclay anticipated making the necessary

---

[52] Swartz and Dumett, *West African Culture Dynamics*, 565.

critical readjustments to navigate and transition from a period characterized by the ending of the slave trade to a modern age of changing market
demands, new loan structures, industrialization, and technological development. In these decades characterized by European colonialism, bad
loans, and growing diasporic protests, Liberia's position relative to the
question of race re-emerged. How leaders addressed these changes would
not only determine the modern course of Liberia's national development
but also address the question of black inferiority and define the state's
nationalist and racialist goals. With the exigencies of the period, leaders
such as Barclay were often caught within forces of multi-directional
pressures.

At the beginning of his term, Barclay's challenges included an economic
depression driven by overwhelming debt obligations and an empty treasury. Through the short-sighted policies of previous administrations, the
country was almost bankrupt. Despite the triumph of independence, in the
emerging decades of hyper-global financializing, the little gains that had
been made would be tested. The racial exclusion of the new financial
economy diminished many of the hard won improvements Liberia had
made. With its independence tied to European financial institutions,
Liberia's sovereignty hung in the balance. In 1898, in his capacity as
Secretary of the Treasury, Barclay had succeeded in reaching
a settlement with British creditors, adjusting the principal on an outstand-
ing loan contracted during the Roye presidency. But there were deeper
implications to this kind of economic dependence. Impatient for expansion, European nations were looking for any pretext to annex and colonize portions of the republic. This left Liberia vulnerable. Negotiations for
trade, loan, or investment could only be made if Liberia offered concessions in exchange for protection against European colonialism, a move
that created a cycle of debt and dependency.

While Barclay tried to heed these warnings, his efforts to develop
Liberia in many ways confirmed Americo-Liberians' anti-West Indian
views. In his efforts to modernize Liberia, he felt the need to bring in
outside help. Barclay became a key political actor who would transform
the tenor of Liberia's political and diplomatic relations. In areas where
a flattened republican subjectivity had shaped Americo-Liberian horizontal citizenship, vertical subjecthood under the empire enabled Barclay to
participate more effectively in diplomatic relationships. In one of his first
of a series of moves, Barclay turned to the British Proconsul Harry
Johnston. In these interactions, European officials did not categorize
him as Americo-Liberian. Consul Braithwaite Wallis, the key British

official in Liberia, identified Barclay as a "West Indian not a Liberian," who still maintained his distinct Barbadian brogue.[53] Once the heightened difference of his race was diminished, if not fully erased, vision and hearing, over the other bodily senses, became the most intuitive means of delineating the different black subjective experiences in Liberia. Henry Wilson also argued that "once divested of America-Liberian status, with all its negative connotations, he [Barclay] could be recognized by Europeans as a statesman of goodwill and talent." Wilson believed that Barclay was credited with transcending the "very American preoccupation with the politics of place, displaying real sympathy with native aspirations, and above all, being free from the 'blancophobia' thought to be characteristic of Americo-Liberians."[54] Such observations and descriptions created an exoticized image of West Indians that was also visible in how the story of Arthur Barclay's leadership was received.

Transnational perceptions of Liberians filled in the racial imaginary about what black people were and how to understand the distinctions between them. Onlookers who saw "blancophobia" as a driving principle among Americo-Liberians and took note of the differences in African Americans' and West Indians' treatment of the natives, were observing the ways in which both groups were seared by their different experiences of racial subjectivity. This act of recognition in Liberia situated people in their appropriate citizenship spaces. American racism perceived by white observers as "blancophobia" drove African American migrants' treaty negotiations and other initiatives. It was possibly for these reasons that Joseph Roberts had suffered many setbacks in his diplomatic negotiations. During his presidency, Roberts had traveled to England to negotiate loan agreements as well as to settle boundary disputes. Roberts experienced little success during his many trips. He was neither able to get better terms nor resolve the boundary question. Indeed, given how race operated, Americo-Liberians like Roberts had largely relied on the Liberian Proconsul, Gerard Ralston, to represent the nation to the outside world and to negotiate treaty obligations. Barclay, on the other hand, partly because of the nature of his subjectivity and liminal positioning, could represent the nation and diplomatically ally with British imperialists. Onlookers surmised that Americo-Liberian racialized republicanism

[53] Wallis to Foreign Office, February 4, 1908, 367/113/7296. 7296 in Swartz and Dumett, *West African Culture Dynamics*, 585.

[54] Henry Wilson, "Nation Building, Ethnicity, and the New Imperialism," in Swartz and Dumett, *West African Culture Dynamics*, 569.

created fears of whiteness while the verticality of imperial subjecthood allowed access to the king and thus opened up access to whiteness in less forceful ways. Because subjects of the empire were all of different races, vertical subjecthood would not be racially bound. Thus, the political presence of the Barbadians in Liberia realigned what blackness signified and what it meant to be Liberian in the mind of the white public.

In his paper "Nation Building, Ethnicity, and the New Imperialism," Henry Wilson compared the philosophies, dispositions, and partisan politics that inserted innovation and vigor into the fight for the Liberian nationality that was occurring at the turn of the century.[55] Wilson focused his exploration on the "middle class nationalism of President Arthur Barclay" and his determination to push Liberia along a path to modernization and progress in the face of the hostilities of European and American rivals. The paper further analyzed and compared Barclay to other personalities such as Sylvester Williams and Edward Blyden. Within these personalities were several "substreams of modern African nationalism, including the pan-Africanist ideologies of West Indian intellectuals such as E. W. Blyden and H. Sylvester Williams, the ethnic nationalisms of rural protest groups and the practical statesmanship of the Americo-Liberians led by Barclay."[56] According to Wilson, "against numerous opponents, internal as well as external, the pioneers of West African nationhood frequently had to play a delaying game and steer a zigzag course." As Wilson puts it, the problem that confronted West African writers and politicians, "nurtured on the nationalist ideas of the founding fathers, was how to adapt their notions of identity, autonomy and nation building to changing constraints and opportunities. All the different nations that had been charged with Liberia's protection and support aimed to influence the young nation both politically and economically."[57]

Sylvester Williams had organized several pan-African congresses in the early 1900s. The first conference, in 1900, lasted three days and took place at Westminster Town Hall in London and featured black delegates from the United States, the West Indies, West Africa, and Southern Africa. In 1908, Williams went to Liberia at the invitation of Barclay. The relationship surrounding the ideology of African nationalism and the challenging circumstances of constructing a cohesive, civilized state were particularly complicated. At a meeting of the African Society at

[55] Ibid., 298–299.
[56] Ibid., 298.
[57] Ibid.

which Sylvester Williams was present, Harry Johnston addressed the gathering, showing pictures from his recent visit to Liberia. Johnston highlighted that not much is known about Liberia, "since until quite recently there had been quite a gulf between civilized Liberians and the uncivilized aborigines." In showing some pictures of Monrovia, he explained that the houses were "nearly as well built as those in Sierra Leone, but that there was still a great deal to be desired in the matter of road-making, a far reaching system of which had now been undertaken."[58]

Among the pictures Johnston had of homes constructed with shingles on raised platforms and government houses were pictures of the official presidential residence, the Liberian House of Representatives, and indigenous buildings. Johnston also showed a picture of Arthur Barclay, highlighting that "he was one of the most remarkable man [*sic*] of African blood he had ever met."[59] He further noted that Barclay was "self-educated and deeply read, and he had done a great deal in recent years to restore the finances of Liberia from the chaos in which they had fallen."[60] Barclay's photograph had also started to circulate as the face of civilization in Liberia (See Figure 7.3). Accompanying these new images of Liberia was a photo illustrating Barclay's role in helping to organize the Liberia Exhibition at the Chicago World's Fair.

In an effort to address these issues, Barclay, during his presidency, sought to strengthen the national government. For more than half of a century, the constitution of Liberia had limited the presidential terms to two years, rendering the position largely ineffectual. That President Roye in his efforts to change the term of the presidency had met his death did not deter Barclay. To address the country's economic sluggishness, debt, and colonial crisis, the Liberian government and the office of the presidency, in particular, had to become more influential in order to command and direct the country's available resources. Barclay sought and received legislative approval to extend the term of president from two to four years. As such, he was able to serve from 1904 to 1912. With increased national power, Liberians started to rally around the political leaders attached to the TWP, within which power was concentrated, and more and more began to move away from the Republican Party that had been formed by the Americo-

[58] *African Affairs: Journal of the Royal African Society*, Vol. 5 (1906): 438.
[59] Ibid.
[60] Ibid.

207. H. E. PRESIDENT ARTHUR BARCLAY,
OF LIBERIA

A native of Barbados, but derived two generations
back from Pōpō, Dahomé

FIGURE 7.3: Arthur Barclay, Barbadian Migrant, 15th President of Liberia
Source: Portrait of H.E. President Arthur Barclay of Liberia by Mr. Raphael, from
the book Harry Hamilton Johnston, *The Negro in the New World* (New York:
Macmillan Company, 1910)

Liberian settlers. Under the TWP, Liberia would become essentially a one-party state until the coup in 1980.[61]

For Barclay, the 1864 Port of Entry Act, enacted one year before the Barbadians' arrival, was the clear source of Liberia's financial and national distress. The Act had been driven in part by Europeans', particularly British merchants' refusal to pay import and export duties when trading with the natives. In response, the government had closed parts of the country to European trading, limiting it to only six areas along the coast which the central government controlled. Though it was meant to curtail trade and to show the force of Liberian sovereignty, the Port of Entry Act was perceived by many, including the indigenous whose trade and livelihood were being curtailed, as a move to merely protect the economic interests of the Americo-Liberian elite. The resulting war between the coastal Kru ethnic group and the Liberian government would also have interventions from the British. The cost to fund expeditions to quell these kinds of rebellions further exhausted the nation's diminishing treasury.

As Barclay forged alliances with natives, he further aggravated the border issues with Britain. Were Liberia to maintain its sovereignty, leaders would have to effectively protect its borders and contain its citizens. In 1907, in a treaty with the French, Liberia agreed that a frontier force was needed to police the established boundaries between Liberia and the French territories of Guinea and the Ivory Coast. Liberia's inability to establish this force led the French to place their own forces on Liberian territories. The British soon also requested a trained police force. Barclay was approached by the British Major MacKay Cadell, who had served in the South African War for some time, to be the head of the Frontier Force. Cadell was employed to create a force that would be comprised of established army personnel in Sierra Leone and Liberian indigenes. Many speculated about the "English" makeup of the force and the French even described it as "a British Army of occupation."[62] With Cadell's increasing power in Liberia, many sought to get rid of him. Liberia almost lost its sovereignty when Cadell refused to resign and instead tried to engineer a coup that almost succeeded.

Barclay took advantage of the French border encroachment issue to promote his program of indirect rule in the hinterland. Faced with British

---

[61] Teah Wulah, *Back to Africa: A Liberian Tragedy* (Bloomington, IN: Author House, 2009), 436.

[62] Starr, *Liberia*, 122.

imperialism, Barclay turned to the United States for help, dispatching a diplomatic mission for the purpose of "soliciting aid in negotiating arbitration treaties and securing the integrity of the Republic, and ascertaining the possibility of floating a new loan."[63] In asking for the United States to essentially extend a protectorate over Liberia, Barclay's bid for assistance to sustain Liberia's independence further complicated the relationship between the two nations and the country's quest for respectability. In a letter to the president of the United States, Barclay wrote: "It is necessary to argue that the duty of the United States towards the unfortunate victims of the slave-trade was not completed by landing them upon the shore of Africa, and that our nation rest under the highest obligation to assist them, so far as they need assistance, toward the maintenance of free, orderly and prosperous civil society."[64] Barclay hoped that by establishing a relationship with the United States he would not only get help in the border disputes with Europeans but also be able to take advantage of the rich resources in the hinterland. President William Howard Taft proved surprisingly sympathetic, sending a three-man delegation to Liberia "to investigate the interests of the United States and its citizens in the Republic of Liberia."[65] The American Commission arrived in Liberia in 1909. It reported to the American Congress in 1910 with an accompanying memoranda going to President Taft.

The commission made six recommendations to the Liberian government. In light of the historical relationship between the two countries, it recommended that the United States extend aid to Liberia promptly. In an effort to settle the boundary dispute with the British and French, the United States would also help to ensure the country's continued sovereignty. The commission further called for the establishment of a customs department, where it would use the funds collected to pay off its debt, an initiative similar to the U.S. policy of "dollar diplomacy" in the Caribbean. It also called for the United States to assist Liberia in overhauling its internal finances as well as lend tactical support in establishing Liberia's Frontier Police Force. They believed that the largest aid that could be rendered Liberia was the establishment of scientific research. This kind of aid would improve Liberia's position in the world, generate interest in agricultural production, help with disease inoculation, and further open up the hinterlands to productive enterprises. The commission also saw the need for

[63] Dunn, *The Annual Messages of the Presidents of Liberia 1848–2010*, 450.
[64] Ibid.
[65] Wulah, *Back to Africa*, 436.

the establishment of a naval coaling station. Mindful of the United States' diplomatic relationship with Europe, Congress, however, refused to interfere in the question of sovereignty as it related to encroaching Europeans. As such, the assistance the United States rendered Liberia was cosmetic at best. Furthermore, the assistance of the United States was bolstered by racist thinking. "The constitutional government by negroes was an experiment," declared the United States Secretary of State, Francis Bacon, "one which so far had failed but which should not be allowed to collapse altogether." Bacon pointed out that "with a little help and tutoring we might help them work out their own salvation." In doing so, he concluded that after the republic secured a regular income, it would "free them from the pressure of foreign debt." After setting up this foundation that would put them on a "sound financial basis," Bacon supposed that "there was good hope that they might succeed in governing themselves."[66]

Ultimately, the relationship would profit the United States more than it would Liberia's efforts towards robust growth, development, and independence. The United States eventually provided an agricultural director, a position that became a part of the early beginnings of the establishment of the Harvey Firestone rubber corporation.[67] The United States further extended military support by sending officers to re-establish the Frontier Force, which eventually came to serve as the machinery that enforced coercive labor tactics on Firestone plantations.[68] It was further agreed that the United States, Britain, France, and Germany would altogether consolidate and liquidate Liberia's debt with a guarantee that they would have joint control over the country's customs department. Liberia's development continued to hinge on the signing of these kinds of unequal contracts. In one instance, France proposed to take over all of Liberia's public debt in exchange for establishing a protectorate over the country. When Liberia refused, France claimed jurisdiction over an area of ninety miles of coastline, east of Cape Palmas, as well as other areas surrounding Cape Mount and Grand Bassa.[69]

In the efforts to transition from the earlier nineteenth-century economic systems, Liberia struggled even more at the dawn of the twentieth century as it entered the global market economy. Barclay sought other

---

[66] Wilson, "Nation Building," 571.
[67] See James Capers Young, *Liberia Rediscovered* (Garden City, NY: Doubleday, Doran, 1934).
[68] *The Firestone Liberian Rubber Scheme: Mr. Harvey S. Firestone, Jnr, in London* (S.l: s.n, 1926), 3.
[69] Kraaij, *The Open Door Policy,* 27.

ways to modernize the country by developing its agriculture-dependent economy. In countries like Liberia, agriculture was needed to reduce the costs of imports and service debt and as a source of revenue. Liberia's dependence on agriculture and the production of primary materials for the developed world showed a distorted and dependent economy and re-enforced the gap between itself and developed economies. As a country tied to the production of primary products, Liberia came to reflect the widening gap between Africa and the West that also reflected the economic inequality between black and white.

Liberia had numerous internal concerns, but its external issues were also important. At the very core of Liberia's dilemmas at the turn of the century were the issues of race, civilization, and modernity, problems that had defined the challenges of post-emancipation for Afro-Barbadians. Liberia had always been represented as a primitive black nationality, unable to modernize and prone to only mimic the ways of Europeans. African Americans, watching from afar as the country slid into bankruptcy and possible annexation, noted, "Liberia is a mighty lens through which the world is looking at the Negro race."[70] Liberians, too, recognized their growing sense of importance in the black world and that their continued independence mattered far beyond the disputed territorial boundaries of a small republic. Toiling to finalize territorial negotiations with both British and French officials while simultaneously struggling to repay financial loans to the British bank, Barclay reminded the legislature exactly what was at stake. "It is a fact," he noted in 1905, that "we do not represent ourselves alone, in this national experiment. Consider what our success or failure will mean for the race."[71]

Liberia existed under the gaze of both the broader black and white worlds. One columnist in the *Crozierville Observer*, likely a Barbadian migrant, noted:

There have been arguments advanced by loyal Liberians that high officials of government should not be severely criticized by citizens because the eyes of the outside world are set upon her and if the men in high positions are found incompetent either from dishonesty, inefficiency, or lack of patriotism the whole citizenry will be considered dishonest, disloyal, inefficient, and not a set of grafters.[72]

---

[70] Wilson, "Nation Building," 571.

[71] Arthur Barclay, "Message of the President of Liberia Communicated to the First Session of the Thirteenth Legislature," December 14, 1905, Dispatches from United States Ministers to Liberia, 1863–1906, Volume 14, Roll T-14. The National Archives, Washington, DC.

[72] *The Crozierville Observer*, February 1930.

He further noted, "These citizens, loyal to individuals rather than to the constituted authority of the state, contend that the white world will welcome any such proof of dishonesty, inefficiency, or disloyalty on the part of high officials of the only Negro Republic in the world, to substantiate their argument that the Negro is incompetent of self-government."[73] Given that Liberia was one of two self-governed black sovereignties in Africa, the other being Ethiopia, he believed that Liberia should try to serve as a symbol of black progress.[74] Turn-of-the-century Liberians felt the demise of Liberia would be detrimental not only to its inhabitants, but also to black people throughout the Atlantic world. Still labeled as an experiment, a failed Liberia would only reinforce the prevailing idea among Europeans and white Americans that blacks were inherently inferior and incapable of self-government.

One year after assuming the presidency, Arthur Barclay, in a letter to Harry Johnston, reminded him of a popular cultural adage: "An African proverb put into the Sierra Leone patois, says, 'Poor man cant vex.'" To Barclay, "Liberia represents the poor man among the nations. She must not get veced [*sic*]. Patience and perseverance must be the watch-word of her policy, internal as well as external."[75] Barclay was keenly aware of Liberia's place among modern nations, but he also knew how important the globalized world had become to Liberia's survival. Perhaps drawing from his Barbadian migratory experiences, Barclay told the Liberian Legislature: "We need external help to develop Liberia."[76] Barclay's remarks embodied the turn-of-the-century tensions surrounding the internal native question, development, modernity, and the country's desire for the acceptance by developed nations. In 1904, Liberia's national debt stood at $800,000, including the $480,000 adjusted 1871 loan principal plus interest. In desperation, Barclay's government contracted a half-million-dollar loan arrangement with the knighted British Proconsul, Harry Johnston, and his Liberian Development Company. To further remedy these problems, Barclay sought the repeal of the Port of Entry Act and made efforts to usher in policies that would bring in more

---

[73] Ibid.

[74] Laura Elizabeth West, "'The Negro Experiment': Black Modernity and Liberia, 1883–1910." Master's thesis, April 25, 2012. (Virginia: Virginia Polytechnic University, 2012), 1.

[75] Arthur Barclay, Letter to Sir Harry H. Johnson, August 26, 1905. Box 3, Liberian Government Archives I, Holsoe Collection.

[76] Dunn, *The Annual Messages of the Presidents of Liberia*, 450.

trade and tax revenue to the government.[77] The repeal of this act may have also been done to consolidate the TWP and as a show of force to the Republican Party. Nonetheless, with its repeal, Barclay's era became known as the era of the "Open Door Policy" in Liberia.[78] Barclay searched for other options to address the growing economic issues and debt. He explored complicated currency regulations, swapping procurement orders for custom revenues. In previous administrations, this had only enriched the foreign merchants and devalued the paper currency, but now under Barclay's control it managed to earn the republic some much needed revenue.

The racialized nature of power structures and dynamics operating to dominate the globalized community worked to restrict Liberians and the nation-state in many ways. This was the crux of Liberians' dilemma. They sought to use the success of the nation to prove that blacks were not contrary to the ideas of civilization, modernity, and progress that seemingly were the preserve of white nations. Barclay desired for Liberians to transcend both the structures of the nation-state and the constraints of ethnicity and particularity.[79] As much as the larger global sphere determined Liberia's place as a nation, it also shaped the factors of racial progress. In addition to shaping how Liberia would be accepted in the larger family of nations, European hegemony also continued to frame transnational racial identities at the turn of the century.

BARCLAY AND THE INDIGENOUS

In Liberia, outside of their crushing and oppressive racial subjectivity, earlier migrants found themselves behaving like colonizers, using their ties and their subjectivity when it suited them. By lugging around their traumas and prejudices, migrants created a universe of advantages but also problems. By their actions, the indigenous had been perceived by Americo-Liberian leadership as sabotaging blacks' post-emancipation progress. Portraying the indigenes in this way reduced their humanity and justified their conquest and colonization. By the turn of the twentieth century, the same beliefs were reassigned and reinterpreted to highlight the indigenous as stymieing

---

[77] Kraaij, *The Open Door Policy*, 150–190.

[78] United States Department of State, Papers Relating to the Foreign Relations of the United States with the Annual Message of the President of the Transmitted to Congress, December 6, 1910. Accessed at the Department of State on March 3, 2017. https://history .state.gov/historicaldocuments/frus1910.

[79] Gilroy, *The Black Atlantic*, 8.

Liberia's modernity and progress. Furthermore, by colluding with the Europeans to the detriment of the Liberian central government and the black race, the ambiguous status and relationship between the indigenes and the central government had proven financially and politically ruinous in a number of ways. For example, in 1879, a German trading ship was attacked by coastal tribes. The German Navy responded by bombarding the Liberian coastline where Americo-Liberians were attempting to carry out governmental business. In the end, the Liberian government was forced to pay indemnities for the stolen, damaged, and lost goods, which amounted to over five thousand dollars.[80] Such actions confirmed in the eyes of many that the indigenous were still acting contrary to the country's interests. They were dangerous to national stability. Edward Blyden alluded to this with a cautionary note: "Let Liberia now consider whether she elects to continue to move with the agencies of civilization or to retire to the bush. If she elects the advantages of civilization, she must accept its responsibilities. ... The world around us, as I have said, is moving, and we must move with it."[81] In addition to causing financial woes, the natives became a source of Liberia's internal unrest. The economic hardships had crippled the government's ability to maintain control over troubled portions of its territory, mainly the southeastern coastal region where the indigenes had rebelled following earlier governmental legislations.

In order to demonstrate a sense of civilization, modernity, and progress, Liberia would have to repair its relationship with the indigenes. With the advent of Barclay's presidency, several significant symbols of citizenship, civil rights, justice, and freedom were employed in speeches or cited in public documents to reflect a change in the government's attitude toward the indigenous population. Unlike his efforts to address the country's economic woes and growing indebtedness, more direct ways were sought by Barclay to tackle its domestic troubles. In 1904, the election of Arthur Barclay ushered in a new era of ethnic relations as he sought to incorporate the natives into the nation-state. In his inaugural address to the senate and the House of Representatives in January of 1904, Barclay noted that a number of questions had "agitated and vexed the minds of thinking citizens." He acknowledged that prior administrations led by Americo-Liberians had focused on the best way to assure "material

---

[80] Kraaij, *The Open Door Policy,* 27.
[81] "A Diplomatic Function at the American Legation," 7. April 13, 1905. *Dispatches from United States Ministers to Liberia, 1863–1906,* Volume 14, Roll T-14. The National Archives, Washington, DC.

prosperity." He, however, planned to turn his attention to bringing the natives more fully into the national fold. As Barclay noted, the development of Liberia could not be divorced from native incorporation. "We cannot develop the interior effectively," he concluded, "until a satisfactory understanding with the resident population is arrived at."[82] Barclay further set a different governmental tone toward the natives for his administration: "We often neglected to make good on our promises, but the native citizen has a very retentive memory and knows exactly what he wants."[83]

As a driving force in the emergence of the TWP, Barclay's presidency represented a maturation of the party ideology about who should be included in the Liberian nation. Barclay apportioned further blame to his predecessors for their failure in this regard. Barclay noted: "The efforts which we have made in the past, made to coerce these populations by arms, have deservedly failed. Government must rest on the consent of the governed."[84] The founders miscalculated in thought:

We sought to obtain, and did not succeed in grasping an enormous mass of territory by neglecting to conciliate and attach the resident populations to our interests. Our present narrow and jealous trade policy initiated in the [18]60's has had the worst possible effects on our political relations with outlying native populations. Take for instance the Manna and Gallinas territories, formerly part of Liberia. Why did we lose these?[85]

Answering his own questions, he reasoned: "Because we neglected to look after and conciliate the populations. We thought their wishes and desires unworthy of serious consideration, and after enduring the situation for many years, they detached themselves from the interest of Liberia, and carried their territories with them." Barclay pointed to other territories, particularly those below the Cavalla, that the nation had also lost because of the treatment of the natives. The country, he insisted, had not learned the lessons of that "great national loss" and has continued to follow the same "mistaken lines." Barclay reminded the legislature that "our attitude of indifference toward the native populations must be dropped." In its place, he advocated "[a] fixed and unwavering policy with respect to the

---

[82] Ibid.
[83] Dunn, *The Annual Messages of the Presidents of Liberia 1848–2010*, 431.
[84] Arthur Barclay, Inaugural address of Arthur Barclay, President of the Republic of Liberia; Delivered January 4, 1904, before the Senate and House of Representatives (Monrovia: Monrovia R.A Phillips, Chief Printer, Government Printing Office, 1904), 29.
[85] Ibid.

natives, proceeding on the lines of interest in local affairs, protection, civilization, and safeguarding their institutions when not brutal or harmful should at once be set on foot."[86]

Barclay expressed his awareness of the duplicity of the Americans and Europeans through his critique of Liberia's issues of debt, colonialism, and imperialism. After all, he noted, Liberia was bought "from its native inhabitants by the Europeans." The colony, in effect, was:

founded by the European. Its expenses paid by the money of the European until it declared its independence. They lavished their money on the establishment of schools, churches and other agencies for the elevation of successive bodies of Negro colonists. It was a European, too, who made possible the annexation of the State of Maryland in Liberia to the Republic.[87]

In doing so, "by organic law we shut him [the indigene] out from citizenship and denied him the right of holding real estate in fee simple." Having "stood shoulder to shoulder with us in the organization and building up of this state," the Europeans naturally expected their reward. Upon independence, Liberians excluded whites from ownership of property in Liberia. But while they were shut out from "privilege and property," Europeans were compensated with what Barclay called "commercial freedom." To Barclay, with this coming to an end in 1862, "our policy of commercial freedom to the European lasted but fifteen short years."[88]

Barbadians' pan-Africanism and black nationalism, as exhibited through Barclay's approach to the indigenes, differed markedly from the previous African American political approach. In the same 1904 speech to the legislature, Barclay made an unequivocal declaration for indigenous inclusion.

The Liberian nation is to be made up of the Negro civilized to some extent in the United States and repatriated, and of the aboriginal tribes. At present it is composed of a small number of civilized and a large number of aboriginal communities in varying degrees of dependence. The problem is how to blend these into a national organism, an organic unity.[89]

This departure from Americo-Liberian modes of relating to the natives was rooted in and reflective of the West Indian-ness of Barclay and the other migrants who had sought similar ways to be included in the British

---

[86] Ibid.
[87] Dunn, The Annual Messages of the Presidents of Liberia 1848–2010, 480.
[88] Ibid.
[89] Ibid.

Empire. As with the post-emancipation aspirations of the Barbadian migrants to civilize and develop Liberia, what made the indigenous visible and subjects to be regenerated again were the pressures of imperialism and colonial expansion.

If race seemed muted in Barclay's approach, efforts to know the natives had become a more pronounced obsession. While there had been hostility and concerns about indigenous trading practices, the Liberian government and the Republican Party had oriented themselves towards the coast, facing outwards rather than inwards to the hinterlands to familiarize themselves with the natives. With Barclay, plans would be necessary to get to know the interior. There had been several efforts carried out by previous administrations. In the Second Session of the Twenty-Ninth Legislature, Barclay mourned the death of H. G. Moore, a statesman who had helped Liberia to tackle its advance into the hinterlands. Barclay said, "During your recess, death has deprived the State of an able, devoted and capable public servant, the Honorable H. J. Moore, Secretary of the Interior."[90] In 1892, Moore had been appointed Secretary of the Interior by President Cheeseman and subsequently directed that department for about twelve years.

As one of the 1865 Barbadian migrants, Moore seemed to reflect Afro-Barbadians' relationship to the natives and the tensions and debates over the place of the indigenous in the Liberian nation. While the early relationship between America-Liberians and natives had been defined by wars over land, Moore and other Barbadians like him in Crozierville had had a long social, economic, and political relationship with the native populations in the interior. His father, G. Moore, had been "a prominent merchant largely interested in the interior trade for many years before the foundation of the interior Department was recognized as the Agent of the Government of Liberia and among the tribes of the hinterland of Montserrado, among whom he was widely known."[91] Barclay recalled that Moore's "attitude toward the native population was sympathetic and his policy conciliatory. It is to be regretted that his ideas were not always popular, especially among the less thoughtful section of our civilized population." Still, Barclay declared, "Secretary Moore made a lasting contribution to the country's prosperity and progress when he succeeded

[90] Ibid.
[91] Arthur Barclay, "Message of the President of Liberia Communicated to the First Session of the Thirteenth. Legislature," December 14, 1905 in Dunn, *The Annual Messages of the Presidents of Liberia 1848–2010*, 430–497.

in eventually convincing the community that the policy he advocated and invariably followed was and is the correct one."[92]

In the late nineteenth century, Moore had indeed played a significant role in signifying the terms that undergirded the wave of new Afro-Barbadian leadership in Liberia by redefining the relationship between the Liberian state and indigenes. Barclay acknowledged that Moore's "tactful management maintained the peace of a great part of the province for many years, especially of the districts contiguous to the Americo-Liberian townships." This was Moore's achievement. As Barclay pointed out, it was through neglect of his advice that "the country between the little Cape Mount and the St. Paul's Rivers has been for over twenty years in a disturbed condition." Barclay contended that Moore had "received from his father much useful information and sound advice as to the manner in which the native population ought to be controlled and governed."[93] To address the challenges with the indigenous, Barclay now attempted to navigate this historic relationship between the settlers and the indigenous as well as consider the necessities of development.

Barclay knew that the new century called for different approaches to modernization, ones in which the natives would play a significant role. In addition to familiarizing himself with the natives, Barclay sought to create policies toward internal development and native incorporation. Naturally, the ever-changing economic and political landscape dictated Barclay's formulations. His style of native incorporation depended on a perception of the indigenous that was decidedly different from that of early Americo-Liberian leaders. "What we need," Barclay said in his inaugural address of 1904, "is wider and deeper culture, and more intimate intercourse with our interior brethren."[94] Like Blyden, Barclay shared a deep respect for and understanding of indigenous cultures. It was widely noted that he possessed encyclopedic knowledge of local ethnography and anthropology. For this reason alone he had been asked to participate in the Liberian Exhibition at the Chicago World's Fair. Now as president, Barclay sought to use this knowledge to incorporate the natives through their political and legal administration.

The president urged the Republic to set to work to repair the cause of the domestic problems. The strengthening of the central government was

---

[92] Messages of the President of Liberia, Monrovia, 1904. Liberia Collection. University of Indiana, Bloomington.
[93] Ibid.
[94] Ibid.

aimed at extending its authority into the hinterland. Barclay proposed the most extensive policy for assimilation, arguing that once the people of the hinterlands had been caught up in modernization and the resulting prosperity, they would attach themselves to the central government. This would transform Liberia from being merely a thought with the possibility of being a potential into an actual nation-state. In Liberia, imperial efforts were strategically aligned with the efforts of the state. By taking on the racially marginalized members, Barclay remapped civilization and redrew lines of race within the black nationality.

Discourses of native incorporation did more than define the bourgeoisie maneuvers of a new imperialism. While new spaces of imperialism were redrawn and secured in the agreement between imperialism and race, Barclay's legislative practices for Liberia were indeed new and dynamic. However, they were ideologies drawn from and erected upon European, not African, epistemological foundations. Barclay's style of native assimilation closely resembled the British colonial policy of "indirect rule," an approach later popularized by the British colonial official Frederick Lugard in his work *Dual Mandate in Tropical Africa* (1922).[95] As a first course of action, the president invited the chiefs to his 1904 inauguration and called the first council of chiefs that same year. Barclay used the findings of Benjamin J. K. Anderson's 1888 explorations to organize the interior for administrative purposes and applied the term Liberian to the unassimilated population for the first time. His aim was to extend the central government and absorb the hinterlands by working through native leaders and using their existing social structures. Barclay consulted regularly with the chiefs of the interior and involved himself in the appointments of paramount chiefs, who were responsible for administering the affairs of a local polity, and clan chiefs, their subordinates.

Barclay proposed that native districts be considered and treated as townships under the government of the native authorities. Under a proposal that very much resembled a plural government, the power to subdivide local authorities was to be the preserve of the president. The native chiefs were to be treated as the local authority.[96] He closed the Second Session of the Twenty-Ninth Legislature noting, "I hope the Legislature will not adjourn before passing a bill to regulate the government of the native communities of the country. This matter cannot be any

---

[95] See Frederick John Dealtry Lugard, *The Dual Mandate in British Tropical Africa* (London: F. Cass, 1922).
[96] Ibid.

longer delayed. A national policy in this regard ought to be initiated."
In putting forward his definition and method for incorporating the natives,
Barclay noted, "The territory should be controlled through the leading
native families. We ought to make it a point to recognize and support
them and get them to work with us." With the establishment of this new
approach to the natives – a form of internal colonialism – Liberians came to
mirror colonial policies adopted by the French in Guinea and Cote d' Ivoire
and the British in Sierra Leone and elsewhere in Africa.

It was perhaps these developments in the neighboring European colonies that prompted Barclay to adopt this new approach. As he noted, "the
Americo Liberians are possibly the greatest travelers of all civilized people
of West Africa. It is a pity, however, that they pay little attention to the
contiguous colonies and protectorates." If they did, Barclay argued, they
would "probably have formed a correct idea of the great improvements
and enormous developments which have taken place around them and
would not be inclined to criticize but rather applaud and assist the efforts
of their own government to keep pace, however lamely with the times."[97]
Barclay was very specific about his plans for native absorption. He
recommended that tribal territory would be assimilated into the townships; inhabitants would have a right to land in a definite area. They were
to be guaranteed limited self-government and "customary native law"
would be recognized both "locally and by courts of the Republic." This
approach, he predicted, would do much to correct the usurpation of
native politics by an encroaching Western-style government. Under these
measures, local authorities seemed to be guaranteed autonomy. But the
promise of full self-sufficiency was illusory. Barclay ordered the "supervision of native population by commissioners living among them."[98]

In 1905, the legislature approved President Barclay's program of active
participation for members of the indigenous population. Chiefs and headmen were commissioned for the first time as officials of the government.
The historical and political methods of rendering what had long been
considered native difference into "normative, national subjecthood in
Liberia" took on multiple dynamics.[99] A bundle of new constitutional
and legislative modifications beckoned in the colonial government's incli-
nation to strengthen the authority of the chiefs. The constitution increased

---

[97] Barclay cited in Swartz and Dumett, *West African Culture Dynamics*, 565.
[98] Dunn, *The Annual Messages of the Presidents of Liberia 1848–2010*, 531.
[99] Nikhil Pal Singh, *Black is a Country: Race and the Unfinished Struggle for Democracy*
(Cambridge, MA.: Harvard University Press, 2004), 13.

the number of seats held by the chiefs on the extended colonial governmental assembly from three to six while the amount of the local intelli-
gentsia remained at three. The chiefs who were to work through the new
council were to be elected by the recently fashioned local councils of
chiefs, a structure for collaboration, negotiation, and policymaking that
advantaged the opinions of the customary figures of authority.
The creation of local councils of chiefs outlined an effort to give a colony-
wide organization and operation to the chieftaincy. The Native
Administration Ordinance that later emerged and that they strongly
supported further increased the influence of high-ranking chiefs.[100]

Barclay made further recommendations for his policy of native incorporation. Following earlier policies, he proposed "the creation of two new courts:
the courts of the native chief, and that of the District Commissioner."[101]
In native communities, the former would take the place of the "Justice of the
Peace in the townships inhabited by the civilized population." The District
Commissioners would hear "appeals from the court of the native chief" and
"settle disputes between members of different sections of the same tribe, or
persons of different tribes" within their jurisdiction. Handling money was an
entirely different matter; it fell outside the realm of native leadership. In this
regard, "jails, fees and costs" were subjects that were to be regulated through
the Attorney-General. Appeals of District Commissioners' decisions were to
be heard in the "Court of Quarter Sessions of each County, which courts
should also deal with crimes of a serious character."[102]

Barclay's policies, though conciliatory towards the indigenes, was not
without an agenda. Among Barclay's primary interests in native assimilation were efforts to find the best ways to "develop and utilize the resources
of the hinterland" and how best to "satisfy, control, and attach the native
populations to the interests of the state." Whig elitist and capitalistic state
plans for commerce and industry rested on the resource and labor exploitation of the indigenous.[103] About six years after Barclay had begun reorga-
nizing the native's governmental structure, in an effort to raise more
revenue, Barclay imposed a one-dollar hut tax on the indigenous population. By 1910, he commenced collecting the hut tax. Barclay imposed the
tax to draw the natives under the purview of the state as well as to raise

---

[100] Blamo, "The Use of Symbolism in National Integration," 6.
[101] Dunn, *The Annual Messages of the Presidents of Liberia 1848–2010*, 531.
[102] Ibid.
[103] Wilson Jeremiah Moses, *Creative Conflict in African American Thought* (Cambridge: Cambridge University Press, 2004), 90.

revenue for his cash-strapped government. The British had imposed a similar hut tax on tribal areas in Sierra Leone, the Gold Coast, and Gambia to finance their imperial administration. Like the hut taxes introduced by the British in other parts of Africa and in the post-emancipation West Indies, this tax effectively forced Africans into a system of wage labor. Levying such taxes forced the indigenes into a cash economy that was linked to the centralized state. Though Barclay set the rate at one dollar per hut, the actual amount differed according to the collector. The chiefs of the villages who actually assessed and collected the taxes became a new set of elite dependent on the Liberian state.[104] As the primary source of revenue, this put great stress on the indigenous population. Similar to the caustic outcomes that had accompanied Americo-Liberian polices, Barclay's hut tax eventually re-ignited the Grebo-Kru uprising, which had begun earlier in the 1870s when they had declared themselves a kingdom independent of the Liberian republic. Peace eventually returned to the Cape Palmas area after the USS *Birmingham* forced an end to hostilities and assisted the government in reaching a negotiated settlement with the Grebo leadership.[105] Nonetheless, this unrest provided more evidence of the multi-tiered nature of tensions with natives that Liberian leaders were forced to navigate.

In an effort to strengthen the central government, Barclay also gave the executive branch additional power. But even in this effort, Barclay unwittingly subordinated the leadership of the native groups to that of the settlers. His proposed bill gave "the Executive the power of issuing such regulations as it may be requested or advised by the native chiefs, which regulations would of course, have the force of law until expressly disallowed by the Legislature." He, however, added the caveat that "it should also be made a misdemeanor for any chief or other person to refuse to obey the summons of the President, Secretary of the Interior or the Superintendent of the County or District when it becomes necessary to investigate matters and things tending to disturb the peace of the country."[106] Indirect rule effectively made the local chiefs of the various ethnicities junior partners in the new order by creating an effective alliance between state bureaucrats in Monrovia and local rural elites;

[104] Augustine Konneh, "The Hut Tax in Liberia: The High Cost of Integration," *Journal of the Georgia Association of Historians*, Vol. 16 (1996): 41–42.

[105] See Jeremy I. Levitt, *The Evolution of Deadly Conflict in Liberia: From "Paternaltarianism" to State Collapse* (Durham, NC: Carolina Academic Press, 2005), 63.

[106] Ibid.

and, as a consequence, this served his political objectives. Given his interactions and policies, the natives came to represent a significant portion of Barclay's political base. This consolidation also served the whims of the TWP and led to their hegemony over Liberia's politics until the party's collapse in 1980. One Gola elder paid tribute to Barclay's internal diplomacy by applying a well-known indigenous adage: "The great king asks of you what he has already taken from you. President Barclay showed us respect by letting us decide to do what he knew we must do."[107]

If the Barbadian migrants were not colonialists before they began to take on political positions in the Liberian government, the policies adopted by Barclay in the twentieth century made Liberians accomplices in the broader European imperial colonial system. Migration to Liberia, particularly by the Barbadians, was driven by the desire to build up a black nation that would bring respectability to the black race. Through Liberia, blacks worldwide were to unite and fight against their enemies in the West. This loyalty to the black race ended with Liberian efforts to incorporate African ethnic groups into the nation-state in ways that mimicked white imperialism.

Yet, Liberia's expansion in this period was driven by motives that were different from those of the European powers. They replaced previous ideas that African ethnic groups were not passive victims of the transatlantic slave trade and European imperialism but collaborators who were deserving of Liberian conquest and civilization. What drove new initiatives of black solidarity that appeared to be Liberian imperialism were efforts to create a bulwark against European aggression to maintain the sovereignty of the country and the respectability of the black race. In continuing its earlier missions, Liberia was forced to control the natives before they could begin to defend themselves against oppressive forms of white racism that accompanied European imperialistic designs in Africa. In the end, it became clear that blacks were not necessarily opposed to the imperialism and inequities of the emerging capitalistic geopolitical system. They sought to be recognized by it, and enter it by harnessing the power and shield of the nation-state to survive.

[107] Warren L. d'Adzevedo, "Tribal Reaction to Nationalism." *Liberian Studies Journal* (1969), Vol. III, No. 1 (1971): 11.

BARCLAY, LIBERIA, AND THE LEAGUE OF NATIONS

Barclay served as president until January 1912. After his retirement, he acted as Secretary of State, Secretary of the Treasury, and Secretary of the Interior and War. But his most important and most challenging assignment came at the age of eighty. Barclay was then in semi-retirement, serving on the legal staff of the Firestone Company of Liberia. In 1929, he was nominated to the administration of President C.D.B. King to be the country's representative to the League of Nations commission of inquiry into the existence of slavery and forced labor in the Republic.[108] Fisk University president Charles S. Johnson was the US representative in the investigation of Liberia by the United Nations for sending laborers into slavery in St. Helena. In his book, *Bitter Canaan: Story of the Negro Republic, 1893–1956*, Johnson highlighted how Barclay handled the international scrutiny and charges. Fascinated by "old man Barclay," Johnson wrote: "As the sole ex-public official whose record inspired international confidence, he was expected to examine impartially those charges against the Republic which he well knew were in very large measure true; he was expected through some miracle of his wisdom to defend the integrity of the state before the world."[109] The chief US diplomat in Monrovia, Clifton Wharton, described the ex-president in a memo to his State Department superiors: "The confidential advisor of the present administration and in times of stress, the government invariably calls upon him ... at present he is practicing law in Monrovia, Dean of the Liberian Bar, best known lawyer in the Republic, is attorney for the Firestone Plantations Company–great experience on commissions."[110]

Due to his age, Barclay was not able to accompany the other members of the commission on their investigatory trips into the interior, but he participated in hearings held in or close to the Liberian capital.[111] Cuthbert Christy, England's representative on the commission, was also

---

[108] League of Nations. International Enquiry into the Alleged Existence of Slavery and Forced Labour in Liberia, 1930, accessed at Hathi Trust Digital Library. https://babel .hathitrust.org.

[109] See Charles Spurgeon Johnson, *Bitter Canaan: The Story of the Negro Republic* (New Brunswick, NJ: Transaction Books, 1987), 87.

[110] Nathaniel R. Richardson, *Liberia's Past and Present* (London: Diplomatic Press, 1959), 5.

[111] International Commission of Inquiry into the Existence of Slavery and Forced Labor in the Republic of Liberia, and Cuthbert Christy. *Communication by the Government of Liberia Dated December 15th, 1930, Transmitting the Commission's Report.* 1930, accessed at Hathi Trust Digital Library. https://babel.hathitrust.org.

fascinated by Barclay's role, which, he noted, was initially one of a defense counsel who questioned the commission's procedure: "His first attitude was one of cheerful non-cooperation on the matter of seating the first witness. His argument on the first day of discussion of testimony was, 'There is nothing before the Commission.'" Christy was convinced that Barclay was "disposed to defend the name of President King and to construe any unfavorable reference to the administration as disloyal, he raised objections to the definition of forced labor, maintaining that there would be no force so long as there was consent of the laborer, however, secured."[112]

In their various diplomatic communications with Britain and the United States, both Christy and Johnson pointed out that it was evident that Barclay knew the history and details of much that was discussed, but he offered no explanations except in defense.[113] They noted that he later changed his stance: "As the proceedings developed and he sensed the fervor and the persistence of the charges, he dropped his defense; still later he showed surprise at the consistency of the revelations made; and finally he shook his hoary head in disgust." Cuthbert was convinced that the proceedings had helped Barclay come to grips with the state of the legal and political systems in Liberia:

On one of his final objections that the chiefs and their people were bringing to the Commission matters which should have been carried to the appropriate departments of government, he was asked to assist a complaining citizen privately to get action on his grievance. Although it was a relatively small matter, Barclay discovered that it took four days merely to get a hearing for the man. He saw the man was intimidated and the case handled between departments with no ultimate effective action taken.

Barclay came to recognize that "what he with all his power and prestige could not do for a common citizen, it was clear to him that a common citizen could not do for himself." Following from this episode, Cuthbert surmised that "the stern logic of the situation eventually overcame his emotional loyalties. With the air of an attorney who has exhausted every reasonable defense, he signed the full report of the Commission without offering amendments." According to Cuthbert, "Barclay faced the new future of Liberia with characteristic courage."[114]

[112] Ibid.
[113] Ibid.
[114] Ibid.

Arthur Barclay died on July 10, 1938, in Monrovia. In his obituary, Charles S. Johnson wrote:

The Old Man, as he is affectionately called, belied his eighty years with his brisk step, firm bearing, active erudition and incredibly incisive wit . . . He probably had read every book that came into Liberia and had a retentive and continuous memory. The laws of Liberia, its international problems, the native question, he knew in detail, and discoursed with familiar knowledge on the activities of the various African societies, archaeology, legal procedure in England and America, aviation, President Hoover's government by commissions etc.[115]

Barclay's body laid in state at the Trinity Memorial Church until the morning of July 13, the day of the burial. Many believed Barclay left an important legacy, including the creation of the modern state machinery, a number of reforms, and a thorough overhaul of the country's bureaucracy to raise what was once a nineteenth-century colony to the standards of effective twentieth-century governance. Reports pointed out that "thousands of persons in all walks of life signed the register and passed paying respects. A military escort comprising the first, fifth and sixth regiments and a detachment from the frontier force under the command of General James Boyer McGill was in attendance." Barclay was remembered as a "Friend of the People," and "Liberia's Grand old man."[116] The funeral oration was delivered by the honorable Dr. G. W. Gibson, who took as his text 2nd Samuel 3:38: "Know ye not that there is a Prince and a Great man fallen in Israel?" Gibson also composed a poem for the occasion.

> He died at his post of duty,
> And the Nation's heart is wrung.
> No death of greater beauty
> By poet has ever been sung,
> In silence deep, he shares the sleep
> That falls on young and old
>
> What are thy thoughts, O nation?
> As he lies calmly dead;
> Who filled thy highest station,
> Thy oft elected head;
> Does despair and grief thy bosom fill?
> Or sadness reign instead

[115] *Liberia Official Gazette*, July 11, 1938.
[116] Ibid.

Out of our grief and sadness,
Out of our anguish and pain
Out of our hearts' deep sorrow
The message of God is plain
That this nation rise through sacrifice
And turn her loss to gain.

Epilogue

British West Indians in Liberia from Edward Blyden to Marcus Garvey

Liberia had been regarded as the black man's republic since its inception. Though black nationalists explored other options at different times, they largely looked to Liberia to nurture nation-building aspirations. Thus, from the mid-nineteenth to the early twentieth century, black West Indian migrants articulated and channeled their popular collective racial consciousness into Liberian nation building, congealing racial and national goals into the ultimate black nationalist endeavor. As a consequence, in its unfolding as a place that united race and nation building, Liberia played a variety of roles in the temporal issues within black nationalism and pan-Africanism. Having evolved through a series of events that consistently placed their black nationalist emphasis into crisis, West Indian migrants to Liberia, from Edward Blyden to Marcus Garvey, provide an avenue for reframing our understanding of the conflicts within ideas of diaspora, blackness, and black racial advancement.

West Indian transatlantic post-emancipation and nation building in Liberia provides a unique epistemological standpoint from which to examine the provocative relationships between freedom, nation building, and citizenship across different segments of the diaspora and Africa as well as how these developments affected conceptions of blackness. Barbadian migration to Liberia outlines some of the broad foundations for conceptions of diaspora, black identity, and pan-Africanism. J. T. Wiles, Arthur Barclay, and the other Barbadian migrants to Liberia signified an underlying shift in the definition and experiences of freedom after emancipation. Together with them in Liberia were African Americans, some free at their own will, others deported, a few voluntary migrants, and slaves freed with the expressed demand that they be sent to

Liberia. Some of the West Indian migrants who were recaptive Africans from the Liberian coast completed that circular migration that many conceive as quintessential to the diaspora by returning to the area from which they had been taken. In these instances, the middle passage and the experience of diaspora became central to new identities. For many recaptive Africans and ethnic indigenes who had not crossed the ocean, they would not be included with African Americans and West Indians in the efforts to project a civilized Liberian nation.

A comparative approach to Liberia's nation building offers a way of understanding Barbadians' and other blacks' experiences of post-emancipation. Over the course of centuries, blacks left various localities for an uncertain existence in what became Liberia. The Liberian nation-building project embodied a new frontier between slavery and freedom for black migrants as they attempted to live out their ideas of freedom, citizenship, and nationhood. Much of their collective consciousness as blacks had long been articulated through a common history of enslavement, freedom, disenfranchisement, and the struggle for equality. Many assumed that from these experiences a collective vision of nationhood would be shaped by the homogenizing process of Liberia's black cosmopolitan society. However, the very act of migration and political developments within the state would put various facets of the migrants' lives in crisis.[1] While common oppression had broken down artificial boundaries within the country and had allowed blacks to come together by race, the need to project a modern black nation exposed the artificiality of those prior connections. The assumptions of black homogeneity quickly evaporated as new issues of identity formed along the intersections of ethnicity, class, and religion.

The motivations that drove Barbadians and other migrants to emigrate were contingent on the pursuit of freedom, social mobility, and the building of a pan-African republic based on the assumption of the homogeneity of the black race. Barbadians advocated a brand of pan-Africanism that was possibly more strategic than genuine, driven more by their socio-historical reality than deep personal convictions. The Barbadian imagination and that of other blacks about building a black republic was driven by the need to bring blacks together under a racial identity so as to break through systems of subjugation. The duplicity of imagination and its transition into praxis revealed the differences between pan-Africanism as an intellectual objective

---

[1] Jaina C. Sanga, *Salman Rushdie's Postcolonial Metaphors: Migration, Translation, Hybridity, Blasphemy, and Globalization* (Westport, CT: Greenwood Press, 2001), 8.

and as a lived experience. The nation-building efforts signaled the limits of pan-Africanism. In many ways, pan-Africanism proved its inability to transcend Africa as a point of reference in the diasporic imaginary. The traditional spatial framework based on Africa as the center and the diaspora as the periphery was outmoded as the Liberian nation-building process brought about new ideas for expressing African-ness.

The very concept of pan-Africanism was transformed, not just culturally, but also practically. Conceived first in the west of the Atlantic as a monolith, the idea of diaspora was re-conceptualized in Africa. For blacks in the diaspora, pan-Africanism discourse implied a commitment to inclusiveness and equality, one in which all blacks were citizens. In the post-independence era, however, experiences previously ideologically determined would take political shape as the lives of migrants became bound up with the struggle to sustain the state. This process would erect boundaries around citizenship. That blacks through migration and Liberia's independence were thought to be free of white racist elements did not mean the absence of competing interests, othering, and difference making. The struggle for rights and equality among the various diasporic ethnicities and their African counterparts would be played out in the political, religious, economic, and social spheres in ways that would destabilize the foundations on which black and African identities were created. This, too, exposed pan-Africanism's underlying paradox.

Blackness in various instances appeared as related in every way, yet proved itself mutable over time and space. So too did ideas that appeared to be etched in the flesh and deeply touted at one time or place that ultimately changed with new circumstances and the arc of time. Many migrants imagined that their journey to a black republic would easily open up access to experiences of freedom, citizenship, and nationhood. However, for many groups of blacks, the migrant road to full citizenship in Liberia would be marked by rough patches and detours and, in some important respects, remained an incomplete journey. Only certain elements of black diasporic identity were privileged in European discourses and configurations in the republic, solidifying hegemonic expectations of racial normativity. Over time, the language of civilization began to assume a prescriptive dimension, a code of sorts, a way of excluding some blacks from the nation-building project by holding them up to Western ideals of proper behavior, and the purist ethics that governed the ideas of the nation.

The shifts in the politics and boundaries of blackness that became evident through West Indian colonization in Liberia show the social construction and contingent dynamic of ethnicity and race. By paying attention to the shifting significations over time, we can consider the ways in which historical context, social demographics, and cultural politics inflect conceptions of race and ethnicity. The Barbadian migration, as an example of how ideas and identity circulated across the Atlantic world, proved race to be shifting, unstable, and a creation of historically, politically, and economically specific relations. With the identity politics that emerged in Liberia, especially in the period of the Scramble for Africa, it became evident that while blacks in diaspora had their African identities at the forefront, it was rather their diasporic identities that took pre-eminence in their lives in Liberia.

In Liberia, freedom, citizenship, and nationhood were imported colonial ideas and only circumscribed and disciplined within the parameters of the state. As imperialist ideology became liberatory for diasporic blacks, and as the evolution of rules for enforcing equality changed over time and space, black migration to Liberia in many ways illustrated the cyclical rebirth of caste in the Atlantic world. The problem of inequality that blacks faced remained an ideological problem that resided in the political structures and policies of blacks and whites alike. Finding equality, freedom, citizenship, and nationhood would not be achieved by the simple act of migrating to and creating a black-only society. Finding freedom and creating equality required serious ideological interventions regarding social and political ideas of community.

Though creating some semblance of cohesion, the nation-building process also produced many fault-lines that proved divisive, often leading to conflict. The extraordinary nature of Barbadians' and African Americans' achievements in Liberia suggests that they had left the old structures of oppression behind, but it did not necessarily mean the end of the caste system. In the relationship between saltwater and Creole ex-slaves, on the Liberian side of the Atlantic, caste had also taken on a different form. The cyclical rebirth of caste in the Atlantic world turned on the evolution of rules for enforcing status as they were challenged over time. What changed in pan-Africanism with the move away from a racist society had less to do with the contours of the ideology and more to do with the basic unequal structures of the new society the migrants founded and the language they used to justify it.

In Liberia, what was thought of as a diaspora consolidated under race became a complex patchwork of interacting and dynamic agents. In a space where race no longer factored largely, race was no longer used as a means of justification, discrimination, and social contempt.

Rather than relying on race, new measures were employed—color, history, class—to label people as second-class and then to engage in all the practices that were supposedly left behind. Competition for interests, polarization, vying for space, and conflict over resources quickly came to bear on emigrants. Dominance by the emigrant elites and other forms of authoritarianism distorted the sense of pan-African community that had motivated many of them to emigrate. In other cases, the values that were being fostered by the emigrants and by the other groups in Liberia failed to respond to the underlying needs of all the members of the society. Indeed, the omission of some groups from the nation-building process also meant their exclusion from the moral dialogue. In many cases, this resulted in not only antisocial behavior but the diminishing of the very ethical order on which pan-Africanism had established itself.

For blacks who had railed against white oppression before emigrating, the vindication offered in Liberia would not be sweet. While life in Liberia provided liberation for many, it simultaneously created subordination for others, an ironic replication of their former lives.[2] Founded as a home for "dispersed and oppressed children of Africa and to enlighten and regenerate this benighted continent," Liberia ignored its native Liberians and created divisions between West Indians and recaptives who also sought freedom in Liberia.[3] Notions of citizenship, color, and labor exacerbated intra-black differences and played a role in establishing hierarchy and creating societal division. At the center of Liberia's nationality was a long-standing tension between the politics of blackness and those of global white supremacy. People like Blyden had long held a deep suspicion of Liberia's split allegiances. Who was the nation projecting to and who was the nation projected for? Why were they projecting at all? And at whose expense? The human cost of placing politics before truth challenged the very goals Liberia sought to achieve. In questioning the humanity of African indigenes and liberated Africans, the immigrants were, in turn, questioning all black humanity. And as a result, they sacrificed their cause at the altar of white supremacy.

Seemingly, as it did every generation or so, the idea of Liberia as a black nationality gathered fresh plausibility and began, gradually, to make its way into the mainstream. In the 1920s, Marcus Garvey reiterated the republic's centrality to black nationalist ambitions when he made Liberia,

---

[2] Derek Phillips, *Looking Backward: A Critical Appraisal of Communitarian Thought* (Newark, NJ: Princeton University Press, 1993), 195.

[3] *The African Repository*, Vol. 49 (1873): 109.

yet again, the focal point of his projects. Garveyism emerged as the twentieth century iteration of black efforts toward self-actualization and self-sufficiency through efforts to repatriate to Africa and develop an economically prosperous black nation. At this juncture, however, in ways similar to and different from past generations who had experienced difficulties in creating a black nationalist agenda in relationship with Liberia, Garvey's racial aspirations and Liberia's national goals stood at an impasse. As Garvey channeled racial issues into a twentieth-century plan for Liberia, new factors contributed to its unmaking.[4]

Social segregation, citizenship rights, and labor, when taken together, provide telling glimpses of the identity crises faced by Liberia and black migrants as they navigated and negotiated issues of identity, the white gaze, and racial authority. The literal sea-change in the underlying function of labor, from the separation of race to the marker of modernity, allowed immigrant blacks to push themselves away from natives on the bottom of the social ladder as whites simultaneously began to pull them toward market solidarity. The subjugation of natives was neither timeless nor explained by slavery alone. Instead, it was an economic and political device that enabled the reconfiguration of a new hierarchy and provided the appearance of modernity pursued by Liberians.

The ultimate undoing of Garveyism in Liberia emerged from a white supremacist foundation that established a series of dynamics and default settings to ensure its continued influence and to neutralize threats to its dominance. At the outset, the republic's white supremacist foundation created an internalized belief in whiteness that inscribed itself into the future via black disunion and self-doubt. To be sure, Liberia's founding investment in whiteness, which created the historical rationale for white superiority, fostered a persistent belief in the necessity of white involvement in solutions to the republic's problems. Thus, when Garvey moved to implement his plans for Liberia, rival white interests called into question the economic strength and ability of black racial bonds to yield substantive returns that could competently address contemporary issues surrounding indebtedness and underdevelopment. With growing antagonism, direct sabotage along with nationalist concerns about sovereignty, diplomatic breakdown, and general mistrust created an atmosphere for the republic's rejection of Garveyism. Ultimately, white supremacy's counter-position to a black nationalism that presented itself as adversarial

---

[4] See "Nationalism and Not Racialism": Liberia in the Making and Un-Making of Garveyism, 76 King Street: Journal of Liberty Hall: The Legacy of Marcus Garvey; Vol III; July, 2017.

and problematic to its dominance meant that in securing white investors, Liberia, by necessity, had to divest nationalism from racialism.[5]

Since its incarnation into the modern era, the depths of white supremacy's impact through blacks' own internalization continues to persist in Liberia. Now it is other blacks, tribal leaders, and politicians who do all the oppressing; meanwhile, black people are conveniently returned to innocence. Liberian colonization of blacks cut black imperialism from the story, extending the presumption of the oppressed blacks well into decades of their existence in Liberia. Except that blacks are not always innocent. These days in Liberia imperialism continues. However, what has changed is the need, the doer, and the mechanism through which this is all accomplished.

[5] Ibid.

Bibliography

ARCHIVES AND MANUSCRIPT COLLECTIONS

Archives of the Episcopal Church, Austin, Texas
Barbados Library Service
Barbados Museum and Historical Society
Barbados National Archives
British National Archives. Kew Gardens
Drew University. Slavery Pamphlet Collection. 1857.
House of Commons Papers
Liberian Government Archives
Rare Books and Special Collections Division. Library of Congress, Washington, DC
Schomburg Center for the Study of Black Culture
Svend Holsoe Collection, Indiana University, Bloomington
University of Indiana, Bloomington. Liberia Collections
University of Liberia
University of the West Indies, Cave Hill Barbados

NEWSPAPERS AND PERIODICALS

African Affairs: Journal of the Royal African Society
The African Repository and Colonial Journal (before 1850)
The African Repository (after 1850)
Anti-Slavery Reporter
African Times
The Baltimore Sun
The Barbadian
The Barbados Advocate
The British and Foreign Anti-Slavery Reporter
The Christian Mirror

The Christian Recorder
The Colored American
The Crozierville Observer
Douglass' Monthly
Frederick Douglass Paper
Journal of the Barbados Museum and Historical Society
Journal of the House of Assembly
The Lagos Weekly Record
The Liberal
Liberia Official Gazette
The Liberian Recorder
The Methodist Herald
The National Era
New Era
The Niles Weekly Register
The North Star
The Observer
The Pennsylvania Freeman
The Provincial Freeman
The Springfield Republican
The Sunday Advocate
The Times

PUBLISHED PRIMARY SOURCES

Anderson, Benjamin J. K. *Narrative of Journey to Musardu. The Capital of the Western Mandingoes*. S. W. Green, Printer, 1870.

Archer, C. V. H. and Wilfred K. Fergusson. *Laws of Barbados*. Barbados: Advocate Co, 1944.

Ashmun, Jehudi, ed. *The African Intelligencer*, Vol. 1, no. 1, July 1820. Rare Books and Special Collections Division. Library of Congress, Washington, DC.

Bacon, Ephraim. *Abstract of a Journal Containing an Account of the First Negotiations for the Purchase of Lands for the American Colony*. Philadelphia, 1824.

Bacon, Ephraim. *Abstract of a Journal Kept by E. Bacon, Assistant Agent of the United States, to Africa: with an Appendix, Containing Extracts from the North American Review, on the Subject of Africa. Containing Cuts, Showing a Contrast between Two Native Towns*. Philadelphia, 1824.

Barclay, Arthur. *Inaugural address of Arthur Barclay, President of the Republic of Liberia; Delivered January 4th, 1904, before the Senate and House of Representatives*. Printed by Authority. Monrovia R.A Phillips, Chief Printer, Government Printing Office, Monrovia 1904.

Barclay, Gerald K. "Brief Life Sketch of the Late Malvina Barclay," In original papers of L.A. Grimes, University of Liberia Library, August 10th, 1973.

Bellman, Beryl Larry. *The Language of Secrecy: Symbols & Metaphors in Poro Ritual*. New Brunswick, NJ: Rutgers University Press, 1984.

Blyden, Edward W. *The Significance of Liberia, an Address Delivered in the Senate Chamber. Monrovia, Liberia, 20th May 1906.* Liverpool: John Richardson and Sons, 1906.

Blyden, Edward W. *Christianity, Islam and the Negro Race.* Edinburgh: Edinburgh University Press, 1967.

Büttikofer, Johann, Henk Dop, and Phillip T. Robinson. *Travel Sketches from Liberia: Johann Buttikofer's 19th Century Rainforest Explorations in West Africa.* Leiden: Brill, 2013.

Buxton, Thomas Fowell. *Private Letter on the Slave Trade to the Lord Viscount Melbourne and the Other Members of Her Majesty's Cabinet by Thomas Fowell Buxton.* London: John Parker and West Strand XXXVIII, 1838.

Buxton, Thomas Fowell. *The African Slave Trade and Its Remedy.* London: Dawsons, 1840.

Carrington, Sean, Henry Fraser, John Gilmore, and Addington Forde. *A-Z of Barbadian Heritage* [1990]. Oxford: MacMillan Caribbean, 2003.

Crowther, Samuel. *Journal of an Expedition up the Niger and the Tshada in 1854.* London, 1855.

Crummell, Alexander. *Africa and America: Addresses and Discourses.* New York: Negro University Press, 1969.

Cuffe, Paul and Rosalind Cobb Wiggins. *Captain Paul Cuffe's Logs and Letters, 1808–1817: A Black Quaker's "Voice from within the Veil."* Washington, DC: Howard University Press, 1996.

Delany, Martin Robison. *The Condition, Elevation, Emigration, and Destiny of the Colored People of the United States; And, Official Report of the Niger Valley Exploring Party.* New York, Arno Press, 1968.

Dispatches from United States Ministers to Liberia, 1863–1906, Volume 14, Roll T-14. The National Archives, Washington, DC.

Dunn, D. Elwood, *Liberia Presidential Papers.* Berlin: De Gruyter, 2011.

Dunn, Elwood D. ed. *The Annual Messages of the Presidents of Liberia 1848–2010: State of the Nation Addresses to the National Legislature: from Joseph Jenkins Roberts to Ellen Johnson Sirleaf.* Berlin: De Gruyter, 2011.

Further Reports from Her Majesty's Diplomatic and Consular Agents Abroad Respecting the Condition of the Industrial Classes and the Purchase Power of Money in Foreign Countries. London: Printed by Harrison & Sons, 1871.

Garrison, William Lloyd. *Thoughts on African Colonization.* New York: Arno Press, 1968.

Garrison, William Lloyd and Truman Nelson. *Documents of Upheaval; Selections from William Lloyd Garrison's the Liberator, 1831–1865.* New York: Hill and Wang, 1966.

Government House. *Laws of Barbados: Laws Statutes and Compilations.* London: William Clowes and Sons, 1875.

Handler, Jerome S., Frederick W. Lange, and Robert V. Riordan. *Plantation Slavery in Barbados: An Archaeological and Historical Investigation.* Cambridge, MA: Harvard University Press, 1978.

Handler, Jerome, Ronnie Hughes, and Ernest M. Wiltshire. *Freedmen of Barbados: Names and Notes for Genealogical and Family History Research.* Published for the Friends of the Barbados Archives. Charlottesville, VA: Virginia Foundation for the Humanities and Public Policy, 1999.

Hawes, B. *West India Colonies: Copies of the Laws, Ordinances and Rules Not Hitherto Printed, No in Force in Each of the West India Colonies, for the Regulation of Labour between Masters and Labourer, and Stating the Dates of Their Being Put in Force.* London: Colonial Office, 1848.

Heard, William H. *The Bright Side of African Life.* New York: Negro Universities Press, 1969.

Huberich, Charles Henry. *The Political and Legislative History of Liberia; A Documentary History of the Constitutions, Laws and Treaties of Liberia from the Earliest Settlements to the Establishment of the Republic, a Sketch of the Activities of the American Colonization Societies, a Commentary on the Constitution of the Republic and a Survey of the Political and Social Legislation from 1847 to 1944; with Appendices Containing the Laws of the Colony of Liberia, 1820–1839, and Acts of the Governor and Council, 1839–1847.* New York: Central Book Company, 1947.

Karnga, Abayomi. *The History of Liberia.* Liverpool: D. Lyle, 1926.

Kemble, Frances Anne. *Journal of a Residence on a Georgian Plantation, 1838–1839.* Ryan Memorial Library of the St. Charles Borromeo Seminary (May 24, 2004 [EBook #12422]).

Lloyd, William. *Letters from the West Indies.* London: Darton and Harvey, 1838.

Lugard, Frederick John Dealtry. *The Dual Mandate in British Tropical Africa.* London: F. Cass, 1922.

Lugenbell, James Washington. Sketches of Liberia: Comprising a Brief Account of the Geography, Climate, Productions, and Diseases of the Republic of Liberia. Washington, DC, 1850.

Marshall, Woodville, "List of Voters for Barbados 1873: A Comment." *Journal of the Barbados Museum and Historical Society,* Vol. 51: (2005): 187–241.

Moak, Nathaniel C. and John T. Cook, *Reports of Cases Decided by the English Courts [1870–1883]: With Notes and References to Kindred Cases and Authorities.* Albany, NY: W. Gould & Son, 1873.

Moses, Wilson Jeremiah, ed. *Destiny and Race Selected Writings, 1840–1898 by Alexander Crummell.* Amherst: University of Massachusetts Press, 1992.

Murdza, Peter J. *Immigrants to Liberia, 1865-1904.* Emigrants Database, Virginia Emigrants to Liberia. Liberian Studies Research Working Paper. No 4. Charlottesville: Virginia Center for Digital History, University of Virginia, 1975. "National Affairs," *The Literary Companion,* Monrovia, Liberia, July 31, 1938.

Parliamentary Papers, 1842 (479). XIII. Appendix VI. Report of Police Magistrates of St. Michael's Parish, June–December, 1841. Grey to Stanley, 18 April, 1842 No. 12, Enc. No. 1 in Select Committee on West India Colonies, 1842.

Pennsylvania Colonization Society. *Meeting Minutes from October 10, 1864 to March 13, 1877,* www.lincoln.edu/library/specialcollections/society/1864-1877.pdf.

Rowson, William. *Census Report of the Population of Barbados 1851–71.* Barbados: Barclay and Fraser Printers, 1872, in Barbados National Archive.

Sherman, Mary Antoinette Brown. "Barclay Women in Liberia: Two Generations: A Biographical Dictionary," *Liberian Studies Journal,* Vol. 30, No. 1 (2005): 28–38.

Shick, Tom W. *Roll of the Emigrants to the Colony of Liberia Sent by the American Colonization Society from 1820–1843* [computer file]. Madison, WI: Tom W. Shick [producer], 1973. Madison, WI: Data and Program Library Service [distributor], 1973 and 1996. 04 June 2011.

Simpson, William. *A Private Journal Kept During the Niger Expedition from May, 1841, Until June, 1842.* London, 1843.

Spurgeon, James Robert. *The Lost Word; or, The Search for Truth; Oration Delivered Before the Grand Lodge of the Most Ancient and Honorable Fraternity of Free Masons in the Republic of Liberia, Dec. 27, 1899, Monrovia.* Monrovia, Liberia: Press of the College of West Africa, 1900.

Starr, Frederick. *Liberia: Description, History, Problems.* Chicago, 1913.

Sturge, Joseph and Thomas Harvey. *The West Indies in 1837: Being the Journal of a Visit to Antigua, Montserrat, Dominica, St. Lucia, Barbadoes, and Jamaica; Undertaken for the Purpose of Ascertaining the Actual Condition of the Negro Population of Those Islands.* London: Hamilton Adams and Co., 1838.

The Firestone Liberian Rubber Scheme: Mr. Harvey S. Firestone, Jnr, in London. S.l.: S.N, 1926.

Thome, James A. and Joseph Kimball, *Emancipation in the West Indies: A Six Months' Tour in Antigua, Barbadoes, and Jamaica in the Year 1837.* [Original. New York: American Anti-Slavery Society, 1838]. New York: Cambridge University Press, 2010.

Thompson, Alvin. *Emancipation I: A Series of Lectures to Commemorate the 150th Anniversary of Emancipation.* Barbados: University of the West Indies, 1984.

Wildman, Captain L. "Minutes of Evidence taken Before the Select Committee on Africa Western Coast." House of Commons Papers, Volume 5, British Parliament. May 3, 1865.

Wiley, Bell I. ed. *Slaves No More: Letters from Liberia 1833–1869.* Lexington: University Press of Kentucky: 1980.

SECONDARY SOURCES

Adderley, Roseanne Marion. *"New Negroes from Africa": Slave Trade Abolition and Free African Settlement in the Nineteenth-Century Caribbean.* Bloomington: Indiana University Press, 2006.

Ajayi, J. F. Ade. *Christian Missions in Nigeria, 1841–1891: The Making of a New Élite.* Evanston, IL: Northwestern University Press, 1965.

Akamisoko, Duke. *Samuel Ajayi Crowther: His Missionary Work in the Lokoja Area.* Ibadan, Nigeria: Sefer, 2002.

Akpan, M. B. "Black Imperialism: Americo-Liberian Imperialism, 1841–1964." *Canadian Journal of African Studies,* Vol. 7, No. 2 (1973): 217–236.

Allsopp, Richard. *Dictionary of Caribbean English Usage*. New York: Oxford University Press, 1996.

Almaguer, Tomas. *Racial Fault Lines: The Historical Origins of White Supremacy in California*. Berkeley: University of California Press, 1994.

Anderson, Benedict. *Imagined Communities. Reflections on the Origin and Spread of Nationalism*. Ithaca, NY: Cornell University Press, 1972.

Appiah, Kwame Anthony. *Identity against Culture: Understandings of Multiculturalism*. Occasional Paper Series. Berkeley: University of California Press, 1994.

Araujo, Ana Lucia, Mariana P. Candido, and Paul E. Lovejoy, eds. *Crossing Memories: Slavery and African Diaspora*. Trenton, NJ: Africa World Press, 2011.

Archibald, A. *A History of Colonization on the Western Coast of Africa*. New York: Negro Universities Press, 1969.

Armah, Ayi Kwei. *The Beautyful Ones Are Not Yet Born*. Boston, MA: Houghton Mifflin, 1968.

Armitage, David and Michael J. Braddick, eds. *The British Atlantic World, 1500–1800*. Basingstoke: Palgrave Macmillan, 2002.

Bailey, Anne C. *African Voices of the Atlantic Slave Trade: Beyond the Silence and the Shame*. Boston, MA: Beacon Press, 2005.

Banton, Caree. "Who is Black in a Black Republic." In *Race and Nation in the Age of Emancipations*, edited by Whitney Nell Stewart and John Garrison Marks, 121–142. Athens: University of Georgia Press, 2018.

Barnes, Diane. *Artisan Workers in the Upper South: Petersburg, Virginia, 1820–1865*. Baton Rouge: Louisiana State University Press, 2008.

Barnes, Kenneth C. *Journey of Hope: The Back-to-Africa Movement in Arkansas in the Late 1800s*. Chapel Hill: University of North Carolina Press, 2004.

Barrow, Alfred Henry. *Fifty Years in Western Africa: Being a Record of the Work of the West Indian Church on the Banks of the Rio Pongo*. London: Society for Promoting Christian Knowledge, 1900.

Beckles, Hilary. *Great House Rules: Landless Emancipation and Workers' Protest in Barbados, 1838–1938*. Kingston, Jamaica, Ian Randle, 2004.

Beckles, Hilary and Verene Shepherd, eds. *Caribbean Freedom: Economy and Society from Emancipation to the Present: A Student Reader*. Princeton, NJ: Wiener, 1996.

Bell, Howard. "Negro Nationalism; A Factor in Emigration Projects, 1858–1861." *Journal of Negro History*, Vol. 47 (January 1962): 42–53.

Bennett, Herman L. "The Subject in the Plot: National Boundaries and the History of the Black Atlantic." *African Studies Review*, Vol. 43, No. 1 (2000): 101–124.

Berlin, Ira. *The Making of African America: The Four Migrations*. New York: Viking, 2010.

Berthoff, Rowland. *British Immigrants in Industrial America, 1790–1950*. Cambridge, MA: Harvard University Press, 1953.

Bettis, Lee Wilson. *The Economics of Sharecropping in NE Brazil*. Columbus: Ohio State University, 1976.

Beyan, Amos Jones. *The American Colonization Society and the Creation of the Liberian State: A Historical Perspective, 1822–1900*. Lanham, MD: University Press of America, 1991.

Blackett, R. J. M., "Martin Delany and Robert Campbell: Black Americans in Search of an African Colony." *The Journal of Negro History*, Vol. 62, No. 1 (1977): 1–25.

Blackett, R. J. M. "Anglo-American Opposition to Liberian Colonization, 1831–1833." *The Historian*, Vol. 41, No. 2 (1979): 276–294,

Blackett, R. J. M. "Return to the Motherland: Robert Campbell, a Jamaican in Early Colonial Lagos." *Phylon*, Vol. 40, No. 4 (1979): 375–386.

Blackett, R. J. M. "The Hamic Connection: African Americans and the Caribbean, 1820–1865." In *Before and After 1865: Education, Politics and Regionalism in the Caribbean*, edited by Brian L. Moore and Swithin R. Wilmot, 317–329. Kingston, Jamaica.: Ian Randle, 1998.

Blackett, R. J. M. *Building an Antislavery Wall: Black Americans in the Atlantic Abolitionist Movement, 1830–1860*. Ithaca, NY: Cornell University Press, 1989.

Blamo, Bernard, J. "Nation-Building in Liberia: The Use of Symbolism in National Integration," *Liberia Studies Journal*, Vol. 4, No. 1 (1971): 21–30.

Blassingame, John W. *The Slave Community; Plantation Life in the Antebellum South*. New York: Oxford University Press, 1972.

Blyden, Nemata Amelia. *West Indians in West Africa, 1808–1880: The African Diaspora in Reverse*. Rochester, NY: University of Rochester Press, 2000.

Breitborde, Lawrence. "City, Countryside and Kru Ethnicity." *Africa: Journal of the International African Institute*, Vol. 61–62 (1991): 186–201.

Breitborde, Lawrence. *Speaking and Social Identity: English in the Lives of Urban Africans*. Berlin: Mouton de Gruyter, 1998.

Brooks, George. *The Kru Mariner in the Nineteenth Century: An Historical Compendium*. Newark, DE: Liberian Studies Association of America, 1972.

Brown, Christopher Leslie. *Moral Capital: Foundations of British Abolitionism*. Chapel Hill: University of North Carolina Press, 2006.

Brown, Kathleen. *Good Wives, Nasty Wenches, Anxious Patriarchs Gender, Race, and Power in Colonial Virginia*. Chapel Hill: University of North Carolina Press, 1996.

Brown, Laurence and Tara Inniss. "The Slave Family in the Transition to Freedom: Barbados, 1834–1841." *Slavery and Abolition*, Vol. 26 (2005): 257–269.

Buell, Raymond Leslie. *The Native Problem in Africa*. New York: Macmillan, 1928.

Burin, Eric. *Slavery and the Peculiar Solution: A History of the American Colonization Society*. Gainesville: University Press of Florida, 2005.

Burroughs, Robert. "[T]rue Sailors of Western Africa: Kru Seafaring Identity in British Traveller's Accounts of the 1830s and 40s." *Journal for Maritime Research*, Vol. 11, (2009): 51–67.

Burrowes, Carl Patrick. *Modernization and the Decline of Press Freedom, 1847 to 1970*. Columbia, SC: Journalism and Mass Communication Monographs, 1996.

Burrowes, Carl Patrick. "Black Christian Republicanism: A Southern Ideology in Early Liberia, 1822 to 1847." *The Journal of Negro History*, Vol. 86, No. 1 (2001): 30–44.

Burrowes, Carl Patrick. *Power and Press Freedom in Liberia, 1830–1970: The Impact of Globalization and Civil Society on Media-Government Relations.* Trenton, NJ: Africa World Press, 2004.

Butler, Judith. *The Psychic Life of Power: Theories in Subjection.* Stanford, CA: Stanford University Press, 1997.

Byrd, Alexander. *Captives and Voyagers: Black Migrants across the Eighteenth-Century British Atlantic World.* Baton Rouge: Louisiana State University Press, 2008.

Campbell, James T. *Middle Passages: African American Journeys to Africa, 1787–2005.* New York: Penguin, 2006.

Campbell, Mavis C. *The Dynamics of Change in a Slave Society: A Sociopolitical History of the Free Coloreds of Jamaica, 1800–1865.* Rutherford, NJ: Fairleigh Dickinson University Press, 1975.

Campbell, Penelope. *Maryland in Africa: The Maryland Colonization Society, 1831–1857.* Urbana: University of Illinois Press, 1971.

Clegg Claude, Andrew. *The Price of Liberty: African Americans and the Making of Liberia.* Chapel Hill: University of North Carolina Press, 2004.

Clegg Claude, Andrew. *Africa and the African American Imagination.* Chapel Hill: University of North Carolina Press, 2006.

Cohen, Richard. "Rethinking 'Babylon': Iconoclastic Conceptions of the Diasporic Experience," *Journal of Ethnic and Migration Studies*, Vol. 21, No. 1 (1995): 5–18.

Cole, Angela. *God Have Mercy: The Codrington Trust.* Barbados: S. N., 2003.

Colley, Linda. *Britons: Forging the Nation, 1707–1837.* New Haven, CT: Yale University Press, 1992.

Connolly, Nathan. *A World More Concrete: Real Estate and the Remaking of Jim Crow South Florida.* Chicago: University of Chicago Press, 2014.

Coutinho, Carlos Nelson. *Gramsci's Political Thought.* Leiden: Brill, 2012.

Cox, Edward L. *Free Coloreds in the Slave Societies of St. Kitts and Grenada, 1763–1833.* Knoxville: University of Tennessee Press, 1984.

Cracknell, Kenneth and Susan J. White. *An Introduction to World Methodism.* Cambridge: Cambridge University Press, 2005.

Cuffe, Paul and Rosalind Cobb Wiggins. *Captain Paul Cuffe's Logs and Letters, 1808–1817: A Black Quaker's "Voice from within the Veil."* Washington, DC: Howard University Press, 1996.

Curtin, Phillip. *Two Jamaicas: The Role of Ideas in a Tropical Colony.* Westport, CT: Praeger, 1968.

Curto, José C. and Paul E. Lovejoy, eds. *Enslaving Connections: Changing Cultures of Africa and Brazil During the Era of Slavery.* Amherst, NY: Humanity Books, 2004.

d'Azevedo, Warren L. "A Tribal Reaction to Nationalism (Part 1)." *Liberian Studies Journal* (1969) Vol. III, No. 1, 1–21.

Davis, Karen F. "The Position of Poor Whites in a Color-Class Hierarchy: A Diachronic Study of Ethnic Boundaries in Barbados." PhD thesis. Detroit: Wayne State University, 1978.

Dawley, Alan. *Class and Community: The Industrial Revolution in Lynn.* Cambridge, MA: Harvard University Press, 1976.

Dayfoot, Arthur Charles. *The Shaping of the West Indian Church 1492–1962.* Gainesville: University Press of Florida, 1999.

Delaney, Ted and Phillip Wayne Rhodes, *Free Blacks of Lynchburg, Virginia, 1805–1865.* Lynchburg, VA: Warwick House, 2001.

Delany, Martin and Robert Campbell. *Search for a Place; Black Separatism and Africa, 1860.* Ann Arbor: University of Michigan Press, 1969.

Dhanda, Karen S. "Labor and Place in Barbados, Trinidad and Jamaica: A Search for a Comparative Unified Field Theory Revisited." *New West Indian Guide,* Vol. 75, No. 3–4 (2001): 229–256.

Drescher, Seymour. *Econocide: British Slavery in the Era of Abolition.* Pittsburgh, PA: University of Pittsburgh Press, 1977.

Drescher, Seymour. *From Slavery to Freedom: Comparative Studies in the Rise and Fall of Atlantic Slavery.* New York: New York University Press, 1999.

Dreyer, Frederick A. *The Genesis of Methodism.* Bethlehem, PA: Lehigh University Press, 1999.

Dubois, Laurent. *Avengers of the New World: The Story of the Haitian Revolution.* Cambridge, MA: Belknap Press of Harvard University Press, 2004.

Dunn, Elwood D., Amos J. Beyan, and Carl Patrick Burrowes. *Historical Dictionary of Liberia.* 2nd ed. Landham, MD: Scarecrow Press, 2001.

Dunn, Richard S. *A Tale of two Plantations: Slave Life and Labor in Jamaica and Virginia.* Cambridge, MA: Harvard University Press, 2014.

Echeverri, Marcela. *Indian and Slave Royalists in the Age of Revolution: Reform, Revolution, and Royalism in the Northern Andes, 1780–1825.* New York: Cambridge University Press, 2016.

Edmondson, Belinda. *Making Men: Gender; Literary Authority, and Women's Writing in Caribbean Narrative.* Durham, NC: Duke University Press, 1999.

Edwards, Brent Hayes. *The Practice of Diaspora: Literature, Translation, and the Rise of Black Internationalism.* Boston, MA: Harvard University Press, 2003.

Egerton, Douglas R. "'Its Origins Is Not a Little Curious': A New Look at the American Colonization Society," *Journal of the Early Republic,* Vol. 5 (Winter 1985): 463–480.

Everill, Bronwen. *Abolition and Empire in Sierra Leone and Liberia.* New York: Palgrave Macmillan, 2013.

Fagan, Benjamin. "Americans as they Really Are": The 'Colored American' and the Illustration of National Identity," *American Periodicals,* Vol. 21, No. 2 (2011): 97–119.

Falola, Toyin and Paul E. Lovejoy, *Pawnship in Africa: Debt Bondage in Historical Perspective.* Boulder, CO: Westview Press, 1994.

Fetter, Bruce. *Colonial Rule in Africa: Readings from Primary Sources.* Madison: University of Wisconsin Press, 1979.

Fields, Karen E. and Barbara Jeanne Fields. *Racecraft: The Soul of Inequality in American Life.* London: Verso, 2012.

Förster, Stig, Wolfgang J. Mommsen, and Ronald Edward Robinson. *Bismarck, Europe, and Africa: The Berlin Africa Conference 1884–1885 and the Onset of Partition.* Oxford: Oxford University Press, 1988.

Foucault, Michel. "The Subject and Power," *Critical Inquiry,* Vol. 8., No. 4 (Summer, 1982), 777–795.

Frantz Fanon. *White Skin, Black Masks.* New York: Grove Press, 1967.

Frazier, E. Franklin. *Black Bourgeoisie, The Book That Brought the Shock of Self-Revelation to Middle-Class Blacks in America.* New York: The Free Press, 1997.

Free, Laura. *Suffrage Reconsidered: Gender, Race, and Voting Rights in the Civil War Era.* Ithaca, NY: Cornell University Press.

Fryar, Christienna, Nicole Jackson, and Kennetta Hammond Perry, "Windrush and Britain's Long History of Racialized Belonging," *Black Perspectives,* July 31, 2018, www.aaihs.org/windrush-and-britains-long-history-of-racialized-belonging/.

Fumerton, Patricia. *Unsettled: The Culture of Mobility and the Working Poor in Early Modern England.* Chicago: University of Chicago Press, 2006.

Gallagher, J. "Fowell Buxton and the New African Policy, 1838–1842." *Cambridge Historical Journal,* Vol. 10, No. 1 (1950): 36–58.

Geiss, Immanuel. "Pan-Africanism." *Journal of Contemporary History,* Vol. 4, No. 1, (1969): 187–200.

Gellner, Ernest. *Nations and Nationalism.* Ithaca, NY: Cornell University Press, 1983.

Gide, Andre. *The Counterfeiters.* France: Alfred K. Knopf, 1925.

Gilchrist, Jennifer Lynn. "Houses on Fire: Late Modernist Subjectivity and Historical Crisis." Thesis. New York: Fordham University, 2008, http://fordham .bepress.com/dissertations/AAI3314561.

Gilroy, Paul. *The Black Atlantic: Modernity and Double Consciousness.* Boston, MA: Harvard University Press, 1993.

Golbert, David L. and Jerome Handler. "Barbados in the Post-Apprenticeship Period: The Observations of a French Naval Officer – 1." *Journal of the Barbados Museum and Historical Society,* Vol. 35, No. 4 (1978): 243–266.

Golbert, David L. and Jerome Handler. "Barbados in the Post-Apprenticeship Period: The Observations of a French Naval Officer – 2." *Journal of the Barbados Museum and Historical Society,* Vol. 36 (1979): 4–15.

Goodridge, Sehon. *Facing the Challenge of Emancipation: A Study of the Ministry of William Hart Coleridge First Bishop of Barbados, 1824–1842.* Bridgetown, Barbados: Cedar Press, 1981.

Gosse, Van. "'As a Nation, the English Are Our Friends': The Emergence of African American Politics in the British Atlantic World, 1772–1861." *American Historical Review,* Vol. 113, No. 4 (2008): 1003–1028.

Goveia, Elsa V. *Slave Society in the British Leeward Islands at the End of the Eighteenth Century.* New Haven, CT: Yale University Press, 1965.

Goyal, Yogita. "Africa and the Black Atlantic." *Research in African Literatures,* Vol. 45, No. 3 (2014): v–xxv.

Greene, Jack P. *Imperatives, Behaviors, and Identities: Essays in Early American Cultural History.* Charlottesville: University Press of Virginia, 1992.

Gurley, Ralph R. *The Life of Jehudi Ashmun, Late Colonial Agent in Liberia.* Washington, DC: J. C. Dunn, 1839.

Gutman, Herbert. *Work, Culture, and Society in Industrializing America: Essays in American Working-Class and Social History.* New York: Knopf, 1976.

Hague, William. *William Wilberforce: The Life of the Great Anti-Slave Trade Campaigner.* Orlando: Harcourt, 2007.

Hahn, Steven. *A Nation Under Our Feet: Black Political Struggles in the Rural South, from Slavery to the Great Migration.* Cambridge, MA: Belknap Press of Harvard University Press, 2003.

Halcombe, J. J. *Mission Life, Vol. IV. Part II.* London: W. Wells Gardner, 1873.

Hall, Stuart. "The Problem of Ideology: Marxism without Guarantees." In *Stuart Hall: Critical Dialogues in Cultural Studies,* edited by David Morley and Kuan-Hsing Chen, 25–46. Abingdon: Routledge: 1986.

Hall, Stuart. "Cultural Identity and Diaspora." In *Identity: Community, Culture, Difference,* edited by Jonathan Rutherford, 227–237. London: Lawrence and Wishart, 1990.

Hall, Stuart. "Old and New Identities." In *Culture, Globalization, and the World-System,* edited by Anthony D. King, 41–68. Binghamton, NY: State University of New York Press, 1991.

Hall, Stuart. *Familiar Stranger: A Life Between Two Islands.* Durham, NC: Duke University Press, 2017.

Handler, Jerome. *The Un-Appropriated People: Freedmen in the Slave Society of Barbados.* Baltimore, MD: John's Hopkins University Press, 1974.

Handler, Jerome S., Frederick W. Lange, and Robert V. Riordan. *Plantation Slavery in Barbados: An Archaeological and Historical Investigation.* Cambridge, MA: Harvard University Press, 1978.

Harcourt, Frank. "Early Post-Emancipation Migration from the Caribbean with Particular Reference to Official Attitudes to Emigrant Agents, 1838–1842." Master's thesis. Kingston, Jamaica: University of the West Indies at Mona, 1998.

Harris, Joseph E. *Global Dimensions of the African Diaspora.* Washington, DC: Howard University Press, 1982.

Harrison, Mark. "'The Tender Frame of Man': Disease, Climate, and Racial Difference in India and the West Indies, 1760–1860." *Bulletin of the History of Medicine,* Vol. 70, No. 1 (1996): 68–93.

Hartman, Saidiya V. *Scenes of Subjection: Terror, Slavery, and Self-Making in Nineteenth-Century America.* New York: Oxford University Press, 1997.

Hartog, Hendrik. "Pigs and Positivism." *Wisconsin Law Review,* Vol. 759, No. 4 (1985): 899–935.

Haskins, James. *The Geography of Hope: Black Exodus from the South After Reconstruction.* Brookfield, CT: Twenty-First Century Books, 1999.

Helg, Aline. *Our Rightful Share: The Afro-Cuban Struggle for Equality, 1886–1912.* Chapel Hill: University of North Carolina Press, 1995.

Hennessy, Thomas. *Dividing Ireland: World War One and Partition.* London: Routledge, 1998.

Heuman, Gad. "Slavery and Emancipation in the British Caribbean." *The Journal of Imperial and Commonwealth History,* Vol. 6, No. 2 (1978): 166–171.

Heuman, Gad. *Between Black and White: Race, Politics, and the Free Coloreds in Jamaica, 1792–1865.* Westport, CT: Greenwood Press, 1981.

Heywood, Linda M. and John K. Thornton. *Central Africans, Atlantic Creoles, and the Foundation of the Americas, 1585–1660.* New York: Cambridge University Press, 2007.

Higginbotham, Evelyn Brooks. "African-American Women's History and the Metalanguage of Race." *Signs*, Vol. 17, No. 2 (1992): 251–274.

Ho, Janis. *Nation and Citizenship in the Twentieth–Century British Novel*. New York: Cambridge University Press, 2015.

Hodges, Graham Russell. *The Black Loyalist Directory: African Americans in Exile After the American Revolution*. New York: Garland Publishers, 1996.

Holder, Burleigh. "A History of Crozierville." *Liberian Studies Journal*, Vol. III, No. 1 (1970–1971): 23–24.

Holsoe, Svend. "Chiefdom and Clan Maps of Western Liberia," *Liberian Studies Journal*, Vol. I, No. 2 (1969), 23–39.

Holsoe, Svend. "A Study of Relations between Settlers and Indigenous Peoples in Western Liberia, 1821–1847", *African Historical Studies*, Vol. 4, No. 2 (1971), 331–362.

Holsoe, Svend and Bernard L. Herman, and Max Belcher. *A Life Remembered: Americo-Liberian Folk Architecture*. Athens: University of Georgia Press, 1988.

Holt, Thomas C. *Black Over White: Negro Political Leadership in South Carolina During Reconstruction*. Urbana: University of Illinois Press, 1977.

Holt, Thomas. *The Problem of Freedom: Race, Labor and Politics in Jamaica and Britain 1832 – 1938*. Baltimore: John Hopkins University Press, 1992.

Holt, Thomas. "Marking: Race, Race-making, and the Writing of History." *American Historical Review*, Vol. 100, No. 1 (1995): 1–17.

Holt, Thomas C. *The Problem of Race in the Twenty-First Century*. Cambridge, MA: Harvard University Press, 2000.

Hornsby, Stephen. *British Atlantic, American Frontier: Spaces of Power in Early Modern British America*. Lebanon, NH: University Press of New England, 2005.

Howard, Philip A. *Changing History: Afro-Cuban Cabildos and Societies of Color in the Nineteenth Century*. Baton Rouge: Louisiana State University Press, 1998.

Howe, Glenford D. and Don D. Marshall, eds. *The Empowering Impulse: The Nationalist Tradition of Barbados*. Barbados: Canoe Press UWI, 2001.

Hoyos, F. A. *Builders of Barbados*. Basingstoke: MacMillan Education, 1972.

Hurley, E. Anthony, Renée Brenda Larrier, and Joseph McLaren, eds. *Migrating Words and Worlds: Pan-Africanism Updated*. Trenton, NJ: Africa World Press, 1999.

Hutton, Frankie. "Economic Considerations in the American Colonization Society's Early Effort to Emigrate Free Blacks to Liberia, 1816–36." *The Journal of Negro History*, Vol. 68, No. 4 (1983): 376–389.

Ihonvbere, Julius Omozuanvbo, and John Mukum Mbaku. *Political Liberalization and Democratization in Africa Lessons from Country Experiences*. Westport, CT: Praeger, 2003.

James, C. L. R. *The Black Jacobins; Toussaint L'Ouverture and the San Domingo Revolution*. New York: Vintage Books, 1963.

Johnson, Charles Spurgeon. *Bitter Canaan: The Story of the Negro Republic*. New Brunswick, NJ: Transaction Books, 1987.

Johnston, Harry Hamilton. *The Negro in the New World*. New York: Macmillan, 1910.

Johnston, Harry Hamilton and Otto Stapf, *Liberia*. London: Hutchinson, 1906.

Jones, H. A. "The Struggle for Political and Cultural Unification in Liberia 1847–1930." PhD thesis. Evanston, IL: Northwestern University, 1962.

Kappel, Robert, Werner Korte, and R. Friedegund Mascher. *Liberia: Underdevelopment and Political Rule in a Peripheral Society*. Hamburg: Institut für Afrika-Kunde, 1986.

Karatani, Rieko. *Defining British Citizenship: Empire, Commonwealth and Modern Britain*. Abingdon: Routledge, 2002.

Karch Brathwaite, Cecilia. "London Bourne of Barbados (1793–1869)." *Slavery and Abolition*, Vol. 28 (2007): 23–40.

Kazanjian, David. *The Brink of Freedom: Improvising Life in the Nineteenth-Century Atlantic World*. Durham, NC: Duke University Press, 2016.

Keagy, Thomas J. "The Poor Whites of Barbados." *Revista de Historia de America*, Vol. 73–74 (1972): 9–52.

Kerr-Ritchie, Jeffrey. *Rites of August First: Emancipation Day in the Black Atlantic World*. Baton Rouge: Louisiana State University Press, 2007.

Kinshasa, Kwando. *Emigration Versus Assimilation: The Debate in the African American Press, 1827 – 1861*. London: McFarland, 1988.

Klingberg, Frank Joseph. *Codrington Chronicle; An Experiment in Anglican Altruism on a Barbados Plantation, 1710–1834*. Berkeley: University of California Press, 1949.

Kolllehlon, Konia, T. "On Race, Citizenship, and Property in Liberia: A Sociologist's Point of View." *The Perspective*, March 19, 2008, www.theperspective.org/2008/0319200803.html.

Konneh, Augustine. "The Hut Tax in Liberia: The High Cost of Integration." *Journal of the Georgia Association of Historians*, Vol. 16 (December 1996): 41–60.

Laidlaw, Zoe. "Heathens, Slaves and Aborigenes: Thomas Hodgkins's Critique of Missions and Antislavery." *History Workshop Journal*, Vol. 64, No. 1 (2007): 133–161.

Lambert, David. "Sierra Leone and Other Sites in the War of Representation over Slavery." *History Workshop Journal*, Vol. 64, No. 1 (2007): 103–132.

Langley, Nina. *Christopher Codrington and His College*. London: SPCK, 1964.

Lao, Agustin. "Decolonial Moves: Trans-Locating African Diasporic Spaces." *Cultural Studies*, Vol. 21, No. 2–3 (2007): 309–338.

Lapp, Rudolph M. "The Ante Bellum Poor Whites of the South Atlantic States." PhD thesis. Berkeley: University of California, 1956.

Laurie, Bruce and Eric Foner. *Artisans into Workers: Labor in Nineteenth-Century America*. New York: Hill and Wang, 1989.

Levitt, Jeremy I. *The Evolution of Deadly Conflict in Liberia: From 'Paternaltarianism' to State Collapse*. Durham, NC: Carolina Academic Press, 2005.

Lewis, Earl. "'To Turn as on a Pivot': Writing African Americans into a History of Overlapping Diasporas." *American Historical Review*, Vol. 100, No. 3 (1995): 765–787.

Lewis, Gordon K. *The Growth of the Modern West Indies*. New York: Monthly Review Press, 1968.

Liebenow, J. Gus. *Liberia; The Evolution of Privilege*. Ithaca, NY: Cornell University Press, 1969.

Lowe, Lisa. *The Intimacies of Four Continents*. Durham, NC: Duke University Press, 2015.

Lynch, Hollis Ralph. *Edward Wilmot Blyden: Pan-Negro Patriot 1832–1912*. London: Oxford University Press, 1967.

Mamdani, Mahmood. *Citizen and Subject: Contemporary Africa and the Legacy of Late Colonialism*. Princeton, NJ.: Princeton University Press, 1996.

Mamigonian, Beatriz Gallotti. *To Be a Liberated African in Brazil: Labour and Citizenship in the Nineteenth Century*. Waterloo, ON: University of Waterloo, 2002.

Mancke, Elizabeth and Carole Shammas. *The Creation of the British Atlantic World*. Baltimore: Johns Hopkins University Press, 2005.

Mann, Kristin and Edna G. Bay, eds. *Rethinking the African Diaspora: The Making of a Black Atlantic World in the Bight of Benin and Brazil*. London: F. Cass, 2001.

Marback, Ricard and Mark Kruman, eds. *The Meaning of Citizenship*. Detroit: Wayne State University Press, 2015.

Marshall, Frank. "Early Post-Emancipation Emigration with particular reference to Official Attitudes." Master's Thesis. Barbados: UWI-Cave Hill, 1998.

Marshall, T. H. *Citizenship and Social Class and Other Essays*. Cambridge: Cambridge University Press, 1950.

Marshall, Woodville. "We Be Wise to Many More Tings: Blacks Hopes and Expectations of Emancipation." In *Caribbean Freedom: Economy and Society from Emancipation to the Present*, edited by Hilary Beckles and Verene Shepherd, 12-20. Princeton, NJ: Wiener, 1996.

Martin, Jane. "Kru men 'Down the Coast': Liberian Migrants on the West African Coast in the 19th and Early 20th Centuries." International Journal of African Historical Studies, Vol. 18 (1995): 401–423.

Mason, Keith. "The Absentee Planter and the Key Slave: Privilege, Patriarchalism, and Exploitation in the Early Eighteenth-Century Caribbean." *The William and Mary Quarterly*, Vol. 70, No. 1 (2013): 79–102.

Mbaku, John Mukum and Julius Omozuanvbo Ihonvbere. *The Transition to Democratic Governance in Africa: The Continuing Struggle*. Westport, CT: Praeger, 2003.

McGraw, Jason. *The Work of Recognition: Caribbean Colombia and the Postemancipation Struggle for Citizenship*. Chapel Hill: University of North Carolina Press, 2014.

McKenzie, P. R. *Inter-Religious Encounters in West Africa: Samuel Ajayi Crowther's Attitude to African Traditional Religion and Islam*. Leicester: University of Leicester, 1976.

Membe, Achille. *On the Postcolony*. Berkeley: University of California Press, 2001.

Metaxas, Eric. *Amazing Grace: William Wilberforce and the Heroic Campaign to End Slavery*. New York: Harper San Francisco, 2007.

Miller, Floyd. *The Search for a Black Nationality: Black Emigration and Colonization, 1787-1863*. Urbana: University of Illinois Press, 1975.

Miller, Ivor. *Voice of the Leopard: African Secret Societies and Cuba.* Jackson: University Press of Mississippi, 2009.

Mintz, Sidney. "The Origins of the Reconstituted Peasantries." In *Caribbean Freedom: Economy and Society from Emancipation to the Present a Student Reader,* edited by Hilary Beckles and Verene Shepherd, 94–98, Princeton, NJ: Wiener, 1996.

Momsen, Janet. "Rural Post-Emancipation Rural Settlement in Barbados." Department of Geography thesis. Newcastle: Newcastle University, 1988.

Monbiot, George. "Neoliberalism – the ideology at the root of all our problems." *The Guardian,* April 15, 2016. www.theguardian.com/books/2016/apr/15/neo liberalism-ideology-problem-george-monbiot.

Mongrue, Jesse N. *Liberia: America's Footprint in Africa: Making the Cultural, Social, and Political Connections.* Bloomington, IN: Universe, 2011.

Moore, Bai T. *Liberian Culture at a Glance: A Review of the Culture and Customs of the Different Ethnic Groups in the Republic of Liberia.* Monrovia: Ministry of Information, Cultural Affairs & Tourism, 1979.

Moore, Henrietta. *Still Life: Hopes, Desires, and Satisfaction.* Cambridge, UK: Polity Publishers, 2011.

Morgan, Edmund. *American Slavery, American Freedom: The Ordeal of Colonial Virginia.* New York: Norton, 1975.

Morris, Rosalind C. ed. *Can the Subaltern Speak? Reflections on the History of an Idea.* New York: Columbia University Press, 2010.

Moses, Wilson Jeremiah. *Alexander Crummell: A Study of Civilization and Discontent.* New York: Oxford University Press, 1989.

Moses, Wilson Jeremiah. *Creative Conflict in African American Thought.* Cambridge: Cambridge University Press, 2004.

Moses, Wilson Jeremiah, ed. *Destiny and Race Selected Writings, 1840–1898 by Alexander Crummell.* Amherst: University of Massachusetts Press, 1992.

Newton, Melanie J. *The Children of Africa in the Colonies: Free People of Color in Barbados in the Age of Emancipation.* Baton Rouge: Louisiana State University Press, 2008.

O'Reggio, Trevor. *Between Alienation and Citizenship: The Evolution of Black West Indian Society in Panama, 1914–1964.* Lanham, MD: University Press of America, 2006.

Olwig, Karen Fog. *Small Islands, Large Questions: Society, Culture, and Resistance in the Post- Emancipation Caribbean.* London: F. Cass, 1995.

Omi, Michael and Howard Winant. *Racial Formation in the United States,* 3rd ed. New York: Routledge, 2015.

Painter, Nell Irvin. *Exodusters: Black Migration to Kansas after Reconstruction.* New York: Knopf, 1977.

Pakenham, Thomas. *The Scramble for Africa, 1876–1912.* New York: Random House, 1991.

Pamphile, Leon D. *Haitians and African Americans: A Heritage of Tragedy and Hope.* Gainesville: University Press of Florida, 2001.

Pannell, Walter. *King Cotton: The Share-Cropper and Tenant Farming in the United States.* Los Angeles: Thor's Book Service, 1943.

Paton, Diana. *A Narrative of Events Since the First of August, 1834.* Durham, NC: Duke University Press, 2001.

Patterson, Orlando. "The Ancient and Medieval Origins of Modern Freedom." In *The Problem of Evil: Slavery, Freedom, and the Ambiguities of American Reform,* edited by Steven Mintz and John Stauffer, 31–66. Amherst: University of Massachusetts Press, 2007.

Perry, Imani. *More Beautiful and More Terrible: The Embrace and Transcendence of Racial Inequality in the United States.* New York: New York University Press, 2011.

Pettigrew, William A. *Freedom's Debt: The Royal African Company and the Politics of the Atlantic Slave Trade, 1672–1752.* Chapel Hill: University of North Carolina Press, 2013.

Phillips, Anthony. "The Parliament of Barbados, 1639–1989." *Barbados Historical and Museum Society,* Vol. 38, No. 4 (1990): 422–451.

Phillips, Derek. *Looking Backward: A Critical Appraisal of Communitarian Thought.* Newark, NJ: Princeton University Press, 1993.

Phillips, Glenn O. "The Beginnings of Samuel J. Prescod, 1806–1843: Afro-Barbadian Civil Rights Crusader and Activist." *The Americas,* Vol. XXXVIII, No. 3 (1982): 363–378.

Pierce, Preston E. *Liberian Dreams, West African Nightmare: The Life of Henry W. Johnson, Part Two.* Rochester, NY: Office of the City Historian, 2005.

Pierre, Jemima. *The Predicament of Blackness: Postcolonial Ghana and the Politics of Race.* Chicago: University of Chicago Press, 2013.

Power-Greene, Ousmane. *Against Wind and Tide: The African American Struggle against the Colonization Movement.* New York: New York University Press, 2014.

Putnam, Lara. *Radical Moves: Caribbean Migrants and the Politics of Race in the Jazz Age.* Chapel Hill: University of North Carolina Press, 2013.

Pybus, Cassandra. *Epic Journeys of Freedom: Runaway Slaves of the American Revolution and their Global Quest for Liberty.* Boston, MA: Beacon Press, 2006.

Racine, Karen and Beatriz G. Mamigonian. *The Human Tradition in the Atlantic World, 1500-1850.* Lanham, MD: Rowman & Littlefield, 2010.

Ragatz, Lowell J. *The Fall of the Planter Class in the British Caribbean, 1763–1833: A Study in Social and Economic History.* New York: Century, 1928.

Reece, James Ebenezer and Charles Guilding Clark-Hunt. *Barbados Diocesan History.* London: West India Committee, 1928.

Reef, Catherine. *This Our Dark Country: The American Settlers of Liberia.* New York: Clarion Books, 2002.

Reffell, Massala. *Echoes of Footsteps: Birth of a Negro Nation.* Bloomington, IN: Xlibris, 2012.

Regosin, Elizabeth Ann. *Freedom's Promise: Ex-Slave Families and Citizenship in the Age of Emancipation.* Charlottesville: University Press of Virginia, 2002.

Richardson, Nathaniel R. *Liberia's Past and Present.* London: Diplomatic Press, 1959.

Roark, James L. *Masters Without Slaves: Southern Planters in the Civil War and Reconstruction*. New York: Norton, 1977.

Rugemer, Edward Bartlett. *The Problem of Emancipation: The Caribbean Roots of the American Civil War*. Baton Rouge: Louisiana State University Press, 2008.

Sanderson, George Neville. *England, Europe & the Upper Nile, 1882–1899: A Study in the Partition of Africa*. Edinburgh: Edinburgh University Press, 1965.

Sandiford, Keith. *Theorizing a Colonial Caribbean-Atlantic Imaginary: Sugar and Obeah*. New York: Routledge, 2011.

Sanga, Jaina C. *Salman Rushdie's Postcolonial Metaphors: Migration, Translation, Hybridity, Blasphemy, and Globalization*. Westport, CT: Greenwood Press, 2001.

Sartre, Jean Paul, *"A Theatre of Situations." Vol IX: Melanges 101*. Paris: Gallimard Press, 1972. Sawyer, Amos. *Beyond Plunder: Toward Democratic Governance in Liberia*. Boulder, CO: Lynne Rienner Publishers, 2005.

Sawyer, Amos. *The Emergence of Autocracy in Liberia: Tragedy and Challenge*. San Francisco: Institute for Contemporary Studies, 1992.

Schama, Simon. *Rough Crossings: Britain, the Slaves, and the American Revolution*. New York: Ecco, 2006.

Schön, James and Samuel Crowther. *Journals of the Rev. James Frederick Schön and Mr. Samuel Crowther: Who, with the Sanction of Her Majesty's Government, Accompanied the Expedition Up the Niger in 1841 on Behalf of the Church Missionary Society*. London: Cass, 1970.

Scott, James C. *Weapons of the Weak: Everyday Forms of Peasant Resistance*. New Haven, CT: Yale University Press, 1985.

Scott, Julius. "The Common Wind: Currents of Afro-American Communication in the Era of the Haitian Revolution." PhD thesis. Durham, NC: Duke University, 1986.

Scott, Julius. *A Common Wind: Currents of Afro-American Communication in the Era of the Haitian Revolution*. New York: Verso Books, 2018.

Scott, Rebecca J. *Slave Emancipation in Cuba: The Transition to Free Labor, 1860–1899*. Princeton, NJ: Princeton University Press, 1985.

Scott, Rebecca J. "Former Slaves: Responses to Emancipation in Cuba." In *Caribbean Freedom: Economy and Society from Emancipation to the Present a Student Reader*, edited by Hilary Beckles and Verene Shepherd, 21–27. Princeton, NJ: Wiener, 1996.

Scott, Rebecca J. *Degrees of Freedom: Louisiana and Cuba After Slavery*. Cambridge, MA: Belknap Press of Harvard University Press, 2005.

Scott, Rebecca and Jean M. Hebrard. *Freedom Papers: An Odyssey in the Age of Emancipation*. Cambridge, MA: Harvard University Press, 2012.

Shaw, Jenny. *Everyday Life in the Early English Caribbean: Irish, Africans, and the Construction of Difference*. Athens: University of Georgia Press, 2013.

Sheppard, Jill. *The Redlegs of Barbados*. New York: KTO Press, 1977.

Sherman, Frank. *Liberia: The Land, Its People, History and Culture*. Dar es Salaam, Tanzania: New Africa Press, 2011.

Shick, Tom W. *Behold the Promised Land: A History of Afro-American Settler Society in Nineteenth-Century Liberia*. Baltimore: Johns Hopkins University Press, 1980.

Sidbury, James. *Becoming African in America: Race and Nation in the Early Black Atlantic*. New York: Oxford University Press, 2007.

Simien, Evelyn M. "Race, Gender, and Linked Fate." *Journal of Black Studies*, Vol. 35, No. 5 (2005): 529–550.

Singh, Nikhil Pal. *Black is a Country: Race and the Unfinished Struggle for Democracy*. Cambridge, MA: Harvard University Press, 2004.

Smallwood, Stephanie. *Saltwater Slavery: A Middle Passage from Africa to American Diaspora*. Cambridge, MA: Harvard University Press, 2007.

Smith, Robert. *Deeds Not Words: A History of the True Whig Party*. Monrovia: University of Liberia, 1970.

Spivak, Gayatri Chakravorty. "Can the Subaltern Speak?" In *Marxism and the Interpretation of Culture*, edited by Cary Nelson and Lawrence Grossberg, 271–313. Urbana: University of Illinois Press, 1988.

Stafford, Patricia. "The Growth of the Black and Brown Middle Class, 1838–1988, and its Role in the Shaping of Modern Barbados." PhD thesis. Cave Hill: University of the West Indies, 2005.

Staudenraus, P. J. *The African Colonization Movement, 1816–1865*. New York: Columbia University Press, 1961.

Stivers, Richard. *The Illusion of Freedom and Equality*. New York: New York Press, 2008.

Stoler, Laura. *Race and the Education of Desire: Foucault's History of Sexuality and the Colonial Order of Things*. Durham, NC: Duke University Press, 1995.

Stuckey, Sterling. *The Ideological Origins of Black Nationalism*. Boston, MA: Beacon Press, 1972.

Stuckey, Sterling. *Slave Culture: Nationalist Theory and the Foundations of Black America*. New York: Oxford University Press, 1987.

Sullivan, Jo Mary and Camille Mirepoix. *Liberia in Pictures*. Minneapolis: Lerner Publications, 1988.

Swartz, B. K. and Raymond E. Dumett. *West African Culture Dynamics: Archaeological and Historical Perspectives*. The Hague: Mouton, 1980.

Temperley, Howard. *White Dreams, Black Africa: The Antislavery Expedition to the River Niger 1841–1842*. New Haven, CT: Yale University Press, 1991.

Tomich, Dale and Michael Zueske, eds. "The Second Slavery: Mass Slavery, World-Economy, and Comparative Microhistories, Part II." Special Issue. *Review: A Journal of the Fernand Braudel Center*, Vol. 31, No. 3 (2008): 251–437.

Tomkins, Stephen. *William Wilberforce: A Biography*. Grand Rapids, MI: Eerdmans, 2007.

Trollope, Anthony. *The West Indies and the Spanish Main*. Cambridge: Cambridge University Press, 1860.

Troutman, Phillip. "Grapevine in the Slave Market: African American Political Literacy and the 1841 Creole Revolt." In *The Chattel Principle: Domestic Slave Trades in the Americas*, edited by Walter Johnson, 203–233. New Haven, CT: Yale University Press, 2004.

Turner, John. "A 'Black-White' Missionary on the Imperial Stage: William H. Sheppard and Middle-Class Black Manhood." *Journal of Southern Religion*, Vol. 9 (2006), https://jsr.fsu.edu/Volume9/Turner.htm.

Tyler-McGraw, Marie. *An African Republic: Black & White Virginians in the Making of Liberia.* Chapel Hill: University of North Carolina Press, 2007.

Valentine, Danyelle. "Embarking on Revolutionary Migrations: The Black Loyalists' Southern Campaign for Freedom during the Revolutionary Era, 1775–1862," PhD thesis in progress. Nashville: Vanderbilt University, in progress.

Van der Kraaij, F. P. M. *The Open Door Policy of Liberia: An Economic History of Modern Liberia.* Bremen: Im Selbstverlag des Museums, 1983.

Wariboko, Waibinte E. *Ruined by "Race": Afro-Caribbean Missionaries and the Evangelization of Southern Nigeria, 1895–1925.* Trenton, NJ: Africa World Press, 2007.

Watson, Karl. "The Redlegs of Barbados." Master's thesis. Florida: University of Florida, 1970.

Watson, Karl, *The Civilised Island, Barbados: A Social History, 1750–1816.* Ellerton, Barbados: Caribbean Graphic Production, 1979.

Welch, Pedro. "An Overlooked Dimension: The Emigration of Barbadian Labourers to Suriname in the Nineteenth Century." *The Journal of Caribbean History,* Vol. 43, No. 2 (2009): 246–264.

Welch, Pedro. "The Forgotten Dimension: Barbadian Emigration to Suriname in the Nineteenth Century." Paper presented at the 41st Annual Conference of the ACH at the University of the West Indies at Cave Hill, May 17, 2009.

Welch, Pedro and Richard A. Goodridge. *"Red" and Black Over White: Free Coloured Women in Pre-Emancipation Barbados.* Bridgetown, Barbados: Carib Research and Publications, 2000.

Wells, Ida B., Frederick Douglass, Irvine Garland Penn, and Ferdinand L. Barnett. *The Reason Why the Colored American Is Not in the World's Columbian Exposition: The Afro-American's Contribution to Columbian Literature* [1893], ed. Robert W. Rydell. Urbana: University of Illinois Press, 1999.

West, Laura Elizabeth. "'The Negro Experiment': Black Modernity and Liberia, 1883–1910." Master's thesis. Virginia: Virginia Polytechnic University, 2012. https://vtechworks.lib.vt.edu/handle/10919/32399.

Wiener, Jonathan M. *Social Origins of the New South: Alabama, 1860–1885.* Baton Rouge: Louisiana State University Press, 1978.

Williams, Eric. *Capitalism and Slavery.* New York: Capricorn Books, 1966.

Wright, Michelle. *Becoming Black: Creating Identity in the African Diaspora.* Durham, NC: Duke University Press, 2004.

Wright, Richard. *Native Son.* New York: Harper Perennial Modern Classics, 1993.

Wulah, Teah. *Back to Africa: A Liberian Tragedy.* Bloomington, IN: Author House, 2009.

Yirush, Craig, ed. *Settlers, Liberty, and Empire: The Roots of Early American Political Theory, 1675–1775.* New York: Cambridge University Press, 2011.

Young, James Capers. *Liberia Rediscovered.* Garden City, NY: Doubleday, Doran, 1934.

Yun, Lisa. *The Coolie Speaks: Chinese Indentured Laborers and African Slaves in Cuba.* Philadelphia: Temple University Press, 2008.

Index

Abokeuta, 115
Abolition Act (1833), 40, 52, 63, 76,
    125, 236, *See also* post-emancipation
    era
abolitionism, 38, 41, 43, 80, 173, 236
    imperialism and, 40, 97, 98, 113, 132
    missionaries and, 89–91
    newspapers and, 121–126
ACS. *See American Colonization Society*
Adamson, John, 51
Addison, Dr., 280
Africa, 283–285, 288–291, 300, *See also*
    Liberia, African diaspora, pan-
    Africanism, Sierra Leone, African
    civilization
    black identity and, 174–175
    European imperialism in, 283–285,
    288–291, 300, 301, 321
    white mortality in, 90
African American migrants, 1, 13, 102, 109,
    112, 118, 171–180, 186, 192–193, *See
    also* Americo-Liberians
    blackness and, 23, 276
    citizenship, 257
    decline in, 8, 129
    escaping slavery, 14, 15
    financial assistance for, 7
    identities, 20
    motivations of, 178–180, 193
    political power of, 245–246, 266–267,
    284
    republicanism, 16, 26, 241–243
    settlements, 201, 202

state divisions, 206–208
    terminology for, 11
    treaty negotiations, 302–303
African Americans
    blackness and, 273
    communication with West Indians,
    105–106, 118–126, 173–174
    free, slave society and, 107–109
    migration to West Indies, 125–126
African civilization, 9, 17–18, 25, 74–101
    Afro-Barbadians and, 157–160, 254
    Barclay, Anthony, Jr. and, 95–96
    Christian missionaries and, 84–92, 95, 96
    colonial identity and, 92–101, 160–171,
    208
    colonization and, 111–114
    motivations, 74–75
    religious ideas and, 78–84, 113
    West Indian migrants to Sierra Leone and,
    75–78
African diaspora. *See also* pan-Africanism,
    black nationalism
    Africa as point of reference for, 174–175,
    328
    framework, 10, 16, 20, 24
    identities, 99, 248–249, 326–327
    Liberia and, 1
    memory of, 274
    return and, 88
African Diaspora Studies, 14
African natives. *See* indigenes
African receptives. *See* recaptives
African religious practices, 79, 220–221

African Repository, The (newspaper), 8, 110–111, 112, 124, 125, 186, 228
African Slave Trade and Its Remedy, The (Buxton), 89
African society, 303
Africanus, 7, 91, 9a, 93, 97, 101
Afro-Barbadian middle class. *See also* Barbadian migrants, free coloreds (mixed-race), free blacks
  colonial identity, 68–69
  education and literacy, 42
  emergence of, 33–39
  ideologies of, 157–160
  legal system and, 64–72
  mobility of, 32
  motives for emigration, 33, 72–73
  political agenda, 64–72
  post-emancipation era, 40–53
  rights and status, 7, 29, 43–53, 72–73, 143, 165–171
Afropolitanism, 23
agency, 13
agrarianism, 267
agriculture, 257–263, 309
Akoo ethnic group, 211
Akpan, M. B., 252
Alfred, Prince, 58
Alger, Horatio, 219
American Anti-Slavery Society, 125
American Colonization Society (ACS), 22, 46, 51, 280, *See also* Liberia
  Barbadian emigrants and, 6–9, 58–59, 127–144, 180, 189
  creation and goals of, 107–109, 238
  criticism of, 121–122, 268
  indigenous slave traders and, 251
  Liberia, control over, 239–240
  Liberian voyages, 198–199
  St. Thomas emigrants and, 192
American Commission to Liberia, 307–308
Americo-Liberians, 230–231, *See also* African American migrants
  political power, 233–234, 236
  use of term, 11, 217
Anderson, Benedict, 255
Anderson, Benjamin J. K., 317
Anderson, J. K., 285
Anglican Church, 79–80, 85
Anti-Administration Party, 267
Antigua, 31, 41, 51
Anti-Slavery Society (England), 67

Anti-Slavery Society (Jamaica), 124
Appiah, Anthony, 215
Applewhaite (Police Magistrate), 62
apprenticeship system
  in Barbados, 30, 43–46
  in Liberia, 263–265
Archer, Edward A., 95, 97
Armah, Ayi Kwei, 19
Armstrong, Geo. L., 134
artisans, 55–56, 57, 257–262
Ashmun, Jehudi, 199
Asian indentured laborers, 52
assimilation, 109, 121, 174, 317–321
Attwell, Joseph, 6, 50, 78, 119, 139
Augustus, Nicholas, 191
Ayres, Eli, 198

back-to-Africa movement, 26
backwardness, 18, 112
Bacon, Francis, 308
Baltimore Sun (newspaper), 120
bankruptcy, 309
baptism, 81–82
Barbadian migrants, 102–145, 326–332, *See also* West Indian migrants, communication, African American and Caribbean
  arrival in Liberia, 189–191, 293–295
  black migration choices, 106–109
  citizenship, 253–266
  class status, 7
  consciousness of, 24
  demographics, 7, 50–51
  foreign aid for, 5, 7
  Liberian consul and, 115–118
  mortality, 203–205, 274
  motivations of, 4, 8, 15, 30, 49–53, 143–145, 178–180
  numbers of, 7, 11, 31, 45
  political and economic privileges, 208–209
  political leadership, 292–300
  political status, 233–241
  ship manifest of, 151
  Sierra Leone migration and, 109–114
  tipping point (1860s), 89, 127–145
  urban, 34
  voyage to Liberia, 149–157
Barbadian, The (newspaper), 80, 86, 88, 119
Barbados
  emancipation, 11–13, 29–33, 118

Barbados (cont.)
  population density, 30, 31, 50, 54
  post-emancipation era, 5, 15, 40–53, 293
  racial codes and laws, 176–177
Barbados Auxiliary Antislavery Society, 97
Barbados Auxiliary Bible Society, 162
Barbados Chamber of Commerce, 52
Barbados Colonization Society, 6, 95, 97,
    103–104
Barbados Company for Liberia (BCL), 10,
    59, 78, 87, 98, 99, 106–109, 131, 189
  assistance from PCS, 127
  Barclay and, 136–139
  creation of, 95
  Jamaican migration and, 71
  leaders of, 6, 162
  requests for assistance, 49–50
barbarity, 18, *See also* savagery
Barclay, Anthony, Jr., 4, 6, 7, 10, 29, 33, 52,
    66, 68, 71–72, 73, 124, 282
  ACS and, 134–139
  African civilization and, 95–96
  Barbados Colonization Society
    resolutions, 95, 97
  on civilizing mission, 74
  colonial subjecthood, 103–104
  criticisms of, 139
  death of, 204
  family, 40–41, 294–295
  Fatherland Union and, 161
  on Haiti, 106–107
  interest in Liberia, 130, 292–293
  Liberian politics and, 236
  pan-Africanism, 92, 104
  political activities in Barbados, 39
  Sierra Leone and, 89
Barclay, Anthony, Sr., 33, 39
Barclay, Antoinette Hope, 224, 270, 296
Barclay, Arthur, 278, 280, 282–325, 326
  baptism, 82
  death of, 324–325
  education, 295–296
  European imperialism and, 288–290
  indigenous Africans and, 311–321
  League of Nations and, 322–323
  Liberian policies and, 300–311
  marriages and family, 224–225
  photograph of, 305
  political career, 296–297
  presidential election, 2–4, 9, 26, 270,
    282–285

  retirement, 322
  transatlantic post-emancipation and,
    292–300
Barclay, Edwin James, 225, 271–272, 277,
    289
Barclay, Ella Mai, 224, 226, 295
Barclay, Ernest, 270
Barclay, Georgia Ann, 226
Barclay, James, 73
Barclay, Mary Augusta, 224
Barclay, Sarah Ann Bourne, 204, 224, 293,
    295
Barclay, Sarah Helena, 224
Barker, A., 49
Barnes, Kenneth C., *Journey of Hope*, 10
Barque Greyhound (ship), 192
Basel Mission, 85
Bassa ethnic group, 196, 198
Belgreave Address and Counter Address,
    38–39, 66, 161–162
Belgreave, Jacob, 38
Benedict, Samuel, 267
benevolence, 143–144, 195, 238
Benson, Stephen Allen, 285
Berlin Conference, 284, 289–290
Best, George Stanfield, 224
Beyan, Amos, 197
black advancement, 109, 273–281,
    310–311, *See also* racial uplift
Black Atlantic theories, 24
black elites, 7, 267–269, 276
black humanity, 330
black identity and subjectivity. *See also*
    blackness, free coloreds (mixed-race),
    free blacks
black identity/subjectivity, 8, 15, 114, 202,
    326, *See also* colonial identity
black nationalism, 3, 9, 16, 109, 178–180,
    See also nationhood
  Afro-Barbadians and, 157–160,
    171–180, 314
  black oppression and, 19
  blackness and, 21
  colonial identity and, 92–93
  Liberian independence and, 110–111
  Liberian nationhood and, 236–238,
    326–332
black racial respectability. *See* respectability
black saviors, 89, 100
Blackett, Edward, 58, 59
Blackett, Mary Elizabeth, 59

Blackett, Richard, 173
Blackman, John W., 138, 161–162
blackness, 25, 190, 244, 327–332, *See also*
	color politics
	Africa and, 100, 162–171
	African diaspora and, 214, 216
	defining, 1, 17–25
	differences in, 171–180
	essentialism, 21
	hierarchy within, 188–189, *See also*
		hierarchies, race and class
	homogeneity in, 25, 327
	labor and, 213–214
	Liberian citizenship and, 244, 253
	Liberian politics and, 234–238
	Liberian representations of, 273–281
	social interactions and, 222–229
	subjectivity and, 175
	vertical subjecthood and, 303
black-owned newspapers, 119–124, 173
Blairmont Plantation, 57
Blamo, J. Bernard, 218, 219
blancophobia, 302
Blankett, H. N. B., 83
Bleby, Henry, 80–81
Blyden, Edward Wilmot, 8, 26, 111,
	130–131, 142, 169, 198, 221, 224, 265,
	267, 291–292, 299, 303, 312, 316, 326,
	330
Blyden, John, 192, 224
Blyden, Joseph, 224
Blyden, Nemata, *West Indians in West
	Africa*, 12
boundary disputes, 302
bourgeoisie, black, 274, *See also* Afro-
	Barbadian middle class
Bourne, Frances Eliza, 83
Bourne, Frances and Susan, 83
Bourne, London, 41, 52, 86, 95, 163–164,
	165
Bourne, William, 41
Bovell, H. H. B., 83
Boyle, Moses S., 279
Bradshaw, John, 83–84, 86
Brathwaite, John, 51
Brazil, 14
Bridgetown, Barbados, 34–35, 136
Brig Cora (ship), 195
	manifest, 150, 151
	voyage to Liberia, 149–150, 185, 293
Brig M.A. Benson (ship), 192

Briggs, James, 50
Bristol, King, 200
British and Foreign Antislavery Society
	(BFASS), 47, 95
British colonialism/imperialism, 16, 26,
	275, *See also* European imperialism in
	Africa, Barbados, colonial identity,
	British Empire
	in Africa, 77, 307
	Afro-Barbadians and, 103–104,
		157–160, 227
	escape from, 1
	ideals of, 16
	internalization of, 17–19
	in Sierra Leone, 77–78
	toward Liberia, 298
British Emancipator (newspaper), 66
British Empire. *See also* British colonialism/
	imperialism, colonial identity
	citizenship in, 115
	royalism, 16
	subjecthood, 25, 34, 177
British Guiana, 31, 55–56, 62
British Virgin Islands, 8
Brooks, J. H., 279
brotherhoods, 57–58
Brown Privilege Bill, 39
Brown, Delia, 51
Brown, Guy, 51
Brown, H. D., 204
Brown, Samuel and Catherine, 83
Brown, Williams Wells, 126
Buchanan, 207
Burgess, Ebenezer, 107
Burin, Eric, 108
	Slavery and the Peculiar Solution, 10
Burke, Rosabella, 205–206
Burke, William C., 129, 205–206
Burnett, W. W., 49
Burrowes, Carl, 237
Bussa Rebellion, 38, 40, 76, 80, 82
Bussa, General, 38, 40
Buxton, Thomas, 80, 89–90

Cadell, MacKay, 306
Cadogan, S. E. F., 270, 272
Campbell, Robert, 115
Canada, 116, 117, 124
Candler, John, 65
Cape Mesurado, 198
capitalist system, 41, 43, *See also* free labor

Carew, Thomas, 77
Caribbean. *See* Barbados
Cavalla, 291, 313
Ceasar, Samson, 210
Central America, 56, 106, 116
centralism, 243
character affidavits, 135
Cheeseman, Joseph James, 292
Cheeseman, Victoria Elizabeth Jelloh, 226
Chicago World's Fair, Liberian Exhibition, 278–281, 297, 304, 316
chiefs, authority of, 318–319
children, under apprenticeship system, 45
Chrinkett, M. C., 83
Christ Church, 135
Christian Recorder (newspaper), 120, 122
Christianity. *See also* missionaries, religion
    gender, 96
    in Barbados, 78–84
    in Liberia, 74–75, 219–221, 280
Christy, Cuthbert, 322–323
Church Missionary Society (CMS), 85, 87, 90, 95, 197
citizenship, American, 177
citizenship, British. *See also* British Empire
    race and, 216
    slavery and, 39
citizenship, Liberian, 17, 22, 26, 32, 49, 53, 115–118, 158, 190, 231–232, 251–252, 327, 328, 329
    blackness and, 233–238, 241
    categories of, 253–266
    defining, 243–253
    indigenous, 249–253
    kinship groups and, 196
    recaptives, 212
    social and religious conduct and, 69
civil rights, 32
Civil War, American, 8, 118, 121–126, 128, 129, 206
Clarke, Helena Jane, 84
Clarkson, Thomas, 95
class, 21, 30, 68, 158, *See also* hierarchies, race and class, Afro-Barbadian middle class, peasant class, lower classes
Clay, Henry, 107–108
Clay-Ashland settlement, 201
Clegg, Claude, *The Price of Liberty*, 10
Coates, J. B., 197
Codrington College, 70, 84, 86
Codrington, Christopher, 84

coercion, 43, 265
Colebrook, William, 84
Coleman, Louisa, 279
Coleman, William David, 292
Collymore, H. M., 83
colonial identity, 25, 103–104, 131
    African civilization and, 96–101, 160–171
    black identity and, 178–180, 230
    British imperialism and, 92–93, 227
    imperial citizenship and, 68–69
    Liberian politics and, 208–209, 233–234, 282–283
    royalist political ideologies and, 158
    slavery and, 38
colonialism, 17, *See also* European imperialism in Africa, British colonialism/imperialism
colonizationists, 193, 236, *See also* American Colonization Society (ACS)
    goals of, 9, 238
    motives of, 121–126, 143–145
    pan-Africanism and, 118
    slavery and, 108–109
    views on blackness, 23, 179
color politics, 52, 167, 212, 227, 238, 266–269, 330
    identity and, 163–164, 230
Colored American (periodical), 119, 124
Commercial Hall, 52
Common Council of Monrovia, 251
communication, African American and Caribbean, 105–106, 118–126, 173–174
Condo ethnic group, 250
"Congo", 217, 231, 262
Congo-Angola, 215
Cooper, Florence, 224
Cooper, Henry, 223, 279
Cooper, Jesse, 225
Cooper-Barclay, Sarah, 224
Coppinger, William, 134, 138
Cornish, Samuel, 119
Cote d'Ivoire, 291, 306
Cox, John Abraham and Molly Ann, 83
creolization, 166
Crowther, Samuel, 91
Crozer, John P., 140, 194
Crozer, Samuel A., 140, 194
Crozierville, 194–195, 200–203, 220, 260–261, 267, 315

Crozierville Observer (newspaper), 309
Crummell, Alexander, 1, 193, 204, 208, 220, 267, 294–296
Cuba, 14, 211
Cuffe, Paul, 107, 109
cultural identities, 217, *See also* identities
Cummins, Thomas J., 68, 96–101, 162
currency, 252
Curtin, Phillip, *Two Jamaicas*, 12
customary native law, 318–319

Darzoe Island, 199
Davis, Euphemia Mary, 225
Davis, Jane Seton, 225
Davis, M., 256–257
Davis, William McCall, 225
Day, David A., 280
Day, Thomas, 62–64, 65
Dayrell, Henry, 68, 162
Dayrell, Jane, 62, 67–68
De Belleh ethnic group, 196
De Coursey, M. T., 279
Defensor, 67
Dei ethnic group, 197, 198
Delany, Martin, 109, 115, 119, 122
Demerara, 8, 31, 54, 62, 73, 210–211
democracy, 116, 243
Dennis, Henry W., 191
Dey ethnic group, 250
diaspora. *See* African diaspora
dignity, 45
Dimery, J. T., 294
diplomatic relations, Liberia, 301–303
discrimination, 37, 213–214
disease, 190, 204–205
dollar diplomacy, 307
Dominica, 51
Donokan, Samuel, 162
double-consciousness, 89
Douglass Monthly (newspaper), 120
Douglass, Frederick, 109, 119–120, 122, 125, 173
Drape, William, 77
Dred Scott ruling, 177
Dunbar, C. B., 223
Duporte, Reverend, 88
Durant, J. N., 89

Eastmond, Thomas Henry and Rebecca Ann, 83
economic privilege, 208–209

economic security, 170
Edina, 207
education, 42, 121, 269–270, 295–296
Edward, William and Sarah Ann, 83
Edwards Brothers, 279
Elder, Dempster & Co., 279
elites
    black, 7, 267–269, 276
    white, 66, 71
Elizabeth (ship), 2–4, 195
Ellis, Thomas, 135
emancipation. *See* freedom, post-emancipation era, abolitionism
Emancipation Act. *See* Abolition Act (1833)
Emancipation Proclamation (US), 9, 15, 236
emigration, 50, 106–109, *See also* Barbadian migrants, West Indian migrants, African American migrants
    costs, 137
    freedom and, 31
    subscription list, 73
Emigration Act, 62, 64
emigration agents, 54–56
emigration laws, 60–64
emigration organizations, 161, *See also* American Colonization Society (ACS), Barbados Company for Liberia (BCL), Fatherland Union-Barbados Emigration Society for Liberia (FUBES), Barbados Colonization Society
equality, 327, 328, 329
essentialism, blackness and, 21
Ethiopia, 310
ethnicity, 217, *See also* hierarchies, race and class, color politics, blackness, identities
    intra-racial rivalry, 187–189
European architecture, 200–206
European gentry, 37
European imperialism in Africa, 283–285, 288–291, 300, 301, 321
European traders, 285–286
Evelyn, Joseph, 47
exile, 76, 78, 108, 114, 133, 268

Fahnbulleh, Ambollai and Jarsie, 226
families, black, 81
farmers, 50–51, *See also* agriculture
Fatherland Union-Barbados Emigration Society for Liberia (FUBES), 6, 7, 10,

52, 87, 95, 98, 103, 106, 120, 135, 137, 189
Ferguson, Samuel D., 279, 280
Fernando Po area, 98–99, 107
Finley, Robert, 108
Firestone Company of Liberia, 308, 322
First Great Awakening, 84
Fitzjames, Alexander, 77
Flill and Moore, 279
foods, in Liberia, 208
force, extralegal, 47
forced labor, 322–323
Forten, James, 123
foster parenting, 225–226
Foucault, Michel, 275
France, 308
Franchise Act (1842), 49, 53
Frederick Douglass Paper (newspaper), 120
free blacks
  identity, 163
  status of, 33–39
  in US slave society, 107–109
  views on emancipation, 30, 32
free coloreds (mixed-race)
  identity, 163
  as oppressors, 37
  as slave owners, 38, 162
  status of, 33–39, 42, 210
free labor
  Barbados plantation economy and, 56
  Barbados tenancy system and, 47
  in Liberia, 263–266
  recaptives in Liberia, 214
freedom, 17, 53, 326–329, See also post-
    emancipation era, Emancipation
    Proclamation (US), Abolition Act
    (1833), abolitionism
  advancement and, 8
  apprenticeship and, 43
  in Barbados, 172
  Liberia and, 143, 157
  in Liberia, 181, 238–239, 265–266
  property ownership and, 72–73
  Sierra Leone as symbol of, 76
  in West Indies, 125
freedom movements, 10, 14, 15, 24
  African American, 15
  Caribbean, 15
  global, 26
Freedom's Journal (periodical), 119
Freemasonry, 227

Frontier Force, 306–308

Gallaudet, Thomas, 110
Gallinas/Gallinhas, 290–291, 313
Gambia, 76
Garrison, William Lloyd, 123
Garvey, Marcus, 26, 326, 330–331
Gaskin, John S., 162
gender, 59–60, 228
  boundaries, 21
  Christianity and, 96
  political rights and, 241, 247–248
George, King, 199, 200
Germany, 308, 312
Getumbe, King, 200
Gibson, G. W., 324–325
Gilroy, Paul, 218
Gittens, James, 33
Globe (newspaper), 66
Gola/Golah ethnic group, 250, 321
Goodridge, Everett Jonathon, 272
Grand Bassa, Monsterrado County, 264–266
Grant, F. B., 82
Graves, Isaac and Rebecca, 81
Graves, Sarah Jane, 81
Great Awakening, 84
Grebo ethnic group, 196, 225, 287, 320
Green, James S., 108
Greene, Jack, 239
Greenleaf, Simon, 240–241
Greenville, 207
Grey, Charles, 78
Greyhound (ship), 193
Griffiths, Samuel, 115
Grimes, Florence Mai, 295
Grimes, Henry Waldron, 224, 226, 276
Grimes, Joseph Rudolph, 271
Grimes, Louis Arthur, 224, 226, 271–272, 295
guardianships, 225
guilds, 57–58
Guinea, 291, 306

H.P. Russell (ship), 192
Haiti, 38, 106, 121
  escaped slaves in, 14
  migration to, 116
Haitian Revolution, 38
Hall, Stuart, 179, 209, 235
Harper, 207

Harris, Joseph, 88
Harris, Thomas, Jr., 29–30, 37, 42, 68, 124, 164
Harte, William, 82
Harvey, Thomas, 44, 47, 164
Havelock, Arthur, 291
Havelock-Blyden Treaty, 291
Hayman, Henry, 279
Heard, William H., 270
heathenism, 80, 227
Henderson, William, 149, 189
hierarchies, race and class, 18, 33, 37, 42, 43–53, 158–160, 173–174, 209, 212, 219, 259, 329–330, *See also* white supremacy
hierarchy, patriarchal, 96
Higginbotham, Evelyn Brooks, 23
Hill, Stephen J., 77, 86
historiography, 13–16
Hoad, John, 135
Holder, Richard N., 272
Holder, Samuel, 58
Holly, James, 116
Holsoe, Svend, 198
Holy Innocents Church, 83, 87
Homestead Act, 228
Hooker, Reverend, 121
House of Assembly, 53
hut tax, 319–320

identities, 20, 160–171, *See also* color politics, blackness, whiteness, colonial identity, racial identity, free coloreds (mixed-race), free blacks
African American, 176
Afro-Barbadian, 163, 180–181
diaspora, 99, 248–249, 326–327
in Liberia, 216–219
West Indian, 20, 25
idolatry, 227
imperialism, 17, *See also* European imperialism in Africa, British colonialism/imperialism
indentureship, 264
independence celebrations, 276
Indians, American. *See* Native Americans
indigenes, 13, 17–18, 186
assimilation, 317–321
citizenship, 243
customary land rights, 243
displacement of, 26

identities, 20, 280–281
rebellions, 306
social relationships with migrants, 225–226
status of, 194–200, 289, 311–321, 331–332
taxes on, 319–320
trade and, 285–286
use of term, 217
indirect rule, 317–321
inequality, 247–248, *See also* hierarchies, race and class
Inniss, Charles, 81, 262
Inniss, Samuel, 55, 81, 262
Inniss, William, 58
Institute for Colored Youths (ICY), 6, 119
intermarriage, 225
Islam, 221
Islander, use of term, 217

Jackson, Andrew, 107
Jamaica, 41
abolition of slavery, 40
economy, 48
maroons (escaped slaves), 14, 76, 108
middle-class economic and political power, 70–71
migration to, 135
missionaries from, 87–88
Jessamy, Holborn, 33
Johnson, C. T., 279
Johnson, Charles S., 322, 324
Johnson, Henry W., Jr., 193, 202–203, 206
Johnson, Hilary R. W., 291, 296
Johnston, Harry, 301, 304, 310

Karnga, Abayomi, 267
Kennedy, Joseph, 68, 162
Key, Francis Scott, 107
Kimball, Thomas, 41–42, 52–53, 54, 70, 119, 125, 164
King, Alfred B., 224, 278, 297
King, C. D. B., 322
King, C. T. O., 277
King, Florence A., 278
King, W. H., 279
kinship groups, 248
citizenship and, 196
land ownership, 253
Knibb, William, 85
Krahn ethnic group, 196

Kru ethnic group, 196, 197–198, 251, 286, 287, 306
Kwa-speaking ethnic groups, 196

labor, 64, *See also* free labor, artisans, plantation economy, wage labor
  blackness and, 213–214
  citizenship and, 253–266
  forced, 322–323
  in Liberia, 188, 231, 237–238
  skilled, 134
labor emigration, post-emancipation, 54–60
labor productivity, 214, 237–238
labor shortage, 54
Lambert, David, 236
land availability in Barbados, 48, 50–51, 54
land ownership in Liberia, 26, 42–43, 49–51, 194–195, 213, 259
  citizenship and, 253
  customary rights to, 243
  grants for migrants, 133
  kinship groups and, 253
Latrobe, Benjamin, 207
Latrobe, John, 114, 128, 131, 132
Lawrence, Charles Aug, 49, 115
laws
  Afro-Barbadian middle class and, 64–72
  customary, 318–319
  on labor emigration, 60–64
  racial codes in Barbados, 176–177
  on voting, 48–49
Leacock, H. J., 86, 88
Lee, Robert E., 205
legitimate trade. *See* trade
Liberal, The (newspaper), 29, 45, 67, 91, 110, 119, 121–126
liberated Africans, 217, *See* recaptives
Liberator, The (newspaper), 123
Liberia. *See also* indigenes, recaptives, land ownership in Liberia
  administrative categories, 216–219
  agriculture, 257–263, 309
  alliances in, 186–189
  apprenticeship system, 263–265
  architecture, 208, 304
  bankruptcy, 309
  black migrants to, 1–26
  blackness in, 1, 17–25, 74–75, 186–188, 234, 273–281
  boundary disputes, 286, 291, 306–307

  constitution, 240–241, 244–248, 253–266
  courts, 319
  debts, 283, 287–288, 300–301, 308, 310–311
  diplomatic relations, 301–303
  diversity among migrants, 189–194
  economic development, 308–311
  exile to, 108
  families migrating to, 46
  forced labor in, 322–323
  founding of, 1
  group identity in, 229–232, *See also* identities
  hinterlands, 290–291, 317, 319
  imperialism and colonialism, 111–114, 194–200, 311–314, 317–321, 329–332
  independence, 102–105, 110–111, 113, 133, 240, 289
  indigenes and, 312
  international public opinion, 300–304
  labor, 331
  landscape, 275
  languages, 195–196
  modernization, 157–160, 170, 215, 273, 292, 303, 309–311, 312, 316–317
  nation-building, 281, 326–332
  political leadership, 2, 266–272, 282–325
  political leadership, post-independence, 285–292
  political parties, 306, *See also* True Whig Party (TWP), Republican Party
  political precedents, 300
  political system, 238–241
  population, 46
  presidential term limits, 304
  rebellions and uprisings, 306, 320
  religion, 219–221, *See also* missionaries
  republicanism, 16, 26, 115, 158, 233–234, 241–243, 300
  settlement patterns, 200–210, 266, 275–276, 277
  social interactions, 222–229
  social plurality in, 206–210
  sovereignty, 283–285
  as symbol, 310
  territories lost, 291
  voting rights, 247–248
Liberia College, 296
Liberian Development Company, 310
Liberian Legislature, 133

Liberian migration, scholarship
  on, 10–13
Light, Henry, 57
Lincoln, Abraham, 128
literacy, 42
Lomax, Jane, 224
lower classes, 37, 65
loyalty. *See also* colonial identity
  Barbadian, to British Empire, 7, 38,
    68–69
  divided, 170
  oath of, 255–256
  of West Indians in Liberia, 293–294,
    298–299
Lugard, Frederick, 317
Lynchburg Emigration Society (LES), 192

MacGregor, Evan John Murray, 60, 66
malaria, 205
Malcolm, Thomas J., 127
male suffrage, 247–248
Mali Empire, 196
Mande group, 196
Manna territory, 313
maroons (escaped slaves), 14, 76, 108, 172
marriage, 222–226
Marshal, 207
Marshall, John Frances, 135
Marshall, Mary, 224–225
Marshall, T. H., 57
Marshall, Woodville, 32
Maryland Colonization Society, 207
Maryland County, Liberia, 287, 314
Massachusetts Colonization Society, 140
Massaquoi, Prince Mommolu, 280
Master and Servant Act, 61
McClain, William, 140, 149–150
McClean, Catharine, 33
McGill, James Boyer, 324
McGregor, John, 48
McNuckles, John, 192
Mel ethnic group, 196
men
  gender roles, 59–60
  voting rights, 247–248
Mercer, Charles, 108
merchant class, 35, 267–269, 286
Methodists, 80–81
middle passage, symbolism of, 149–181
migration. *See* Liberia, Barbadian migrants,
  West Indian migrants, African

American migrants, Sierra Leone,
  emigration
millenarianism, 113, 159, 293
Mills, Samuel, 107
Mirror (newspaper), 55–56
missionaries, 6, 133
  Afro-Barbadian, 84–92
  recaptives as, 262–263
  views on Liberians, 179
  white, 85
Mitchell, R. H., 279
mixed-race individuals. *See* free coloreds
  (mixed-race)
mobility, 14, *See also* emigration
  freedom and, 50
  laws restricting, 60–64
modernity, 93, 100, 157–160, 170,
  260–261, 273, 312
  blackness and, 215
  indigenes and, 312, 316–317
Monroe, James, 107–108, 238
Monrovia, 108, 202, 266, 280, 304
Moore, Amelia, 83
Moore, Edward and Maud, 83
Moore, G., 315
Moore, H. G., 315–316
Moort, Paulus, 280
Morant Bay Rebellion, 12
Moravians, 80
Muslims, 221

National Era (newspaper), 120
national frameworks, 12
nationhood, 17, 32, 111, 158, 190,
  236–241, 327, 329, *See also* black
  nationalism
Native Administration Ordinance, 319
Native Americans, 112, 225
natives. *See* indigenes
Naturalization Act (US), 177
Negro Republic, 2
Negro Era (newspaper), 260–261
New Times (newspaper), 119
New York State Colonization Society, 270
newspapers, black-owned, 119–124, 173
Newton, Melanie, 162
  The Children of Africa in the Colonies,
    12, 13
Niger Expedition, 90–91, 95
Nigeria, 115
nomenclature, 188, 216–219

North Star, The (newspaper), 119, 122
Nova Scotia, 14, 106
Nurse, John, 50

oath of loyalty, 255–256, *See also* loyalty
Old Whig Party, 267
Omi, Michael, 175
one-drop rule, 176
Open Door Policy, 311
oppression. *See also* racism
  escape from, 1
  in Liberia, 3, 332
  resistance to, 14
  victims turned victimizers, 16–19, 164,
    209

Padmore, George S., 271
Padmore, Jacob, 59, 83, 135, 219–221, 259
Padmore, James B., 224, 271
Padmore, John, 185, 194–195, 210
Padmore, Lucretia, 59, 83
Padmore, Ruth, 83
paganism, 227
pan-African congresses, 303–304
pan-Africanism, 3, 9, 16–17, 326–330
  Afro-Barbadian views on, 157–160
  Barbadian emigrants' commitment to,
    171–180, 314
  blackness and, 21
  debates on, 109
  differing views of, 178–180
  in Liberia, 273
  limits of, 328
  millenarianism and, 113
  prophetic traditions in, 299
paternalism, 36, 47, 65, 214
patriarchy, 59–60, 96, 158, 170, 240
Payne, James Spriggs, 127, 223, 251, 255,
  286
Peal, Burgess, 279
peasant class, 48, 71
pejorative terms. *See* nomenclature
Pennsylvania Colonization Society (PCS),
  127, 137, 140
Pennsylvania Freeman (newspaper), 124
Peter, King, 197, 198–199, 200
petitions, 69–71
Phillips, Reverend, 88
Phipps, Charles, 78, 95, 96, 97, 162
Pierre, Jemima, 217
Piper, John, 163

Pitman, C. A., 222–224
plantation economy, 42–43
  labor emigration and, 56–57, 61
  low-wage work, 50–51, 64
political power, 49, 53, *See also* Liberia,
  power
political rights, 32
Pongas Mission, 85–89, 95
Port of Entry Act (1864), 306
Porte, Conrad, 224
Porte, Lillian, 224
Ports of Entry Act (1864), 286
post-emancipation era, 5, 10, 15, 25, 29–33,
  293
  Barclay, Arthur, and, 292–300
  discontents and decline, 40–53
  labor emigration, 54–60
power, 18, 159, 170
  construction of, 275
  imbalances in, 179
Prescod, Samuel, 29, 42–43, 47–48, 119
  abolitionism, 173
  on apprenticeship, 45
  background, 53
  politics and, 65–72, 73
primitivism, 280
property ownership, 49–51, *See also* land
  ownership in Liberia
property rights, 241
  blackness and, 244–248
  of whites, 314
  of women, 228
Protestant work ethic, 87
Puritans, 112

Queah ethnic group, 250

race
  biologically deterministic arguments
    about, 23
  social construction of, 329
racial exclusion, 177–178, *See also* British
  Empire:subjecthood
racial hierarchy, 52, 212, *See also*
  hierarchies, race and class
racial identity, 16, 187, *See also* color
  politics, blackness, whiteness, colonial
  identity, free coloreds (mixed-race),
  free blacks
  Liberian citizenship and, 244–253
  solidarity and, 188, 229

subjectivity and, 175
racial uplift, 172, 174, 178, *See also* black advancement
racism, 16, 72, 143, 195, 209, 240, 302, 308, *See also* oppression
 British colonial policies and, 77–78
 systematic, 16–19
Ralston, Gerald, 115–118, 302
Ralston, Robert, 108
Randolph, Jesse, 223
Randolph, John, 107
Rankin, F. Harrison, 110
Rawle, Reverend, 84, 86
rebellions and uprisings, 38, 40, 80
recaptives, 13, 230, 327, 330
 as apprentices, 263–265
 citizenship, 243–244
 identities, 20
 in Liberia, 186, 193–194, 210–216
 status of, 17–18
Redwar, H. R., 82
Reef, Catherine, 143
Reeves, Conrad, 162
regional frameworks, 12
religion. *See also* Christianity, missionaries
 African, 227
 African civilization and, 113
 in Barbados, 78–84
Republican Party, 236, 241–243, 268–269, 311, 315
republicanism, 16, 26, 115, 158, 233–234, 241–243, 300
respectability, 7, 8, 32, 68, 178–180, 273
 colonization and, 19
 families and, 46
 imperialism and, 93
 Liberia and, 134
 Liberia as black republic and, 114
 Liberian, 307
 religion and, 79, 81
 royalist appeals and, 160–171
Richards, W. M., 224
Rix and Lomax, 279
Roberts, Joseph Jenkins, 102–105, 128, 191, 210, 229, 242
 Barclay, Arthur and, 296
 on Barbadian migrants, 233–234, 258
 on British colonial politics, 282
 political leadership, 269, 285
 treaties, 302

Roberts, Z. B., 297
Robertsport, 207
Rodney, Walter, 32
Roebuck Street, 35
Rothery, William E., 278
Royal Navy, 98
royalist political ideologies. *See* colonial identity
Roye, Edwin J., 287–288, 297, 299, 301, 304
rubber companies, 292
Russell, Alfred F., 221, 296
Russell, John, 68
Russwurm, John Brown, 107, 210

Sain, Mr., 166–167
St. Croix, 31
St. Joseph's parish, 35
St. Kitts, 8, 51
St. Mary's Anglican Church, 82
St. Mary's Chapel, 82–83
St. Michael's parish, 34, 79
St. Phillip's parish, 35, 83
St. Thomas, 8, 192, 299
St. Thomas's parish, 35, 83
St. Vincent, 56
Sandiford, Samuel, 162
savagery, 18, 80, 166, 199, 209, 231–232
saviors, 92, 114
 black, 89, 100
 white, 195
Sawyer, Amos, 287
Scramble for Africa, 283–285, 288–291, 300, *See also* European imperialism in Africa
seasoning period, 190–191, 274
Second Great Awakening, 84
self-determination, 73
self-sacrifice, 181
sexual standards, 227
Seys, John, 140–142
Shannon, J. H., 54–56, 73
sharecropping, 264
Sharpe, Granville, 75
Sheafe, John, 162
Sherman, Mary Antoinette Brown, 225
Sherman, R. A., 279
Shick, Tom, *Behold the Promised Land*, 11
ships to Liberia (1865), 186, *See also* Brig Cora (ship)
Shipwrights and Bricklayers Union, 58

Shrewsbury, William, 80
Sierra Leone, 121
  Barbadian migration to, 6, 8, 88–89,
    109–114, 233
  as British colony, 105
  boundary disputes, 286, 291
  enslaved Africans exiled to, 76
  escaped slaves in, 14
  establishment of, 75–76
  missionaries in, 85–89
  recaptive Africans in, 210–211
  West Indian migration to, 11, 75–78
Skeete, Samuel, 35, 81, 204
skilled labor, 134, *See also* artisans
Skinner, B. R., 225
slave owners, free coloreds as, 38, 162
slave ships, 150
slave trade
  abolition efforts, 95
  African participation in, 197–198, 228,
    248–251, 275, 286
  Africans rescued from, 194
  on Liberian coastline, 76, 195, 239
slavery, 33, 37, 38, 174–175
  British subjecthood and, 177
  civilization and, 93, 100
  colonizationists and, 121–126
  escape from, 1, *See also* maroons (escaped
    slaves)
  in Liberia, 322–323
  proximity to, 214, 227–228
  shared experiences of, 188
Smith, Mary, 53
Smith, Robert, 268
Snetter, E. A., 279
social ascriptions, 188, 216–219
social equality, 209
social exclusion, 330
social hierarchy, 169, 207, 224, *See also*
  hierarchies, race and class
  in Liberia, 226–228, 264–266, 267,
    274–276, 329–332
  patriarchal, 96
social mobility, 32, 49, 71, 170, 327
social segregation, 188, 201, 276, 331
Society for the Extinction of the Slave Trade,
  90, 162
Society for the Propagation of the Gospel in
  Foreign Parts, 84
Soulouque, Faustin, 116
sovereignty, 288–291, 301, 306–308, 321

Springfield Republican (newspaper), 120
Steward, J. G., 122–123
Stivers, Richard, 213
Stockton, Robert, 198
Strutt, Charles Henry, 56
Sturge, Joseph, 44, 47, 164
Sunderland, Dr., 280
Suriname, 14

Taft, 307
Tappan, Charles, 165–166
taxes, 319–320
Taylor, Charles Henry, 289
Teage, Hilary, 240–241
tenancy system
  in Barbados, 47
  in Liberia, 263–265
terror, 47
Theresa (ship), 192
Thomas, H., 135
Thomas, William F., 68
Thome, James, 41–42, 52–53, 54, 70, 119,
  125, 164
Thorne, James, 162
Thorne, Joseph, 164
Thorpe, Adrianna Alberta Louise, 83
Thorpe, I. J., 270
Thorpe, John Isaac and Elizabeth Maria, 83
Thoughts on African Colonization
  (Garrison), 123
Times (newspaper), 54–56, 81, 88
Tobago, 51
Toussaint, 106
townships, 317–318
Tracy, Joseph, 110, 140
trade, 285–286, *See also* slave trade
  legitimate, 251–252, 275
  limits on, 306
transatlantic analysis, 11–12
Trinidad, 51
Trinity P. Episcopal Church School, 224
Trollope, Anthony, 166
True Black Man's Party, 267
True Liberian Party (TLP), 242
True Whig Party (TWP), 26, 236–237,
  267–272, 287, 297, 306
  emergence of, 313
  indigenes and, 321
Tull, Henry Herdle, 83
Tull, Sarah Ann, 50
Tull, William Edward, 50

Tuning, J. A., 2, 9, 282, 284–285, 294, 297–299
Turner, H. M., 280
Tyler-McGraw, Marie, *An African Republic*, 10

unemployment, 30
unions, 57–58
United States. *See also* American Commission to Liberia, African American migrants, American Colonization Society (ACS), African Americans
   in 1860s, 127–130
   abolition of slavery, 118
   aid to Liberia, 307–308
   blackness in, 176–177
   citizenship, 177
   Civil War, 8, 118, 121–126, 128, 129, 206
   imperialism in Africa, 114
   imperialism in North America, 199
   political traditions, 241–243
   slavery and black emigration, 107–109
uprisings. *See* rebellions and uprisings

Vai ethnic group, 196–197, 225, 226
valorization, 188–189
victims turned victimizers, 16–19, 164, 209
Victoria, Queen, 48, 58
Virginia, migrants from, 210
voting laws, 48–49

wage labor, 41, 43, *See also* free labor
wages, 43, 50, 54
Walcott, Edward, 55–56
Walker, Daniel, 193
Walker, David, 171–180
Walker, James, 9, 30, 49, 74, 130
Wallis, Braithwaite, 301
Ward, Samuel, 124
wardships, 225
Warner, Daniel, 130–133, 142, 189–190, 211, 225, 257, 285–286, 293–294
Washington, Bushrod, 107
Watts, Frederick, 66–67
Webster, Daniel, 107–108
Weeks, James Milton, 272
Weeks, John Braithwaite, 50
Weeks, Rocheforte L., 272
Wesley, John, 80

West Indian (newspaper), 119
West Indian Church for the Furtherance of the Gospel in Western Africa, 85
West Indian migrants, 1, 11, 186, 326–332, *See also* Barbadian migrants
West Indians
   communication with African Americans, 105–106, 118–126, 173–174
   identities, 20, 25
   labor rivalries, 64
   post-emancipation, 10
   white perceptions of, 302–303
West Indies and the Spanish Main, The (Trollope), 166
Western culture, 226–228
Wharton, Clifton, 322
Whig liberalism, 40, 178, *See also* True Whig Party (TWP)
white elites, 66, 71
white planters. *See also* plantation economy
   land ownership, 42–43
   opposition to emancipation, 40
   wage labor and, 41
white saviors, 195, *See also* missionaries
white supremacy, 4, 115, 168, 170, 213, 217–219, 241, 276, *See also* race and class
   escape from, 1
   internalization of, 17–19
   Liberia and, 299, 330–332
whiteness, 23
   fears of, 302–303
   as ideal, 163
   proximity to, 93, 165, 209, 215, 249
whites. *See also* European imperialism in Africa, British colonialism/imperialism, colonizationists
   black emigration and, 107–109
   in Liberia, 2, 109
   mortality rates in Africa, 90
   paternalism, 109
   poor, 45
   status and privileges of, 34, 37
Wilberforce, William, 75, 89
Wiles, Florence Irene, 223, 228
Wiles, James T., 6, 33, 49, 95, 138, 223, 228–229, 271–272, 295, 298, 326
   family, 82–83, 225
   mixed-race status, 33
   Sierra Leone and, 89
Wiles, Richard Jones, 295

Wiles, Richard Stanley, 272
Williams Brothers, 279
Williams, H. A., 297
Williams, Sylvester, 303–304
Williamson, Charles, 117
Wilson, Henry, 302, 303
Wilson, Thomas, 280
Winant, Howard, 175
Woerrman, A., and Co., 279

Wolmers Free School, 70
women
  gender roles, 59–60
  legal rights, 228
  political rights, 241
Woodley Park Plantation, 57
Worrell, John T., 33, 49–51, 115

yellow fever, 205

CPSIA information can be obtained
at www.ICGtesting.com
Printed in the USA
LVHW090441171220
674409LV00007B/139